The
SPSS GUIDE to
Data
Analysis
for SPSS/PC+™, 2nd Edition

MARIJA J. NORUŠIS
Rush-Presbyterian-St. Luke's Medical Center

SPSS Inc.

For more information about SPSS/PC+ Studentware Plus™, the SPSS/PC+™ system, and other software produced and distributed by SPSS Inc., please write or call

Marketing Department
SPSS Inc.
444 North Michigan Avenue
Chicago, IL 60611
Tel: (312)329-3500
Fax: (312)329-3668

In Europe and the Middle East, please write or call

SPSS International B.V.
P.O. Box 115
4200 AC Gorinchem
The Netherlands
+31.1830.36711
Fax: +31.1830.35839

The SPSS Guide to Data Analysis for SPSS/PC+™, 2nd Edition
Copyright © 1991 by SPSS Inc.
All rights reserved.
Printed in the United States of America.

1 2 3 4 5 6 7 8 9 0   93 92 91

ISBN 0-923967-34-6

Library of Congress Catalog Card Number: 91-066147

Preface

"The business of a poet is to examine not the individual but the species; to remark general properties and large appearances. He does not number the streaks of the tulip, or describe the different shades of verdure of the forest; he is to exhibit . . . such prominent and striking features as recall the original to every mind." (Samuel Johnson, *Rasselas.*)

It is not often that anyone compares a statistician to a poet. Yet it is fitting to do so. The statistician, like Johnson's poet, searches for "general properties and large appearances." The goal of data analysis is to describe the species based on observations of individuals. The data analyst must identify patterns from thousands of fragments and then speak of the whole. For that is what is of interest.

In this book we consider how to proceed from individual observations to the whole. There are many ways in which the fragments may be assembled, and these can result in different views of the whole. Statistics books differ in what parts of the assembly process they emphasize. This book tries to give students the skills that they need to become informed consumers or producers of statistical information. Therefore this book emphasizes what the statistical process is all about: how to conduct studies, what the results mean, and what can be said about the whole from the pieces.

With SPSS/PC+ students can practice using the tools for analyzing data that the professionals use, and gain experience in analyzing data the way professional researchers do. They need these skills if they pursue graduate degrees, and equally if they enter the working world.

Using this Book

The book is divided into four main parts: Getting Started, Describing Data, Testing Hypotheses, and Examining Relationships. Examples from the NORC General Social Survey are used throughout. Of course, the best way to learn about anything is to actually do it. That's especially true for data analysis, so each chapter closes with exercises that reinforce and extend the material in three major areas: syntax, statistical concepts, and data analysis. These exercises test understanding of both the mechanics of statistical analysis and the interpretation of the results. The data used in the data analysis exercises, a subset of the General Social Survey data, are available from SPSS Inc. Appendix B contains selected answers to the exercises. Appendix A explains how to correct some of the errors commonly made by users of Studentware. Appendix A explains how to format summary statistics for presentation. Appendix F presents nonparametric procedures not covered in the main text.

Acknowledgments

I wish to thank the members of the SPSS staff who have participated in the preparation of this book. I have benefited from their expertise. I also wish to thank my students and other users of previous versions of this book and software for helpful suggestions. Finally, I wish to thank Liz Adams for her editorial contributions.

Marija J. Norušis

Contacting SPSS Inc.

If you would like to be on our mailing list, write to us at one of the addresses below. We will send you a copy of our newsletter and let you know about SPSS Inc. activities in your area.

SPSS Inc.
444 North Michigan Avenue
Chicago, IL 60611
Tel: (312) 329-3500
Fax: (312) 329-3668

SPSS Federal Systems (U.S.)
800 K St., N.W.
Suite 300
Washington, DC 20001
Tel: (202) 408-7626
Fax: (202) 408-7627

SPSS Latin America
444 North Michigan Avenue
Chicago, IL 60611
Tel: (312) 329-3568
Fax: (312) 329-3668

SPSS Benelux BV
P.O. Box 115
4200 AC Gorinchem
The Netherlands
Tel: +31.1830.36711
Fax: +31.1830.35839

SPSS UK Ltd.
SPSS House
5 London Street
Chertsey
Surrey KT16 8AP
United Kingdom
Tel: +44.932.566262
Fax: +44.932.567020

SPSS GmbH Software
Steinsdorfstrasse 19
D-8000 Munich 22
Germany
Tel:+49.89.2283008
Fax: +49.89.2285413

SPSS Scandinavia AB
Sjöängsvägen 21
S-191 72 Sollentuna
Sweden
Tel: +46.8.7549450
Fax: +46.8.7548816

SPSS Asia Pacific Pte. Ltd.
#26-01
78 Shenton Way
Singapore 0207
Singapore
Tel: +65.221.2577
Fax: +65.221.9920

SPSS Japan Inc.
Gyoen Sky Bldg.
2-1-11, Shinjuku
Shinjuku-ku
Tokyo 160
Japan
Tel: +81.3.33505261
Fax: +81.3.33505245

SPSS Australia
P.O.Box 879
345 Pacific Highway
Crows Nest
Sydney, NSW 2065
Australia
Tel: +61.2.954.5660
Fax: +61.2.954.5616

Contents

PART ONE
Getting Started

Running SPSS/PC+:
A Quick Example

How do you run SPSS/PC+?

- How do you start the program?
- What is displayed on the screen?
- What happens when you run a set of commands?
- How do you get out of SPSS/PC+?

he SPSS/PC+ system installed on your computer is one of many software products available for the storage, retrieval, and analysis of data. Database products provide for the efficient storage and retrieval of individual pieces of information. Spreadsheet programs specialize in the flexible display and manipulation of rows and columns of data. Statistical software programs such as SPSS/PC+ help you summarize data and draw conclusions from them. For a particular problem, you may choose to use more than one software package. For example, you can create and maintain a database or spreadsheet and then use SPSS/PC+ to analyze it, since SPSS/PC+ can read data from many database and spreadsheet programs.

STARTING SPSS/PC+

Before we discuss the operation of SPSS/PC+ in detail, let's run a simple analysis. You'll interact with the system by entering and running a few simple commands.

Creating a Data Directory

The explanations and commands in this book assume that you have stored your data in the directory \spss\data. If your files are to be in another directory, use the name of that directory in the following steps and when entering commands listed throughout the remainder of this book. Follow these steps to create the data directory:

1. Turn on your computer, following the directions in the manual. We are assuming that SPSS/PC+ is installed in the directory c:\spss. You should see a DOS prompt, something like C:>.

2. To change to the SPSS directory, at the DOS prompt type

```
cd \spss
```

and press ⏎Enter

3. Then type

```
md data
```

and press ⏎Enter. This command creates a subdirectory named data.

Starting SPSS/PC+

The steps for starting SPSS/PC+ are always the same:

❶ To get into your SPSS/PC+ data directory, at the DOS prompt type

`cd \spss\data`

and press (⏎Enter).

❷ To start the program, type

`spsspc`

and press (⏎Enter) again. First you will see the SPSS/PC+ logo on your screen, followed by the screen shown in Figure 1.1.

The screen is divided into two large areas called **windows,** plus a message line at the bottom:

■ **Upper window.** The upper window displays the Menu on the left and a Help window on the right, which describes items on the Menu. After you have run a command, you can turn off the menus and see the results in this space, in the **listing window.**

■ **Scratch pad.** The lower window is called the **scratch pad.** The scratch pad is where you enter the commands that tell SPSS/PC+ what to do. When you first start SPSS/PC+, the cursor is blinking in the scratch pad, at the point where commands will be entered.

■ **Message line.** The message line (sometimes referred to as the "status line") at the bottom displays messages and other information from SPSS/PC+.

Figure 1.1 SPSS/PC+ windows

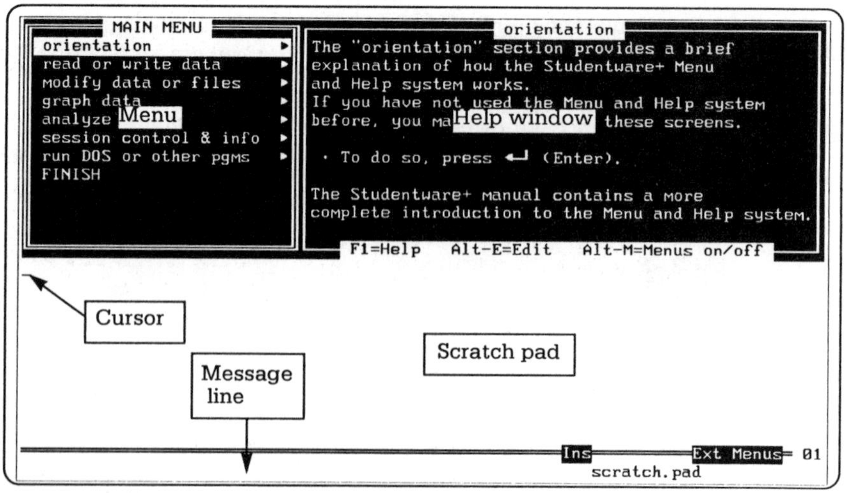

RUNNING AN ANALYSIS

To see how easy it is to run an analysis in SPSS/PC+, you can practice entering and reviewing data collected from interviews with seven individuals during a national survey.

Entering Variable Names

Attributes such as age vary from one individual to the next. They are called **variables**. To tell SPSS/PC+ which variables you are going to enter, you need the DATA LIST command.

After you start SPSS/PC+, the item orientation is highlighted on the menu.

➊ Since you want to read data into the system, press ⊕ to highlight read or write data and then press (┙Enter) to select the item. A menu appears containing a list of command names (in capital letters), as well as the item labels and formatting. In the Help window on the right is information about the highlighted command, GET. If you press ⊕, the Help window displays information about the next command.

➋ Press ⊕ until DATA LIST is highlighted. Then press (┙Enter) to select the command and paste it into the scratch pad. The cursor is blinking where the next item will be pasted.

➌ Press ⊕ until FREE is highlighted, and press (┙Enter) to paste it. Another menu appears, listing two items that can be used after FREE and a variety of examples. The item variables is highlighted. Press (┙Enter) to select it and a typing window appears, as shown in Figure 1.2

Figure 1.2 Typing window

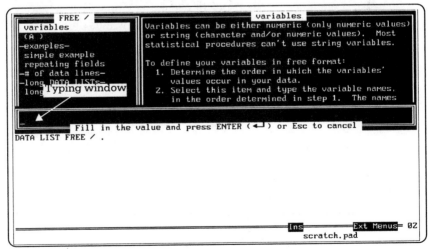

④ Type the variable names and specifications

```
age sex educ hompop agewed state (a20)
```

and press ⏎Enter. The contents of the typing window are pasted into the scratch pad, after FREE /, as shown in Figure 1.3.

Figure 1.3 Pasted DATA LIST command

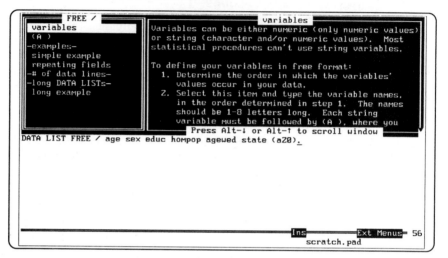

DATA LIST. The DATA LIST command in Figure 1.3 assigns names to the six variables in the analysis. You'll use these names whenever you want to refer to these variables in SPSS/PC+. A variable name can contain up to eight characters. The order in which the variables are listed on the DATA LIST command is the order in which the values will be entered. The keyword FREE indicates that the data values will be entered sequentially but not necessarily in fixed column locations.

The last variable is assigned the name *STATE*. The *a20* in parentheses after the name indicates that the values of the variable can contain letters as well as numbers (a for alphanumeric) and can be up to 20 characters long. A variable that can contain letters is known as a **string variable.** The remaining variables are **numeric variables,** since their values are numbers. *AGE* is the person's age, *SEX* is their sex, *EDUC* is the highest year of education, *HOMPOP* is the number of people in the household, and *AGEWED* is the age of first marriage. In this example, *SEX* is a numeric variable because we assigned it numeric codes: 1 for *male* and 2 for *female*. You will learn more about assigning codes to variables in Chapter 5.

Entering Data Values

Next, you need to tell SPSS/PC+ the values of each variable for each person.

● Press ⏎ twice to go back to the read or write data menu.

② Press ⤓ to highlight BEGIN DATA and then press ⏎Enter. The underscore cursor is blinking in the scratch pad between BEGIN DATA and END DATA. The borders on the upper window have turned dark gray, indicating that the scratch pad is the active window, not the menus.

❸ Type the following data, pressing ⏎Enter at the end of each line before the last.

```
33 2 16 1 19 "Illinois" ·
43 2 15 2 21 "Ohio"
47 1 16 4 23 "North Carolina"
35 2 17 1 21 "Oregon"
65 1 18 2 26 "New Mexico"
19 1 12 5 22 "Kansas"
70 2 16 4 23 "Massachusetts"
```

If you need to make corrections, use the backspace key to delete any unwanted characters and the arrow keys to move the cursor.

BEGIN DATA—END DATA. The command BEGIN DATA signals that the following lines contain, for each individual, the actual values for the six variables. The first person is 33 years old and female. She has completed 16 years of education, and lives alone in Illinois. Her first marriage was at age 19. The name of the state is enclosed in quotation marks because it is a string variable. Note that at least one blank space separates each value. The command END DATA follows the values for the last person, indicating the end of the data values.

Running Commands

● Press ⬆ until the cursor is somewhere in the DATA LIST line.

② To run all the commands from the cursor on down, press F10 and then ⏎Enter.

SPSS/PC+ reads the variable names and the data values and holds them in the computer memory. Results of running the commands are displayed on the screen and written to a disk file called the listing file.

The MORE Prompt

When the word MORE appears in the upper right corner of your screen, you can move to the next page of output by pressing the space bar. When the analysis is completed, the message This procedure was completed at appears, along with the time of completion. Press the space bar once more to return to the scratch pad. The Main menu appears again and the box cursor is blinking in the scratch pad, ready for the next pasted command.

Labeling the Variables

Although you should always try to choose descriptive variable names, it's sometimes difficult to do so in eight characters. The command VARIABLE LABELS allows you to supply additional identifying information for each variable.

1. Press ⊕ to highlight read or write data and press (⏎Enter).

2. Highlight labels and formatting and press (⏎Enter).

3. Since VARIABLE LABELS is already highlighted, press (⏎Enter) again. The command is pasted into the scratch pad and a new menu appears with variable(s) highlighted. The tilde (~) to the left of the item indicates that the item is required, as the note at the bottom of the menu reminds you.

4. Press (⏎Enter). The Variables window pops open, listing all of the variables in the current file in the system. The window also lists ALL, TO and some system variables beginning with dollar signs. Use the arrow keys to move from one variable to another.

5. Press the arrow keys until AGE is highlighted and press (⏎Enter).

6. Then press (Esc), highlight the apostrophes, and press (⏎Enter). The typing window opens. Type a label that explains whose age is being listed

```
Age of respondent
```

and press (⏎Enter). This label will be used to identify the variable later, so that anyone reading the results of an analysis will know what you are talking about.

7. Select variable(s) again, select SEX, press (Esc), select the apostrophes, type Sex, and press (⏎Enter).

8. In a similar manner, enter the following labels:

```
EDUC 'Highest year of school completed'
HOMPOP 'Number of people in household'
AGEWED 'Age of first marriage'
STATE 'State of residence'.
```

9. To run the command, press (F10) and then (⏎Enter).

VARIABLE LABELS. Up to 40 characters of text for a variable label can be supplied between the apostrophes. SPSS/PC+ uses this additional text, when possible, to label the results of your analysis. This makes it easier for you and anyone else to read your results. For example, the label *Number of people in household* is given to the variable named *HOMPOP*. The rules for specifying labels are outlined in Chapter 5.

Listing the Data

Having entered the data, you should check to see if they are correct. One way to do this is to list them in a table, which is a simple form of analysis.

1. Press ⬇ until analyze data is highlighted and press ⏎Enter.
2. Select reports and tables. The LIST command is highlighted.
3. Press ⏎Enter to paste it in the scratch pad.
4. To run the command, press F10 and ⏎Enter.

LIST. The LIST command instructs SPSS/PC+ to list the values of all the variables for all of the individuals. This allows you to check that you have entered the information correctly.

THE INPUT

Now that you see how easy it is to run SPSS/PC+, let's consider what you've just done. Look at Figure 1.4, which shows the commands, or **input,** for this analysis.

Figure 1.4 Input

```
DATA LIST FREE / age sex educ hompop agewed state (a20).
BEGIN DATA.
33 2 16 1 19 "Illinois"
43 2 15 2 21 "Ohio"
47 1 16 4 23 "North Carolina"
35 2 17 1 21 "Oregon"
65 1 18 2 26 "New Mexico"
19 1 12 5 22 "Kansas"
70 2 16 4 23 "Massachusetts"
END DATA.
VARIABLE LABELS AGE 'Age of respondent' SEX 'Sex'
EDUC'Highest year of school completed'
 HOMPOP 'Number of people in household'
 AGEWED 'Age of first marriage'
 STATE 'State of residence'.
LIST.
```

These commands analyze data for seven individuals. For each individual, six **variables,** or pieces of information, are recorded: age, sex, highest year of school completed, number of people in the household, age of first marriage, and state of residence. The variable labels come next, telling precisely what type of information is in each variable. Finally, the LIST command produces a listing of all the information you entered.

THE OUTPUT

The results from running one or more commands are called the **output**. To review the output, you can display the listing window by closing the menus.

① Press Alt M.

The end of the output is visible in your listing window and the cursor is at the bottom of the scratch pad. To see all of the output, you need to switch the cursor to the listing window.

② Press F2 and Enter. Press F2 again, and then Z, which "zooms" the window. Now use the ↑ key to move the cursor to the line that begins with AGE. The output is shown in Figure 1.5.

Figure 1.5 Output from the LIST command

```
     AGE      SEX     EDUC   HOMPOP   AGEWED STATE

    33.00    2.00    16.00    1.00     19.00 Illinois
    43.00    2.00    15.00    2.00     21.00 Ohio
    47.00    1.00    16.00    4.00     23.00 North Carolina
    35.00    2.00    17.00    1.00     21.00 Oregon
    65.00    1.00    18.00    2.00     26.00 New Mexico
    19.00    1.00    12.00    5.00     22.00 Kansas
    70.00    2.00    16.00    4.00     23.00 Massachusetts


Number of cases read =       7    Number of cases listed =       7
```

Notice that each column of values is labeled with the name assigned by the DATA LIST command. Errors in the listing of the data values must be corrected before you perform any statistical analyses. Otherwise, your results will be incorrect.

If your data values are correct, go on to the next section. If they are incorrect, switch the cursor back to the scratch pad by pressing F2 and Enter. Use the arrow keys and the backspace to remove unwanted characters and then type the correct characters. Run the commands again, by placing the cursor in the command you want to start with and pressing F10 and then Enter.

RUNNING ANOTHER COMMAND

When the data values are correct, you can practice entering another analysis command and running it. Position your cursor below the LIST command and follow these steps:

① Return to the menus by pressing Alt M.

② Select analyze data and then descriptive statistics.

③ Select the DESCRIPTIVES command.

④ Select VARIABLES. When the Variables window pops open, paste ALL.

⑤ To run the command, press F10 and ↵Enter.

⑥ Press the space bar when MORE appears.

DESCRIPTIVES instructs SPSS/PC+ to calculate basic summary statistics for each variable listed after the command name. In this case you've asked for descriptive statistics for all variables. Figure 1.6 shows the output from the DESCRIPTIVES command.

Figure 1.6 Output from DESCRIPTIVES

```
Number of Valid Observations (Listwise) =        7.00

Variable      Mean    Std Dev   Minimum   Maximum    N  Label

AGE          44.57     18.04     19.00     70.00     7  Age of respondent
SEX           1.57       .53      1.00      2.00     7  Sex
EDUC         15.71      1.89     12.00     18.00     7  Highest year of scho
HOMPOP        2.71      1.60      1.00      5.00     7  Number of people in
AGEWED       22.14      2.19     19.00     26.00     7  Age of first marriag
STATE       This is a String (Alphanumeric) variable.    State of residence
```

Since descriptive statistics can't be calculated for a string variable, SPSS/PC+ displays a message reminding you that *STATE* is a string variable. For each of the five remaining variables you see the arithmetic mean (*Mean*), the standard deviation (*Std Dev*), the smallest (*Minimum*) and largest (*Maximum*) values, and the number of observations (*N*). (If you're not familiar with these statistics, they are all described in Chapter 9.)

The last column contains part of the label assigned on the VARIABLE LABELS command. Since your screen can display only 80 characters, the label is truncated to the maximum length that will fit on the screen.

SAVING AND GETTING AN SPSS/PC+ SYSTEM FILE

Once you've entered the data values, variable names, and labels, it's a good idea to save all of the information in a **system file**. A system file contains the data, the variable names, and labels in a format that SPSS/PC+ can read very efficiently. To save a system file:

① Select read or write data and then the SAVE command.

② Select OUTFILE. The typing window opens.

③ Type

```
educ.sys
```

and press ↵Enter. The file name is pasted between the apostrophes.

④ To run the command, press F10 and ⏎Enter. There is now a file educ.sys in your \spss\data directory.

If you want to save the file on a diskette in the A: drive, type

`a:educ.sys`.

To retrieve the file later, from read or write data enter and run the command

`GET /FILE 'educ.sys'.`

and press F10 and ⏎Enter. To retrieve the file from a diskette in the A: drive, run the command

`GET /FILE 'a:educ.sys'.`

These commands are discussed further in Chapter 5.

LEAVING SPSS/PC+

To end an SPSS/PC+ session and return to the DOS prompt, highlight FIN-ISH and press ⏎Enter to paste the command. Then press F10 and ⏎Enter to run the command.

WHAT'S NEXT?

In this chapter you ran a simple SPSS/PC+ analysis. You saw that you communicate with SPSS/PC+ by running commands. The next chapter describes SPSS/PC+ commands in more detail.

Summary

How do you run SPSS/PC+?

To start SPSS/PC+, you type spsspc and press ⏎Enter.

To tell SPSS/PC+ what you want it to do, you enter commands in the scratch pad.

To run commands, you press F10 and ⏎Enter.

When MORE appears on the screen, you press the space bar.

To leave SPSS/PC+, you enter FINISH and then press F10 and ⏎Enter.

EXERCISES

1 The SHOW command provides information on SPSS/PC+ running options, such as
   the length and width of a page, screen colors, the command prompt, and so forth.
   You can change these options using the SET command.

   a. Using SPSS/PC+, enter and run the SHOW command. You can paste it from the
      menu session control & information.

   b. Use the FINISH command to return to DOS.

   c. If there is a printer connected to your PC, turn it on and type

   ```
   print spss.lis
   ```

   to obtain a printed copy of the information produced by SHOW.

2 a. Start up SPSS/PC+ again. If you already ran the commands in this chapter, en-
      ter and run the command

   ```
   GET /FILE 'educ.sys'.
   ```

   If you did not previously save educ.sys, run the commands in this chapter now.

   b. Press Alt V to see a list of the variable names. While the Variables menu is open,
      press ⊕ until AGE is highlighted. Use the arrow keys to see what information is
      available for each variable named on the DATA LIST command. This variable list
      is a good place to check the spelling of variable names and to see variable labels.

3 Ask five students the number of hours of class they have each week, the number
   of hours they study each week, their age in years, and their home town.

   a. Enter and run the commands shown below. Between BEGIN DATA and END DATA,
      enter values for the data you gathered. A typical case describing a student from
      Peoria is shown as an example.

   ```
   DATA LIST FREE
    /hometown (a20) age classhrs studyhrs.
   BEGIN DATA
   "Peoria" 19 15 30
   fill in the rest of the values here
   END DATA.
   VARIABLE LABELS HOMETOWN 'City or town'
       /AGE 'Age of student'
       /CLASSHRS 'Class hours per week'
       /STUDYHRS 'Hours of study per week'.
   ```

   b. Run a LIST command and check your data.

   c. Run the command

   ```
   DESCRIPTIVES AGE CLASSHRS STUDYHRS.
   ```

SPSS/PC+ Commands and Sessions

How do you communicate with SPSS/PC+?

■ How should SPSS/PC+ commands look?

■ Does spelling matter? What about spaces between words?

■ How does SPSS/PC+ know where the end of a long command is?

■ What kinds of commands are typically used in an SPSS/PC+ session?

■ What statistical procedures are available?

I n Chapter 1 you saw that you operate SPSS/PC+ by giving it instructions that it has been programmed to understand. The word or group of words that SPSS/PC+ understands are known as **commands**. In this chapter we'll consider the components of a single SPSS/PC+ command and how a group of commands together make up a session.

COMMANDS AND SPECIFICATIONS

Each command must begin with a command name. DATA LIST, BEGIN DATA, END DATA, VARIABLE LABELS, LIST, and DESCRIPTIVES are all SPSS/PC+ command names.

In a few situations, the entire command consists of just the command name. For example, the LIST command in Chapter 1 consisted of only the word LIST. It didn't need any additional specifications since, by default, it lists the values of all variables for all cases, which is what we wanted. (The word **default** refers to the action taken by a command when you do not provide instructions to the contrary.)

However, command names are usually followed by additional specifications. For example, to override the default and list only the values for *STATE* and *EDUC*, you would specify these variables on the LIST command:

```
LIST STATE EDUC.
```

In some cases, additional specifications, such as a list of variables, are required; in other cases, as in the LIST command, they are not.

Subcommands and Keywords

Like command names, subcommands and keywords are words that SPSS/PC+ has been programmed to recognize. Subcommands and keywords allow you to customize your commands. For example, if you want to number the output from the LIST command, you can use the FORMAT subcommand with the NUMBERED keyword, as shown in Figure 2.1. The slash (/) before FORMAT indicates the start of a subcommand.

Figure 2.1 Parts of a command

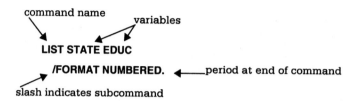

The output from this LIST command is shown in Figure 2.2. You can compare this listing with the output from the LIST command in Chapter 1.

Figure 2.2 Listing

```
Case#  STATE                  EDUC
    1 Illinois               16.00
    2 Ohio                   15.00
    3 North Carolina         16.00
    4 Oregon                 17.00
    5 New Mexico             18.00
    6 Kansas                 12.00
    7 Massachusetts          16.00

Number of cases read =      7    Number of cases listed =      7
```

There are hundreds of subcommands and keywords in SPSS/PC+, but you do not need to worry about most of them. Procedures are designed so that most of the time you get what you need without having to give lengthy specifications. Complete command specifications appear on the reference card at the back of this book. You can also view information about each command and its subcommands in the menus.

RULES FOR CONSTRUCTING COMMANDS

When you are entering commands you must follow these rules:
- Each command must begin on a new line.
- All commands must end with a period or be followed by a blank line.
- A subcommand must be separated from the previous subcommand by a slash.
- One or more blanks must separate all words and symbols on a command.
- Some command specifications use additional punctuation, such as parentheses, quotation marks, and equals signs. Equals signs are usually

optional, but parentheses and quotation marks or apostrophes are required.

Some shortcuts:

- Command names and keywords can be abbreviated to the first three characters. Variable names cannot be abbreviated.
- You can enter commands in upper or lower case.
- You can use as many lines as you want for entering a command as long as you use a period to indicate the end of a command. However, you can't split a word across two lines.

THE SPSS/PC+ SESSION

To do anything useful with your data, you need at least two SPSS/PC+ commands, one to describe your data and another to analyze it. In a typical SPSS/PC+ session, you usually have more than two commands. You can do any or all of the following:

Identify and describe your data. This includes giving names to the variables and supplying descriptive information so the output is easier to read.

Modify your data. You can compute new variables from existing ones. For example, you can add two variables together or square them. You can also change the data values. For example, you can create a new variable that has a value of 1 if the highest year of education is less than or equal to 8, 2 if the highest year is greater than 8 and less than or equal to 12, and 3 if it is greater than 12. Then the value 1 would represent elementary school, 2 high school, and 3 at least some college. You can also analyze a subset of the data.

Analyze your data. This is your main objective. Table 2.1 lists the commands that are available to analyze your data. In Chapters 8 through 27, you'll find descriptions of many different types of analyses you can perform.

Save your data. You can save the data you defined or modified for easy subsequent use.

Table 2.1   Statistical procedures discussed in this book

Command name	What the command does
ANOVA	Computes a multi-way analysis of variance or covariance.
CORRELATION	Computes Pearson correlation coefficients and their observed significance levels.
CROSSTABS	Counts the number of cases with distinct combinations of values and computes chi-square tests of independence and measures of association.
DESCRIPTIVES	Computes descriptive statistics.
EXAMINE	Provides stem-and-leaf plots, boxplots, robust estimates of location, normal probability plots, and other descriptive statistics and plots.
FREQUENCIES	Computes frequency tables, histograms, and descriptive statistics.
MEANS	Computes descriptive statistics when cases are subdivided into groups based on one or more grouping variables.
NPAR TESTS	Computes nonparametric tests that require minimal assumptions about the data.
ONEWAY	Computes a one-way analysis of variance and multiple comparison tests.
REGRESSION	Estimates a bivariate or multivariate regression model and calculates diagnostics to see how well the model fits.
PLOT	Produces a scatterplot of two variables. Points can be identified by their values on another variable.
RANK	Produces new variables containing ranks and scores.
T-TEST	Tests the equality of two means and produces descriptive statistics.

WHAT'S NEXT?

In this chapter you learned that you use commands to communicate with SPSS/PC+. You also saw that SPSS/PC+ commands consist of command names, subcommands, keywords, and additional specifications such as lists of variables. In the next chapter you'll see an example of a complete session and an alternative method of entering commands.

Summary

How do you tell SPSS/PC+ you want it to analyze your data?

You communicate with SPSS/PC+ by using commands.

SPSS/PC+ commands are made up of command names, subcommands, keywords, additional specifications such as variable names and labels, and punctuation.

You can abbreviate a command or keyword to its first three letters. Spelling doesn't matter after the third letter. You must spell out variable names in full.

You can enter commands in upper or lower case, and you can vary the number of blanks between words.

Each command must begin on a new line and end with a period. You can split a command across lines, as long as you don't split a word.

In addition to the period, SPSS/PC+ commands contain slashes, parentheses, and equals signs. Slashes and parentheses are required.

A typical SPSS/PC+ session includes commands that identify, modify, analyze, and save your data.

SPSS/PC+ has many commands for analyzing data.

EXERCISES

Syntax

1 Find the error in each of the following commands:

a. `List cases 5`

b. `list cases5.`

c. `list 5 cases.`

d. `LIST STATE educ /CASES 5 FORMAT NUMBERED.`

Data Analysis

1 A survey was sent out asking writers in and around Chicago about their salaries. Answers given by five of the writers are listed as follows.

Sex	Years experience	Annual salary	Work location
2	4	30,000	city
1	20	38,000	suburb
1	7	34,000	city
1	6	39,000	city
2	8	38,000	suburb

a. Following the example in Chapter 1, enter these data using the commands DATA LIST, BEGIN DATA, END DATA, and VARIABLE LABELS. Be sure to use the same punctuation as in Chapter 1.

b. Run a LIST command to check the data.

c. Run a DESCRIPTIVES command to calculate summary statistics.

3 A Data Analysis Session

What goes into a typical data analysis session?

- What types of commands are usually included?
- How do you know what subcommands are required?
- How do you save and print files?
- Can you get a list of variables?
- Can you just type the commands instead of pasting?
- How do you run just one command from the middle of a list?
- How do you find a specific command in the menus?

I n Chapter 1, you entered commands into the scratch pad from the menus. This chapter will describe how some of these functions might work together in a session.

In most of the examples in this book, the examples start with the GET command to read a system file instead of a DATA LIST command. You obtain the same results if you use DATA LIST and the other commands every time, but GET is easier and a lot faster. Just remember—after defining your data with DATA LIST or TRANSLATE, save the data with the SAVE command.

A SAMPLE SESSION

In this sample session, we will create a simple bar chart of a variable called *SATJOB*, save the results, and print them.

Starting SPSS/PC+

1 At the DOS prompt, type

cd \spss\data

and press ⏎Enter.

2 To start the program, type

spsspc

and press ⏎Enter again.

Identifying your data

There are three ways to get your data into SPSS/PC+:

- You can use GET if the data have been saved into a system file with the SAVE command.
- You can use DATA LIST to read data contained in a separate data file or included with your commands between the BEGIN DATA and END DATA commands (see Chapter 5).
- You can use TRANSLATE to read a file from a spreadsheet or database program (see Chapter 5).

The most efficient of these three is to use GET and SAVE. For example, in Chapter 1 you defined the data using DATA LIST and saved a system file with the SAVE command. When you want to use these data again, just start SPSS/PC+ from the c:\spss\data directory, enter the command

```
GET /FILE 'educ.sys'.
```

press F10, and press ⏎Enter to run the command. (GET is from read or write data.) If the file is on diskette in the A: drive, use the command

```
GET /FILE 'a:educ.sys'.
```

The GET command creates an **active file** containing all the data, variable names, and labels. You can then proceed with your analysis. You don't have to enter DATA LIST, BEGIN DATA, or VARIABLE LABELS again.

This time you are going to retrieve a system file called gss.sys. Ask your instructor if this file is available on your system. It contains data from the General Social Survey and is described in more detail in Chapters 6 and 7. This is a file we will be using throughout the book for examples and exercises.

1. Press ⬇ to highlight read or write data, and press ➡.

2. Press ⏎Enter to select GET, and then press ⏎Enter again to select FILE.

3. Type

```
gss.sys
```

in the typing window and press ⏎Enter.

4. Press F10 and ⏎Enter to run the command.

Analyzing your data

Often you want to describe the data by counting how frequently people gave each answer to a question asked during interviews.

1. Select analyze data and descriptive statistics. The FREQUENCIES command is highlighted at the top of the list. Press ⏎Enter to paste it.

The tilde (~) in front of VARIABLES indicates that this item is required.

2. Highlight VARIABLES and press ⏎Enter to paste it. The Variables window pops open.

3. Use the arrow keys to highlight the variable SATJOB and press ⏎Enter to paste it. Then press Esc to close the Variables window.

4. Highlight and paste BARCHART, and press Esc to return to the FREQUEN-CIES menu.

⑤ Paste FORMAT and then NOTABLE. The command now looks like this:

`FREQUENCIES SATJOB /BARCHART /FORMAT NOTABLE.`

This command requests a bar chart of *SATJOB* and suppresses the tables usually displayed by FREQUENCIES.

⑥ Press F10, and then ↵Enter.

You can watch the case counter in the upper right corner and then press the space bar when MORE appears. The resulting bar chart is shown in Figure 3.1.

Figure 3.1   Bar chart of job satisfaction

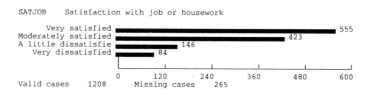

```
SATJOB      Satisfaction with job or housework

      Very satisfied  ███████████████████████████████████ 555
Moderately satisfied  ████████████████████████████ 423
A little dissatisfie  █████████ 146
   Very dissatisfied  █████ 84
                      ┼──────┼──────┼──────┼──────┼──────┼
                      0     120    240    360    480    600
Valid cases    1208   Missing cases   265
```

Saving Your Results

Normally, the output from a command goes to a file named spss.lis.

❶ To see the file in the listing window, press F2 and ↵Enter, as in Chapter 1.

However, each time you start a new session, SPSS/PC+ deletes the previous spss.lis file and starts a new one. If you want to keep your results, you need to save them in a file with another name. Follow these steps:

❷ Press ↑ to move the cursor up to the line containing the FREQUENCIES command in the listing window and press F7 and then ↵Enter. This is the beginning of the area you want to save.

❸ Move the cursor to a line below the bar chart and press F7 again. Now the area you want to save is highlighted.

❹ Press F9, use the ← key to highlight write Marked area in the mini-menu, and press ↵Enter. The mini-menu displays REVIEW.TMP.

❺ Type a new name right over REVIEW.TMP. Although you can use any three-letter extension, if you always use the extension lis for a listing file, you can remember what kind of file it is. In this instance, you might use barchart.lis.

❻ Press ↵Enter and SPSS/PC+ saves the highlighted area into the file barchart.lis. The file is saved in the DOS directory you were in when you started SPSS/PC+.

Saving Your Commands

If you think you might want to use the same commands again, you can save them in another file. The process is the same as saving a listing file.

❶ If the cursor is not in the scratch pad, press F2 and ⏎Enter. The cursor switches windows.

❷ Press F9 and then ⏎Enter.

❸ Type a name for the file. In this case, you might type barchart.job, using the extension job to help you remember that this file contains a series of commands.

❹ Press ⏎Enter. SPSS/PC+ saves the file.

To run these commands again, all you need to do is enter the following command in the scratch pad (INCLUDE is on the session control & info menu)

```
INCLUDE 'barchart.job'.
```

and press F10 and then ⏎Enter.

Printing a File

If your computer is attached to a printer, you can print the listing file after you run the FINISH command to leave SPSS/PC+.

❶ To end the session, paste FINISH. Then press F10 and then ⏎Enter.

❷ At the DOS prompt, type

```
print barchart.lis
```

and press ⏎Enter.

This is the usual method of printing the file. You may have different instructions, either in your computer manual or from a computer-system supervisor.

You can also print output as you generate it by entering the command

```
SET PRINTER ON.
```

at any time during your SPSS/PC+ session. (SET is on the menu session control & info.) To stop printing within a session, use

```
SET PRINTER OFF.
```

If your printer prints rows of question marks instead of bars, it is not recognizing the extended ASCII characters. To get bars composed of Xs, use the SET SCREEN OFF command before you run the FREQUENCIES command. The commands look like this:

```
SET SCREEN OFF.
GET FILE 'gss.sys'.
FREQUENCIES SATJOB /BARCHART /FORMAT NOTABLE.
```

The output is sent to the file and not shown on the screen, although you can access the listing window after the commands have been run.

TYPING AS AN ALTERNATIVE TO PASTING

Up until now, we have showed you how to paste commands and their specifications into the scratch pad while you typed only filenames and variable names that SPSS/PC+ did not already know. It is also possible to type commands and their subcommands directly into the scratch pad without using the menus. We will get the system file saved in Chapter 1 and create a bar chart comparing the number of males and females.

After starting SPSS/PC+, turn off the menus:

❶ Press Alt M.

❷ Type

```
get file 'educ.sys'.
```

Be sure the apostrophes and the period are in the right places.

❸ To run the command, press F10 and ⏎Enter. You can press Alt V to see the names of the variables.

After you run the command, the menus return; the blinking box cursor indicates that pressing any keys will affect the menus, not the scratch pad.

❹ Press Alt M again to turn off the menus.

❺ Type and run the command

```
frequencies sex /barchart /format notable.
```

The output is shown in Figure 3.2.

Figure 3.2   Bar chart showing value codes

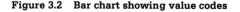

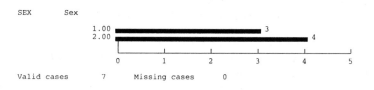

It is apparent that we never told SPSS/PC+ that values 1 and 2 are codes for male and female.

⑥ Press ⒜ⓛⓣ ⓜ to turn off the menus and type the following command:

```
value labels sex 1 'Male' 2 'Female'.
```

For more information on the VALUE LABELS command, see Chapter 5.

⑦ Turn off the menus again and move the cursor back up to the FREQUEN-CIES command. Press ⒡⒎, ⒠⒩⒯⒠⒭, and ⒡⒎ again, to highlight the command.

⑧ To run only the highlighted command, press ⒡⒑⒪, use the arrow keys to highlight run marked Area in the mini-menu, and press ⒠⒩⒯⒠⒭.

Now the bar chart has labels that make it easy to interpret, as shown in Figure 3.3.

Figure 3.3   Bar chart showing value labels

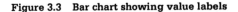

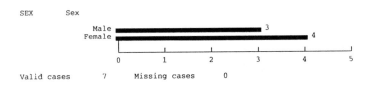

FINDING A COMMAND IN THE MENUS

Suppose you know that you want to paste a particular command, but don't know where to find it in the menus. For example, you might want to sort the cases in the educ.sys file by years of education, from highest number to lowest number of years.

① Turn off the menus by pressing ⒜ⓛⓣⓜ.

② In the scratch pad, type

```
sort
```

③ To open the menus, press ⒜ⓛⓣⓜ again. The SORT menu pops up, and you don't have to find it from the Main menu.

④ Select sort variable(s), paste EDUC, and press ⒠⒮⒞ to close the Variables window.

⑤ Press ⬇ to highlight (D) and then paste it. D stands for descending order.

⑥ Turn off the menus by pressing ⒜ⓛⓣⓜ and type a period to end the command. Run the command.

⑦ Turn off the menus. Type and run the command

```
list.
```

The cases are now listed in descending order.

Any time you want to paste a particular command or want to read its help windows, you can type it in the scratch pad and press (Alt)(M) to open the menus to the correct menu. If you type a command with one or more sub-commands and press (Alt)(M), the menus will open to the menu of the subcommand in which the cursor is positioned.

RUNNING SPSS/PC+ WITH MENUS OFF

If you want to type all your commands directly in the scratch pad without pasting from the menus, run the following command:

```
set automenu off.
```

Then the menus will not be displayed unless you specifically open them. You can put this command in an initialization profile, as described in Appendix C.

Entering Commands in Examples and Exercises

To run commands shown in this book, you can enter them either by pasting or by typing. If you know exactly what commands you want to run, typing may be faster.

SUMMARY OF MENU FEATURES

Below is a list of features, most of which were illustrated in this chapter. The menus themselves contain information on how to use the system in the orientation section. Complete information on using the Menu system is in the *SPSS/PC+ 4.0 Base Manual*.

- You can highlight menu items by pressing (↑) and (↓). Whenever a menu item is highlighted, a description appears in the Help window to the right of the menu.

- An arrowhead to the right of a menu entry indicates that there is a submenu. To see the submenu, press (↵Enter) or (→). (↵Enter) pastes; (→) places the highlighted keyword in a holding area, so you can paste a whole series later by pressing (↵Enter).

- Required items are preceded by a tilde (~).

- All subcommands that you can paste are in uppercase letters and are preceded by a slash.

- Other keywords are in uppercase with no slash.

- A lowercase item that begins and ends with hyphens is an informational item. A Help window describes the items beneath it on the menu list.

- A lowercase item with no hyphens can be selected by pressing ⏎Enter or ⊕. It leads to another menu.

- When a subcommand requires the name of one or more current variables, pasting it from the menus causes the Variables window to open.

- To paste a variable from the Variables window, use the arrow keys to highlight it; then press ⏎Enter.

- If a subcommand contains a pair of single quotes, pasting it opens the typing window. Whatever you type is pasted between the quotation marks when you press ⏎Enter.

- If a keyword or subcommand contains a pair of parentheses, pasting it opens the typing window. Whatever you type is pasted between the parentheses when you press ⏎Enter.

- Pressing Alt Esc takes you back to the Main menu.

- To close the menus, press Alt M.

- It is possible to edit the scratch pad without closing the menus: press Alt E. The border around the menu turns gray, and you can type in the scratch pad. Press Esc or Alt E to activate the menus again. When using this method, be sure that you know whether you are in the menus or the scratch pad before you start typing.

WHAT'S NEXT?

In this chapter you became more familiar with the REVIEW editor and the mechanics of running SPSS/PC+ efficiently. In the next chapter you'll see how to take advantage of more SPSS/PC+ features.

Summary

What features are used in a typical data analysis session?

A tilde (~) on the menus indicates a required item.

To get a list of variables, press (Alt)(V).

To use data from a system file that was saved with the SAVE command, run a GET command.

To save text on the screen into a new file, highlight it with (F7) and then press (F9) to specify the filename.

You can print a file after leaving SPSS/PC+ by using the DOS PRINT command.

You can turn off the menus by pressing (Alt)(M) and type commands in the scratch pad.

To run a command in the middle of a list, highlight it with (F7) and press (F10) (A).

To find a command in the menus, turn off the menus, type the command name, and press (Alt)(M) to turn the menus back on.

EXERCISES

1 From the DOS directory c:\spss\data, start SPSS/PC+ by typing spsspc and then pressing (←Enter). In the scratch pad, enter the command

```
get file 'gss.sys'.
```

This retrieves the file gss.sys, which contains data from the General Social Survey. The rest of the exercises use the file gss.sys.

2 Press (Alt)(V), highlight MARITAL, and read its label at the top left of the box. Then press (Alt)(↓) and read the value labels for the codes 1 through 5 and 9. Press (Esc) to clear the Variables menu.

3 Enter and run the command

```
descriptives educ agewed.
```

When you finish reading the descriptive statistics, press the space bar to move on to the next screen. When you see MORE, press the space bar again until you see the cursor in the scratch pad.

4 Press [F2]. The Windows mini-menu at the bottom of the screen highlights Switch. Press [↵Enter] and the cursor moves to the listing window at the top of the screen. The cursor should be on a new line in the scratch pad. Enter and run the command

```
list sex age educ/cases from 11 to 20.
```

In this group of 10 individuals, three are male and seven are female. If you want to check the value labels, go back to the scratch pad and use [Alt][V] to look at the Variables window. Highlight *SEX* and press [Alt][↓] to see the value labels. Press [Esc] to close the window.

5 Now you can mark a block of text in the output and save it in a file. Switch to the listing window by pressing [F2] and [↵Enter]. Press [↑] to move the cursor up the screen. If you keep pressing [↑] when the cursor reaches the top of the screen, the output scrolls down. Stop when the cursor is on the line containing the LIST command that matches the one you typed in the scratch pad. To highlight the line in the output, press [F7] and [↵Enter]. The line blinks, waiting for you to mark the end of a text block. Move the cursor down and stop on the line starting with Number of cases read.

Press [F7] again. SPSS/PC+ tells you how many lines are marked. Press [F9] and use the arrow keys to highlight write Marked area. Press [↵Enter]. SPSS/PC+ waits for you to type a filename. Type a filename (for example, sxaged.lis) right over RE-VIEW.TMP. You can use lower case. When you press [↵Enter], the output you marked is saved in a file. The cursor is still in the Listing window. Press [F2] and [↵Enter] to switch windows.

6 To leave SPSS/PC+, paste the command

```
FINISH
```

press [F10], and then press [↵Enter]. If you have a printer, you can print the file sxaged.lis from DOS by typing the DOS command

```
print sxaged.lis
```

and pressing [↵Enter]. DOS commands don't have periods at the end.

4

Using SPSS/PC+ Efficiently

What features will help you run SPSS/PC+ efficiently?

- Are there special keys to help with editing?
- What if you can't remember what each special key does?
- What other functions does the REVIEW editor provide?
- Can you get a list of saved files?
- How can you find definitions of statistical terms?
- Are there shortcuts to make editing faster?
- How do you modify the number of decimal places in a value?

In Chapters 1 and 3, you pasted or typed commands into the scratch pad. REVIEW, the text editor built into SPSS/PC+, provides simple editing functions, as well as a number of specialized functions designed to make your work in SPSS/PC+ easier. This chapter will describe the functions available in REVIEW.

EDITING TEXT IN THE SCRATCH PAD

To communicate with SPSS/PC+, you paste or type commands into the scratch pad. But what if you want to change something or you make a mistake? You need to know how to move the cursor around and how to change what you have typed. If the menus are on, press (Alt)(M) to turn them off temporarily.

Moving the cursor. To move the cursor up, down, right, or left on the screen, you can use the keys with arrows on them. You can also do the following:

- If the cursor is at the end of a line, press (←Enter) to move the cursor to a new blank line.
- To make the cursor jump to the end of a line, press (Ctrl)(→).
- To jump back to the beginning of the line, press (Ctrl)(←).

Insert or overtype. The REVIEW editor, like many other computer editors, can operate in two modes: insert and overtype. When you start SPSS/PC+, it is in **insert** mode. That means that when you start typing, the letters and numbers are *inserted* at the position of the cursor. Any text to the right of the cursor is pushed further to the right.

- To change from insert mode to **overtype** mode, you press (Ins). Then the characters you type *replace* the ones that are already there.
- To change back to insert mode, just press (Ins) again. This key acts like a toggle switch—whenever you press it, the mode changes.

Deleting text. To delete a character, you can use one of these methods:

- Move the cursor to the character following the one you want to delete and backspace over it.

- Move the cursor to the character you want to delete and press (Del).

Joining lines. If you press (←Enter) by mistake when the cursor is positioned within a line, the line splits into two separate lines at the cursor position.

- To join two lines together, move the cursor into the upper line, press (Ctrl)(→) and then press (Del). The cursor jumps to the end of the line and the two lines are joined together.

After your changes are made, you can run commands in the scratch pad or position the cursor where you want the next entry and press (Alt)(M) to turn the menus back on.

USING FUNCTION KEYS AND MINI-MENUS

A lot of what you do in a text editor is typing. However, when you need to give a command like "save all this into a disk file" or "switch from the scratch pad to the listing window," you use the **function keys** labeled (F1), (F2), and so forth, on your keyboard. You have already used (F10) to run SPSS/PC+ commands.

When you press a function key, the REVIEW editor displays a one-line **mini-menu** at the bottom of the screen, offering a choice of related commands. For example, if you press (F1), the mini-menu shown in Figure 4.1 appears at the bottom of your screen.

Figure 4.1 Mini-menu for info

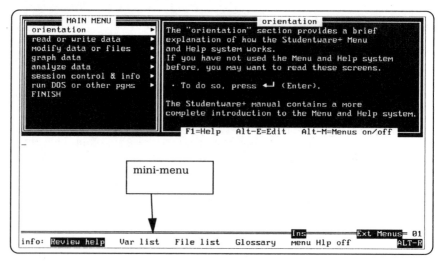

The mini-menu shows the general topic for the function key you pressed (the topic for F1 is info) followed by a list of commands related to that topic. One command, here the first one, Review help, is highlighted.

■ To accept the highlighted command, press ↵Enter.

■ To select another command, press the left or right arrow (← or →) and then press ↵Enter.

■ Another way to run a command from a mini-menu is to type the letter that is capitalized in the command. This is usually, but not always, the first letter of the command.

Let's look at Review help. Press ↵Enter to select Review help from the mini-menu. The help screen in Figure 4.2 appears.

Figure 4.2 Help screen

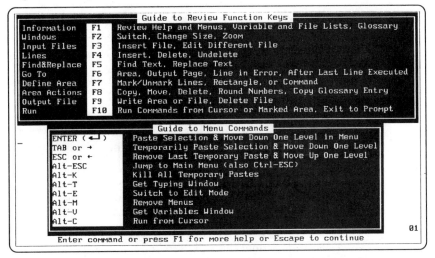

```
┌─────────────────── Guide to Review Function Keys ───────────────────┐
│ Information      F1   Review Help and Menus, Variable and File Lists, Glossary │
│ Windows          F2   Switch, Change Size, Zoom                       │
│ Input Files      F3   Insert File, Edit Different File                │
│ Lines            F4   Insert, Delete, Undelete                        │
│ Find&Replace     F5   Find Text, Replace Text                         │
│ Go To            F6   Area, Output Page, Line in Error, After Last Line Executed │
│ Define Area      F7   Mark/Unmark Lines, Rectangle, or Command        │
│ Area Actions     F8   Copy, Move, Delete, Round Numbers, Copy Glossary Entry │
│ Output File      F9   Write Area or File, Delete File                 │
│ Run              F10  Run Commands from Cursor or Marked Area, Exit to Prompt │
└─────────────────────────────────────────────────────────────────────┘
        ┌─────────────── Guide to Menu Commands ───────────────┐
│       │ ENTER ( ↵ )   Paste Selection & Move Down One Level in Menu │
─       │ TAB or →      Temporarily Paste Selection & Move Down One Level │
        │ ESC or ←      Remove Last Temporary Paste & Move Up One Level │
        │ Alt-ESC       Jump to Main Menu (also Ctrl-ESC)      │
        │ Alt-K         Kill All Temporary Pastes              │
        │ Alt-T         Get Typing Window                      │
        │ Alt-E         Switch to Edit Mode                    │
        │ Alt-M         Remove Menus                           │
        │ Alt-V         Get Variables Window                   │
        │ Alt-C         Run from Cursor                        │
        └──────────────────────────────────────────────────┘  01
        Enter command or press F1 for more help or Escape to continue
```

The top part of the screen lists the general topics (on the left) and the specific commands (on the right) associated with each function key. The rest of the screen reminds you which keys to use when you want to access other features. If you press F1 again, you see which keys to use when you want to move the cursor around or modify the file you're editing. Press Esc to clear the help screen.

Function Key Commands

As shown in Figure 4.2, the following commands are available by pressing the function keys:

Information   F1 provides REVIEW help, access to SPSS/PC+ menu screens from within REVIEW, information on your variables, and the SPSS/PC+ glossary (see the next section on "Additional Help").

Windows   F2 lets you switch the cursor between the listing window and the scratch pad or adjust the size of the windows.

Input Files   F3 lets you insert the entire contents of another file into the file you're editing, or edit a different file altogether.

Lines   F4 lets you insert a line before or after the line the cursor is on, delete a line, or recover the last line you deleted.

Search & Replace   F5 lets you search the file for specific text or replace text (selectively or globally) with different text.

Go To   F6 lets you move the cursor immediately to a specific page number in the SPSS/PC+ output file, or to a marked area if you have marked one (see F7).

Define Area   F7 is used to mark an area (either a group of lines, a rectangular area, or an SPSS/PC+ command) for use with the F8 commands. Position the cursor on the first line of the area to be marked and press F7 and then ENTER. Then position the cursor on the last line to be marked and press F7.

Area Actions   F8 lets you copy, move, or delete a marked area; round all of the numbers in the marked area to a specific number of decimal places; or (when the glossary is active) paste a glossary definition into the file you are editing.

Output File   F9 lets you save the file (or a marked area within it) onto disk or delete an existing file from disk.

Run   F10 lets you submit commands to SPSS/PC+ for processing or move to a prompted session, as discussed in Appendix C.

Additional Help

In addition to the REVIEW help screens, you can obtain the following additional help from the info mini-menu (F1), shown in Figure 4.1:

- **Varlist.** If you have executed a DATA LIST or GET command (see Chapter 5), this feature displays a window that lists all the variable names you have defined. By pressing (Alt) with ↓, you can view the label for each value.

- **File list.** SPSS/PC+ asks for a DOS file specification (such as *.sys or a:*.*) and then displays a window containing the names of all disk files meeting that specification. As you highlight the name of each file, SPSS/PC+ displays its size and creation date.

- **Glossary.** SPSS/PC+ asks for the Item to look up. Type a word used in statistics and data analysis. (If your cursor is on a word, SPSS/PC+ automatically fills in that word. You can use this feature as a shortcut to avoid retyping a statistical term that appears in your output.) SPSS/PC+ then displays the definition if it's in the glossary. If not, SPSS/PC+ displays the definition of the closest matching term—which may or may not be similar to the one you're looking for. If you press (F8) while the definition is visible, SPSS/PC+ pastes it into the editing window. Clear the definition by pressing (Esc), or browse through neighboring definitions with (Ctrl)(PgDn) and (Ctrl)(PgUp).

- **Menus.** The Menu system contains all the commands and their subcommands along with explanations and examples. Instructions for using the menu system are in the Orientation window at the top of the Menu system. To close the menus, press (Alt)(M). If you then type a command name in the scratch pad and press (Alt)(M) again, the Menu system opens at the level of the typed command, displaying help for the typed command.

Shortcuts

Some REVIEW commands have keyboard shortcuts, which let you bypass the mini-menus by pressing (Alt) along with a letter. Obviously, you're not going to memorize all these commands at once. Refer to this list if you use a command frequently and want a shortcut.

(Alt)(B)	Inserts a line before the cursor location.
(Alt)(C)	Runs SPSS/PC+ commands, starting at the command where the cursor is.
(Alt)(F)	Opens the file list.
(Alt)(G)	Opens the glossary.

(Alt)(I)   Inserts a line after the cursor location.

(Alt)(M)   Opens or closes the Menu system for SPSS/PC+ commands.

(Alt)(R)   Opens the REVIEW help display.

(Alt)(S)   Switches to the other window when you are editing two files.

(Alt)(V)   Opens the variable list.

(Alt)(W)   Writes the file you are editing to disk.

(Alt)(Z)   Zooms the window to fill the screen. Press (Esc) to "unzoom."

MODIFYING DATA FORMATS

Another way to make output easier to read is to modify the number of decimal places in numeric values. In Chapter 1, the values for HOMPOP were printed in the output as *1.00*, *2.00*, and so forth. Two decimal places is the default format for numerals. Since these values represent the number of people in the household, there's no need for the decimal places. To change the display format, follow these steps:

1 From the menus, enter and run the command

```
GET /FILE 'educ.sys'.
```

2 Select labels & formatting from the read or write data menu and paste the FORMATS command.

3 Select variable and paste the variable HOMPOP. Press (Esc) to return to the FORMATS menu.

4 Paste (F) and type 2.0 in the typing window. The 2 indicates a width of two characters and the zero indicates that no characters are wanted after the decimal point. The width of two characters was chosen in case anyone lives with ten or more people; on the other hand, three digits for 100 or more people would be unreasonable, unless you defined a large dormitory as a household.

5 Press (↵Enter) to paste the number. Then run the command.

6 Select analyze data, descriptive statistics, and paste the FREQUENCIES command with VARIABLES HOMPOP.

7 Paste the BARCHART subcommand and run the FREQUENCIES command.

The output is shown in Figure 4.2.

Figure 4.3 Frequencies output

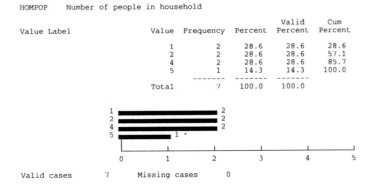

```
HOMPOP      Number of people in household

                                                  Valid      Cum
Value Label                  Value  Frequency  Percent  Percent  Percent

                                1        2      28.6     28.6     28.6
                                2        2      28.6     28.6     57.1
                                4        2      28.6     28.6     85.7
                                5        1      14.3     14.3    100.0
                                      -------  -------  -------
                     Total              7     100.0    100.0

            1 ████████████████ 2
            2 ████████████████ 2
            4 ████████████████ 2
            5 ████████ 1 .
              ┴─────────┴─────────┴─────────┴─────────┴
              0         1         2         3         4         5

Valid cases      7     Missing cases      0
```

The values for number of people in the household are now listed as 1, 3, 4, and 5, in the frequencies table as well as on the bar chart. If you save the new system file, the new format for HOMPOP will be used each time you get the file again. If you open the Variables window and highlight HOM-POP, Width is listed as 2 and Decimals as 0.

WHAT'S NEXT?

In this chapter you became more familiar with the REVIEW editor and the mechanics of running SPSS/PC+ efficiently. In the next chapter you'll see the details of how data can be entered in SPSS/PC+.

Summary

What features will help run SPSS/PC+ efficiently?

Pressing a function key ([F1], [F2], etc.) displays a mini-menu at the bottom of the screen. You can highlight and run any selection.

You can display a list of variables in the current active file by pressing [Alt][V].

A list of files is available by pressing [Alt][F].

Definitions of statistical terms are in the glossary, available by pressing [Alt][G].

Many other REVIEW commands are available by pressing [Alt] and a letter.

To save text on the screen into a new file, highlight it with [F7] and then press [F9] to specify the filename.

To modify numeric display formats, use the **FORMAT** command.

EXERCISES

To do the following exercises, you should have the file gss.sys in the \spss\data directory.

1 From the DOS directory c:\spss\data, start SPSS/PC+. Then press [Alt][F], type *.sys, and press [↵Enter]. A window appears, showing you the files in the current DOS directory that end with sys. The asterisk (*) is a "wild card" and can substitute for any character or characters. Press [Esc] to clear the window.

2 In the scratch pad, enter and run the command

    GET /FILE 'gss.sys'.

3 Press [Alt][M] to turn the menus off. Type and run the command

    descriptives age educ hompop.

Press the space bar when MORE appears.

4 To see the listing file, press [F2] and [↵Enter]. Use the arrow keys to move the cursor to the word Mean and press [Alt] [G] for the Glossary. The word *Mean* is already entered in the message line. When you press [↵Enter], you can see the entry for Mean. press [F8] to paste it into the listing window.

Press (Alt)(G) again and type n and then (↵Enter). This gives you the definition for another column heading in the output.

Press (Ctrl)(PgUp) to see the glossary entry which is alphabetically just above the current item. Press (Esc) to leave the glossary.

The definition of *Mean* in the listing file is highlighted. Press (F9) and save the marked area to a file meandef.lis. You can print it later from the DOS prompt.

5 Switch back to the scratch pad. Get the file educ.sys, created in Chapter 1. With the menus off, type plot and open the menus. Finish entering and run the following command:

```
plot /plot educ with age.
```

From the plot, how old is the person with 12 years of education?

6 To leave SPSS/PC+, enter

```
FINISH.
```

press (F10), and then press (↵Enter). If you have a printer, you can print the file meandef.lis from DOS by typing the DOS command

```
print meandef.lis
```

and pressing (↵Enter).

5 Defining Data

How do you tell SPSS/PC+ about your data file?

■ What are cases, variables, and values?

■ How can you enter data from spreadsheets and databases into SPSS/PC+?

■ What are variable names and why are they necessary?

■ How do you indicate that data values are unavailable or missing?

■ What is a system file and why is it useful?

I n this chapter you'll see how to prepare data for entry into SPSS/PC+ and how to set up the necessary commands for describing your data.

CASES, VARIABLES, AND VALUES

A data file consists of cases, variables, and values. A **case** is the basic unit for which you obtain measurements. In a survey of political opinions, a case is the person you question. In a study of company performance, the case is the company. For each case you record information about **variables.** Variables can be age, type of product purchased, or attitude about a particular issue. You obtain information about the same variables for all cases. What differs for the cases are the actual **values** of the variables.

Consider the example in Chapter 1. The data are shown in Figure 5.1. In this data set there are seven individuals, or cases. For each case, the following variables are recorded: age, sex, education, number of people in the household, age of first marriage, and state of residence. The first case has a value of 33 for age, a code of 2 for sex, 16 years of education, and 1 person in the household who married at 19 and is living in Illinois.

Figure 5.1 Education data

```
      AGE      SEX      EDUC     HOMPOP   AGEWED STATE
     33.00     2.00    16.00     1.00     19.00 Illinois
     43.00     2.00    15.00     2.00     21.00 Ohio
     47.00     1.00    16.00     4.00     23.00 North Carolina
     35.00     2.00    17.00     1.00     21.00 Oregon
     65.00     1.00    18.00     2.00     26.00 New Mexico
     19.00     1.00    12.00     5.00     22.00 Kansas
     70.00     2.00    16.00     4.00     23.00 Massachusetts

Number of cases read =      7    Number of cases listed =      7
```

Before entering data into SPSS/PC+, you must decide how to code the data, how to represent missing data, and what variable names to use. Missing values and variable names are discussed below. Data coding is discussed in Chapter 7.

Missing Values

For some cases you may not be able to obtain values for some of the variables. In such situations you must enter a special code known as a **missing-value code** to indicate that the value is unavailable.

For each variable you can select one code to represent missing values. The code you choose for a variable should be one that can't possibly occur in the data. For example, for a variable like age you can use a negative number, such as –1, as the missing-value code, since only positive ages are possible. For every case where you don't know the age, you would enter the value –1. On the other hand, if you have a variable like change in income, you can't use a negative number to indicate missing values, since it's certainly possible for income to drop, resulting in a negative income change.

To tell SPSS/PC+ what codes you have selected for each variable to designate missing values, you must use the MISSING VALUES command, which is discussed later in this chapter.

Variable Names

You must assign each variable in your file a name by which you will refer to it when requesting analyses. Follow these rules when assigning variable names:

- Give every variable a different name.
- Don't use more than eight characters.
- Start the name with a letter. The rest of the characters can be letters or numbers.
- Choose names that help you remember what the variable is. For example, *PRICE* is more descriptive than *XYZ*.
- The words in the following list have special meaning in SPSS/PC+ and cannot be used as variable names:

ALL	EQ	LE	NOT	TO
AND	GE	LT	OR	WITH
BY	GT	NE	THRU	

Variable names are specified on the DATA LIST command, or they are translated directly from a spreadsheet or database when you use the TRANSLATE command. Both of these commands are discussed below.

READING THE DATA INTO SPSS/PC+

Before you can analyze your data, you have to read it into SPSS/PC+. There are several ways you can accomplish this, depending on what form the data are in:

- The TRANSLATE command reads data from spreadsheets (with each case in a row and each variable in a column) and databases in dBASE format.

- The DATA LIST command reads data contained in a text file, such as one created by a word processor and saved in "text" or "ASCII" format.

- Finally, there is a special SPSS/PC+ format for data files. If you have used the SAVE command to create a file in this special format, you can read it very efficiently with the GET command. GET and SAVE are discussed at the end of this chapter.

Spreadsheets and Databases: The TRANSLATE Command

If your data are in a spreadsheet or database on the computer, you can tell SPSS/PC+ to read the data directly from the spreadsheet or database file. SPSS/PC+ uses the file extension to know what kind of file to expect. Table 5.1 lists the different formats that SPSS/PC+ knows how to read and the filename extensions. Most spreadsheet and database programs can save a file in one of these formats.

Table 5.1 Spreadsheet and database formats

Format	File extension
Lotus 1-2-3 Rel. 1A	.WKS
Lotus 1-2-3 Rel. 2.x	.WK1
Lotus 1-2-3 Rel. 3	.WK3
Symphony 1, 1.01	.WRK
Symphony 1.1, 1.2, 2	.WR1
Multiplan (SYLK)	.SLK
Excel (SYLK)	.SLK
dBASE II, III, IV	.DBF

For example, if you've entered the compensation profiles of various companies into a Lotus spreadsheet named pay.wk3 with each company in a row and compensation in a column, you can read the data with the command

```
translate from 'pay.wk3'.
```

If you have a database saved in dBASE format in a file named educ.dbf, you can read it all into SPSS/PC+ with the command

```
translate from 'educ.dbf'.
```

Variable Names

SPSS/PC+ takes variable names directly from the spreadsheet or database when you use the TRANSLATE command. When translating from a database, SPSS/PC+ uses the database variable names (fieldnames). When translating from a spreadsheet, by default SPSS/PC+ uses column names as its variable names. With a Lotus 1-2-3 spreadsheet, this produces variables named *A*, *B*, *C*, and so on.

Since column names are not very descriptive, you may want to use the column headings (titles) as variable names instead. If your spreadsheet contains column headings in the first row, you can use them as variable names by adding the FIELDNAMES subcommand to your TRANSLATE command:

```
translate from 'pay.wk3' /fieldnames.
```

Ranges

By default, SPSS/PC+ tries to read the entire spreadsheet or database file. In the case of spreadsheets, every row in the spreadsheet becomes a case. (If you use the FIELDNAMES subcommand, every row after the first becomes a case.) Rows that don't contain data or that contain column labels become problem cases.

Often you can solve such problems by telling SPSS/PC+ to read only a certain range from the spreadsheet. If you've given a name to a range in the spreadsheet program, you can use that name:

```
translate from 'pay.wk3' /range=current.
```

If the range that contains the data you want to analyze doesn't have a name, specify it directly. For Lotus 1-2-3 and Symphony spreadsheets, use the usual range notation with two periods separating the beginning and end of the range:

```
translate from 'pay.wk3' /range=b6..k119.
```

For SYLK files saved from Excel or Multiplan, use a colon:

```
translate from 'pay.slk' /range=r2c6:r11c119.
```

If the spreadsheet has column headings that you want to use as variable names, just include the headings within the range and specify the FIELD-NAMES subcommand, too:

```
translate from 'pay.wk3' /range=b5..k119 /fieldnames.
```

If you still have unwanted rows within your range (for example, if you have a blank row or a row of hyphens between your column headings and your data), just delete the unwanted rows and columns in the spreadsheet program and save a trimmed-down copy to read into SPSS/PC+.

Text Files: The DATA LIST Command

If you don't have a spreadsheet or database program, you can type the data into a text file and then read it into SPSS/PC+ using the DATA LIST command. You can use any word processor or text editor, or you can turn off the menus (Alt M) and type directly into the scratch pad and edit the file within SPSS/PC+ (see Appendix C).

The easiest way to enter your data into a text file is to use what is called "free" format. The rules are simple:

- Enter all the variables for each case in the same order, separating each value with a blank space (or a comma).

- You must enter a value for every variable for every case. If you don't have a value, enter the code specified on the MISSING VALUE command for that variable.

- If there are blanks or commas within a string variable, enclose the values in quotes.

- Press ↵Return at the end of each case. (This isn't strictly necessary, but it's a good idea.)

- Save the file as a plain text file. Your word processor may call this "unformatted," "text," "ASCII format," or something similar. Most text editors automatically save plain text files. If you are using the SPSS/PC+ editor in the scratch pad, press F9, type the filename, and press ↵Return.

Once you have a text file containing only your data, with blank spaces separating each value, you read the data into SPSS/PC+ with the DATA LIST command. On the DATA LIST command you specify the name of the file that contains the data, and you assign variable names to the values in the data file. A typical DATA LIST command looks like this:

```
data list free file 'educ.dat'
 /age sex educ maeduc paeduc state (a20).
```

After the DATA LIST command name you specify FREE for free format. Next is the FILE subcommand, where you specify the name of your text file between apostrophes. Then comes a slash and your list of variable names. The variable names must be specified in the same order that you entered the data for each case. Otherwise SPSS/PC+ will not be able to match up the correct values with each variable. After string variables, you must specify the letter *a* and the length of the longest value in parentheses.

Data in the Same File with Commands

For small data sets you may want to include the data in the same file as the SPSS/PC+ commands. If you do this, you omit the FILE specification from the DATA LIST command, since the data are not in a separate file. Instead, the data are included between the BEGIN DATA and END DATA commands. For an example, see Chapter 1.

DESCRIBING THE DATA

Once you have read your data into SPSS/PC+ and assigned variable names, you can provide additional descriptive information, such as missing-value codes and variable and value labels.

Missing Values

To define the codes used to represent missing data, use the MISSING VALUES command. List the name of each variable followed by its missing-value code in parentheses. For example, if you use a missing-value code of 0 for *EDUC*, *MAEDUC*, and *PAEDUC* and a code of –1 for *AGE*, use the following command:

```
missing values educ (0) maeduc(0) paeduc (0) age (-1).
```

If you use the same code for several variables, you can list all variables that have the same code and then specify the code once. For example, the previous command can be simplified to

```
missing values educ maeduc paeduc (0) age (-1).
```

Variable Labels

Although you should try to choose variable names that are descriptive, it's hard to identify a variable in just eight characters. You can use the VARIABLE LABELS command to assign descriptive labels to variable names. These labels are printed on your output whenever the variables are used. Although variable labels are not required, they're often helpful, especially if your output is going to be read by others.

For example, to assign a label to the *EDUC* variable, run the command:

```
variable labels educ 'Highest year of school completed'.
```

After the command name, list the variable followed by a label in quotes. Be sure the label does not have more than 40 characters, including spaces and punctuation marks.

If you want to assign labels to several variables, you can list them all on the same VARIABLE LABELS command:

```
variable labels educ 'Highest year of school completed'
   maeduc "Mother's highest year of school".
```

If you want to include an apostrophe as part of a label, enclose the label in quotation marks. Instead of pasting apostrophes from the menu, turn the menus off ((Alt)(M)) and type the quotation marks and the label.

Value Labels

A variable label helps you remember what variables are. However, a variable label doesn't tell you anything about the meaning of the values for the variable. To assign labels to each value, use the VALUE LABELS command.

For example, if the *SEX* variable is coded 1 for male and 2 for female, use the command

```
value labels sex 1 "Male" 2 "Female"
```

After the command name, give the name of a variable followed by each value and the label in quotes. A label cannot be longer than 20 characters and it cannot be split across command lines.

When you have several variables with the same coding scheme, you can list all of the variable names together before you start identifying the values. You can also assign different labels to different variables on a single VALUE LABELS command. Separate the labels for one variable from the labels for another with a slash.

If the values are letters, the variables are string variables, and you must put the letters in quotes everywhere you use them in your SPSS/PC+ commands. For example, if *SEX* has the values M and F, these values must be specified in quotes on the VALUE LABELS command:

```
value labels sex "M" "male" "F" "female".
```

SAVING AND RETRIEVING SYSTEM FILES

Once you've read your data into SPSS/PC+ and assigned missing-value codes and descriptive labels, it's sometimes convenient to save it all as an SPSS/PC+ system file. A system file contains the data plus variable names, variable labels, value labels, and missing-value definitions in a format that SPSS/PC+ can read very efficiently.

To create a system file, use the SAVE command:

```
save outfile 'educ.sys'.
```

This command saves the data and the data descriptions in a file named educ.sys.

To read in data from a system file you've previously saved, use the GET command:

```
get file 'educ.sys'.
```

After the GET command, you can proceed immediately with your analysis. You don't need to use the DATA LIST or TRANSLATE command, and you don't need to redefine labels and missing values.

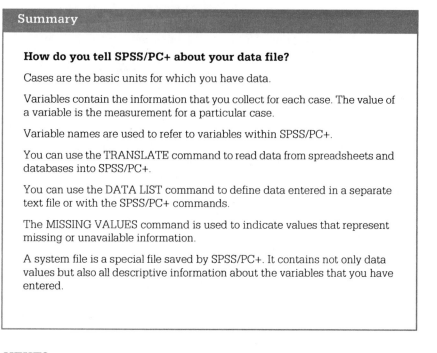

Summary

How do you tell SPSS/PC+ about your data file?

Cases are the basic units for which you have data.

Variables contain the information that you collect for each case. The value of a variable is the measurement for a particular case.

Variable names are used to refer to variables within SPSS/PC+.

You can use the TRANSLATE command to read data from spreadsheets and databases into SPSS/PC+.

You can use the DATA LIST command to define data entered in a separate text file or with the SPSS/PC+ commands.

The MISSING VALUES command is used to indicate values that represent missing or unavailable information.

A system file is a special file saved by SPSS/PC+. It contains not only data values but also all descriptive information about the variables that you have entered.

WHAT'S NEXT?

In the last five chapters you were introduced to the mechanics of operating SPSS/PC+. In the next two chapters you'll learn about some of the issues associated with designing studies and preparing data for analysis.

EXERCISES

Syntax

1 Which of the following are not valid SPSS/PC+ variable names? Identify what's wrong.
   a. PORCUPINE
   b. MA EDUC
   c. EDUC12YR
   d. 89GRADE
   e. &345AB
   f. VYTAUTAS

2 Correct the errors in the following commands:
   a. `translate from mydata.dbf.`

b. `translate from 'mystuff.slk' /range c3 to c14.`

c. `tanslate from 'datafile.wk1' /fieldnames A1..K14.`

d. `data list free file=mydata/ a b c.`

e. `data list free age race sex.`

f. `variable labels satis Satisfaction with Product.`

g. `value labels '1' male '2' female.`

h. `missing values satis (1, 99, -5).`

3 The following commands are meant to enter the grades of 10 students on an exam. What's wrong with these commands?

```
datalist free / score
variable labels scores "Score on Midterm Exam".
100
23
95
72
88
99
67
89
62
53
```

4 a. Think up four variables for a study you might be interested in conducting. Make up data for a dozen or so cases on the four variables. Enter the data into a data file.

b. Write the DATA LIST command needed to read your data file.

c. Write VARIABLES LABELS and (if appropriate) VALUE LABELS commands for your study.

d. Run an analysis including the DATA LIST, VARIABLE LABELS, and VALUE LABELS commands. Include a LIST command to print a list of the values in your data file. Check to make sure they agree with what you entered. If not, correct your commands and run them again.

6 Designing a Study

How should you proceed if you want to explore an idea?

- What information do you want to obtain?
- Who or what do you want to be able to draw conclusions about?
- Who will you include in your study?
- Will it be an experiment or a survey?

If it's an experiment:

- How will you decide who goes into which group?
- How will you decrease the chance that the subjects or experimenters influence your results?
- How will you choose a comparison group?

Y ou must state your ideas clearly if you plan to evaluate them. This advice applies to any kind of work and especially to research design and statistical analysis. Before you begin working on design and analysis, you need to have a clearly defined topic to investigate.

ASKING A QUESTION

You may have a general suspicion that smoking less makes people feel better. Or you may have an idea for a study method that will make people learn more. Before you begin a study about such intuitions, you should replace vague concepts such as "feeling better" or "smoking less" or "learning more" with definitions that describe measurements you can make and compare. You might replace "feeling better" with an objective definition such as "the subject experiences no pain for a week." Or you might record the actual dosage of medication required to control pain. If you're interested in smoking, you need a lot of information to describe it. What does each of the subjects smoke—a pipe, cigars, or cigarettes? How much tobacco do the subjects consume in a day? How long have they been smoking? Has the amount they smoke changed?

On the other hand, you must balance your scientific curiosity with the practical problems of obtaining information. If you must rely on people's memory, you can't ask questions like "What did you have for dinner ten years ago?" You must ask questions that people will be able to answer accurately. If you're trying to show a relationship between diet and disease, for example, you can't rely on people's memory of what they ate at individual meals. Instead, you have to be satisfied with overall patterns that people can recall. Some information is simply not available to you, however much you'd like to have it. It's better to recognize this fact before you begin a study than when you get your questionnaires back and find that people were not able to answer your favorite question. If you think about your topic in advance, you can substitute a better question, one that will give you information you can use, even if it's not the information you *wish* you could have.

What Information Do You Need?

A critical step in any study is the decision about what information you are going to record for each participant. Of course, you can't record every possible piece of information about your subjects and their environment. Therefore, you should think hard about what information you will try to get. If you accidentally forget to find out an important characteristic of your subjects, you may be unable to make sense of the patterns you find in your data. When in doubt, it is usually better to record more information than less. It's easy to leave unnecessary variables out of your data analysis, but it's often difficult (and expensive) to go back and gather additional information. For example, if you're studying what types of people are likely to buy a high-priced new product, you may not be able to adequately describe buyers versus nonbuyers if you forget to include information about income.

DEFINING A POPULATION

When you conduct a study, you want your conclusions to be far reaching. If you're a psychology student, you may want your results to apply to all laboratory rats, not just the ones in your lab. Similarly, if you're doing a market research survey on whether people in Los Angeles would buy disposable umbrellas, you may want to draw conclusions about everybody in the city. The people or objects about whom you want to draw conclusions are called a **population.** One of the early steps in any study is nailing down exactly what you want your population to be.

Defining a population may seem straightforward, but often it isn't. Suppose that you are a company personnel manager and you want to study why people miss work. You probably want to draw conclusions only about employees in your particular company. Your population is well defined.

However, if you're a graduate student writing a dissertation about the same topic, you face a much more complicated problem. Do you want to draw conclusions about professionals, laborers, or clerical staff? About men or women? Which part of the world is of interest—a city, a country, or the world as a whole? No doubt, you (and your advisor) would be delighted if you could come up with an explanation for absenteeism that would apply to all sorts of workers in all sorts of places. You're not likely to come up with that kind of explanation, though, and even if you do, you're not likely to come up with the evidence to support it. People miss work for lots of reasons (besides being sick), and the reasons are quite different for different kinds of employees. For example, the president of a major corporation probably doesn't need to stay home waiting for a phone to be installed. And the afternoons he takes off to play golf are probably not recorded in the personnel office as absenteeism.

To be realistic, you should study only a part of the labor force. Absenteeism among laborers in auto factories in Detroit, for example, is a problem with a well-defined population about which you'd have a fighting chance to draw some interesting conclusions.

Even when the population of interest seems to be well defined, you may not actually be able to study it. If you're evaluating a new method for weight loss, you would ideally like to draw conclusions about how well it works for all overweight people. You can't really study all overweight people, though, or even a group that is typical of all overweight people. You will probably be able to try out your new method only on people who want to lose weight. People who don't want to lose weight or who have been disheartened by past efforts to reduce may not agree to try yet another method.

A population that includes only people who want to lose weight may be lighter, younger, or healthier than the ideal population of all overweight people. Therefore, your conclusions from studying people who want to lose weight don't necessarily apply to people who are not motivated. For example, the treatment may have some unpleasant consequences, such as making people want to chew on the nearest thing available, like gum, a pencil, or the corner of a desk. People who really want to lose weight will be willing to put up with such minor inconveniences to reach their goal. People who don't much care about their weight may toss in the scale quickly. Thus, the new treatment may work quite differently for those who are motivated versus those who are not.

Sampling

If you have decided that your population of interest is all rats or all residents of Los Angeles, you certainly don't want to have to train all of the world's rats or personally visit every Los Angeles home. What you want to do is study *some* rats or people, draw conclusions based on what you've observed in them, and have the conclusions apply to the population in which you're really interested.

The rats or people (or other creatures or objects) that you actually observe in your study are called the **sample.** You can select a sample from a particular population in countless ways. How you do it is very important, because if you don't do it right, you won't be able to draw conclusions about your population.

Random Samples

What is a good sample? A sample is supposed to let you draw conclusions about the population from which it's taken. Therefore, a good sample is one that is similar to the population you're studying. But you should *not* go out and look for animals, vegetables, or minerals that you think are "typical" of your population. With that kind of a sample (a **judgment** sample) the reliability of the conclusions you draw depends on how good your judgment was in selecting the sample—and there's no way to assess the selection scientifically. If you want to back up your research with statistics, you need a **random sample.** Statisticians have studied the behavior of random samples thoroughly. As you will learn in later chapters, the very fact that a sample is random means that you can determine what conclusions to draw about the population from which the sample is taken.

? *So what is a "random sample" if it's so important?* It is a sample in which every member of the population (animal, vegetable, mineral, or whatever) has a fair chance of being selected. No particular type of creature or thing is systematically *excluded* from the study, and no particular type is more likely to be *included* than any other. Each unit is also selected independently: including one particular unit doesn't affect the chance of including another.   ■■■

If you are interested in the opinions of all the adults in Los Angeles, do not rely on a door-to-door poll in midafternoon or ask questions of people as they leave church services on a rainy Sunday. Such samples exclude many of the types of people about whom you want to draw conclusions. People who have jobs are usually not home on weekday afternoons, so their opinions would not be included in your results. Similarly, people standing in the rain may express different opinions—especially about umbrellas, for example—than they would if they were warm and dry. Polling in the rain may lead you to the wrong conclusion about the proportion of the city's residents interested in your new product, disposable umbrellas. To make things worse, you *can't tell* what the effects of excluding dry people will be. You can't tell whether your observed results are biased one way or another, and you can't tell by how much. You might even be on target, but you don't know that either.

From any particular random sample, of course, the results are not exactly the same as the results you would get if you included the entire population. Later chapters will show you how statistical methods take into account the fact that different samples lead to somewhat different results. You will then understand how much you can say about a population from the results you observe in a sample.

Volunteers

To make it easier to have people participate in your study, you may be tempted to rely on volunteers. But you should not rely on any special types of people, and volunteers are one of those special types. Many studies have shown that people who volunteer are different from those who don't. Often, volunteers are different in important ways.

For example, when Ann Landers conducts a survey by asking people to write in and express their opinions, she is relying on people who write to her voluntarily. These people are probably quite different from the people who don't. The people who do bother to write in about topics like having children or dealing with noisy neighbors or interacting with the opposite sex form a special type of sample.

The results from this kind of voluntary sample don't even apply to the population of all people who read the column, and the results certainly don't apply to any wider population. Who is likely to take up a pen and write to a columnist? Certainly not students cramming for finals. Most likely, the respondents are people with time on their hands, people who have very strong feelings one way or another, and people who read papers that carry that particular column. (Then, too, the respondents are limited to people who can read and write.) You can't generalize the results of a columnist's survey like this to *any* larger group.

Similarly, if you stand in a shopping center with your newly invented disposable umbrella in one hand and a clipboard in the other, and you wait for people to voluntarily come up and talk to you, your results probably won't apply to any well-defined larger group. Only when a sample is selected randomly, so that all members of the population have the same likelihood of being included, can you relate the sample results back to the target population. Sampling strategies are important in many different kinds of studies.

USING SURVEYS

Two categories of studies that are often undertaken are **surveys** and **experiments.** Other categories of studies are also done, but these two differ in a fundamental way. In a survey, unlike an experiment, you just record information about the participants (or perhaps ask them to record the information themselves). You ask questions or take measurements. You don't actually do anything to the people. In fact, you try as much as possible not to exert any influence.

To conduct a good survey, you must phrase your questions so they don't suggest "correct" answers. If you're interviewing a person, you must make sure that you don't smile and thus encourage a particular response.

For the same reason, you must not frown or even raise an eyebrow when you disapprove. In legal jargon, you must not "lead the witness."

You must also make sure that you question all people with the same eagerness and not elicit more thorough information from one type of person than from another. If you think too much education makes people neurotic, you must make sure that you question those who have advanced degrees and those who don't with the same fervor about their neuroses. You must be careful not to dig deeper in the psyches of people with advanced degrees.

You can get survey data in two different ways. You can conduct your own survey, or you can get the data from a survey that somebody else has already done.

Conducting Your Own Survey

The great advantage of conducting your own survey is that you can tailor it for your own research project. You can ask the questions you want to ask in the way you want to ask them. You can choose exactly the population you want to study and select just the kind of sample you need. You can control the training of interviewers, and you can deal with all of the problems that come up during the survey itself. In short, you can do everything possible to make sure the survey will help you answer your questions.

Doing all of these things takes a great deal of time and often a great deal of money. If you're going to invest a lot of time and money in a study, you owe it to yourself to get expert advice. Show your plans to someone who has actually carried out similar surveys, and ask for advice—*before* you take any big steps like printing the questionnaires.

A book on data analysis—like this one—can't tell you all you need to know to carry out a serious survey. But Chapter 7 does tell you some of the principles for designing the form for a questionnaire to simplify the task of analyzing your data.

Analyzing an Existing Survey

Without a doubt, the best way to get survey data is to design and carry out a survey focused on precisely the research questions you want to study. Realistically, though, you often have to settle for "re-using" a survey that somebody else has carried out. In fact, that is the strategy of most of the examples in this book (see Chapter 7). Using data from a survey that wasn't designed for your study is often called **secondary analysis** to distinguish it from the **primary analysis** that was the purpose of the original survey.

Secondary analysis lets you do research that you couldn't otherwise do all on your own. But you must keep in mind that the data were not collected specifically for your own interests. The survey questions may not have measured exactly what you wanted them to, but you're stuck with them nonetheless. Remember to interpret them as they were asked, not as you wish they were asked.

When you plan to use existing data, you don't have to worry about the thousands of details that go into conducting a survey. Instead, you have to make sure that the survey was carried out properly in the first place. Was it conducted by a reputable organization? Were the questions well phrased, was the sample well chosen, were the forms carefully processed? Most important, have you formulated research questions that you can reasonably hope to answer with the existing data?

DESIGNING EXPERIMENTS

Unlike a survey, an experiment involves actually doing something to the subjects rather than just soliciting answers to questions. For example, instead of asking people whether they think that vitamin C is effective for preventing colds, you might give them vitamin C and observe how many colds they develop. Sometimes you study the subject before and after your experimental treatment. Sometimes, instead, you take several groups of subjects, do something different to each of the groups, and then compare the results.

Experimentation on people poses ethical questions that deserve careful thought. Many responsible institutions have committees that regulate experiments involving human subjects. If an experiment exposes a subject to risks, such as possible side effects from a new drug, you must certainly inform the subjects in advance. Usually you must have them sign forms to give their consent.

In experiments as well as surveys, the subjects must come from the population you're interested in. (As you can probably guess, proper sampling is much easier with laboratory animals than with people in a survey.) If you are comparing different treatments or techniques, you must also make sure that the groups receiving them are as similar as possible. Again, randomness is the key. The best way to make groups similar is to assign subjects to the groups randomly. This procedure doesn't guarantee that the groups will be exactly the same, but it does increase the likelihood.

Random Assignment

Random does not mean "any old way." You can't assign subjects to groups according to whatever strikes your fancy or let others make the assignment decisions for you. On the contrary, randomness requires a very specific, systematic approach to minimize the chance that groups will contain particular types of individuals. For example, if you wanted to study the effect of personal computers on learning and allowed school teachers to select which students received the computers, the teachers might select well-behaved students to reward them. These students may be more intelligent or more diligent than the students who don't get to use the special equipment. Any evaluation of the effect of personal computers would be tainted by the differences between the students.

A good way to assign people, animals, or objects to the groups in an experiment is to use a table of random numbers. You can't just make up a table of numbers that you think are random. You're likely to have certain number biases, such as birthdays, license plates, lucky numbers, and so forth. In a properly constructed table of random numbers, every number from 0 to 9 has the same chance of appearing in any position in the table.

Figure 6.1   A table of random numbers

```
8588 5171 0775 7818 8683 3168 1557 8319 8733 0678
7185 8645 1537 3754 0201 2450 5757 3479 6619 7297
1053 9728 3028 8725 4855 0218 8771 8711 5227 0172
75⑦ 0826 7257 5527 2668 8157 9188 9087 3322 9672
3551 3316 3584 9439 0011 7365 7787 2771 1246 3253
0540 5837 3791 5113 9965 1547 8996 2194 5726 7744
8465 5569 3735 9040 5370 9659 3204 8690 7635 0260
7596 3890 9413 0714 3739 6928 9430 1803 4582 6382
1975 2561 0757 4942 9724 4448 1938 8763 8070 4775
6568 4150 2359 9998 8336 1032 2512 4846 5662 0727
5663 0845 9992 1232 1894 8111 1875 5363 6654 4690
5752 0513 5976 5158 3309 6280 9070 4958 4529 9911
5289 1813 2026 5226 5053 6380 5452 2842 9163 0307
1025 1437 1879 5550 9449 7903 5308 6931 6937 2185
4487 6412 5533 7740 2590 2580 0091 1993 1185 7311
7362 1779 3391 5349 7330 6562 8946 2329 3123 8516
7848 7974 6174 8014 7262 2689 8035 8546 0975 4533
8752 9071 8844 8708 4724 9788 9572 1540 3772 0495
8139 0471 5303 2611 9669 3966 0300 6057 2510 0498
```

The table of random numbers in Figure 6.1 has the numbers grouped into fours, but the grouping is just for convenience. It has no other significance. To randomly assign subjects to groups, you start at an arbitrary place in the table and assign the digit at that place to the first subject. Each new subject gets a digit from successive places in the table. If you start at the circled location in Figure 6.1, for example, the first subject gets the number 7, the next subject the number 0, and the next subject the number 8. Since everything is random, it really doesn't matter whether you read the table across or down. However, once you've selected a starting point, stay in sequence. Using the table in this systematic way prevents you from choosing "favorite" numbers as starting points or as the next numbers in the sequence. You can never be too careful when you're trying to be random.

You use the numbers you assigned to the subjects to assign them to experimental groups. For example, if you have two groups, you can assign subjects with even numbers to one and subjects with odd numbers to the other. This procedure should result in about the same number of subjects in the two groups. But if you want the groups to be exactly equal in size, you can assign two- or three-digit random numbers to each of the subjects. Then arrange the numbers in order, from smallest to largest. Subjects with numbers in the lower half go to one group, and subjects with numbers in the upper half go to the other. You can use all sorts of systems with a random number table to assign subjects to groups, even in very complicated experimental designs.

? *Why is randomness so important? Does it really matter?* Yes, it does. Unless you use a procedure that assigns your subjects randomly, the results of your study may be difficult or impossible to interpret. Many assignment schemes that appear random to the inexperienced investigator turn out to have hidden flaws. On one occasion, researchers at a hospital compared two treatments for a particular disease. Patients who were admitted on even-numbered days received one treatment, and those admitted on odd-numbered days received the other. That assignment sounds random enough, but it failed. The number of patients admitted with the disease on even days gradually became larger than the number admitted on odd days. Why? What happened is that some of the physicians figured out the scheme and made it a point to admit their patients on days when the procedure they preferred was being used. Such biases make it possible for the patients admitted on even and odd days to be quite different. You can't rely on the results of such a study that used nonrandom assignment.   ■■■

"Blind" Experiments

In experiments, as in surveys, you must not bias your observations or treatments with your own opinions or preconceptions about which group or treatment should yield better results. Some events, of course, are not disputable, such as the fact that a rat has died. However, when making observations that are not as clear-cut, such as assessing the happiness of a person's marriage, it is all too easy to let unreliable judgment creep in— even though you're trying to be objective and "scientific."

Not only you as an experimenter but also your subjects (especially if they're humans) can influence the outcome of an experiment without even trying. An example of a biasing influence is the **placebo effect,** a well-known effect in medical research. The placebo, such as a brightly colored pill that has no real effect, and a (costly) pep talk from a sympathetic physician are enough to cure many ailments. In an experiment on alertness, for example, if students know that the vitamin supplements they get with their math lessons are intended to make them less sleepy during class, they may actually feel more alert (or more drowsy if they have a bias against the experiment's success).

The placebo effect can occur in many kinds of experiments, not just in medical research. To avoid the effect, prevent subjects from knowing which experimental group they're in, and don't tell them anything about the expected results. Keep them "blind" as much as possible. Ethical considerations require that they know about any risks and that they give "informed consent." However, you can still design the treatments to avoid biasing the results. For example, if one treatment requires a group of people to take pills, make sure that all of the other groups get pills too, even if they're just sugar.

The people who record the experimental results should also be unaware of the assignment of subjects to groups. They, too, should be "blind." Make sure they know exactly what to measure, such as weight without clothes, learning time to the nearest second, or anxiety on a particular scale. But avoid explaining more than they need to know. If you satisfy their curiosity by explaining what is going on while the study is in progress, you will never be sure whether they unconsciously affected the results. Explain the issues after the study is complete. Even if you're making the observations yourself, you can still keep yourself blind by not knowing which subject is in which experimental group. Have an assistant assign the subjects randomly to the various groups.

Medical studies are often characterized as being single blind or double blind. When only the subjects don't know to which groups or treatments they've been assigned, the experiment is called **single blind.** When both the experimenter and the subjects don't know the assignment, the study is called **double blind.** Double-blind studies are the most reliable.

Control Groups

If you're conducting a study to evaluate a new experimental method or treatment, make sure you include a group that *doesn't* receive the new treatment. This **control group** will provide you with measurements to which the results of the new treatment can be compared. If you're evaluating a new instructional method, for example, the appropriate control

treatment may be the standard instructional method. If you're doing a medical experiment, the appropriate control treatment may be the standard medication or procedure for a particular ailment.

Don't compare the new treatment's results just to historical information or "commonly held beliefs." Doing so can create a variety of problems. For example, a surgeon who is pioneering a new technique can't simply compare the survival rates of patients who were given the new operation with those of patients from previous years. Differences may occur for many reasons. Current patients may have been diagnosed earlier than previous patients, so they have a better chance of surviving. Another possibility is that the surgeon's skills may have improved with time, making the newer patients more likely to survive.

There are all kinds of differences between groups that are treated at different times. You don't know—you can't know—what all of these differences are and how they affect a study. To avoid this problem, make sure that a control group is part of your study's design, and don't rely on historical controls.

WHAT'S NEXT?

This chapter has briefly discussed some important points to think about when designing a study. There are many others. For further discussion of basic design issues, read N. M. Bradburn and S. Sudman's *Asking Questions* (1982) and B. Williams' *A Sampler on Sampling* (1978).

The next chapter focuses on survey research. You will learn about an extensive study known as the General Social Survey, which we will use in the examples throughout this book. You will also learn how to set up questionnaire forms so they are useful for interviews and for data analysis.

Summary

How should you proceed if you want to explore an idea?

You should carefully formulate a question and decide exactly what pieces of information are necessary to answer the question.

You must determine what the population of interest is and select a random sample of objects of people from the population.

You must be sure that you don't unintentionally bias your sample by making it more likely that some members are included than others.

The procedure for gathering the information must be objective and standardized. Questions must be unambiguous.

If several different conditions are being compared, you must ensure that the subjects are randomly allocated to the groups.

You must prevent the subjects and investigators from allowing their personal prejudices to influence the outcome of the investigation.

EXERCISES

1 If there are 50 children in a classroom and you wish to randomly select 10 of them to participate in a study, how would you go about selecting the sample?

2 A candidate for political office is interested in finding out what percentage of the city's voters support him. He has obtained bids from two survey organizations to conduct a poll for him. Both organizations plan to canvass about 1000 residents. The first, using a register of households, proposes to select a random sample of 400 households and then question all family members. The second plans to randomly select 1000 people from the population. Explain to the candidate which poll will probably be more informative and why.

3 Your former high-school principal is interested in why some of his graduates are successful and others not. He commissions you to develop a plan for studying this question.

   a. What is your population?

   b. Discuss several ways for selecting a sample.

   c. How would you define "success"?

   d. If you do a mailing to graduates and receive questionnaires returned as "undeliverable," discuss problems with just throwing them away.

   e. If you do a mailing, how will you deal with people who do not return your form? That is, how will you deal with the problem of non-response?

   f. What do you think of the strategy of distributing questionnaires at a class reunion?

4 Which of the following procedures should result in a random sample of a city's adult population?

   a. Random-digit dialing (a computer places calls to randomly generated phone numbers).

   b. Randomly selecting 10 places of employment and then randomly selecting employees within each.

   c. Selecting every fifth person entering a grocery store.

   d. Randomly selecting children in all schools and then including their parents in the study.

5 In the 1936 Presidential race between Roosevelt and Landon, the *Literary Digest*, a magazine that ran the largest polls of that time, predicted a Landon victory on the basis of 2,376,523 mail questionnaires (out of about 10,000,000 mailed). In fact, Roosevelt won by a margin of 19 percentage points. What possible reasons can you think of for their missing the mark so badly?

6 In the 1954 clinical trial of the Salk polio vaccine, many different study designs were considered.

   a. One possible approach would be to select a random sample of children and vaccinate them. What problems do you see with this approach?

   b. Another approach would be to vaccinate a group of children whose parents have volunteered them for the study, and then compare the polio rate for vaccinated children with the rate for unvaccinated children in the same area. What problems do you see with this approach?

   c. Many trials of medical agents must rely on volunteers. Can you think of a better strategy than giving all of the volunteers the new treatment and then comparing their results to known results in the general population?

   d. Knowing that polio is an epidemic disease in which clusters of cases occur, what do you think of vaccinating only all children in Chicago and then comparing their rate to all unvaccinated children in Detroit?

7 U.S. employment and unemployment statistics are based on results from the monthly Current Population Survey. One of the questions not included in the survey is, "Were you unemployed?" What would be wrong with asking the question in that way?

8 Suppose you want to determine how self-made millionaires differ from the general population.

   a. What problem do you see with just taking a random sample of the population?

   b. There are more complex types of random samples than those in which each unit has the same chance of inclusion. (In all of them, however, every member of the population has a known, non-zero chance of inclusion and this chance is taken into account in analyzing the data.) Suggest an alternative sampling strategy to deal with the problems you mentioned in part a.

9 List some problems you see with attempting to take random samples from large populations. What happens when you can't identify all the members of your population?

Designing Forms for Studies

How should you design the form that will be used for recording the data?

- What information will you gather for each respondent?

- How will you record the answers?

- How will you assign codes to answers?

- How will you indicate that a respondent refuses to answer a question or that the information is unavailable?

- How will you prepare the form to make it easy to enter the information into the computer?

B ecause it's much easier to follow explanations when they are tied to an example, the remainder of this book focuses on one large-scale study, the General Social Survey, or GSS. The General Social Survey is conducted by the National Opinion Research Center, NORC, a social science research organization at The University of Chicago. By examining parts of the General Social Survey in this book, you will learn about form design and coding, data entry, and especially about statistical analysis of the results. This chapter discusses design of the forms for collecting the data.

THE GENERAL SOCIAL SURVEY

The General Social Survey is administered every year to a sample of about 1,500 persons. This sample represents the population of adults living in the United States but not in institutions such as mental hospitals and college dormitories. Members of the military are also excluded. An interviewer visits each selected household and questions the chosen person, the **respondent,** about present and past experiences, behavior, and opinions.

The method that the National Opinion Research Center uses to select people for inclusion in the sample is complex. It involves first selecting a random sample of cities and counties, then a random sample of neighborhoods, then a random sample of households, and finally a person within a household. In this book, this sampling scheme will be treated as equivalent to a random sample of the population.

The General Social Survey was designed to include questions on many different topics, particularly questions previously asked on older surveys during the 1940s, 1950s, and 1960s. Having data for the same questions asked over the years lets people study how attitudes and opinions have changed. Data from the General Social Survey are distributed at nominal cost and are widely used by researchers and students. (See *General Social Surveys, 1972-1985: Cumulative Codebook.*)

Is Life Exciting?

So many questions are included in the General Social Survey that it would be hard to show the analysis of all of them. Instead, we will focus on one of the questions:

- In general, do you find life exciting, pretty routine, or dull?

We'll look at responses to this question and see how they relate to responses to several other questions, such as those about education, age, sex, marriage, and belief in life after death. But before looking at the actual data from these questions, let's start at the beginning.

DESIGNING THE FORM

Before you accumulate survey data, you must design an appropriate form. For many questionnaires, the respondent fills out the form. However, an interviewer might fill it out, or the respondent might fill out some parts and the interviewer might fill out other parts. For the General Social Survey, a trained interviewer fills out the form. This procedure adds to the cost of the study but makes it easier to control the way in which the questions are presented. In any case, the form must clearly specify what information is to be recorded and how it is to be recorded. To minimize the number of errors that occur when the form is used, you should make it easy to understand and reasonably simple.

Take the time to design your form so that the information from it can be easily entered into a computer. If you don't think about the data entry in advance, you'll be stuck with stacks of forms and no easy way to start analyzing them. You'll spend needless hours or even days recopying numbers from one form to another. This kind of work is tedious and—to make things worse—it increases the number of errors in the data. You won't make this mistake twice; plan ahead and don't make it at all.

Arranging the Form

Figure 7.1 shows a form like the one used for recording the results of a General Social Survey interview. Only some of the questions are shown, and they are rearranged from the original.

Interviewers fill out this form, or one like it, in the homes of the respondents. Interviewers are trained to read each question *exactly* as it appears, without varying a word and without indicating approval or dismay at the respondents' answers. All of the respondents must be asked the questions in the same say. If the interviewers don't ask the questions in a standard way, differences in their personalities or attitudes can contaminate the results.

As shown in Figure 7.1, there is a place on the form to record each piece of information. The *way* it is to be recorded is also clearly specified. For example, instead of asking directly for a person's age, the interviewer is to request the actual month, day, and year of birth. Since people are not always truthful about their age, asking for the date of birth instead of asking directly for age increases the likelihood of a correct answer. The computer will calculate the exact age later.

Never ask interviewers or respondents to calculate anything themselves. Get the raw numbers and let the machine do the arithmetic. If you're interested in the ratio of a person's weight to height, for example, have the interviewer or respondent record weight and height. Then have the computer calculate the ratio. This procedure saves time and increases the accuracy of the results. Computers divide better than distracted people with calculators.

Coding the Data

The answers to many questions are numbers. If you ask how much people weigh, how many cigarettes they smoke daily, or how many brothers and sisters they have, the answers will be numbers, and you can simply leave space on the questionnaire form to write in each one. You should leave enough room for the biggest number possible, even if you don't expect to get it. If you ask enough people how many children they have, for example, you will certainly find somebody who has 10.

When the answer to a question isn't a number, you should try to figure out in advance what answers are possible. Respondents would then select among the alternatives. If you don't think of the possible responses before the survey, you'll be in serious trouble. For example, if you let people supply their own answers to a question about how they view life in general, you'll probably end up with as many different answers as there are people in the survey. How are you going to analyze "Kinda OK," "Could be worse," "Great, except for my job," "Today exciting, yesterday not"? You would spend hours deciding what to do with hundreds of such answers. By forcing people to choose among specific alternatives (such as "Exciting," "Pretty routine," or "Dull"), you can get data that are easier to analyze.

? *What if you really are interested in the way people say things in their own words?* Sometimes you simply don't know in advance what people will say, and you want to allow them to say exactly what they please. You can certainly have interviewers write down exactly what the respondents say, word for word. Questions like these, which don't specify the possible responses, are known as **open-ended questions.** A computer won't be much help in analyzing open-ended questions directly, though, so you should either study the answers and assign codes to them before you enter your data or else ask the same questions again in a different way, with specified choices for responses. ■■■

Figure 7.1 Sample form with questions from the General Social Survey

---

```
1. Case Number  □□□□

2. What is your date of birth?

   □□    □□    □□□□
   Month  Day    Year

        Numerical Notations of Months

   January  01    May     05    September  09
   February 02    June    06    October    10
   March    03    July    07    November   11
   April    04    August  08    December   12

3. Circle Respondent's Sex:

   Male......1      Female.....2

4. Are you currently--married, widowed, divorced,
   separated, or have you never been married?

   Married.........1    Separated.......4
   Widowed.........2    Never married...5
   Divorced........3

5. On the whole, how satisfied are you with the work you
   do--would you say you are very satisfied, moderately
   satisfied, a little dissatisfied, or very dissatisfied?

   Very satisfied..........1
   Moderately satisfied....2
   A little dissatisfied...3
   Very dissatisfied.......4
   Don't know.............8

6. Taking things all together, how would you describe your
   marriage? Would you say that your marriage is very happy,
   pretty happy, or not too happy?

   Very happy...........1    Not too happy........3
   Pretty happy.........2    Don't know...........8

7. In general, do you find life exciting, pretty routine,
   or dull?

   Exciting.............1    Dull.................3
   Pretty routine.......2    No opinion...........8

8. Do you believe there is life after death?

   Yes..............1       Undecided........8
   No...............2

9. What is the highest grade in elementary school or
   high school that you finished and got credit for?
   CODE EXACT GRADE.

   No formal school....00    7th grade.......07
   1st grade..........01    8th grade.......08
   2nd grade..........02    9th grade.......09
   3rd grade..........03    10th grade......10
   4th grade..........04    11th grade......11
   5th grade..........05    12th grade......12
   6th grade..........06

10. IF FINISHED 9TH-12TH GRADE OR DON'T KNOW:

   Did you ever get a high school diploma
   or a GED certificate?

   Yes .................1
   No...................2
   Don't know...........8
```

11. Did you ever complete one or more years of college for credit--not including schooling such as business college, technical or vocational school?

    Yes 1
    No...............2
    Don't know.......8

    IF YES TO PREVIOUS QUESTION:

12. How many years did you complete?

    1 year............13   6 years...........18
    2 years...........14   7 years...........19
    3 years...........15   8 or more years....20
    4 years...........16   Don't know........98
    5 years...........17

13. Do you have any college degrees?

    Yes.................1
    No..................2
    Don't know..........8

    IF YES TO PREVIOUS QUESTION:

14. What degree or degrees? CODE HIGHEST DEGREE EARNED

    Associate/Junior college............2
    Bachelor's..........................3
    Graduate............................4
    Don't know..........................8

15. In which of these groups did your total family income, from all sources, fall last year--1983-- before taxes, that is. Just tell me the letter.

    A. Under $1,000 01
    B. $1,000 to 2,999..................02
    C. $3,000 to 3,999..................03
    D. $4,000 to 4,999..................04
    E. $5,000 to 5,999..................05
    F. $6,000 to 6,999..................06
    G. $7,000 to 7,999..................07
    H. $8,000 to 9,999..................08
    I. $10,000 to 12,499................09
    J. $12,500 to 14,999................10
    K. $15,000 to 17,499................11
    L. $17,500 to 19,999................12
    M. $20,000 to 22,499................13
    N. $22,500 to 24,999................14
    O. $25,000 to 34,999................15
    P. $35,000 to 49,999................16
    Q. $50,000 or over..................17
       REFUSED..........................97
       DON'T KNOW.......................98

    TOTAL INCOME INCLUDES INTEREST OR DIVIDENDS, RENT, SOCIAL SECURITY, OTHER PENSIONS, ALIMONY OR CHILD SUPPORT, UNEMPLOYMENT COMPENSATION, PUBLIC AID(WELFARE), ARMED FORCES OR VETERAN'S ALLOTMENT.

16. Would you say your own health, in general, is excellent, good, fair, or poor?

    Excellent.........1   Poor..............4
    Good..............2   Don't know........8
    Fair..............3

For questions that require choosing among alternatives, think about all the possibilities. Anticipate the unusual. For example, if you want to ask about housing, remember that not everyone lives in a house or an apartment. It is especially important to make provisions for responses such as "Don't know" or even "None of your business." Don't leave it up to an interviewer to decide what to do when somebody can't or won't answer a difficult question. Anticipate these problems, and write clear instructions on the form in the places where such answers can occur. Whenever there is a real possibility of answers that don't fit into your scheme, include an "Other" category, and leave space on the form for writing out the unusual answers. You may be able to do something with this written information later.

On the General Social Survey form, all acceptable answers to a question are listed. Each answer has a code with it, a number that represents that answer. For the view-of-life question, a code of 1 is circled for the answer *Exciting*, 2 for *Pretty routine*, and 3 for *Dull*. The code number 8 is reserved for the answer "Don't know." These numerical values are the **coding scheme** for the variable. For each respondent, one of these numbers will go into the computer to represent the answer to this question.

Coding schemes are arbitrary. A code of 3 could just as well have been assigned to the *Exciting* response and a code of 1 to *Dull*. What's important is that each possible response has a code that is different from the others. For example, you wouldn't code the states of the union by their first letters, because the first letters for the names of many states are the same.

Tips on Form Design

Here are a few hints about designing a form that will make your life a lot easier when it comes time to analyze the data.

Split up complicated questions. Some questions are best asked in parts. Questions 9–14 in Figure 7.1 were carefully designed to find out a respondent's level of education. Instead of just asking for total years of education, the General Social Survey asks about the highest year completed in grammar school or high school and then separately asks about college. This is so that someone who spent five years mastering first grade won't count them as five years of education. Because years of education don't always correspond to diplomas and degrees, the General Social Survey also asks for the highest degree received.

Record numbers when you can. Record information in as much detail as possible, using actual numbers. Don't group family size into small, medium, and large. Instead, get the exact number of people in the family. Later, you can use the computer to create categories like small, medium, and large based on the exact numbers. If you've recorded only the categories, you won't be able to try different grouping schemes or to analyze the data in more detail.

You may notice that the General Social Survey question about income doesn't follow this advice. That's because income is a sensitive matter for many people, and they may refuse to give their income as an exact dollar amount; or they may not know their yearly income to the nearest dollar. The General Social Survey softens the question by letting the interviewer hand a card to the respondent with preprinted income categories. That way, the respondent never needs to give an exact figure. Analyzing income categories may be harder than analyzing the exact incomes—but the problem would be even worse if people refused to answer at all or if they gave false answers.

Use a numeric coding scheme. When items require coding, assign numbers instead of letters to the responses. Numbers simplify both data entry and data analysis. For example, coding sex as 1 and 2 is simpler than coding sex as M and F.

Put an identification number on the form. You can use the identification number to locate forms that you later find to have errors or unusual values. Even if you're running a confidential survey and each form isn't linked to a particular person, put an identification number on the respondent's form *before* you enter the data into the computer. Then enter the identification number with the rest of the data. This number links the paper form and the computer record.

COLLECTING THE DATA

After you determine the questions you want to ask and the way you want to record the answers, and you design a clear form that's easy to use, you can begin to collect the data. In many studies, much of the work comes here. Remember that the interviewers must carry out your well-designed survey exactly as you specified. They must ask the questions in a standardized way, without leading the respondents, and they must use your coding schemes by entering the proper types of information in the right places. Unless the interviewers (or you yourself) gather the data well, all the work you did to prepare the study and any work you do to analyze it will be for naught.

REVIEWING AND PREPARING FORMS FOR DATA ENTRY

After you've collected your data but before you enter it, you should check through the forms to see if anything strange has happened. People who fill out forms or respond to questionnaires are very creative in coming up with ways to confound your expectations. They forget to answer questions, refuse to answer questions, answer questions twice, and make up their own alternatives rather than choose from the ones you gave them. You need to find out about these problems and decide how to handle them before anyone tries to enter your data into the computer.

Make sure that the special codes for missing and illegible answers are entered on the forms. You may have to expand the master list of codes to include new ones for unanticipated situations. If your study was conducted shortly after a blizzard, for example, you may find that snow removal ranked unexpectedly high among people's concerns. If you didn't have a preassigned code for snow removal, you may want to include one, so you can distinguish it from the rest of the *Other* concerns.

Remember, if *you* can't decipher a questionnaire, neither will the person who enters the data into the computer. Even if you enter the data yourself, you'll do a better job if you decide what to do with the problems in advance.

WHAT'S NEXT?

When you have the completed forms from your study and entered the data into a computer, you are ready to begin analyzing your data. That's what the rest of this book is about.

Summary

How should you design the form that will be used for recording the data?

Indicate a specific place on the form to record each piece of information.

Include an identification number on the form for each respondent.

Record the actual values for numeric data.

If necessary, assign codes to possible answers.

Assign special codes for missing or unavailable information.

Split up complicated questions into parts.

Make sure the data can be entered into a computer directly from the form.

EXERCISES

1 In question 3 in Chapter 6 we discussed a study to identify why some high-school graduates are more successful than others. Choose five measures of "success." Write the question, answers, and coding scheme you will use for obtaining the information.

2 A survey was conducted to examine voter preference in a mayoral campaign. The three viable candidates are Jane, Harry, and Rich. The following table contains responses for six of the persons interviewed:

Person	Sex	Age	Candidate	Registered to vote	Employment status
Rogers	male	52	Harry	yes	looking
Boyd	male	25	Rich	doesn't remember	full-time student
Paul	female	38	Svetlana	no	not on market
Kelley	male	no answer	Marija	yes	employed
Shoot	female	45	Rich	no	laid off
Harman	female	68	undecided	yes	retired

Decide how you will code each of the variables.

3 What improvements would you make to the following form, which was designed to measure insomnia after administration of a drug?

```
Name_____

Age  1. under 20  Race_____    Sex_____
     2. 21-70
     3. 71-99
     4. other

How well did you sleep last night?_____

Did you wake up during the night? 1. yes 2. no 3. maybe

Do you think you slept better last night than you
usually do?

       1. yes, much
       2. yes, somewhat better
       3. yes, but not much
       4. no

How many hours did you sleep last night?

       1. more than 8
       2. 4-8
       3. fewer than 4

Describe your dreams if they troubled you.
```

4 Devise coding schemes for the following variables:

a. Miles driven to work per year

b. Hours of television viewing per month

c. Favorite type of television program

d. Daily alcohol consumption

e. Grandfather's income

f. Respondent's income

g. Attitude toward violence on television

5 Here are some additional questions from the General Social Survey. Suggest coding schemes.

a. Were you living with both your own mother and father around the time you were 16?

b. What hours do you usually work?

c. How often do you attend religious services?

d. Many people who want to volunteer for service in the armed forces do not have the necessary basic skills like reading, writing and arithmetic. Do you think the armed forces should refuse to accept such volunteers, or should they accept them and give them the necessary education?

6 Improve the following coding schemes and questions:

a. Circle the number of meals you typically eat in a restaurant each week:

1. 0-1

2. 1-3

3. 5-6

4. More than 7

b. At what type of restaurants do you eat?

    1. Inexpensive
    2. Expensive
    3. Very expensive
    4. All of the above

c. Which of the following influence your selection of a restaurant?

    1. Cost not food not service
    2. Food not cost not service
    3. Service not cost not food
    4. Cost and food not service
    5. Food and service not cost
    6. Service and cost not food
    7. Other

d. Rate the last restaurant you ate at on the following scale:

    ——————————
    0   75

e. Given economic contingencies and inflation, as well as cost escalation, difficulties in staff acquisition, in conjunction with variegated consumer consumption preferences, how would you optimize restaurant performance in this establishment?

PART TWO
Describing Data

8 Counting Responses for a Single Variable

How can you count the various responses people give to a question?

- What is a frequency table, and what can you learn from it?
- How can you tell from a frequency table if there have been errors in coding or entering data?
- What are percentages and cumulative percentages?
- What is a bar chart, and when do you use it?
- How can you tell if a variable is measured on a nominal, ordinal, interval, or ratio scale?

Y ou're finally ready to get answers to your questions. How many people find life exciting? How many believe in a life after this one? How many marriages are happy? How many people are satisfied with their jobs?

COUNTING FREQUENCIES

You can answer all of these questions and many similar ones by just counting the number of times various answers occur. For example, to find out how people view life, all you have to do is count the number of people who selected response 1 (*Exciting*), response 2 (*Pretty routine*), and response 3 (*Boring*).

Fortunately, since you're analyzing the survey with SPSS/PC+, you don't have to count anything. Tell the computer to count by using these commands.

```
get file 'gss.sys'.
frequencies life.
```

The FREQUENCIES command counts the number of times each of the codes occurs. You supply the names of the variables for which you want counts; everything else is done for you.

Figure 8.1 Frequency table

```
LIFE        Is life exciting or dull?

                                              Valid     Cum
    Value Label           Value  Frequency  Percent  Percent  Percent
Exciting                    1        684     46.4     46.8     46.8
Pretty routine              2        704     47.8     48.2     95.0
Dull                        3         73      5.0      5.0    100.0
Missing data                9         12       .8    MISSING
                                    -------  -------  -------
                     TOTAL         1473    100.0    100.0

Valid Cases     1461    Missing Cases     12
```

? *What about that other command, GET?* We talked about the GET command in Chapters 3 and 5. It tells SPSS/PC+ how to read a system file containing the GSS (General Social Survey) data.

You need to use either a DATA LIST or a GET command in your sessions, depending on whether you use a raw data file or a system file. You don't have to use them before each analysis command, though. Once you've read the system file, you can continue to use it over and over until you leave SPSS/PC+ with the FINISH command.   ■ ■ ■

Interpreting a Frequency Table

When you run a job with the above FREQUENCIES command, you get back something very much like Figure 8.1. It's called a **frequency table** because it tells you how frequently each response occurs. The first line identifies the variable. The variable name, *LIFE*, and the variable label, *Is life exciting or dull?*, appear here. Then starts the actual frequency table.

Each line of the frequency table describes a particular code. For each code, the first column, called *Value Label*, is the descriptive label you attached to the code. If you didn't give a value label to a code, this space is left blank. The second column, headed *Value*, is the actual code used to represent the response in the data file. The third column, headed *Frequency*, is the number of cases who chose that response.

The first line of this table is for the first code, which corresponds to a person saying life is exciting. This response has a code of 1 and the label *Exciting*. You can find the number of cases who gave this answer (684) in the third column.

The last line describes the code used for missing responses, if one was defined. For the *exciting-routine-dull* question, a code of 9 designates missing values. Perhaps these people didn't know what answer to give, or perhaps the interviewer forgot to ask the question or to record the answer. In any of these situations, code 9 is used. From the last line of Figure 8.1, you see that twelve questionnaires had missing values for this question.

Checking the Data

If you find codes in the frequency table that are not supposed to occur in the data—say a value of 6 for the *exciting-routine-dull* question—you must go back and look for the cases with the offending values. Maybe the data were entered incorrectly, or maybe the answer on the form was wrong. Go back and check. Unless you clean up the data, all subsequent analyses will be incorrect. Finding these bad codes is one important reason why you should look at frequency distributions before beginning other analyses. (Another reason is simply to get a good, basic look at your data so you won't be surprised later.)

PERCENTAGES

If you tell a friend that 684 people find life exciting, chances are your friend will reply, "Yeah? Out of how many?" The number itself isn't very informative. It means one thing if 100,000 people were questioned, and another if 685 people were questioned. A group of 684 people out of 100,000 suggests that the excited people are a very small minority. But if 684 out of 685 people find life exciting, that's almost everyone.

One way to make a count more meaningful is to express it as a percentage of the entire sample. The percentage tells how many people out of each 100 gave the response you're talking about. For example, 2 out of 5 is 40%—and so is 400 out of 1,000.

You can find percentages in the fourth column of your SPSS/PC+ frequency table. The 684 people who found life exciting were 46.4% of the total sample of 1,473. Almost half of the people questioned found life exciting. (You can find the total number of cases in your study by looking at the line labeled *TOTAL* at the bottom of the frequency table. The first number in that line, under the column labeled *Frequency*, is the total number of cases. As you can see, 1,473 people were part of the 1984 General Social Survey.)

Similarly, you can see fromFigure 8.1 that 47.8% of the people found life pretty routine. A mere 5% of the sample found life dull. The twelve missing answers are about 0.8% of the total sample. The sum of the percentages across all possible codes is 100%.

Valid Percentages

Sometimes you wish to compute percentages using only cases who actually answered a question. Suppose you ask 100 people whether life is exciting or routine, and 25 say that it's exciting, 25 say that it's routine, and 50 tell you to bug off. It's a bit misleading, though it's correct, to state that 25% of those people think that life is exciting. A naive reader or listener would probably assume that the other 75% of the people find life routine. That's not really true, since the remaining 75% includes people who declined to answer as well as those who find life routine. You can describe the results better by saying that half of the people *who answered the question* find life exciting and half find life routine. You should also mention that half of the people in your sample refused to answer the question.

The percentages based only on the cases who actually answered the question (called **valid cases**) are in the column labeled *Valid Percent* in the frequency table. For our example, since so few cases had missing responses, the columns labeled *Valid Percent* and *Percent* are almost identical. If you have many cases with missing values, the two columns can be quite different. Since cases with codes declared missing are not included in the calculation of the "valid" percentages, the word *MISSING* appears for them in the *Valid Percent* column. (The last column, labeled *Cum Percent*, is described later.)

Bar Charts

Turning a frequency table into a picture often makes the data easier to understand. Look at Figure 8.2, which is a frequency table of the responses to the question about marital status. You can see that 56% of the sample were currently married, 10% were widowed, 11% were divorced, and 19% were never married.

Figure 8.2 Frequency table of marital status

```
MARITAL    Marital status

                                          Valid     Cum
    Value Label         Value  Frequency  Percent  Percent  Percent

Married                   1        829     56.3     56.3     56.3
Widowed                   2        154     10.5     10.5     66.7
Divorced                  3        166     11.3     11.3     78.0
Separated                 4         42      2.9      2.9     80.9
Never married             5        282     19.1     19.1    100.0
                                 -------   -------  -------
                 TOTAL            1473     100.0    100.0
```

To transform this frequency table into a picture, you merely add a slash and the word BARCHART to your FREQUENCIES command. Run the following command:

```
frequencies variables = marital /barchart.
```

This command produces the bar chart in Figure 8.3. The display is called a **bar chart** because each line in the frequency table is turned into a bar. The length of the bar depends on the number of cases. (The actual frequency is given beside the bar.) At a quick glance, you can tell how often each of the responses was selected. You can also see whether one of the responses was an overwhelming favorite, and which responses are about equally likely.

Since computer screens and printers have a limited ability to show detail, responses that have similar frequencies may end up with bars of equal length—even though the actual frequency counts are slightly different. In this example, the bars for *Widowed* and *Divorced* have the same length, although the actual frequencies are a bit different. This doesn't really matter. The point of a bar chart is to provide a visual summary of the data, and such minor distortions do not change the overall impression. If you want precision, look at the numbers, not the chart.

Figure 8.3 Bar chart of marital status

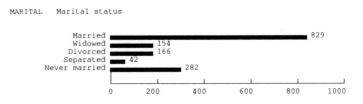

MARITAL   Marital status

Married ▬▬▬▬▬▬▬▬▬▬▬▬ 829
Widowed ▬▬▬ 154
Divorced ▬▬▬ 166
Separated ▬ 42
Never married ▬▬▬▬ 282

0   200   400   600   800   1000

Cumulative Percentages

The last column in the frequency table is entitled *Cum Percent*. To see what this column tells you, look at the frequency table for another variable, *EDUC*, which shows the highest year of school completed. Run the following command:

```
frequencies educ.
```

? *Where did this EDUC variable come from?* The questionnaire in Chapter 7 had two variables, one with highest year of elementary and high school and one with highest year of college. *EDUC* was made by combining the variables named *YRSEDUC* and *YRSCOLL*. Combining, shuffling, and otherwise altering variables is easy on a computer. More about that in Chapters 11 and 14. ∎∎∎

From Figure 8.4, can you tell what percentage of the sample completed 7 or fewer years of school? Since there is a separate entry in the table for each year of school completed, the number you want is the sum of the percentages of those whose highest year completed was 0, 1, 2, 3, 4, 5, 6, or 7. You can compute this with a calculator using the *Valid Percent* column. But don't bother. Just look at the entry in the *Cum Percent* column for 7 years. It tells you that 5.9% of the sample stopped at 7 or fewer years of school. The **cumulative percentage** for a response is the sum of the valid percentages for that response, plus all responses that precede it in a frequency table. By looking at the cumulative percentage for the value of 11, you can tell that 28% of the sample had 11 or fewer years of school.

Figure 8.4   Frequency table for education

EDUC   Highest year of school completed

Value Label	Value	Frequency	Percent	Valid Percent	Cum Percent
	0	3	.2	.2	.2
	1	3	.2	.2	.4
	2	4	.3	.3	.7
	3	9	.6	.6	1.3
	4	11	.7	.7	2.0
	5	11	.7	.7	2.8
	6	19	1.3	1.3	4.1
	7	26	1.8	1.8	5.9
	8	77	5.2	5.2	11.1
	9	58	3.9	3.9	15.0
	10	99	6.7	6.7	21.8
	11	91	6.2	6.2	28.0
	12	491	33.3	33.4	61.4
	13	108	7.3	7.3	68.7
	14	121	8.2	8.2	76.9
	15	74	5.0	5.0	82.0
	16	149	10.1	10.1	92.1
	17	40	2.7	2.7	94.8
	18	31	2.1	2.1	96.9
	19	20	1.4	1.4	98.3
	20	25	1.7	1.7	100.0
Missing data	99	3	.2	MISSING	
	TOTAL	1473	100.0	100.0	

All frequency tables produced by the FREQUENCIES procedure contain a column with the cumulative percentages. For years of education, cumulative percentages are very useful and easy to interpret. For some variables, such as marital status, race, state of birth, or father's occupation, cumulative percentages are of little use or interest (although they are printed anyway).

Look again at Figure 8.2, the frequency table for marital status. The cumulative percentage for code 3—*Divorced*—is 78%. It's the sum of the valid percentages for the categories *Married*, *Widowed*, and *Divorced*. If you had interchanged the coding scheme for *Married* and *Never married*—that is, if you had assigned a code of 1 to *Never married* and a code of 5 to *Married*, leaving the other codes alone—the cumulative percentage for code 3 would be the percentage of people who were never married, were widowed, or divorced. For a variable like marital status, cumulative percentages don't convey useful information.

LEVELS OF MEASUREMENT

Variables can be classified into different groups based on how they are measured. Marital status, degree of excitement, and years of education are all different types of variables. Marital status is called a **nominal** variable since the numerical code assigned to the possible responses convey no information. The fact that *Never married* is assigned a bigger number (code 5) than *Divorced* (code 3) means nothing. The codes are merely labels or names. (That's why the level of measurement is called *nominal*—from the Latin word for "name.") Birthplace, color of hair, position on the football team, and species of animal are all examples of nominal variables. Codes assigned to possible responses merely identify the response. The actual code number means nothing.

Sometimes the order of numbers is significant. Think about the *exciting-routine-dull* variable. The responses to the question can be arranged in a meaningful order. If we arrange them in terms of decreasing excitement, then the response *Exciting* comes first, followed by the response *Pretty routine*, and finally the response *Dull*. Of course, we could have arranged the responses in the other order as well (from low excitement to high excitement). In both orders, the response *Pretty routine* falls between the others. For the marital status variable, it means nothing that the *Widowed* response falls between *Married* and *Divorced*, because there is no *order* to those categories; but it does mean something that *Pretty routine* is between *Exciting* and *Dull*.

If the possible responses can be arranged in order, as with the *exciting-routine-dull* variable, the variable is called **ordinal**: its codes have an order, nothing more. (*Ordinal* is from——you guessed it——a Latin word meaning "order.") Variables such as job satisfaction, condition of health, and happiness with one's social life, all of which are usually measured on a scale going from much to little, are ordinal variables. The numbers assigned to the responses allow you to put the responses in order.

Although the codes assigned to the *exciting-routine-dull* variable are ordered from high to low, we can do little else with the actual codes. They merely convey order. Someone who was bored with life (code 3) didn't differ by two "excitement units" from someone who found life exciting (code 1). Subtracting or dividing the codes makes no sense.

A variable like weather temperature can be measured and recorded on a scale that is much more precise than the *exciting-routine-dull* variable. The interval, or distance, between values is meaningful everywhere on the scale. The difference between 100 degrees Fahrenheit and 101 degrees Fahrenheit is the same as the difference between 102 degrees and 103 degrees. However, since temperature measured on the Fahrenheit scale does not have a true zero, you can't say that an 80-degree day is twice as hot as a 40-degree day. A temperature of zero does not mean there is no heat. The zero point is determined by convention. (If you insist, I'll admit that temperatures do have an absolute zero point; but that has very little to do with the measurement of weather temperatures.) Thus, weather temperature can be called an **interval** variable.

The last type of measurement scale is called a **ratio** scale. The only difference between a ratio scale and an interval scale is that the ratio scale has an absolute zero. Zero means *zero*. It's not just an arbitrary point on the scale that somebody happened to label with zero. Height, weight, distance, age, and education can all be measured on a ratio scale. For example, someone with 8 years of education has twice the number of years of education as someone with 4 years. Zero education means no education at all. On a ratio scale, the proportions, or ratios, between items are meaningful.

? *Why all the fuss? Why have we spent all this time describing these "levels of measurement"?* The reason is straightforward—the way in which you analyze your data depends on how you've measured it. Certain analyses make sense with certain types of data. Even something as simple as interpreting cumulative percentages requires you to know what scale your data are measured on. You've seen that cumulative percentages don't make much sense for variables measured on a nominal scale. In the next chapter, you'll learn some additional techniques for describing variables measured on different scales.   ■■■

MORE ABOUT THE FREQUENCIES PROCEDURE

You can use the SPSS/PC+ FREQUENCIES procedure to:
- Make a frequency table.
- Make a bar chart.
- Make a histogram (described in Chapter 9).
- Calculate descriptive statistics (also described in Chapter 9).

A Frequency Table

To make a frequency table, run the command

```
frequencies yourvar.
```

where *YOURVAR* is the name of the variable for which you want to make the frequency table.

If there are several variables for which you want frequency tables, list all of their names separated by at least one blank or a comma:

```
freq yourvar1 yourvar2 yourvar3.
```

Notice that we have abbreviated FREQUENCIES to FREQ. SPSS/PC+ keywords can be abbreviated to three or more characters.

A Bar Chart and a Frequency Table

To make both a frequency table and a bar chart, add a slash and the word BARCHART:

```
frequencies yourvar /barchart.
```

A Bar Chart without a Frequency Table

If you want to make a bar chart but don't want to get a frequency table, add a slash and the words FORMAT NOTABLE:

```
frequencies yourvar
  /format notable /barchart.
```

A Frequency Table in a Condensed Format

If you want to make a table and print it in a condensed format, use the CONDENSE keyword. This format takes up less space than the usual one:

```
frequencies yourvar /format condense.
```

WHAT'S NEXT?

You've seen that using the FREQUENCIES procedure is a handy way get a good impression of your data. In Chapter 9, you'll see how you can use FREQUENCIES to obtain an additional display for variables that are not nominal. You'll also see how to calculate numbers that summarize your data.

Summary

How can you count the various responses people give to a question?

A frequency table tells you how many people (cases) selected each of the responses to a question. For each code, it contains the number and percentages of the people who gave each response, as well as the number of people for whom responses are not available.

If you find codes in the frequency table that weren't used in your coding scheme, you know that an error in data coding or data entry has occurred.

Variables are classified into different categories based on the coding scheme:

If there's no order to a coding system and a particular code only identifies a category, the variable is measured on a nominal scale.

If the categories can be ordered on some basis, the variable is measured on an ordinal scale.

If you can interpret the actual distances between the ordered categories, the variable is measured on an interval scale.

If you can interpret distances and can also speak of a zero value, the variable is measured on a ratio scale.

EXERCISES

Syntax

1 To get a frequency table for the variable *LIFE*, you run this command

```
frequencies for life.
```

and get this error message:

```
Warning 10045, Text: LIFE
Valid keywords on FREQUENCIES FORMAT subcommand are
CONDENSE, ONEPAGE, NOTABLE, LIMIT, NOLABELS, DVALUE, AFREQ, DFREQ,
DOUBLE, and NEWPAGE.
```

Indicate what's wrong with the command and write it correctly.

2 How can you simply the following set of commands?

```
frequencies    life.
frequencies    marital.
frequencies    sex.
frequencies    race.
```

3 You run the command

```
frqencies life.
```

and get the following error message:

```
ERROR       1   Text:  FRQENCIES LIFE
Invalid command.  Check spelling.  If this is intended as a continuation
of a previous line, be sure that you did not end the previous line
with a period.
```

Fix the command.

4 Fix the following commands:

a. `frequencies life  /barchart life.`

b. `frequencies   life   barchart.`

c. `frequencies life. barchart.`

Statistical Concepts

1 For which of the following variables would frequency tables be useful?

a. Calories consumed per day

b. Ideal number of children for a family to have

c. Belief in life after death

d. Mileage on family automobile

e. Political party membership

f. ID numbers of forms

2 Below is a frequency table for the job satisfaction variable from the General Social Survey. Fill in the missing entries.

```
SATJOB     Satisfaction with job or housework
```

Value Label	Value	Frequency	Percent	Valid Percent	Cum Percent
Very satisfied	1	▒▒▒▒	37.7	▒▒▒▒	45.9
Moderately satisfied	2	423	28.7	35.0	81.0
A little dissatisfied	3	146	9.9	12.1	▒▒▒▒
Very dissatisfied	4	84	5.7	7.0	100.0
	.	208	▒▒▒▒	MISSING	
Missing data	9	57	3.9	MISSING	
TOTAL		1473	100.0	100.0	

```
Valid Cases    1208    Missing Cases   ▒▒▒▒
```

3 The following data represent the number of periodicals read by 25 college students: 1, 1, 1, 1, 1, 1, 2, 2, 2, 3, 3, 3, 3, 3, 3, 4, 4, 5, 5, 5, 5, 8, 9, 9, 10.

a. Fill in the following frequency table:

Value Label	Value	Frequency	Percent	Valid Percent	Cum Percent
	1.00				
	2.00				
	3.00				
	4.00				
	5.00				
	8.00				
	9.00				
	10.00				
TOTAL		25	100.0	100.0	

b. Using the same data, fill in the following bar chart:

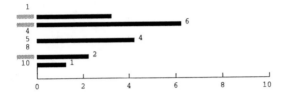

4 For which of the following variables would cumulative percentages be easily interpreted?
   a. Number of adults in a household
   b. Brand of car ownership
   c. College major
   d. Number of illnesses during the past year

5 Which scale of measurement (nominal, ordinal, interval, or ratio) are the following variables measured on?
   a. Ethnic origin
   b. Satisfaction with family life
   c. Breed of dog
   d. Likelihood of buying a product
   e. Days of hospitalization
   f. Hours worked per week

Data Analysis

Use the gss.sys system file to answer the following questions.

1 Make frequency tables and bar charts for *HAPMAR* (happiness of marriage) and *RACE*. On the output, indicate how the different columns of the frequency table are calculated.

2 a. Based on the output you obtained in question 1, how many people are very happy with their marriage?
   b. What percentage is this of all currently married people who answered the question?
   c. What percentage of the total sample are happily married people?
   d. What percentage of the married people who answered the question are either very happily married or pretty happily married?
   e. Can you tell from the tables what percentage of people in the various race categories are happy with their marriage?

3 Give an example of a question that can be answered by looking at the cumulative percentage column for *HAPMAR*.

Summarizing Data

How else, other than by making a frequency table, can you summarize the responses to a question?

■ What is the mean? The median? The mode? What does each of them tell you about the distribution of a variable?

■ When is each of these statistics most appropriate? What characteristics of the data make each one more or less useful?

■ How can a graphical display summarize the distribution of a variable? What kinds of graphical displays are used, and what are the advantages of each?

■ Aside from the mean, median, and mode, what other statistics might provide helpful information?

■ In what way can you describe how concentrated—or how dispersed—the values are?

I n Chapter 8, you saw that a frequency table is a convenient way of looking at the responses to a question. Frequency tables are easy to read, and they provide complete and detailed information about the answers. You know exactly how many people gave each of the responses. But sometimes that's just too much information.

SUMMARIZING VARIABLES

Think about a variable like age, height, or weight. If you recorded actual heights in inches or weights in pounds, a lot of different responses are possible. The more finely you measured the variables, the larger the number of possible responses. If you recorded height only to the nearest foot, the number of different heights is fairly limited. However, if you measured height to the nearest millimeter, it's possible that everyone in your sample had a different measurement. What would happen if you made a frequency table for such a variable? You'd probably end up with an enormous table with a lot of different values. Most of the codes in the table would show only a single case with that particular value. In fact, if every case had a different value, you'd end up with nothing more than a list of all the responses. That kind of frequency table doesn't do much for you. You need some way to summarize the data further. The way to further summarize a variable depends on how it is measured.

Nominal Variables

If you have a variable that records the number of people who were born in each of 400 cities, you may not be able to summarize further at all. Since the name or ID number of the city is a nominal variable, you can't very well group the cities into larger categories without further information, such as what state they're in. In other words, you can't really summarize a name effectively. All you can do with the name or ID number is *count* the number of people for each one.

If you're going to report the results to an audience that has a short attention span, you might organize the frequency table so that it goes from the most frequently occurring city to the least frequently occurring. Then you could mention only the "top ten" cities. The "top" city has a statistical term you can use to describe it—the **mode**. The mode is the most frequently occurring value.

Nominal variables with many categories can be difficult to summarize. If you need to summarize, you have to rearrange the coding system. For example, you can combine cities in the same state, or you can group them by population. You can then make frequency tables based on the new, more compact classification. (Chapter 11 tells you how to use the computer to rearrange your coding system.)

Ordinal Variables

It's easier to summarize an ordinal variable than a nominal variable. If you make a frequency table and decide that you have too many categories (*Extremely exciting, Greatly exciting, Moderately exciting, Mildly exciting, Slightly exciting, Almost but not quite exciting,* ...), you can combine adjacent categories. One way to do this is to convert all the different codes that stand for varying degrees of excitement to a single code—*Exciting*. Similarly, you can combine the various codes for *Routine* and for *Dull*. The frequency table for the less elaborate coding scheme will be easier to read and probably just as informative.

A variable with ordered categories also gives you more choice in descriptive statistics. You can still report the mode (the category that has the largest number of cases) for an ordinal variable as you can for a nominal variable. The mode, remember, tells you which response occurred most frequently. In addition, there's another number, often more informative, that you can compute for an ordinal variable. It's called the **median**. The median is the "middle" value, the value that divides the observations into equal halves. Notice that you can't have a middle value unless it makes sense to put the values in order. That's why the median is a useful statistic for ordinal variables but not for nominal variables.

For example, if you ask five people to rate the President's performance on a scale of 1 to 5 and you get the answers 1, 1, 3, 4, 5, the median answer is 3. The median is the middle observation when the values are ordered from smallest to largest (or largest to smallest, for that matter). The median provides you with some idea of what a *typical* response is.

? *What if you have an even number of observations? There may not be a single median, since two numbers are in the middle.* That's true. With the numbers 1, 2, 3, 4, the numbers 2 and 3 are equally in the middle. If this happens, you can still calculate the median. Find those two middle numbers and figure out what number would be in the middle of them:

- Add the two middle numbers together.
- Take half of their sum. This is the median.

In this example, you would add the middle numbers 2 and 3 to get 5. Half of 5, or 2.5, is the median of 1, 2, 3, 4. SPSS/PC+ does this for you automatically. ■■■

Interval or Ratio Variables

If your variable is measured on an interval or ratio scale, there are many different ways to summarize it. You could still make a frequency table, but it would probably be unwieldy and not particularly informative.

For example, the commands

```
get file 'gss.sys'.
frequencies age /format condense.
```

produce the frequency table for the *AGE* variable shown in Figure 9.1. It looks different from the previous tables since it's printed in a condensed format (see the end of Chapter 8). Both the valid percent (*PCT*) and the cumulative percent (*CUM PCT*) are rounded to the nearest integer. The percent based on all cases, including missing, does not appear. If this table had not been printed in condensed format, it would continue for many pages and you would have a hard time looking at it. Even in condensed format, it doesn't really grab your attention. In such situations, a histogram, discussed in the following section, is a more useful display.

HISTOGRAMS

The frequency table contains all of the information about the *AGE* variable—too much information to scan easily. A bar chart sure wouldn't help, since it would have as many bars as there are different values. What you could do is make another frequency table in which each line represents not a single age but several ages. For example, you can count the number of people in their teens, twenties, thirties, forties, and so on. This is a more manageable way to look at the data. You could then use a modification of the bar chart, called a **histogram**, to display the number of cases occurring

Figure 9.1 Frequency table for age

AGE   Age of respondent

VALUE	FREQ	PCT	CUM PCT	VALUE	FREQ	PCT	CUM PCT	VALUE	FREQ	PCT	CUM PCT
18	2	0	0	42	21	1	55	66	14	1	85
19	20	1	1	43	25	2	56	67	25	2	87
20	23	2	3	44	23	2	58	68	24	2	88
21	37	3	6	45	20	1	59	69	9	1	89
22	29	2	8	46	18	1	60	70	18	1	90
23	50	3	11	47	19	1	62	71	12	1	91
24	47	3	14	48	22	1	63	72	14	1	92
25	39	3	17	49	21	1	65	73	6	0	93
26	32	2	19	50	8	1	65	74	15	1	94
27	44	3	22	51	16	1	66	75	9	1	94
28	37	3	25	52	21	1	68	76	14	1	95
29	33	2	27	53	14	1	69	77	13	1	96
30	28	2	29	54	17	1	70	78	6	0	96
31	28	2	31	55	19	1	71	79	4	0	97
32	37	3	33	56	19	1	72	80	6	0	97
33	39	3	36	57	19	1	74	81	12	1	98
34	31	2	38	58	24	2	75	82	8	1	98
35	37	3	40	59	16	1	76	83	5	0	99
36	41	3	43	60	27	2	78	84	4	0	99
37	38	3	46	61	20	1	80	85	2	0	99
38	31	2	48	62	20	1	81	86	2	0	99
39	24	2	50	63	15	1	82	87	1	0	99
40	28	2	51	64	13	1	83	88	2	0	100
41	25	2	53	65	18	1	84	89	7	0	100

M I S S I N G   D A T A

VALUE	FREQ	VALUE	FREQ	VALUE	FREQ
99	6				

in each decade. To make both a frequency table and a histogram, run the following command:

```
frequencies age
  /histogram minimum(10) maximum(90) increment(10).
```

Figure 9.2 is the histogram for the *AGE* variable. The first line represents cases in their teens; the second represents cases in their twenties; and so on. For each ten-year group of ages, the histogram shows a bar whose length depends on the number of cases that belong to the group. The actual number of cases appears in the column labeled *Count*. The middle value for each interval is printed in the column labeled *Midpoint*. For example, the midpoint age for people in their forties is 45, and there were 222 cases in the sample with ages in the forties. If you add up all of the counts in Figure 9.1 for ages 40 to 49, you get the number 222. Try it.

Figure 9.2 Histogram for age

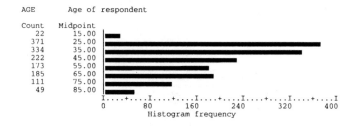

```
AGE            Age of respondent

Count    Midpoint
   22      15.00
  371      25.00
  334      35.00
  222      45.00
  173      55.00
  185      65.00
  111      75.00
   49      85.00
         I....+....I....+....I....+....I....+....I....+....I
         0        80       160      240      320      400
               Histogram frequency
```

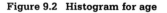 *Why did it take such a long specification to get the histogram?* It doesn't really. Just a slash and the word HISTOGRAM on the FRE-QUENCIES command will tell SPSS/PC+ to produce a histogram. The MIN-IMUM, MAXIMUM, and INCREMENT specifications are optional. They determine the lowest and highest values shown, as well as the size of the interval. We used them here so that the groups would come out in convenient intervals: teens, twenties, and so on. If we'd just said HISTOGRAM, SPSS/PC+ would have selected the intervals. ▪▪▪

By looking at Figure 9.2, you get a pretty good idea of the ages of the people in your sample. You see that not many people were in their teens. This is because the General Social Survey was restricted to adults 18 or older. The greatest numbers of people were in their twenties and thirties. The numbers of people in their fifties and sixties were roughly the same. As expected, there were not very many people in their eighties. You could tell all of this from the frequency table, but not as easily.

The number of intervals you should use in a histogram depends on the data. If the intervals are very wide, you may not be able to see important differences. On the other hand, if they are too narrow, you may have more detail than you want to see. Often it's a good idea to make several histograms and see which one summarizes the data most clearly. The command

```
frequencies age
   /histogram minimum(10) maximum(90) increment(5).
```

produces the histogram in Figure 9.3. The ages are grouped into five-year intervals: 15–19 years, 20–24 years, 25–29 years, and so on. Even though this histogram shows more detail than the other one, it's not really more informative. A grouping of cases into decades of age seems to be sufficient. Another display, similar to the histogram, is discussed in Chapter 13.

Figure 9.3   Another histogram for AGE

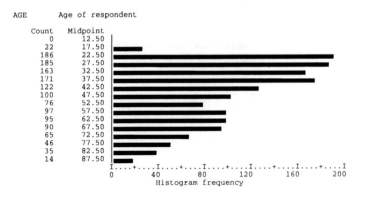

Differences Between Bar Charts and Histograms

As you've noticed, a histogram looks pretty much like a bar chart. There are only two real differences:

1 In a bar chart, each bar represents a single code, while in a histogram the bars often represent the combined frequencies of several codes.

2 Bar charts and histograms treat codes with *no* cases (frequencies of zero) in different ways.

To make a bar chart, you don't have to assume anything about what the codes actually mean. Since you can use whatever codes you want for nominal and ordinal variables, there's no way that the computer can tell what codes were possible but did not occur. If a value has no cases, no bar appears for it in a bar chart. So, for example, if you're using codes from 1 to 3 and there are no cases with the value 3, there simply is no bar for that code. The same applies to frequency tables.

On the other hand, if the variables are measured on an interval or ratio scale, you do want to know when some of the values do not occur in your data. When some of the values do not occur, a histogram leaves a space for them with no bar. For example, if there were no people in their thirties in the sample, there would be room in the histogram for the "thirties" bar but no bar would be displayed. If you made a bar chart of the ages, on the other hand, no space would be left for the thirties. The "holes" in the histogram tell you that some possible values didn't occur at all. That makes it easier for you to see what the real distribution of values looks like. It is essential to know about the "holes" when you have an interval or ratio variable.

Uses of Histograms

Histograms are useful whenever:

- A variable has many different values.
- It's reasonable to group adjacent values.

Never use a histogram to summarize a nominal variable. If you have codes from 1 to 121 that identify different religions (see Appendix J of the General Social Survey *Codebook* if you can), it makes no sense to group the codes into intervals. The Hungarian Reformed Church (code 1) probably has little to do with the Evangelical Congregational Church (code 2), so there's no logical reason to combine them in a histogram.

By looking at a histogram, you can see the *shape* of the distribution:

- How often the different values occur.
- How much spread, or variability, there is among the values.
- Which values are most typical of the data.

These things are important, first of all, because they tell you a lot about your data. Also, some of the statistical procedures that we'll be using later shouldn't be used unless the data come from particular types of distributions.

Different Types of Distributions

A variable like age can have many different types of distributions, depending on what population you study. If you're studying first-graders, their ages are fairly similar. If you made a histogram of the ages, you'd most likely end up with two long bars, one for 5-year-olds and one for 6-year-olds, with a few short fragments for 7- or 8-year-olds.

On the other hand, if you study college freshmen, the distribution of the ages spreads out more. Although the majority of college freshmen are either 18 or 19, there are always a few younger students who skipped grades, and surprisingly often there is an octogenarian catching up on what he or she missed. You find people in all different age groups in this sample. Some values are more likely than others, but many different ones occur.

Finally, if you're studying the entire U.S. population, your sample includes people of all ages. The distribution of their age would not look anything like that of the first-graders or of the college students.

DESCRIPTIVE STATISTICS

If you want to describe the distribution of ages in each of the three samples just referred to, you can always show the three histograms. That's a fine way to display the results. But often you want to summarize the data even further. You'd like to be able to report some numbers that describe the distributions more precisely.

What sorts of descriptions might these be? The mode—the most frequently occurring value—is the simplest way we can represent "typical." For a nominal variable, it's about the only thing we can use. The median— the middle value when values are arranged from smallest to largest—is another way of representing "typical." Of course, you can only calculate the median for a variable that's measured at least on an ordinal scale. There's no way you can arrange religions and find a "middle" one. (Strictly speaking, you can calculate a median for nearly anything. What I really mean is that you can only make sense of a median when the variable is measured at least on an ordinal scale.)

In addition to the mode and the median, there are other handy statistics you can use to describe your data.

Other Percentiles

The median is the value that splits the sample into two equal parts. Sometimes, though, it's useful to look at values that split up the cases in other ways. What's the value that cuts off the bottom quarter of the cases, or the top quarter? These values are called **percentiles** since they give the percentages of cases above and below them. The median is the 50th percentile, since 50% of the cases have larger values and 50% have smaller values. The 25th percentile is the value that splits the cases so that one quarter of them have values below it. (It follows that 75% of the cases exceed the 25th percentile.) If you've made a frequency table, you can locate percentiles in the cumulative frequencies column. However, there's a simpler way to go about it:

```
frequencies age /format condensed
/percentiles=25 50 75.
```

This command asks for the 25th, 50th, and 75th percentiles for the *AGE* variable. As shown in Figure 9.4, 25% of the cases have ages less than or equal to 29; 50%, less than 40; and 75%, less than 58.

Figure 9.4 Frequency table with percentiles

AGE   Age of respondent

VALUE	FREQ	PCT	CUM PCT	VALUE	FREQ	PCT	CUM PCT	VALUE	FREQ	PCT	CUM PCT
18	2	0	0	42	21	1	55	66	14	1	85
19	20	1	1	43	25	2	56	67	25	2	87
20	23	2	3	44	23	2	58	68	24	2	88
21	37	3	6	45	20	1	59	69	9	1	89
22	29	2	8	46	18	1	60	70	18	1	90
23	50	3	11	47	19	1	62	71	12	1	91
24	47	3	14	48	22	1	63	72	14	1	92
25	39	3	17	49	21	1	65	73	6	0	93
26	32	2	19	50	8	1	65	74	15	1	94
27	44	3	22	51	16	1	66	75	9	1	94
28	37	3	25	52	21	1	68	76	14	1	95
29	33	2	27	53	14	1	69	77	13	1	96
30	28	2	29	54	17	1	70	78	6	0	96
31	28	2	31	55	19	1	71	79	4	0	97
32	37	3	33	56	19	1	72	80	6	0	97
33	39	3	36	57	19	1	74	81	12	1	98
34	31	2	38	58	24	2	75	82	8	1	98
35	37	3	40	59	16	1	76	83	5	0	99
36	41	3	43	60	27	2	78	84	4	0	99
37	38	3	46	61	20	1	80	85	2	0	99
38	31	2	48	62	20	1	81	86	2	0	99
39	24	2	50	63	15	1	82	87	1	0	99
40	28	2	51	64	13	1	83	88	2	0	100
41	25	2	53	65	18	1	84	89	7	0	100

M I S S I N G   D A T A

VALUE	FREQ	VALUE	FREQ	VALUE	FREQ
99	6				

Percentile	Value	Percentile	Value	Percentile	Value
25.00	29.000	50.00	40.000	75.00	58.000

Valid Cases   1467   Missing Cases   6

Why don't the percentiles based on the cumulative percent column match the percentiles at the bottom of the table? The cumulative percents printed in the condensed table are rounded to the nearest integer. For example, for age 28, the real cumulative percent is 24.54, which is given in the table as 25. The 25th percentile is therefore not 28 but 29. ■■■

The Average or Arithmetic Mean

For interval and ratio variables, the arithmetic **mean**, or average, is usually a better measure of central tendency than either the mode or the median. It's simple to calculate. Just add up all of the values and divide the sum by the number of cases. Since you're using SPSS/PC+ for analyzing the data, you don't even have to bother doing that. Just run the command

frequencies age **/statistics mean median mode.**

and SPSS/PC+ prints the mean, median, and mode for the *AGE* variable.

As shown in Figure 9.5, the mean value for age is 44, the median is 40, and the mode is 23.

Figure 9.5   Central tendency

```
AGE       Age of respondent
Mean        44.005     Median     40.000     Mode        23.000
```

? *Why are all of these "typical" values different?* There's no reason for these numbers to be identical, since they all define "typical" in different ways. The mode is the value that occurs most often; the median is the middle value when the numbers are arranged from smallest to largest; and the mean is the familiar "average" value. ■■■

Mean, Median, or Mode?

For *AGE*, the mean and the median values are pretty similar. The mode is quite different. Which number should you report if you are describing the age data?

Usually the mode is a poor measure of central tendency for an interval or a ratio variable. Looking at Figure 9.4, you can see that age 23 does have the highest frequency (50 cases), but many other ages have large frequencies as well. If you look at the percentage, you'll see that only 3% of the sample is 23 years old. So you can pretty much eliminate the mode as a good number to report in this situation. Though it satisfies one of the definitions of "typical," it ignores much available information about the data.

Although the median is a good measure of "typicalness" (called **central tendency** in more formal language), it also ignores a lot of the information that you've collected about a variable measured on an interval or ratio scale. For example, the median of the five ages 28, 29, 30, 31, and 32 is 30. The median for the five ages 28, 29, 30, 98, and 99 is also 30. The actual values of ages above and below the median are ignored. The median is 30 regardless of whether everyone is close to 30 or whether the values vary quite a bit.

When should you report the median, and when should you report the mean? If a variable is measured on an ordinal scale, the median is the statistic of choice. If a scale doesn't have intervals of equal length, it doesn't make sense to compute a mean. For a variable measured on an interval scale, the mean and the median are both useful numbers to report. The mean makes maximum use of the data since all of the values are actually used in computing it. (Remember, you add up *all* the numbers, then divide by how many numbers there are.) In some situations, however, the mean may not really represent the data well.

Suppose you ask five people how many parking tickets they've received in the last year, and you get the following replies: 2, 5, 6, 7, 90. The mean number of tickets for this sample is 22. (The sum is 110, and 110 divided by 5 is 22.) That statistic does not describe the data well. The person who never feeds a meter is making the people in the sample look more delinquent than they really are. The median, 6, describes the data better.

Whenever there are cases that have values much larger or smaller than the others, the mean is usually not a good measure of central tendency. It is unduly influenced by extreme values (called **outliers**). In such situations, you should report the median and mention that some of the cases had extremely large or small values. For example, you could say "The median number of tickets for the sample is 6. Eighty percent had 7 or fewer tickets a year. One person reported 90 tickets."

HOW MUCH DO THE VALUES DIFFER?

Measures of central tendency provide information only about "typical" values. They tell you nothing about how much the values vary within the sample. Suppose you ask 10 students on the Dean's List and 10 students on academic probation how many hours of TV they watched last week, and you get the answers shown in Table 9.1.

Table 9.1   A TV log

Dean's List students Hours	Probation students Hours
4	0
4	0
5	0
5	0
5	0
5	3
5	10
5	10
6	12
6	15
Sum: 50	50

The average number of hours for the two groups of students is the same—5 per week. However, the distributions of values differ. All of the Dean's List students watched between 4 and 6 hours of TV during the week. There's little variation in the numbers from student to student. The students on probation, however, differ from each other much more. Some seem to have devoted themselves entirely to other pursuits, while others watched a lot of TV.

How can you measure this variability? One of the more obvious ways is to report the smallest and largest values in each of the samples. The minimum number of hours in the first sample is 4 and the maximum is 6. In the second sample, the minimum number of hours is 0 and the maximum is 15. The distance between the largest and smallest values is called the **range**. For the first sample the range is 2, while for the second sample it is 15. That's quite a difference. By comparing the ranges of the two samples, you can tell that the students in the second sample differed more from each other than did those in the first.

The range is not a particularly good measure of variability, though. It depends only on the smallest and largest numbers and pays no attention to the distribution of the numbers in between. For a variable measured on an ordinal scale, it's the best you can do. For a variable measured on an interval or ratio scale, you can compute some better measures.

The Variance

For each case, you can compute how much it varies from the mean of all the cases. Just subtract the overall mean from the case's value. For the

first case in Table 9.1, the difference is:

4 (the case's value) – 5 (the mean) = –1

This indicates that the person watched one less hour of TV than the average. Table 9.2 shows the differences for all of the data. From the table, you can see that the differences are much smaller for the Dean's List students than for the students on probation.

Table 9.2 The TV log with differences from the mean

	Dean's List students		Probation students	
Hours	Difference		Hours	Difference
4	-1		0	-5
4	-1		0	-5
5	0		0	-5
5	0		0	-5
5	0		0	-5
5	0		3	-2
5	0		10	5
5	0		10	5
6	1		12	7
6	1		15	10
Sum: 50	0		50	0

How can you use these differences to measure variability? The simplest tactic that comes to mind is just to add up the differences and compute a mean difference for each group. Like many great ideas we've all had, this one has a flaw. The sum of the differences from the mean is always zero. Some of the differences are positive and some are negative, so when you add up all of the positive and negative numbers the result is always zero. You need a better way to assemble all of the differences from the mean.

There are several ways to do this. For example, you could treat all the differences as if they were positive and compute a mean difference for them. It turns out, though, that a better way is to:

- Square the differences.
- Add them up.
- Then divide the sum by the number of cases minus one.

This measure is called the **variance.**

? *Why divide by the number of cases minus one, instead of just the number of cases?* You are working with a sample taken from a larger population, and you are trying to describe how much the responses vary from the mean of the entire population. However, since you don't know the population mean, you have to use the sample mean in your calculation—and using the sample mean makes the sample seem less variable than it really is. When you divide by the number of cases minus one, you compensate for the smaller variability that you observe in the sample. ■ ■ ■

Large values for the variance tell you that the values are quite spread out. Small values indicate that the responses are pretty similar. In fact, a value of zero means that all of the values are exactly equal. For Table 9.2, the variance for the Dean's List students is 0.44, while for the students on probation it is 36.44. This supports our observation that there is more variability in TV watching for students on probation.

The Standard Deviation

Since you calculate the variance by squaring differences from the mean, it is expressed in some unit of measurement like squared hours, squared children, or something similar. To express the variability in the same units as the observations, just take the square root of the variance. This is called the **standard deviation**. The standard deviation is expressed in the same units as the original data.

For the Dean's List students in Table 9.2, the standard deviation is the square root of 0.44, or 0.66. For the students on probation, it is the square root of 36.44, or 6.04.

Computing the Variance with SPSS/PC+

Although it's good to know how to compute the different measures of variability so you know how to interpret them, you don't have to worry about doing the actual math. Just run the command

```
frequencies age
    /statistics minimum maximum range variance stddev.
```

and you will obtain the measures of variability for the *AGE* variable. They are shown in Figure 9.6.

Figure 9.6 Measures of variability from SPSS/PC+

```
AGE        Age of respondent

Std Dev     17.811    Variance    317.220    Range     71.000
Minimum     18.000    Maximum      89.000

Valid Cases    1467    Missing Cases      6
```

The youngest person in the sample is 18 and the oldest is 89, resulting in a range of 89 minus 18, or 71. The variance of *AGE* is 317 squared years. Its square root, the standard deviation, is 17.8 years.

? *What's this? Nobody in the General Social Survey sample was 90 years old or older?* Actually, this is just a quirk in the way ages were coded. For obscure historical reasons, the General Social Survey assigned an age of 89 to everyone with an age of 89 or older. Because not many people are that old, this quirk has very little effect on analysis of *AGE*. Still, it's better to record actual ages. When you design *your* study, leave room for ages of 100 or more. ■■■

MORE ABOUT THE FREQUENCIES PROCEDURE

You can use the SPSS/PC+ FREQUENCIES procedure to make frequency tables and bar charts. These are described in Chapter 8. You can also use FREQUENCIES to make histograms and to calculate:

- The mean, median, and mode.
- The minimum, maximum, and range.
- The variance and standard deviation.
- Percentiles.

Basic Statistics

If you just want to calculate the mean, standard deviation, minimum, and maximum, as well as a frequency table, run the command:

```
frequencies age /statistics.
```

Replace *AGE* with the names of the variables for which you want the statistics. The keyword STATISTICS tells SPSS/PC+ to calculate the mean, standard deviation, minimum, and maximum.

No Frequency Table

If you want to calculate the basic statistics but don't want a frequency table, run the command:

```
frequencies age /format notable /statistics.
```

The variables for which you want statistics must be listed first. It doesn't matter in what order you give the remaining instructions.

Histograms without Frequency Tables

When a variable such as age, weight, or income can have many different values, you may want to make a histogram to see what the distribution of the variable looks like. However, you don't want to make a frequency table since it would be very large and not very useful. Run the command:

```
frequencies age /format notable /histogram.
```

Additional Statistics

If you want to calculate all of the descriptive statistics available in the FREQUENCIES procedure, run the command:

```
frequencies age /statistics all.
```

This will give you the mean, median, mode, standard deviation, variance, range, minimum, maximum, and the sum. It will also give you some additional statistics we haven't discussed, such as skewness and kurtosis. (These statistics will be discussed in Chapter 16.)

You can calculate any of these statistics individually by entering their keywords after the STATISTICS subcommand. The following statistics keywords are available in FREQUENCIES:

KURTOSIS	*Kurtosis.*
MAXIMUM	*Maximum.*
MEAN	*Mean.*
MEDIAN	*Median.*
MINIMUM	*Minimum.*
MODE	*Mode.*
RANGE	*Range.*
SESKEW	*Standard error of skewness.*
SKEWNESS	*Skewness.*
STDDEV	*Standard deviation.*
SUM	*Sum.*
VARIANCE	*Variance.*

If you just enter STATISTICS by itself, you get the mean, standard deviation, minimum, and maximum.

Percentiles

To get the 25th, 50th, and 75th percentiles for a variable, run the command:

```
frequencies age /percentiles 25 50 75.
```

If you want both percentiles and descriptive statistics but no frequency table, run the command:

```
frequencies age /statistics
    /percentiles 25 50 75 /format notable.
```

If you want percentiles other than 25, 50, and 75, list their numbers after the word PERCENTILES. To get the 33d and 66th percentiles, run the command:

```
frequencies age /statistics
    /percentiles 33 66 /format notable.
```

WHAT'S NEXT?

This chapter was about summarizing your data. The next chapter shows you how to look at two or more variables at the same time. This will be your first look at the very important topic of relationships between variables.

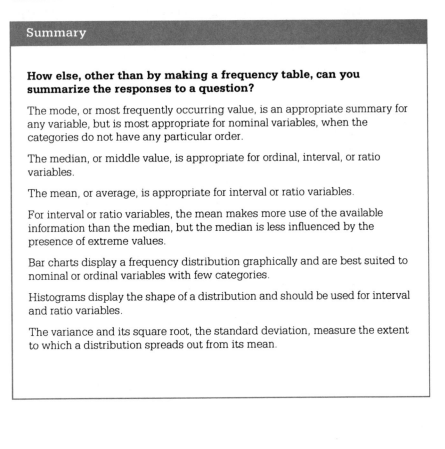

Summary

How else, other than by making a frequency table, can you summarize the responses to a question?

The mode, or most frequently occurring value, is an appropriate summary for any variable, but is most appropriate for nominal variables, when the categories do not have any particular order.

The median, or middle value, is appropriate for ordinal, interval, or ratio variables.

The mean, or average, is appropriate for interval or ratio variables.

For interval or ratio variables, the mean makes more use of the available information than the median, but the median is less influenced by the presence of extreme values.

Bar charts display a frequency distribution graphically and are best suited to nominal or ordinal variables with few categories.

Histograms display the shape of a distribution and should be used for interval and ratio variables.

The variance and its square root, the standard deviation, measure the extent to which a distribution spreads out from its mean.

EXERCISES

Syntax

1 The weight losses, in pounds, of five students during finals week are 0, 2, 1, 5, and 3. Write out all the SPSS/PC+ commands, including data definition, needed to compute descriptive statistics and a frequency table for the weight-loss variable.

2 Modify one of the commands in your previous answer to get a histogram, as well as the frequency table and descriptive statistics.

3 How would you change the FREQUENCIES command if you didn't want a frequency table?

4 Correct the following commands:

   a. `frequencies weight /notable /barchart.`

   b. `frequencies weight /format histogram.`

   c. `frequencies weight /hist and statistics.`

Statistical Concepts

1 A sample consists of 5 consumers who are not satisfied with a new product (coded as 0), 21 consumers who are somewhat satisfied (coded as 1), and 10 consumers who are completely satisfied (coded as 2). Does it make sense to calculate the following statistics? If so, compute them.

   a. Modal satisfaction

   b. Median satisfaction

   c. Mean satisfaction

   d. Variance of satisfaction

2 A sample consists of 11 graduates of the University of Texas (coded 1), 10 graduates of the University of Michigan (coded 2), and 10 graduates of the University of Hawaii (coded 3). Which of the following statistics are appropriate for describing these data? Calculate the statistic if you think it is interpretable.

   a. Modal college attended

   b. Median college attended

   c. Mean college attended

3 A sample contains 5 families who own no car (coded 0), 20 families who own 1 car (coded 1), and 10 families who own 2 cars (coded 2). Indicate which of the following statistics are appropriate and then calculate them.

   a. Modal number of cars owned

   b. Median number of cars owned

   c. Mean number of cars owned

4 If a sample has 237 observations ranked from largest to smallest, which observation is the median? What if the observations are ranked from smallest to largest?

5 If you calculate the mean for a variable which has two categories coded as 0 and 1, what, if anything, does the mean tell you? For example, if the "average sex" of a sample is 0.75 (males are coded as 0 and females as 1), what does this mean?

6 In a corporation, a very small group of employees has extremely high salaries, while the majority of employees receive much lower salaries. If you were the bargaining agent for the employees, what statistic would you calculate to illustrate the low pay level, and why? If you were the employer, what statistic would you use to demonstrate a higher pay level, and why?

7 The number of dogs owned by 10 families are as follows: 0, 1, 1, 1, 2, 2, 2, 2, 2, 4. Fill in the following table based on these values:

Mean		Median		Mode	
Std Dev	1.059	Variance		Range	
Minimum		Maximum			

8 Compute the missing entries in the following table:

a.
Variable	Std Dev	Variance	Valid N
VARA	6.529		10

b.
Variable	Range	Minimum	Maximum	Valid N
VARB		.000	19.000	10

c.
Variable	Mean	Sum	Valid N
VARC		85.000	10

9 An absent-minded instructor calculated the following statistics for an examination: mean=50; range=50; number of cases=99, minimum=20; and maximum=70. She then found an additional examination with a score of 50. Recalculate the statistics, including the additional exam score.

10 The following data represent the number of periodicals read by 25 college students: 1, 1, 1, 1, 1, 1, 2, 2, 2, 3, 3, 3, 3, 3, 3, 4, 4, 5, 5, 5, 5, 8, 9, 9, 10.

   a. Using these data, fill in the following histogram:

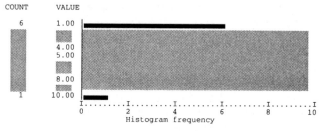

   b. Which is more appropriate for summarizing the data, the histogram above, or the bar chart in Chapter 7, Statistical Concepts question 3?

11 Which measures of central tendency are appropriate for each of the following variables? If several can be calculated, indicate which makes most use of the available information.

   a. Number of siblings

   b. Political party affiliation

c. Satisfaction with family

d. Vacation days per year

e. Type of car driven

f. Weight of father

12 For each of the variables in question 11, would you make a bar chart or a histogram?

13 The number of pairs of shoes owned by 7 college freshmen are 1, 2, 2, 3, 4, 4, and 5.

   a. Compute the mean, median, mode, range, and standard deviation.

   b. An eighth student, the heir to a shoe empire, is added to the sample. This student owns 50 pairs of shoes. Recompute the statistics.

   c. Which of the statistics are not much affected by the inclusion of an observation which is far removed from the rest?

Data Analysis

Use the gss.sys system file to answer questions 1 and 2.

1 AGEWED (age at first marriage), SATJOB (satisfaction with job or housework), and RACE (respondent's race) are all variables that characterize the respondents.

   a. Determine the level of measurement of each of these variables.

   b. Calculate appropriate descriptive statistics for each of the variables. Make histograms or bar charts as needed.

   c. For each of the variables, compare the values of the different measures of central tendency. Indicate why and when you would prefer one measure over another.

   d. Based on your previous analysis, write a brief paragraph describing the participants in the GSS.

2 Consider the variable for total family income (INCOME82).

   a. Obtain a frequency table for the variable.

   b. Examine the coding scheme used to report the income value. Using this scheme, is INCOME82 a nominal, ordinal, interval, or ratio variable?

   c. What descriptive statistics are appropriate for describing this variable, and why? Does it make sense to compute a mean?

   d. Discuss the advantages and disadvantages of recording income in this manner. Would you record income in the same way if you were doing a study? Describe some other ways of recording income.

3 Below are data for 10 cases from a study of heart disease in male workers. For each case we have recorded the number of cigarettes smoked per day in 1958 (CGT58), whether there is a history of heart disease (HISTORY, 0=no, 1=yes), and the average diastolic pressure in 1958 (DBP58). Write the SPSS/PC+ commands that will read the data and compute appropriate descriptive statistics for each of the variables. Be sure to include variable labels and value labels in your data definition commands. Write a paragraph describing your results.

CASEID	CGT58	HISTORY	DBP58
13	0	1	70
30	60	0	87
53	0	0	89
84	15	1	105
89	25	0	110
102	30	0	88
117	0	0	70
132	30	0	79
151	0	0	102
153	0	1	99

10 Counting Responses for Combinations of Variables

How can you study the relationship between responses to two questions that have a small number of possible answers?

- Why is a frequency table not enough?

- How can you make a table that displays the responses to the two questions together?

- What kinds of percentages can you compute for a table, and how do you choose among them?

- Can one of the variables be considered a dependent variable?

- What if you want to examine more than two variables together?

In Chapter 8, we established that about 47% of our sample found life exciting. From the frequency table, we can tell nothing more. We can't tell whether the men found life more exciting than the women, or whether the single people were more excited than the people who were married or widowed, or whether those who believed in an afterlife were more likely to be excited by *this* life. We'd like to be able to explore these questions and more like them.

TWO FREQUENCY TABLES

Frequency tables, bar charts, and histograms aren't of much help in answering questions that involve relations among several variables, since they look at variables one at a time. From Figure 10.1, the frequency table for the *exciting-routine-dull* variable, and Figure 10.2, the frequency table for the sex variable, we still can't say whether the men found life more exciting than the women.

```
get file 'gss.sys'.
frequencies life sex.
```

Figure 10.1 Frequency table for LIFE

```
LIFE        Is life exciting or dull?

                                            Valid      Cum
        Value Label          Value  Frequency  Percent  Percent  Percent

Exciting                       1        684     46.4     46.8     46.8
Pretty routine                 2        704     47.8     48.2     95.0
Dull                           3         73      5.0      5.0    100.0
Missing data                   9         12       .8   MISSING
                                      -------  -------  -------
                             TOTAL     1473    100.0    100.0

Valid Cases     1461     Missing Cases     12
```

Figure 10.2 Frequency table for SEX

```
SEX        Respondent's sex

                                              Valid      Cum
    Value Label           Value  Frequency  Percent  Percent  Percent

Male                        1        598      40.6     40.6     40.6
Female                      2        875      59.4     59.4    100.0
                                   -------   -------  -------
                         TOTAL      1473     100.0    100.0

Valid Cases    1473   Missing Cases    0
```

What we need to do is take each line of the *LIFE* frequency table and *subdivide* it into the number of males and females.

CROSSTABULATIONS

We want to know how many of the 684 people who found life exciting were men and how many were women. Of the 704 people who found life pretty routine, how many were men and how many were women? Similarly, how many of the 73 people who found life dull were men and how many were women?

To answer these questions, just use the CROSSTABS command:

```
crosstabs life by sex.
```

This command makes a table showing *LIFE* by *SEX*: the categories of the variable before BY become the rows, and the categories of the variable after BY become the columns. Look at the results in Figure 10.3. The 1,461 people who answered the question about excitement are subdivided by whether they are males or females. The little boxes in Figure 10.3 are called **cells**, and they are arranged in rows and columns. Labels at the left and the top of the table describe what's in each of the rows and columns. To the right and at the bottom of the table are totals—often called **marginal totals** because they are in the table's margins.

Because the categories of the two variables are "crossed" with each other, this kind of table is called a **crosstabulation**. A crosstabulation contains a cell for every combination of categories of the two variables. Inside the cell is a number showing how many people had that combination of responses. The table is a very efficient way to present a lot of numbers. Let's look at what's in the cells.

The number in the first cell of the table, 300, tells you that 300 males found life exciting. The next number is in the column labeled *Female*, and it tells you that 384 females found life exciting. The sum of these two numbers—684—is shown in the margin. This is the same number that appears in Figure 10.1 for the total number of people who found life exciting. Each

Figure 10.3 Crosstabulation of LIFE and SEX

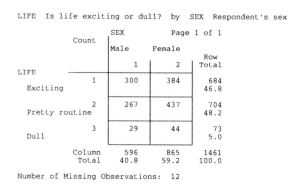

```
LIFE   Is life exciting or dull?   by  SEX   Respondent's sex

                      SEX              Page 1 of 1
              Count
                    |Male       Female
                    |                       Row
                    |   1    |    2    |  Total
    LIFE    _____|        |         |
               1    |  300   |   384   |   684
    Exciting        |        |         |   46.8

               2    |  267   |   437   |   704
    Pretty routine  |        |         |   48.2

               3    |   29   |    44   |    73
    Dull            |        |         |    5.0

            Column     596       865      1461
            Total     40.8      59.2     100.0

Number of Missing Observations:  12
```

line of the figure tells you the number of men and the number of women who gave a particular answer about the excitement of their life.

The margins of the table show the same information as the frequency tables in Figure 10.1 and Figure 10.2. In the right-hand margin, labeled *Row Total*, you have the total number of people who gave the responses *Exciting*, *Pretty routine*, and *Dull*. The right-hand margin also shows what percentages those counts are of the total sample. In the bottom margin, labeled *Column Total*, you have the total number of males and of females, and what percentage each is of the sample. So a crosstabulation contains a lot of information. Besides telling you the number of males and females who gave each of the responses, it has frequencies in the margins.

Percentages

More women gave the answer *Exciting* than did men: 384 women compared to 300 men. The answer is clear. More women than men found life exciting. Wait—is that really what you want to know? From the column totals of Figure 10.3, you see that a lot more women than men were in the sample. Almost 60% of the sample were women. That difference makes it hard to compare just the counts in the cells. Even if men and women find life equally exciting, you would expect to see more women in the *Exciting* cell simply because more women were in the sample.

Determining the Percentages

To compare the excitement rates among men and women, you need percentages. You need to figure out how many men would say they find life exciting if your sample had 100 men, and similarly how many women would say they find life exciting if your sample had 100 women. Then you can compare these two percentages. To get SPSS/PC+ to compute the percentages for you, type:

```
crosstabs life by sex /cells count column.
```

The CELLS subcommand tells SPSS/PC+ to calculate the percentages so that the column totals are 100 (keyword COLUMN) and also to display the number of cases in each cell (keyword COUNT). That's what we want in order to compare 100 men to 100 women.

The table with the percentages is shown in Figure 10.3. Each cell of the table now contains two numbers: the count of the cases in the cell and the percentage that the count is of the column total (called a **column percentage**). A **directory** of all of the numbers in a cell appears in the upper left-hand corner of the table. The directory shows that each cell contains a count (*Count*) followed by a column percentage (*Col Pct*).

Figure 10.4 Crosstabulation with column percentages

```
LIFE   Is life exciting or dull?  by  SEX  Respondent's sex

                    SEX              Page 1 of 1
           Count
           Col Pct  Male     Female
                                        Row
                     1         2      Total
      LIFE
                1    300       384      684
      Exciting     50.3      44.4     46.8

                2    267       437      704
   Pretty routine  44.8      50.5     48.2

                3     29        44       73
      Dull          4.9       5.1      5.0

           Column   596       865     1461
           Total    40.8      59.2    100.0

Number of Missing Observations:  12
```

Results of Percentaging

Looking at the percentages in the table, you see that 50.3% of the men reported their life as exciting, but only 44.4% of the women reported the same thing. These percentages are just the opposite of what the counts show. It's easy to mislead yourself if you compare just the counts in the cells of a crosstabulation. Turn the counts into percentages. Percentages eliminate the differences that show up when you have more people in one group than in another.

Column Percentages and Row Percentages

If you add up the percentages in the *Male* column in Figure 10.3, they sum to 100. The percentages in the *Female* column also add to 100. That's what we wanted. We wanted to be able to compare the responses to the excitement variable as if there were 100 men and 100 women in the sample. (Don't be confused by the percentages in the margins of the table. We are talking here about percentages *inside* the cells of the table.)

There's another way you could have computed percentages for the same table. If 100 people give the answer *Exciting,* how many of these are men and how many are women? The calculations are pretty easy. Of the 684 people who said life is exciting, 300 are men, or 43.9% (300 divided by 684 is 0.439, or 43.9%). The 384 women made up the other 56.1% of the people who said life is exciting. Because these percentages are based on a row total (684), they are called **row percentages**.

What do these numbers tell you? They tell you how likely it was that a person who considered life exciting was a male or a female. But you're probably interested in knowing how likely it was that a male or female found life exciting—and in this table the row percentages don't tell you that. It's usually true in a crosstabulation that either row percentages or column percentages answer your question. Deciding to use one or the other is often based on whether you consider one variable dependent and the other independent.

DEPENDENT AND INDEPENDENT VARIABLES

Sometimes you look at two variables together because you think that one influences the other. In our example, the sex of the respondent may have influenced his or her perception of life. We know that the influence can't go in the other direction—your sex can't be determined by your views on how exciting life is. The variable doing the influencing is called the **independent variable**, and the variable being influenced is called the **dependent variable**.

? *How can you remember which variable is called independent and which is called dependent?* Those are important terms, which you'll run into again and again. Actually, it's easy to remember which is which:

■ The *dependent* variable *depends* on the other one.

■ The *independent* variable doesn't depend on the other one; it goes its own way, *independently.*

With a moment's thought, you should always be able to figure out whether to consider a variable dependent or independent.   ■■■

If you can identify one of your variables as independent and the other as dependent, then you should compute percentages so that they sum to 100 for each category of the *independent* variable. If the values of the indepen-

dent variable are at the tops of the columns, use column percentages.
Until you're comfortable with these ideas, you can use this system:

1 Figure out which variable is dependent on the other.

2 Type crosstabs (dependent variable) by (independent variable).

3 Type a slash, and then cells count column for cell counts and column percentages.

AN EXAMPLE: IS MARRIAGE EXCITING?

We've seen that the men were somewhat more likely to find life exciting than the women were. How about married people? Were they more likely to feel that life is routine than those who were still exploring? If you were analyzing your data without a computer, each question you wanted to look at would require someone going through all the forms again and counting. *With* a computer, all you have to do is run this command.

```
crosstabs life by marital /cells count column.
```

Here, *MARITAL* is the independent variable, so we put it second on the CROSSTABS command. (People got married sometime before the interview; they're excited or bored during the interview. Marital status is surely the independent variable.) We wanted to see how many people in each marital category found life exciting or routine, so we calculated percentages to make it look as if there were 100 people in each marital category. Since marital status is the independent variable and is in the columns, we asked for column percentages with the keyword COLUMN on the CELLS subcommand. When you run this command, a table like that shown in Figure 10.5 appears on your screen.

You should have no trouble reading the table. About 48% of the married people found life exciting. How does this compare to the other categories? There doesn't appear to be much of a difference between those who were married and those who were divorced. Almost 47% of the divorced people thought that life was exciting. People who hadn't ever been married were the most likely to find life exciting: 52% of them said so. Only 34% of the widowed reported that their lives were exciting. The percentage for separated people—43%—was between the percentages for the widowed and the married.

Figure 10.5 Excitement and marriage

```
LIFE   Is life exciting or dull?  by  MARITAL  Marital status

                         MARITAL                                    Page 1 of 1
              Count
              Col Pct  Married  Widowed  Divorced Separate Never ma
                                                     d       rried     Row
                          1       2       3         4        5       Total
     LIFE     ─────
                 1       392      51      77        18       146       684
        Exciting        47.6     33.8    46.7      42.9     52.3      46.8

                 2       401      82      77        20       124       704
    Pretty routine      48.7     54.3    46.7      47.6     44.4      48.2

                 3        31      18      11         4         9        73
        Dull             3.8     11.9     6.7       9.5      3.2       5.0

              Column     824     151     165        42       279      1461
              Total      56.4    10.3    11.3       2.9      19.1     100.0

Number of Missing Observations:  12
```

MORE THAN TWO VARIABLES

The popular press often reports that marriage is good for men and not as good for women. Married men even have much lower death rates than their single counterparts. Let's see whether the differences we've observed among the marital groups were similar for men and women. The simplest way to begin exploring this question is to type

```
crosstabs life by marital by sex /cells count column.
```

Instead of getting a single table, you now get two partial tables or **subtables**, as shown in Figure 10.6. One of the subtables is for men and the other is for women. The subtables show some interesting differences. The divorced men found life a lot less exciting than the men who were married or never married. Of the married men, about 51% described their lives as exciting, and of the never-married men, 54%. Of the divorced men, only 42% reported life exciting. In contrast, divorced women and women who had never been married were *more* likely to report life exciting than their married counterparts. Only 45% of the married women classified their lives as exciting, but 51% of the never-married women and 49% of the divorced women thought that life was exciting.

Both men and women who were widowed were less likely to report life exciting than were any of the other marital groups. There were not very many separated people, so you have to be careful in what you say about them.

Figure 10.6 Is marriage good for men?

LIFE   Is life exciting or dull? by MARITAL Marital status
Controlling for..
SEX Respondent's sex Value = 1 Male

		MARITAL					Page 1 of 1
	Count Col Pct	Married	Widowed	Divorced	Separate d	Never ma rried	Row
		1	2	3	4	5	Total
LIFE							
	1	182	6	22	10	80	300
Exciting		51.1	30.0	41.5	55.6	53.7	50.3
	2	161	11	27	7	61	267
Pretty routine		45.2	55.0	50.9	38.9	40.9	44.8
	3	13	3	4	1	8	29
Dull		3.7	15.0	7.5	5.6	5.4	4.9
	Column	356	20	53	18	149	596
	Total	59.7	3.4	8.9	3.0	25.0	100.0

LIFE   Is life exciting or dull? by MARITAL Marital status
Controlling for..
SEX Respondent's sex Value = 2 Female

		MARITAL					Page 1 of 1
	Count Col Pct	Married	Widowed	Divorced	Separate d	Never ma rried	Row
		1	2	3	4	5	Total
LIFE							
	1	210	45	55	8	66	384
Exciting		44.9	34.4	49.1	33.3	50.8	44.4
	2	240	71	50	13	63	437
Pretty routine		51.3	54.2	44.6	54.2	48.5	50.5
	3	18	15	7	3	1	44
Dull		3.8	11.5	6.3	12.5	.8	5.1
	Column	468	131	112	24	130	865
	Total	54.1	15.1	12.9	2.8	15.0	100.0

Number of Missing Observations: 12

Control Variables

When we split up a table in this way—into a separate subtable for each category of a third variable—we say that we **control** for the third variable. In the example, we controlled for *SEX*. Controlling for variables is a very important concept in data analysis. Here it meant that we were mainly interested in the *LIFE* by *MARITAL* relationship, but we suspected that another variable (*SEX*) might influence the relationship between *LIFE* and *MARITAL*. We controlled this influence in the crosstabulation by simply producing a separate subtable of the main relationship (*LIFE* by *MARITAL*) for each category of the control variable (*SEX*). Even if *SEX* affects the main relationship, it certainly doesn't affect it in the subtables—because everybody in a subtable has the *same* sex.

You could subdivide your sample on the basis of all kinds of different things. You could build a table that classifies cases on the basis of sex, health, belief in the afterlife, and job satisfaction, in addition to the question about life being exciting. Such a large table would be difficult to read and interpret, especially since most of the cells would have few cases. When you use SPSS/PC+, you can have as many as 10 of these classifications, but whenever you include another classification, you are dividing up the same number of cases into more and more cells. Building tables is most useful when you have a *small* number of variables that you want to examine together.

MORE ABOUT THE CROSSTABS PROCEDURE

You use the CROSSTABS procedure to count the number of times different combinations of values for two or more variables occur in the data. You can get:

- Crosstabulations for two or more variables.
- Row percentages.
- Column percentages.

Crosstabulations of Two Variables

If you want to tabulate the number of males and females who believe in life after death, type:

```
crosstabs sex by postlife.
```

The first variable forms the rows of the table. The second variable forms the columns. The word BY separates the variables. If you want to make *POSTLIFE* the row variable, just reverse the order of the variable names:

```
crosstabs postlife by sex.
```

If you have several variables that you want to crosstabulate with *SEX*, list them before the word BY and separate them with commas or blanks:

```
crosstabs postlife hapmar life by sex.
```

More than Two Variables in a Table

To calculate separate tables of *POSTLIFE* and *SEX* for several categories of marital status, type:

```
crosstabs postlife by sex by marital.
```

A separate table of *POSTLIFE* and *SEX* is displayed for each marital category. To include additional variables in the table, list each of them after BY. For example, to make a table of *POSTLIFE* by *SEX* for marital status categories within each excitement category, type:

```
crosstabs postlife by sex by marital by life.
```

Percentages

If you want to see the number of cases in each cell and the number in the cell as a percentage of all cases in the row or column, you must use the CELLS subcommand. The subcommand must be preceded by a slash. Following the CELLS subcommand, type the keyword ROW to get row percentages. The command

```
crosstabs postlife by sex
   /cells count row.
```

gives you a crosstabulation that contains the number of males and females who believe and don't believe in life after death. Categories of *POSTLIFE* are the rows of the table. The keyword ROW indicates that row percentages are to be computed. For each category of *POSTLIFE*, the percentage of men and the percentage of women who hold that belief is calculated.

If you type

```
crosstabs postlife by sex.
   /cells count column.
```

you get column percentages. For each cell, the percentage of all men or women who hold that belief is calculated.

Cell Contents

Here is a complete list of the keywords available for the CELLS subcommand on the CROSSTABS command.

COUNT	*Cell counts.*
ROW	*Row percentages.*
COLUMN	*Column percentages.*
TOTAL	*Total percentages.*
EXPECTED	*Expected frequencies.*
RESID	*Residuals (observed minus expected).*
SRESID	*Standardized residuals.*
ARESID	*Adjusted standardized residuals.*
ALL	*All cell information.*

By default, CROSSTABS displays cell counts if there is no CELLS subcommand.

You can also use a STATISTICS subcommand on the CROSSTABS command to request statistics for the table. The keywords for the STATISTICS subcommand are given at the end of Chapter 21, where the statistics are discussed. Additional features of the CROSSTABS procedure are discussed in Chapters 19 and 21.

WHAT'S NEXT?

A crosstabulation is a very effective way of displaying the values of two or more variables at the same time. However, a crosstabulation becomes large and difficult to use when a variable has many categories. In the next chapter you will learn how to change the way your variables are coded to solve this and similar problems.

Summary

How can you study the relationship between responses to two questions that have a small number of possible answers?

A crosstabulation shows the numbers of cases that have particular combinations of responses to two or more questions.

The number of cases in each cell of a crosstabulation can be expressed as the percentage of all cases in that row (the row percentage) or the percentage of all cases in that column (the column percentage).

The variable that is thought to influence the values of another variable is called the independent variable.

The variable that is influenced is called the dependent variable.

If there is an independent variable, percentages should be calculated so that they sum to 100 for each category of the independent variable.

When you have more than two variables, you can make separate crosstabulations for each of the combinations of the other variables.

EXERCISES

Syntax

1 For the two variables called *RACE* and *SATJOB*, write out the SPSS/PC+ command that would produce:

a. A crosstabulation table with *RACE* as the row variable and *SATJOB* as the column variable.

b. A crosstabulation table with *RACE* as the column variable and *SATJOB* as the row variable.

c. The table in question a with row percents.

d. The table in question b with column percents.

e. The table in question b with row and column percents.

2 Correct the error in the following SPSS/PC+ commands:

```
a. crosstabs rowvar by colvar
b. cross zodiac with life.
c. crosstabs zodiac by life cells=row.
d. crosstabs zodiac by life for marital.
```

3 Write the commands that produced the following crosstabulation.

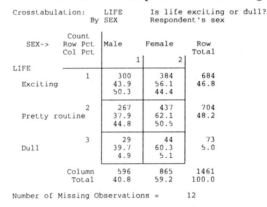

```
Crosstabulation:    LIFE      Is life exciting or dull?
              By SEX      Respondent's sex

              Count
    SEX->    Row Pct  Male      Female      Row
             Col Pct                        Total
                           1         2
LIFE         ───────
                  1    300       384       684
     Exciting       43.9      56.1      46.8
                   50.3      44.4

                  2    267       437       704
 Pretty routine    37.9      62.1      48.2
                   44.8      50.5

                  3     29        44        73
     Dull          39.7      60.3       5.0
                    4.9       5.1

             Column   596       865      1461
             Total    40.8      59.2     100.0

Number of Missing Observations =        12
```

Statistical Concepts

1 Identify the dependent and independent variables, if possible, for each of the following pairs of variables:

a. Satisfaction with job and race

b. Belief in life after death and sex

c. Astrological sign and excitement with life

d. Mother's highest degree and daughter's highest degree

e. Happiness with one's marriage and belief in life after death

2 If you construct a crosstabulation for each of the pairs of variables in the previous question, with the first variable forming the rows of the table and the second variable forming the columns, should you calculate row or column percentages? An-

swer for all five pairs.

3 The following table indicates whether each of twenty people owns or rents a home
(1=*own*, 2=*rents*) and how satisfied they are with city services (1=*not satisfied*;
2=*satisfied*; 3=*very satisfied*).

Person	Owner	Satisfied
1	1	1
2	1	1
3	1	1
4	1	1
5	1	1
6	1	2
7	1	3
8	1	3
9	2	2
10	2	2
11	2	3
12	2	3
13	2	3
14	2	3
15	2	3
16	2	3
17	2	3
18	2	3
19	2	3
20	2	3

a. Summarize the data by filling in the values for the cell counts and marginals of
the following crosstabulation.

```
Crosstabulation:     OWNER      Home ownership
                By SATISFY    Satisfaction with services

             Count
SATISFY->  Row Pct  Not sati Satis-    Very sat   Row
           Col Pct  sfied    fied      isfied     Total
                       1.00     2.00      3.00
OWNER
             1.00
    Owns


             2.00
    Rents


           Column
           Total

Number of Missing Observations =      0
```

b. Calculate the row and column percentages.

c. What percent of the sample are homeowners?

d. What percent of the sample are very satisfied with city services?

e. What percent of homeowners are very satisfied with city services? Of non-
owners?

4 A study to determine the effect of grade point average on performance on a test resulted in the following table:

PERFORM-> Count	Poor	Fair	Good	Row Total
GPA	1	2	3	
1 Below average	56	54	12	122 36.2
2 Average	31	65	43	139 41.2
3 Above average	12	25	39	76 22.6
Column Total	99 29.4	144 42.7	94 27.9	337 100.0

a. What is the independent variable? What is the dependent variable?

b. Would you look at row percentages or column percentages to see whether the independent variable seems to affect the dependent variable?

5 Fill in the missing information in the following table:

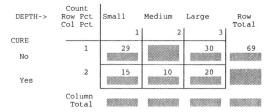

DEPTH-> Count Row Pct Col Pct	Small	Medium	Large	Row Total
CURE	1	2	3	
1 No	29		30	69
2 Yes	15	10	20	
Column Total				

6 Your local newspaper's Sunday supplement contains an article on job satisfaction and marital status. The article contains the following table. The authors conclude that marriage makes people more satisfied with their jobs, since 63 percent of the very satisfied people are married, while only 14 percent have never been married. Comment on the conclusions from the study.

Crosstabulation: MARITAL   Marital status
          By SATJOB   Satisfaction with job or housework

SATJOB-> Count Col Pct	Very satisfied 1	Modratly satisfi 2	A little dissati 3	Very dis satisfie 4	Row Total
MARITAL					
1 Married	351 63.2	242 57.2	73 50.0	36 42.9	702 58.1
2 Widowed	44 7.9	31 7.3	7 4.8	5 6.0	87 7.2
3 Divorced	68 12.3	55 13.0	16 11.0	13 15.5	152 12.6
4 Separated	15 2.7	12 2.8	5 3.4	6 7.1	38 3.1
5 Never married	77 13.9	83 19.6	45 30.8	24 28.6	229 19.0
Column Total	555 45.9	423 35.0	146 12.1	84 7.0	1208 100.0

Number of Missing Observations =   265

7 Below is a crosstabulation of belief in life after death and highest degree achieved. Calculate the appropriate percentages, and write a few sentences summarizing the table.

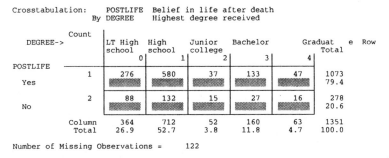

```
Crosstabulation:    POSTLIFE  Belief in life after death
                 By DEGREE    Highest degree received

             Count
    DEGREE->          LT High  High     Junior   Bachelor       Graduat  e  Row
                      school   school   college               Total
                           0|       1|       2|       3|       4|
    POSTLIFE   ─────────
                 1     276      580      37       133      47      1073
    Yes                                                            79.4

                 2     88       132      15       27       16      278
    No                                                             20.6

           Column      364      712      52       160      63      1351
           Total       26.9     52.7     3.8      11.8     4.7     100.0

Number of Missing Observations =      122
```

8 For which of the following pairs of variables do you think a crosstabulation would be appropriate?
   a. Weight in pounds and daily intake in calories
   b. Number of cars and highest degree achieved
   c. Body temperature in degrees and survival after an operation
   d. Eye color and undergraduate grade point average

Data Analysis

Use the gss.sys system file to answer the following questions.

1 You're interested in examining the relationship between the happiness of a person's marriage and whether they find life to be exciting, routine, or dull. Generate the SPSS/PC+ output that you need to investigate the question.

2 Discuss whether row or column percentages tell you what you want to know, and why.

3 Write a brief paragraph summarizing your results.

4 Write the SPSS/PC+ command to interchange the rows and columns of your table. That is, if in your previous table *HAPMAR* was the row variable, make it the column variable.

5 Would you still look at the same percentages?

6 Write a brief paragraph summarizing the relationship between a person's job satisfaction (*SATJOB*) and whether he or she perceives life to be exciting.

Changing the Coding Scheme

How can you change the way your variables are coded?

- How can you switch the code numbers that stand for particular responses?

- How can you combine groups of codes into a smaller, more convenient number of codes?

- Can you preserve the original variable and make a new, recoded version, too?

- What happens to value labels when you recode the values?

- What happens to missing-value codes when you recode the values?

A variable like *AGE* has too many categories to use in a crosstabulation. The table would contain hundreds of cells, and most of them would be empty or nearly empty. To use a variable like *AGE* in a crosstabulation, you need to create broader categories from the original data. The RECODE command lets you combine values into a single new code. This is sometimes called **collapsing** the codes. For example, you can group people's ages into decades or perhaps just into *Young*, *Middle-aged*, and *Old* categories. Then you can make a crosstabulation comparing excitement among people in the different age groups. You can also use RECODE simply to rearrange a coding scheme.

THE RECODE COMMAND

The RECODE command works in a straightforward manner. You enter specifications that say, "If the value is now this, make it equal to that." Recoding is useful in several circumstances.

Changing Individual Values

Remember that *LIFE* has three valid responses, coded 1–3:

1 Exciting

2 Pretty routine

3 Dull

Suppose you want to change the order to go from least excitement to most excitement:

1 Dull

2 Pretty routine

3 Exciting

In effect, you want to swap the values 1 and 3. You can do this easily by typing:

```
recode life (1 = 3) (3 = 1).
```

Before the swap, the frequency table for *LIFE* looks like Figure 11.1, which by now should be familiar. After the swap, all the original 1s for *LIFE* have changed to 3s, and the original 3s have changed to 1s. However, the value labels are still the same. Code 1, which now stands for the *Dull* category, still has the label *Exciting*—a confusing situation. When you tinker with the way a variable is coded, you don't affect the variable label or value labels you may have given it. You can fix this problem easily, though, just by issuing a new VALUE LABELS command (and VARIABLE LABELS, if you want to) along with your RECODE command:

```
recode life (1 = 3) (3 = 1).
value labels life 1  'Dull' 2  'Pretty routine'
  3  'Exciting'    8 "Don't know" 9 'No answer'.
```

Now a frequency table showing the recoded variable, *LIFE*, will have the right assignment of labels. The new frequency table is in Figure 11.2. Compare it to Figure 11.1, especially in the way that the *Cum Percent* column has changed. Also, if you list out the actual values in the file (see Chapter 2), you'll see that cases that had value 1 for *LIFE* have value 3 instead, and vice versa.

Figure 11.1 LIFE frequency table before recoding

```
LIFE        Is life exciting or dull?

                                            Valid      Cum
       Value Label         Value  Frequency  Percent  Percent  Percent

Exciting                     1        684     46.4     46.8     46.8
Pretty routine               2        704     47.8     48.2     95.0
Dull                         3         73      5.0      5.0    100.0
Missing data                 9         12       .8   MISSING
                                    -------  -------  -------
                    TOTAL            1473    100.0    100.0
```

Figure 11.2 LIFE frequency table after recoding

```
LIFE        Is life exciting or dull?

                                            Valid      Cum
       Value Label         Value  Frequency  Percent  Percent  Percent

Dull                         1         73      5.0      5.0      5.0
Pretty routine               2        704     47.8     48.2     53.2
Exciting                     3        684     46.4     46.8    100.0
Missing data                 9         12       .8   MISSING
                                    -------  -------  -------
                    TOTAL            1473    100.0    100.0
```

Collapsing Values

You can also use RECODE to collapse a variable like *AGE* (the respondent's age at the time of the interview) into a small number of categories:

```
recode age (18 thru 29=1) (30 thru 45=2)
   (46 thru 59=3) (60 thru 89=4) (else=9).
variable labels age  'Age collapsed into categories'.
value labels age 1  '18 - 29 years' 2  '30 - 45 years'
   3  '46 - 59 years' 4  '60 or more years'.
missing values age (9).
```

This RECODE command combines the values 18 through 29 into a single category with the code of 1; 30 through 45 into a category with the code of 2; 46 through 59 into a category with the code of 3; and 60 through 89 into a category with the code of 4. Everyone else is assigned a code of 9.

? *What about people younger than 18 or older than 89? Is that who "everyone else" is?* There aren't any valid ages less than 18 or more than 89. The General Social Survey doesn't include anyone younger than 18, and it reports an age of 89 for people 90 or over. Ages outside of the range 18–89 are all missing values. In the RECODE command, therefore, values that aren't in the range 18–89 are recoded to 9, and then 9 is declared missing.   ■■■

Without recoding, the frequency table for *AGE* would be pretty long, containing one line for every age between 18 and 89, resulting in 72 lines in all. But after the recoding (and a new VALUE LABELS command for clarification), the frequency table is more compact and easier to interpret. It looks like Figure 11.3.

Figure 11.3 AGE frequency table after recoding

```
AGE        Age collapsed into categories

                                        Valid     Cum
   Value Label           Value  Frequency  Percent  Percent  Percent

18 - 29 years              1        393      26.7     26.8     26.8
30 - 45 years              2        476      32.3     32.4     59.2
46 - 59 years              3        253      17.2     17.2     76.5
60 or more years           4        345      23.4     23.5    100.0
                           9          6       .4     MISSING
                                  -------   -------  -------
                  TOTAL            1473     100.0    100.0
```

How Does It Work?

The RECODE command operates on one case at a time. It takes a case's value on the variable you are recoding and then starts searching through the recode specifications. If it finds a specification telling it what to do with the value, it makes the switch and stops processing the RECODE command for that case. This means that a RECODE command never changes the value of a case twice. The command

```
recode life (1 = 3) (3 = 1).
```

changes the 1s to 3s and leaves them there. It doesn't recode them a second time, back to 1s. Only the cases that were originally 3 for the *LIFE* variable get recoded to 1.

Another important point to remember is that if you don't recode a value, the value doesn't change. In the example above, cases for which the variable *LIFE* doesn't equal 1 or 3 are totally unaffected by the RECODE command.

Specifying the RECODE Command

The RECODE command is easy to read. The examples so far have had the following general form:

```
recode variable name (current codes = new code)
  (current codes = new code)
```

RECODE works on one variable before it starts on any others. You put the variable name after the word RECODE and then enter as many recode specifications as you want—each enclosed in parentheses. A **recode specification** is a current code (or a list of current codes), followed by an equals sign (=), followed by the single new code that you want the current one(s) changed to. If you have a list of codes, you can enter each of them separately:

```
recode age (18 19 20 21 22 23 24 25 26 27 28 29 = 1)
  (30 31 32 33 34 35 36 37 38 39 40 41 42 43 44 45 = 2)
  ...and so on.
```

You can also enter them as a range of codes, like the earlier example:

```
recode age (18 THRU 29 = 1) (30 THRU 45 = 2) ...and so on.
```

Or you can mix the two styles. RECODE is very flexible that way:

```
recode age (18 19 20 21 22 23 24 25 26 27 28 29 = 1)
  (30 thru 45 = 2) (46 47 48 49 thru 59 = 3)
  ...and so on.
```

AGE AND EXCITEMENT WITH LIFE

Now that *AGE* is in a usable form for crosstabulations, we'd like to know whether young, middle-aged, and older people in the sample had different feelings about how exciting life is.

We'll group the men and the women into categories based on age and then make a crosstabulation of age categories and excitement categories:

```
get file 'gss.sys'.
recode age (18 thru 29=1) (30 thru 45=2)
   (46 thru 59=3) (60 thru 89=4) (else=9).
variable labels age  'Age collapsed into categories'.
value labels age 1  '18 - 29 years' 2  '30 - 45 years'
   3  '46 - 59 years' 4  '60 or more years'.
missing values age (9).
crosstabs life by age /cells count column.
```

The results are in Figure 11.4, and they are as you might expect. Of the young people, aged 18–29, 54% found life exciting; but of the old people, aged 60 or over, only 37% did.

Figure 11.4 Age and life's excitement

```
LIFE  Is life exciting or dull?  by  AGE  Age collapsed into categories

                 AGE                                Page 1 of 1
           Count
           Col Pct  18 - 29  30 - 45  46 - 59  60 or mo
                    years    years    years    re years   Row
                       1        2        3        4      Total
   LIFE            ┌────────┬────────┬────────┬────────┐
              1    │  211   │  219   │  125   │  128   │  683
    Exciting       │ 54.1   │ 46.3   │ 49.6   │ 37.5   │ 46.9
                   ├────────┼────────┼────────┼────────┤
              2    │  168   │  237   │  115   │  180   │  700
  Pretty routine   │ 43.1   │ 50.1   │ 45.6   │ 52.8   │ 48.1
                   ├────────┼────────┼────────┼────────┤
              3    │   11   │   17   │   12   │   33   │   73
    Dull           │  2.8   │  3.6   │  4.8   │  9.7   │  5.0
                   └────────┴────────┴────────┴────────┘
           Column    390      473      252      341     1456
           Total     26.8     32.5     17.3     23.4    100.0
```

Let's introduce *SEX* as a control variable again, as in Chapter 10. That way, we can tell whether the pattern of declining excitement is the same for both men and women.

```
crosstabs life by age by sex /cells count column.
```

The separate crosstabulations for men and women are shown in Figure 11.5. The men's enthusiasm for life doesn't seem to decline until age 60 or so. In both of the age groups 18–29 and 30–45, 52% of the men reported that life was exciting. The percentage actually increases somewhat in the age group 46-59. However, only 42% of those over 60 reported being excited with their lives.

Figure 11.5 Controlling for sex

```
LIFE  Is life exciting or dull?  by  AGE  Age collapsed into categories
Controlling for..
SEX  Respondent's sex  Value = 1  Male
                      AGE                                  Page 1 of 1
           Count
           Col Pct  18 - 29  30 - 45  46 - 59  60 or mo
                    years    years    years    re years   Row
                      1        2        3        4       Total
 LIFE     ─────────
            1          89      102       58       51      300
 Exciting             51.7     52.0     54.2     42.1     50.3

            2          76       87       45       59      267
 Pretty routine       44.2     44.4     42.1     48.8     44.8

            3           7        7        4       11       29
 Dull                  4.1      3.6      3.7      9.1      4.9

           Column     172      196      107      121      596
           Total      28.9     32.9     18.0     20.3    100.0
```

```
LIFE  Is life exciting or dull?  by  AGE  Age collapsed into categories
Controlling for..
SEX  Respondent's sex  Value = 2  Female
                      AGE                                  Page 1 of 1
           Count
           Col Pct  18 - 29  30 - 45  46 - 59  60 or mo
                    years    years    years    re years   Row
                      1        2        3        4       Total
 LIFE     ─────────
            1         122      117       67       77      383
 Exciting             56.0     42.2     46.2     35.0     44.5

            2          92      150       70      121      433
 Pretty routine       42.2     54.2     48.3     55.0     50.3

            3           4       10        8       22       44
 Dull                  1.8      3.6      5.5     10.0      5.1

           Column     218      277      145      220      860
           Total      25.3     32.2     16.9     25.6    100.0
```

The pattern for women is different. In the age group 18–29, 56% of the women reported being excited by life. In the age group 30–45, only 42% still classified their lives as exciting. This is a drop of 14%. Of the women over 60, only 35% were excited by life. For the younger age groups, age appears to have dampened the women's enthusiasm for life, but not the men's.

You can offer many explanations for this finding. Women may be discriminated against in the work force and rapidly lose their youthful enthusiasm. Women in the intermediate age group 30-45, especially those with children, may have greater demands on their time and therefore feel less enthusiastic than their younger counterparts (or less industrious husbands).

In any event, we couldn't have found this difference between men and women without entering all three variables (*LIFE*, *AGE*, and *SEX*) into the analysis at once.

MORE ABOUT RECODE

Now that you've seen an application of the RECODE command, here is some more information about how you can use it.

Recoding Several Variables

If you have more than one variable to recode, you can do one of two things. Either enter a RECODE command for each variable; or just put a slash after the specifications for the first one and then enter the name and specifications for the next:

```
recode life (1 = 3) (3 = 1)
  /age (18 thru 29=1) (30 thru 45=2)
(46 thru 59=3) (60 thru 89=4) (else=9).
```

If you want to recode several variables in the same way, you can simply list the names of all of them before the recode specifications. The next example recodes four variables representing the education of the respondent, spouse, father, and mother. We want to recode all four in the same way:

```
recode educ speduc paeduc maeduc (0 thru 6 = 1)
  (7 thru 9 = 2) (10 thru 12 = 3)
  (13 thru 16 = 4) (17 thru 20 = 5) (97,98,99 = 9).
```

What Happens to the Original Data?

When you recode a variable, you change its values to new ones. For the rest of the SPSS/PC+ session, your data will contain the new values.

? *If you collapse the values of AGE as in the earlier example, have you lost the original codes forever?* Certainly not—they're still out there in the data file you read with DATA LIST or in the system file you read with *GET*. You *have* lost them for the duration of the SPSS/PC+ session. RECODE really does change the data in your active file—but not in the data file or in the system file it read to create the active file.   ■■■

If you want to have both versions of a variable, say *AGE*, then you can use COMPUTE to create a copy of the variable, leaving your original *AGE* values alone. (We'll talk more about COMPUTE in Chapter 14.) Let's say you want to call the new variable *AGECAT*, for age categories:

```
compute agecat = age.
recode agecat (18 thru 29=1) (30 thru 45=2)
  (46 thru 59=3) (60 thru 89=4) (else=9).
variable labels agecat  'Age collapsed into categories'
value labels agecat 1  '18 - 29 years' 2  '30 - 45 years'
   3  '46 - 59 years' 4  '60 or more years'.
missing values agecat (9).
```

Since the RECODE command uses the new *AGECAT* variable, you end up with a new variable named *AGECAT* and the original, unrecoded variable *AGE*.

What ELSE?

Suppose you have 50 numeric state codes, and you want to recode *New York* (code 36) to code 1, *California* (code 6) to code 2, *Texas* (code 48) to code 3, and the other 47 states to code 4. Do you have to list all 47 state codes in one enormous recode specification? You could, but there's an easier way:

```
recode state (36=1) (6=2) (48=3) (else=4).
value labels state 1  'New York' 2  'California'
               3  'Texas'  4  'Other'.
```

The handy keyword ELSE means just what it ought to mean. Anything *else*—anything that hasn't been recoded by a previous specification in this RECODE command—gets caught up and put into the new code 4.

Missing Values

One common way to use ELSE is to recode all the values you're interested in, and toss the rest into the system-missing value. (System-missing values are codes that SPSS/PC+ assigns when it encounters values that are not valid. For example, if a variable is numeric and SPSS/PC+ finds a string value for a case, the variable is assigned the system-missing value for that case. System-missing values are never included in the computation of statistics.)

For example, the following command recodes everything except original values 36, 6, and 48 to system-missing:

```
recode state (36=1) (6=2) (48=3) (else=sysmis).
value labels state 1  'New York' 2  'California' 3  'Texas'.
```

The keyword ELSE catches everything that hasn't been recoded yet, including the values you've declared missing and the system-missing values. So be careful when you use ELSE.

The keyword SYSMIS (for system-missing) also works in the opposite direction. For example, if you left blanks in your data file for a variable named *SALES* when there were no sales, the cases with blanks will turn up as system-missing. You may decide later that you want to use those cases in your analysis, with the understanding that their sales are zero. You can use RECODE to turn *SYSMIS* into the zero value you want:

```
recode sales (sysmis=0).
```

The RECODE command never determines which values are defined as user-missing. Thus the command above does not make zero a missing value. If zero was already a user-missing value, however, it remains one.

For the user-missing value (the one specified on the MISSING VALUE command) you use RECODE just as you would for any other values.

```
recode life (8 = 2).
value labels life 1  'Exciting' 2 "Routine, don't know"
                  3  'Dull'.
```

Even though code 8, *Don't know,* was originally declared missing, the above command recodes it to 2. Because RECODE doesn't affect the definition of missing values, 8 is still missing (although no cases have the value 8 after the recode) and 2 is not missing.

To recode *both* system-missing and user-missing values, you can use the keyword MISSING. You can only recode from MISSING to some other code (not the reverse):

```
recode state (36=1) (6=2) (48=3) (missing=0) (else=4).
value labels state 1  'New York' 2  'California'
                   3  'Texas'    4  'Other'.
missing values state (0).
```

Lowest and Highest Values

Two useful shortcuts for the RECODE command are the keywords LOWEST and HIGHEST. You use them in a range of values to mean just what they say—the lowest and highest values in your data, whatever those values are. Use the keywords like this:

```
recode income (missing=0) (lowest thru 10000=1)
  (10000 thru 30000=2) (30000 thru highest=3).
value labels income 1  'Low' 2  'Moderate' 3  'High'.
missing value income (0).
```

LOWEST and HIGHEST stand for current codes that will be changed into new ones. You can't use these keywords to refer to new codes.

Overlapping Values

You may have noticed in the last example that the values in the recode specifications overlap. The values for $10,000 and $30,000 each occur twice. Why should this be? A value of exactly $10,000 is recoded by the *first* specification to include that value—in this example, it is recoded to 1. But consider what happens if someone's income is $10,000.01. As the example is written, that person's income is recoded to 2. If the values in the specifications did *not* overlap, and the second specification were (10001 thru 30000=2), the income of $10,000.01 wouldn't be recoded at all. Because of this type of problem, it's often a good idea to have overlapping values in the specifications.

SUMMARY OF KEYWORDS USED IN RECODE

The keywords you can use are:

SYSMIS   *Refers to system-missing values.* You can recode to or from SYSMIS (that is, it can be on either side of the equals sign).

MISSING   *Refers to all missing values, whether user-missing or system-missing.* You can only recode from MISSING to some other code, as shown above.

LOWEST   *Refers to the lowest value in your data (including user-missing values).* LOWEST is used to specify the bottom of a range of codes. You cannot recode values into LOWEST. It's an input specification only.

HIGHEST   *Refers to the highest value in your data (including user-missing values).* HIGHEST is used to specify the top of a range of codes. You cannot recode values into HIGHEST. It's an input specification only.

ELSE   *Refers to any value not yet recoded by the* RECODE *command.*

Notice that ELSE must be the last specification on a RECODE command. Specifications are checked in order, and ELSE grabs all values that are left unrecoded, so there's no point in having further specifications. They won't ever be used.

In fact, when you use more than one of these keywords, you should almost always use them in the order in which they're listed above: SYSMIS, then MISSING, then ordinary values (perhaps including LOWEST and HIGHEST in range specifications), and last of all ELSE.

WHAT'S NEXT?

To use *AGE* in a crosstabulation, we had to combine its codes into a manageable number of categories. That worked fine, but we did lose some information about people's exact ages. In the next chapter, we'll compare the *average* ages of the people who said their lives were exciting, routine, or dull.

Summary

How can you change the way your variables are coded?

You can use the RECODE command to switch or combine the codes for any of your variables. RECODE takes values, lists of values, or ranges of values, and assigns them to new values according to your specifications.

RECODE changes the values for the remainder of your SPSS/PC+ session. It doesn't change the data file or the system file from which you read the data. You can use the keyword INTO on the RECODE command to create a new variable, leaving the original unchanged.

You must reassign value labels and missing values if your recoding makes the existing ones inappropriate.

EXERCISES

Syntax

1　Correct the syntax errors in the following RECODE commands:

```
a. recode life '1 = 3' '3 = 1'.
b. recode life (1 = 3, 3 = 1).
c. recode educ (0 - 8 = 1)(9 - 12 = 2)(13 - 16 = 3)
        (16 - 20 = 4).
d. recode age (else = 9) (18 thru 29 = 1) (30 thru 45 = 2)
        (46 thru 59 = 3)(60 thru 89 = 4).
```

2　Explain whether this command

```
recode life (1 = 3) (3 = 1).
```

does or does not have the same effect as these two commands:

```
recode life (1 = 3).
recode life (3 = 1).
```

3 The following RECODE commands are syntactically correct. Describe their effect, including their effect upon missing values.

a. `recode score (lowest thru 50 = 1)(51 thru highest = 2).`

b. `recode opinion (3 = 1) (else = 2) (missing = 9).`

4 Why do the following commands not make sense? Don't just state a rule; show why the commands request something impossible.

a. `recode age (1 = 18 thru 29) (2 = 30 thru 45)`
   `             (3 = 46 thru 59)(4 = 60 thru 89) (9 = 99).`

b. `recode sales (lowest thru 1000 = 1)(1000 thru 4000 = 2)`
   `             (4000 thru highest = 3) (sysmis = missing).`

c. `recode income (0 = lowest) (1 = 4000) (2 = 8000) (3 = 12000)`
   `             (4 = 16000) (5 = 20000) (6 = 30000) (7 = highest).`

Looking at Means

How can you summarize the relationship between two
variables when one is measured on an interval or ratio
scale and the other has a limited number of distinct
categories?

- Why can't you make a table showing the number of times each combination of responses occurs?

- What are good summary measures for a variable measured on an interval scale?

- How can you display separate summary statistics for each of the different categories?

I n Chapter 11 we used a crosstabulation to look at the relationship between age and excitement with life. People were assigned to one of four
age categories based on their actual ages. It's always possible to group the
values of variables like age into a smaller number of categories. But the
grouping ignores some of the available information. All cases with values
in the same range are treated as the same. In our example, people who
were 30 years old were grouped into the same category as people who
were 45. Using *individual* ages in the crosstabulation would have been
cumbersome because there were so many different ones.

You can look at the relationship between age and excitement in another
way that still produces compact tables but is based on each person's actual
age. You can look at the average ages for people in each of the excitement
categories.

COMPARING AVERAGES

To examine the relationship between the *AGE* variable and the *LIFE* variable, you can use SPSS/PC+ to compute the average age of the people in
each of the categories *Exciting*, *Pretty routine*, and *Dull*. This should give
you some idea of whether the average ages in the excitement categories
are different. You should also look at the standard deviation (see Chapter
9) for each category. That way, you'll have some idea of the spread of the
age values. Just run the commands:

```
get file 'gss.sys'.
means age by life.
```

The MEANS command calculates means for the variable before the BY for
each of the categories of the variable after BY. (The second variable
shouldn't have too many categories.) For this example, you get the results
shown in Figure 12.1.

On the output, the variable whose means you're calculating, *AGE*, is
named on the line that says *Summaries of.* The variable that determines
the groups for which the means are calculated, *LIFE*, is listed where it says
By levels of.

The line labeled *For Entire Population* gives the mean and standard
deviation of *AGE* for all cases in the sample. (Since we haven't included our

Figure 12.1 Means of AGE by levels of LIFE

```
Summaries of    AGE         Age of respondent
By levels of    LIFE        Is life exciting or dull?

Variable        Value  Label                  Mean    Std Dev    Cases

For Entire Population                        43.9760   17.7752    1456

LIFE              1   Exciting               41.9473   16.8140     683
LIFE              2   Pretty routine         45.0300   18.1265     700
LIFE              3   Dull                   52.8493   19.6869      73

   Total Cases =       1473
Missing Cases =         17 OR    1.2 PCT.
```

entire population in the study, this line describes our entire sample, not the population.) The average age of the 1,456 cases in the sample was 44 years, and the standard deviation was almost 18. Now what about the ages of the people who found life exciting, routine, and dull?

The average age of the 683 people who found life exciting was about 42. The people who found life pretty routine were older. Their average age was close to 45. The 73 people who found life dull were by far the oldest. Their average age was almost 53. The variability in the groups, as measured by the standard deviation, is pretty similar. The bored people had the largest standard deviation, close to 20.

From this table you can see that, on the average, the younger people found life more exciting than the older people. There was over a 10-year difference in average ages between the people who found life exciting and those who found it dull. Is this true for both men and women? Before we try to answer that, we should check for an overall age difference between the sexes, since it's generally true that women live longer than men. Use this command:

means age by sex.

This command gives the results in Figure 12.2.

Figure 12.2 Means of AGE for men and women

```
Summaries of    AGE         Age of respondent
By levels of    SEX         Respondent's sex

Variable        Value  Label                  Mean    Std Dev    Cases

For Entire Population                        44.0048   17.8107    1467

SEX               1   Male                   42.6064   17.0232     597
SEX               2   Female                 44.9644   18.2793     870

   Total Cases =       1473
```

Sure enough, the average age of the women in the General Social Survey sample was almost 45, while the men averaged only about 42.6 years old.

Now let's find out whether our previous finding—that younger people find life more exciting than older people—holds for both sexes. Try this:

means age **by sex by life.**

This gives you Figure 12.3. As a result of adding the specification BY LIFE to the MEANS AGE BY SEX command, we have a table that divides up each of the categories in Figure 12.2 into three smaller categories according to whether they are excited by life. (The maximum number of BY keywords allowed is five.)

Figure 12.3 Means of AGE by SEX by LIFE

```
Summaries of   AGE      Age of respondent
By levels of   SEX      Respondent's sex
               LIFE     Is life exciting or dull?


Variable       Value  Label                 Mean    Std Dev   Cases

For Entire Population                      43.9760   17.7752   1456

SEX              1   Male                  42.5805   17.0258    596
  LIFE           1   Exciting              41.4033   16.0691    300
  LIFE           2   Pretty routine        43.3408   17.6493    267
  LIFE           3   Dull                  47.7586   19.8794     29

SEX              2   Female                44.9430   18.2237    860
  LIFE           1   Exciting              42.3734   17.3841    383
  LIFE           2   Pretty routine        46.0716   18.3574    433
  LIFE           3   Dull                  56.2045   19.0429     44

    Total Cases =    1473
```

The first line in Figure 12.3, after the values for the whole sample, gives the average age (and the standard deviation) for all the men in the sample. This line is similar to the corresponding line in Figure 12.2. The next three lines divide the men into those who find life exciting, pretty routine, and dull. Then follows the same information for women. Men who found life exciting had an average age of 41.4, while those who found life routine averaged 43.3 years old. Similarly, women who found life exciting averaged 42.4 years old, while women who found life routine were over 46 years old on average. The groups who found life positively dull had the oldest average age for both men and women. There's a 14-year age difference between *Exciting* and *Dull* for the women and a 6-year difference for the men.

Since the women in the sample were older than the men, we can't really compare the average ages for the men and the women in each of the categories of excitement. We can see that the bored women were older than the bored men, but this doesn't necessarily mean that the women became bored later in life than the men. It could mean that the men and the women became bored at the same age, but the bored women grew older while the bored men died.

> *Why aren't the average ages for all men and all women exactly the same in Figure 12.2 and Figure 12.3?* The reason for the slight discrepancy is that Figure 12.2 is based on all cases with non-missing values of AGE, while Figure 12.3 is based on cases that have valid values for *both* AGE and LIFE. ■■■

SIMPLE SOLUTIONS

The last several chapters weren't meant to explain a problem as complex as "Why are some people excited by life and others not?" These chapters just show you that using *simple* procedures—such as making tables of frequencies, percentages, and means—can help you look for answers. Don't think that for a complicated problem you always need some exotic statistical analysis. You might. But your first step should always be to look at the data carefully with simple but powerful methods. Make tables and look at them carefully. Think about the problem. No statistical procedure can substitute for thought. And always start simply.

MORE ABOUT THE MEANS PROCEDURE

You can use MEANS to:
- Compute means of a variable for each category of one or more other variables.

Order of Variables

The order of the variables you name on the MEANS command determines their order on the output. The first variable is always the one for which the means are computed. If you type

```
means age by life by sex.
```

you'll get a line showing the mean age for each of the three categories of *LIFE*, followed by a line showing the mean age for men and another showing the mean age for women within each category. This arrangement is different from what you see in Figure 12.3, which was produced by:

```
means age by sex by life.
```

More Than One Table

If you have more than one variable before the first BY on the MEANS command, you'll get a separate table of means for each variable. If you type

```
means age educ by sex by life.
```

you'll get one table for *AGE* by *SEX* by *LIFE* and another table for *EDUC* by *SEX* by *LIFE*.

Options for MEANS

You can use the OPTIONS subcommand with MEANS to control some of the features of a table and the statistics it shows. To do so, type a slash and the word OPTIONS after your table specification. Then type one or more option numbers after the word. Here is a list of the option numbers and what they mean. (In the list, *independent variable* refers to a grouping variable, as opposed to a *dependent variable*, which is one for which group means are displayed.)

1	Include user-missing values	8	Suppress value labels
2	Exclude cases with user-missing dependent values	9	Suppress independent variable names
3	Suppress all labels	10	Suppress independent variable values
5	Suppress group counts		
6	Display group sums	11	Suppress group means
7	Suppress group standard deviations	12	Display group variances

You can also use a STATISTICS subcommand with MEANS. Statistic 1 gives you an **analysis of variance**, the type of statistical procedure described in Chapter 20.

WHAT'S NEXT?

Procedure MEANS calculates descriptive statistics for groups of cases. In the next chapter, you'll see how these summary variables can be converted into visual displays. Instead of having to pore through lists of numbers, you'll be able to examine your data with boxplots and stem-and-leaf plots.

Summary

How can you summarize the relationship between two variables when one is measured on an interval or ratio scale and the other has a limited number of distinct categories?

If cases are classified into several groups, you can study the relationship between the variables that form the groups and other variables.

For each of the groups, you can compute descriptive statistics such as the mean and standard deviation of a variable of interest.

By examining how the means and standard deviations vary among the groups, you can study the relationships among the variables.

In SPSS/PC+, the descriptive statistics for each of the groups can be displayed in a table.

EXERCISES

Syntax

1 Write the command to calculate average ages (variable *AGE*) for people who have different degrees of job satisfaction (*SATJOB*).

2 You want to calculate the average number of years of education (*EDUC*) for people who believe in life after death and those who don't (*POSTLIFE*). You type in

```
means postlife by educ.
```

Describe the results this will produce.

3 An investigator is studying the relationship between systolic blood pressure (variable *SYSTBP*), smoking (*SMOKE*, coded 0=*no*, 1=*yes*), and drinking more than 4 ounces per day of alcohol (*DRINK*, coded 0=*no*, 1=*yes*). How would you instruct SPSS/PC+ to calculate the average blood pressure for people who don't smoke and don't drink much; don't smoke but drink much; smoke but don't drink much; and smoke and drink much?

4 How would you change the previous command if the investigator wanted to obtain the means of the four smoking-drinking groups separately for females and for males (variable *SEX*)?

5 If there are any syntax errors in the following commands, correct them. Describe the table(s) produced by each. (*AGECAT* is a variable representing four categories of age.)

a. means educ by agecat.

b. means educ age by sex.

c. means educ by agecat by sex.

d. means sex by age by educ.

6 Which of the MEANS commands below produced the following table?

```
Summaries of    SALNOW      Current Salary
By levels of    MINORITY    Minority Classification
                SEX         Sex of Employee


Variable          Value  Label              Mean      Std Dev    Cases

For Entire Population                     13767.8270  6830.2646    474

MINORITY            0    White            14409.3243  7217.6382    370
  SEX               0    Males            17790.1649  8132.2646    194
  SEX               1    Females          10682.7159  3204.7575    176

MINORITY            1    Nonwhite         11485.5769  4568.6551    104
  SEX               0    Males            12898.4375  5223.9525     64
  SEX               1    Females           9225.0000  1588.9474     40

  Total Cases =    474
```

a. means salnow by sex minority.

b. means salnow by minority by sex.

c. means minority by salnow by sex.

Statistical Concepts

1 Indicate whether you would use procedure FREQUENCIES, CROSSTABS, or MEANS to find the following:

a. The average age for members of different political parties

b. The number of married, single, widowed, divorced, and never married people in each of the political parties

c. The number of members in each of the political parties

d. The average age of men and women in each political party

e. The number of men and women in each of the marital categories within each of the political parties

2 A market research company is trying to decide what color to make a new brand of breath mints. They ask 100 consumers to choose among the colors white, yellow, green striped, and red striped. A research analyst assigns the codes 1 through 4 to the possible choices and uses the MEANS command to find average color preferences for men and women in each of four income categories. How would you interpret the resulting table?

3 Below is a MEANS table that shows the average ages of men and women who believe in life after death and those who don't or are uncertain.

```
Summaries of   AGE        Age of respondent
By levels of   SEX        Sex of employee
               POSTLIFE   Belief in life after death


Variable         Value  Label                    Mean    Std Dev   Cases

For Entire Population                          ▓▓▓▓▓▓    17.8107    1467

SEX                1   Male                   42.6064    17.0232   ▓▓▓▓▓
   POSTLIFE        1   Yes                    42.0341    16.8936     410
   POSTLIFE        2   No or uncertain        43.8610    17.2833     187

SEX                2   Female                 44.9644    18.2793     870
   POSTLIFE        1   Yes                    45.3323    18.2541     662
   POSTLIFE        2   No or uncertain        43.7933    18.3543   ▓▓▓▓▓

   Total Cases =    1473
```

a. Fill in the missing information.

b. Based on the previous table, what is the average age of women in the sample?

c. What is the average age of men who don't believe in life after death?

d. From the table, can you tell what the average age is of people who believe in life after death?

4 You are interested in studying the relationship between highest degree received by a person in school, the person's marital status, and several other variables. Describe how you might investigate the relationship of these two variables and

a. The number of hours of television watched per week

b. Religious affiliation

c. Job satisfaction

d. Number of siblings

e. Zodiac sign

5 Two students are investigating the relationship between college grade point average and the number of cars owned five years after graduation. The first student plans to use the SPSS/PC+ RECODE command to recode the actual grade point averages into the A range, the B range, the C range, and the D and lower range. He then plans to obtain a crosstabulation of the number of cars by recoded grade point average. The second student plans to calculate the mean grade point average for people who have different numbers of cars. How are these two approaches similar and how do they differ?

Data Analysis

Use the gss.sys system file to answer the following questions.

1 You want to examine the relationship between the happiness of a person's marriage and their years of education. Run the appropriate analyses. (Use the *EDUC* variable, which tells you the number of years of education a person has, and *HAPMAR*, which tells the happiness of the marriage.)

2 Summarize your results.

3 Rerun your analysis including an additional variable, the respondent's sex. Do there appear to be differences between men and women?

4 Make a crosstabulation of the highest degree received *(DEGREE)* and the happiness of a marriage *(HAPMAR)*. Summarize your results.

5 For each of the categories of the *DEGREE* variable, find the average years of father's education *(PAEDUC)*. Does there appear to be a relationship between a person's highest degree and the amount of education the person's father has?

Additional Ways of Displaying Data

What additional displays are useful for summarizing the distribution of a variable for several groups?

- What is a boxplot?
- What can you tell from the length of a boxplot?
- How is the median represented in a boxplot?
- What is a stem-and-leaf plot?
- How do stem-and-leaf plots differ from histograms?

I n Chapter 12, you saw how the tables produced by the MEANS procedure are used to look at average values of a variable when the cases
are subdivided into groups based on one or more grouping variables. In
this chapter, we'll see how this table can be turned into a picture with the
EXAMINE procedure. We'll look at boxplots and stem-and-leaf plots.

THE BOXPLOT

If you wish to visually compare the distribution of a variable, you need a
display that will convey information about both central tendency and variability. The histogram, a display we've already considered, gives us a fairly detailed picture of the values in our sample. In fact, a histogram may
present too much information, especially if we want to compare the distribution of a variable for several groups. It's certainly possible to arrange
several histograms side-by-side and compare them, but that can involve
considerable effort. Often, it's more useful to abstract the information
from a histogram and construct what's called a **boxplot**. To get boxplots,
you just run the commands:

```
get file 'gss.sys'.
examine age by life /plot boxplot.
```

Figure 13.1 A boxplot

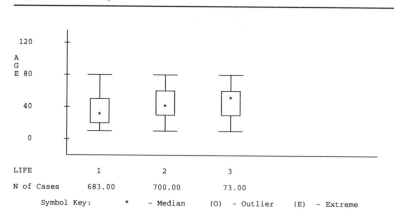

A boxplot is based on several summary measures that we have already discussed: the median, the 25th percentile, the 75th percentile, and the largest and smallest values. Look at Figure 13.1, which contains three boxplots for the *AGE* variable, one for each category of *LIFE*. (It appears indecipherable at first glance, but it's a display that's really quite easy to understand once you've been introduced.)

To figure out which box belongs to which *excitement* category, look at the labels underneath the plot. The variable or variables that form the groups are identified on the far left immediately under the display. In this case the grouping variable is *LIFE*. The first "box" is for cases that fall in the first category of *LIFE* (value 1), the second is for cases in the second category, and similarly for the third. The vertical axis on the plot is for the variable whose distribution you are summarizing, in this case, *AGE*. Unlike the horizontal scale where distances don't convey information (if you had coded the excitement categories 1, 3, and 20, the display wouldn't change, except that the new values would be given underneath the plot), the vertical axis has a meaningful scale. In this case it ranges from 0 to 120. You can only use boxplots to summarize variables for which percentiles are meaningful measures. Remember, you can't interpret a median for variables like religion or automobile color.

In each of the boxes you see an asterisk (*). The asterisk identifies the median of each of the groups. To determine the age value that corresponds to an asterisk, you must see where the asterisk lies on the *AGE* scale. For the first group, the asterisk corresponds to a median age value around 38. For the second group, the median is approximately 40, while for the third group, it is around 55.

> **?** *How am I supposed to figure out what the medians really are when the axis for age is so sparsely labeled?* The point of the boxplot is not to determine the actual medians. You can easily get SPSS/PC+ to display them. (In fact, the EXAMINE procedure displays them by default.) In a boxplot, you're interested in seeing the relationship of the medians for the different groups. In this case, you see that the bored people have a higher median age than both of the other groups. Excited people and those who find life routine have similar median ages.   ■■■

Now let's consider the box itself. The width of the box doesn't tell you anything. All boxes on the display have the same width. What does matter is the length of the box. The lower boundary of a box is the 25th percentile, while the upper boundary is the 75th percentile. That means that 50% of the cases have values within the box, 25% have values less than the lower boundary of the box, and 25% have values larger than the upper boundary. By looking at the length of the box, you can tell how much spread there is in the data values. If one box is much longer than the others, that means the data values in that group have more variability. In our example, the lengths of the boxes are pretty similar. (The length of the box—the difference between the 75th percentile and the 25th percentile—is called the **interquartile** range.)

> **?** *How come the medians aren't in the middle of the boxes?* The median is in the middle of the box only if the distribution is fairly symmetric. (A **symmetric** distribution is one that can be split down the middle into two parts that are mirror images of each other.) If the median is not in the middle of the box, the distribution is not symmetric. If the asterisk is closer to the bottom of the box than to the top, the data are positively skewed. That means there are more cases toward the upper end of the distribution; there is a "tail" toward larger values. If the median is closer to the top of the box than the bottom, the opposite is true. The tail is toward smaller values. (There's more discussion of this in Chapter 16.)   ■ ■ ■

Extreme Values

Sometimes you have data values in a group that are quite different from the others. That's useful information to include in a boxplot. The SPSS/PC+ boxplot has two categories for values far removed from the rest. Cases with values more than 3 box lengths from the upper or lower edge of the box are called extreme values and labeled with an *E* on the plot. Cases with values between 1.5 and 3 box lengths from the upper or lower edge of a box are called outliers and are labeled with an *O* on the plot. In Figure 13.1, there are no *O*s or *E*s on the plot. This indicates that there were no very unusual data points.

> **?** *What should I do if I find Os or Es on a plot?* Together with the symbols, you'll also find case numbers, or other identifying information, for the extremes and outliers. Examine each of the extremes and outliers to make sure that the data values have been correctly entered into the computer. If you find errors, correct them. If the extremes and outliers are not the results of data entry or coding errors, make sure that you choose appropriate measures to describe the data. For example, use the median instead of the mean, since the median is less influenced by outlying values.   ■ ■ ■

You'll notice that the boxes have lines coming out of the tops and bottoms. (These are known as **whiskers,** and the plot is sometimes called a **box-and-whiskers plot**.) For each group, the top whisker stops at the largest value that is not an outlier, and the bottom whisker ends at the smallest value that is not an outlier. In Figure 13.1, since there are no outliers or extremes, the whiskers start and end at the smallest and largest values for a group. These values are pretty much the same for each of the groups. That's not very surprising. It just means that there is an 18-year-old and a 90-year-old in each of the groups.

Why Use Boxplots?

You will find that boxplots are a compact, informative way of summarizing data. By scanning a set of boxplots, you can quickly determine how groups differ from each other. At a glance, you can compare medians and spread, as well as the ranges of the data values. That's much more convenient than poring over tables of means and standard deviations.

STEM-AND-LEAF PLOTS

You've already seen that a histogram is a good way of examining the distribution of a variable that has many ordered values. There's another display, closely related to the histogram, that can be used in place of a histogram. The advantage of a **stem-and-leaf plot** is that it preserves more information about the data than does a histogram.

We've previously seen that people who find life to be dull have a higher mean and median age than people who do not find life dull. Let's look at both a histogram and a stem-and-leaf plot of the ages of people who find life dull. First, let's get a histogram from the EXAMINE procedure.

```
select if (life eq 3).
examine age /plot histogram.
```

We used the SELECT IF command so we would get the plots only for the people who find life dull.

Figure 13.2 Histogram of AGE for LIFE=3

```
      AGE        Age of respondent

  Frequency    Bin Center
       2.00       15.0    **
       9.00       25.0    *********
      13.00       35.0    *************
       5.00       45.0    *****
      11.00       55.0    ***********
      16.00       65.0    ****************
      12.00       75.0    ************
       5.00       85.0    *****

  Bin width :   10.0
```

Look at the histogram in Figure 13.3. There's a row for each decade of age. Each of the stars in a row represent a person with an age that falls into that decade. You see that there are 9 people who are in their twenties. Can you tell whether these people are in their early twenties or late twenties? Of course not, since the same symbol is used to represent all of the cases.

Let's look at a stem-and-leaf plot for the same data:

```
examine age /plot stemleaf.
```

Figure 13.3 Stem-and-leaf plot of AGE for LIFE=3

```
     AGE        Age of respondent

 Frequency    Stem &  Leaf
      2.00       1  .  99
      9.00       2  .  001244688
     13.00       3  .  0022355667899
      5.00       4  .  00048
     11.00       5  .  01123334899
     16.00       6  .  0112334667778889
     12.00       7  .  033444456688
      5.00       8  .  11256

 Stem width:   10
```

You see that Figure 13.3, the stem-and-leaf plot, looks very much like a histogram. There's a row for each decade of age. The number of cases in a row depends on the number of people with ages in that decade. The stem-and-leaf plot differs from the histogram in that the same symbol is not used to represent all of the cases. Instead, the symbol used for a case is the last digit of the age. Look at the row for the nine people in their twenties. You can immediately see that there are two people who are exactly 20 years old, one person who is 21, one person who is 22, two people who are 24, one person who is 26, and two people who are 28.

In a stem-and-leaf plot, each observed value is subdivided into two components—the leading digit or digits, called the **stem**, and a trailing digit, called the **leaf**. For example, the age 74 has a stem of 7 and a leaf of 4. Each row of the plot represents a stem, and each case is represented by its leaf value. Within each stem, the leaves are ordered from smallest to largest.

> **?** *How would you make a stem-and-leaf plot of a variable like in-
> come?* For a variable like income that has many digits, it is un-
> wieldy and unnecessary to represent each case by the last digit of income.
> Instead, we can take a number like 25,323 and subdivide it into a stem of 2
> and a leaf of 5. In this case, the stem is in ten thousands and the leaf is in
> thousands. We no longer retain the entire value for a case, but usually that
> isn't important. Income differences in the hundreds seldom matter much.
> EXAMINE always displays the stem width under the plot.   ■ ■ ■

From both the stem-and-leaf plot and the histogram we can see that the
age distribution for the bored people is somewhat unusual. There appear
to be two peaks, the thirties and the sixties. Compare this histogram to the
one for all cases that we obtained in Chapter 8. The distribution looks different, doesn't it?

MORE ABOUT THE EXAMINE PROCEDURE

With the EXAMINE procedure you can calculate many different statistics
and plots. In this chapter we've covered only the simplest. Here's how to
get the displays that we discussed.

To make a stem-and-leaf plot and get descriptive statistics for *AGE* for
all cases, specify:

```
examine age /plot stemleaf.
```

If you want the cases subdivided into groups, specify a grouping variable
name after the keyword BY, as in:

```
examine age by life /plot stemleaf.
```

This will result in four stem-and-leaf plots—one for all cases and one for
each of the values of the *LIFE* variable.

If you want to get both histograms and boxplots, specify:

```
examine age by life /plot histogram boxplot.
```

Statistics Displayed by EXAMINE

Using EXAMINE, you can compute a variety of descriptive statistics for your
data. The following keywords can appear on the STATISTICS subcommand:

DESCRIPTIVES   *Basic descriptive statistics.*

EXTREMES(n)   *The* n *cases with the largest values and the* n *cases with
the smallest values.* If you don't give a value for *n*, the
5 smallest and 5 largest cases are displayed.

| **ALL** | *Descriptive statistics and extremes.* |
| **NONE** | *No statistics.* |

Unless you specify STATISTICS NONE, EXAMINE will display descriptive statistics.

Plots

In the EXAMINE procedure, plots are requested with the PLOT subcommand. The following keywords can appear on the PLOT subcommand:

BOXPLOT	*Boxplots.*
STEMLEAF	*Stem-and-leaf plots.*
HISTOGRAM	*Histograms.*
SPREADLEVEL	*The Levene test (see Chapter 20).*
NPPLOT	*Normal probability plots (see Chapter 18).*
ALL	*All available plots.*
NONE	*No plots.*

Identifying Extreme Cases

To use a variable other than the sequence number of the case in the data file to identify extreme cases, you must specify a variable name on the ID subcommand.

For example, if you want to identify cases on the basis of their phone numbers, specify:

```
examine age by life /id phone /statistics extreme.
```

This will result in a list of the cases with the five youngest and oldest ages. Each case will be identified by its phone number. (But only if you have entered the phone numbers into the file and called the variable *PHONE*.)

WHAT'S NEXT?

You've already seen how to use RECODE to change your original data. Chapter 14 describes some additional ways to do so. It's best to start simply, but sometimes you have to transform the original data to find out what you want to know.

Summary

What additional displays are useful for summarizing the distribution of a variables for several groups?

Boxplots and stem-and-leaf plots can be used to summarize data.

A boxplot is a display that shows both the central tendency and variability of the data.

The length of the box in a boxplot is the distance between the 25th percentile and the 75th percentile. Fifty percent of the data values fall in this range.

The median is represented by an asterisk in a boxplot. If the median is not in the center of the box, the distribution of values is skewed.

A stem-and-leaf plot, like a histogram, shows how many cases have various data values. A stem-and-leaf plot does not use the same symbol to represent all cases. Instead, the symbol depends on the actual value for a case.

EXERCISES

Syntax

1 Find the syntax errors in the following EXAMINE commands:

  a. `examine income IQ`
    `/plot histogram`
    `/plot stemleaf.`

  b. `examine attnspan with tvhours.`

2 Write the EXAMINE command to produce boxplots—with no additional plots or statistics—for *INCOME* within categories of *RELIGION* and for *INCOME* broken down by both *RELIGION* and belief in an afterlife (*POSTLIFE*).

Statistical Concepts

1 Consider the following twenty ages: 21, 22, 22, 22, 25, 28, 30, 31, 32, 34, 35, 35, 35, 35, 38, 39, 40, 40, 41, and 80. Complete the following stem-and-leaf plots for them:

```
Frequency    Stem &  Leaf
              2   .
              3   .
              4   .
            Extremes
```

```
Frequency     Stem &  Leaf
```

```
                 2  *
                 2  :
                 3  *
                 3  .
                 4  *
              Extremes
```

2 Complete the following histogram for the data in question 1:

```
Frequency    Bin Center
```

```
                25.00
                35.00
                45.00
              Extremes
Bin width :       10.00
Each star:         1 case(s)
```

3 Compared to a histogram, what are the advantages of a stem-and-leaf plot?

4 Answer the following questions based on the accompanying boxplot. The boxplots represent the time it took to ship products from three warehouses.

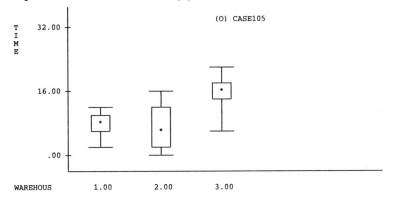

a. Estimate the median for warehouse 1.

b. Estimate the interquartile range for warehouse 2.

c. For warehouse 3, what is the largest value that is not an outlier?

d. Which warehouse has the most variability?

e. If you were to choose one of the warehouses to ship your product, which warehouse would you select and why?

5 Based on the following stem-and-leaf plot, complete the frequency table below.

```
Frequency     Stem &  Leaf

   5.00        15  .  03469
   8.00        16  .  11235788
   4.00        17  .  0022
   2.00        18  .  08
   1.00        19  .  0
   1.00        20  .  4
   1.00        21  .  5
   3.00        22  .  228

Stem width:       10.00
Each leaf:         1 case(s)
```

```
                    Frequency Table
                    --------- -----

    Bin                                    Cum
    Center      Freq      Pct              Pct

    <150.0
     162.5
     187.5
     212.5
     237.5
```

6 The following is a stem-and-leaf plot for the starting salaries of 25 men.

```
    Frequency     Stem &  Leaf

        2.00        21  .  56
        3.00        22  .  344
        4.00        23  .  0168
        4.00        24  .  2355
        5.00        25  .  04789
        1.00        26  .  7
        2.00        27  .  07
        1.00        28  .  5
         .00        29  .
        2.00        30  .  05
        1.00  Extremes     (35150)

    Stem width:      1000
    Each leaf:       1 case(s)
```

a. From the plot, can you tell what the actual salaries are for all of the men?

b. List the salaries in as much detail as you can.

7 Based on the summary statistics shown in the table below, sketch a boxplot.

```
Mean       44.0048  Std Err       .4650  Min      18.0000  Skewness     .5317
Median     40.0000  Variance  317.2203  Max      89.0000  S E Skew     .0639
5% Trim    43.2546  Std Dev    17.8107  Range    71.0000  Kurtosis    -.8026
                                         IQR      29.0000  S E Kurt     .1277

                              Percentiles
                              -----------
    Percentiles     10.0000  25.0000  50.0000  75.0000  90.0000
    HAVERAGE        23.0000  29.0000  40.0000  58.0000  70.0000
    TUKEY'S HINGES           29.0000  40.0000  58.0000
```

Data Analysis

Use the gss.sys system file to answer the following questions.

1 Select only cases who claim that their marriage is not too happy (*HAPMAR*=3). Use the stem-and-leaf plot to obtain a distribution of their ages. From this display, list the ages of all the people who think their marriage is not too happy. How does the age of the people who are unhappy compare to the age distribution of all people in the study?

2 Obtain boxplots for *AGE* for the three categories of *HAPMAR*. From the boxplots, estimate the median age in each of the three groups.

a. Which of the groups has the most variability?

b. Do you think the age distribution is symmetric for each of the three groups?

c. For each of the groups, below what value do 25% of the ages fall?

3 Using the displays available in the EXAMINE procedure, look at the relationship between *AGE* and *HEALTH*. Write a brief paragraph summarizing your conclusions.

14 Modifying Data Values

How can you use SPSS/PC+ and the computer to create new variables and to change the values of the ones you have?

■ How can you create a new variable for all the cases?

■ How can you perform calculations using the values of your variables?

■ How can you tell the computer to make decisions about whether to carry out a calculation, based on the values of your variables?

■ What happens if a case has a missing value for one of the variables involved in a calculation?

■ What happens if a case has a missing value for one of the variables involved in a decision about whether to carry out a calculation?

■ Does it matter in what order transformation commands are entered?

■ How can you choose a smaller group of cases from your file for analysis?

B efore you can even begin to analyze your data, you may have to switch them around somehow. You asked for the respondent's year of birth, but you want to analyze age. You asked for years of education in two separate questions, but you want to combine them into a single variable. Perhaps you want to take the two variables for the education of the respondent and the respondent's spouse and then make two variables that always contain husband's education and wife's education.

Changes like these are called **transformations**. SPSS/PC+ lets you do them easily with a few commands. In Chapter 11, you saw how to use the RECODE command to change the way your data are coded. In this chapter, you'll look at some commands that do transformations you can't do with RECODE.

AN EXAMPLE: COMPUTING AGE

Back in Chapter 7, you saw that the General Social Survey asks for date of birth rather than age. Most of the time, though, you want to use a person's age in your analysis. Determining age from year of birth seems simple enough: subtract the birth year from the year the survey question was asked. The SPSS/PC+ system file gss.sys has a variable named *AGE* that was calculated with the COMPUTE command. The following command created the new variable:

```
compute age = 1984 - byear.
```

After SPSS/PC+ runs this command, each case in the file has a new variable, *AGE*, that didn't exist before. If you save a system file, *AGE* is saved with the other variables. That is exactly what was done with the system file gss.sys.

? *Why ignore the actual month and day of birth?* A variable such as *AGE* usually doesn't need to be precise within a fraction of a year. If you do want to know an exact age, or if you want to know the exact interval of time between any two dates, you can use the YRMODA function explained in "More about Transformations" at the end of this chapter. ∎∎∎

THE COMPUTE COMMAND

This is the general form of the COMPUTE command:

```
compute   variable name = instructions.
```

It includes:

- The word COMPUTE.
- A variable name, either for a variable you've already defined or for a brand-new variable.
- An equals sign.
- Instructions telling SPSS/PC+ what you want to compute.

What kind of instructions can you use? You can add, subtract, multiply, divide, or do a lot of other things. You can do these things to variables in your file or to numbers. To add or subtract, use the plus sign or the minus sign (+ or –). To multiply, use an asterisk (*). To divide, use a slash (/). You can also use functions that are built into the SPSS/PC+ language and perform useful calculations automatically—such as rounding a number to the nearest integer or taking a square root. Here are some examples that show COMPUTE used in various ways:

```
compute survyear = 1984.
compute onevar = another.
compute whole = part1 + part2 + part3 + part4 + part5 + 100.
compute receipts = numsold * (cost + markup).
compute predict = .7204 * educ + .0937 * age + 16.25.
compute logincom = ln(income).
```

How Does It Work?

When you use a COMPUTE command, it is executed on every case. For each case, SPSS/PC+ first computes whatever you instructed it to compute (whatever's on the *right* side of the equals sign). It then sets the variable named on the *left* side of the equals sign to the results of the computation. If this variable is a new one, SPSS/PC+ adds it to the list of variables in your file, and you have one more variable than you had before. If the variable to the left of the equals sign already exists, SPSS/PC+ forgets the value that the variable had before the COMPUTE command and gives it the new value.

Let's look again at the examples in the previous list and see how COMPUTE works for all of them.

Neither of the following examples involves actual computation:

```
compute survyear = 1984.
compute onevar = another.
```

The variable *SURVYEAR* is set to 1984 for every case, and the variable *ONE-VAR* becomes a copy of the variable *ANOTHER* for every case. (We already used a simple COMPUTE command like this to copy a variable near the end of Chapter 11.)

A calculation for COMPUTE can involve several different parts:

```
compute whole = part1 + part2 + part3 + part4 + part5 + 100.
```

This command just adds up each *PART* variable and then adds 100.

The next examples show how things can start to get complicated:

```
compute receipts = numsold * (cost + markup).
compute predict = .7204 * educ + .0937 * age + 16.25.
```

The first of these commands computes *RECEIPTS* as *NUMSOLD* times the sum of *COST* and *MARKUP*. The second command multiplies *EDUC* by 0.7204 and then multiplies *AGE* by 0.0937, then adds those two products to the number 16.25. These commands illustrate some basic rules:

- When the instructions include parentheses, SPSS/PC+ performs the part inside the parentheses first. Remember that you can always use parentheses to specify operations in the order that you want.

- When parentheses don't specify the order, SPSS/PC+ performs multiplication and division before it performs addition and subtraction. In a series of multiplications and divisions, or a series of additions and subtractions, SPSS/PC+ works from left to right.

The next example uses the built-in function LN:

```
compute logincom = ln(income).
```

This function gives the natural logarithm of the value inside the parentheses. Here the variable name *INCOME* is inside the parentheses, so the command takes the logarithm of *INCOME* and assigns it to a variable named *LOGINCOM*. If this variable didn't already exist, SPSS/PC+ creates it as it executes the COMPUTE command. The value in parentheses is called the **argument** of the function. You can use either numbers or variable names as arguments.

Missing Values and COMPUTE

Missing values are always important to consider when you transform data. SPSS/PC+ does not use missing values in carrying out a COMPUTE command. If a case has a missing value for any variable used in a computation, the variable being computed is set to the system-missing value for that case. This happens when the computation runs into either a system-missing value or a user-missing value. In the command

```
compute receipts = numsold * (cost + markup).
```

the *RECEIPTS* variable is set to system-missing if *NUMSOLD*, *COST*, or *MARKUP* has either a system-missing or a user-missing value for the case.

Keeping User-Missing Values

When you compute one variable equal to another, the copy you get isn't always exact: user-missing values are converted into system-missing. Usually this is a good thing, because you may not have declared those values missing for the new variable. However, if you want to preserve the user-missing values, use the VALUE function, like this:

```
compute yearborn = value(byear).
```

If 9999 is a user-missing value for *BYEAR*, then cases coded 9999 for *BYEAR* are also coded 9999 for *YEARBORN*. The VALUE function *does not* make 9999 a missing value for *YEARBORN*. If you want to do that, enter a MISSING VALUE command.

THE IF COMMAND

The COMPUTE command works on every case. Sometimes, though, you want to treat different cases in different ways. If you need a variable containing the husband's education for every married respondent in the General Social Survey, you want to take respondent's education for male respondents but spouse's education for female respondents. You want a missing value for respondents who aren't married. You must check the value of the two variables *SEX* and *MARITAL* to see what action is required for each case. The IF command lets you do this.

An IF command looks much like a COMPUTE command except that in place of the word COMPUTE, you have the word IF followed by the condition under which the calculation should be performed. You put parentheses around the condition. It all reads very naturally. The general form of the command is:

```
if ( something is true ) variable name = instructions.
```

The "something is true" part of this command is the **condition**, which determines whether or not the instructions should be computed and stored in the variable that's named. A condition is a logical expression, something that is either true or false. Some examples of conditions are:

- If the variable *SEX* equals 1.
- If the string variable *STATE* equals 'TN'. (Remember, the values of string variables should always be in quotes.)

- If the variable LIFE equals 1 and the variable *EDUC* is greater than the variable *PAEDUC*.
- If the sum of the variables *TEENS* and *ADULTS* is greater than 4.

When you're stating conditions like this, use the abbreviations shown in Table 14.1. You can use either a two-letter form or a symbolic form, whichever one you feel more comfortable with. When there's more than one condition, you can use the keywords AND and OR to combine them.

Table 14.1 Abbreviations in IF conditions

EQ	or	=	means equal to
LT	or	<	means less than
GT	or	>	means greater than
NE	or	<>	means not equal to
GE	or	>=	means greater than or equal to

With these abbreviations and keywords, you can state the above conditions like this:

```
if (sex eq 1)
if (state = 'TN')
if (life = 1 and educ > paeduc)
if (teens + adults > 4)
```

To make a complete SPSS/PC+ command, of course, you include the variable name, the equals sign, and the instructions, just as on a COMPUTE command. For example,

```
if (sex eq 2) salary = .59 * salary.
```

Anything you can put after the word COMPUTE on a COMPUTE command is also legal after the parentheses on an IF command.

How Does It Work?

An IF command, like a COMPUTE command, is executed for every case—or at least it *starts* to be executed for every case. The difference is that IF commands come in two parts: a condition followed by a computation. If the condition is false, the command is not completed and the case is not changed. Like a COMPUTE command, an IF command can also create an entirely new variable.

Let's create *HUSED* (husband's education) out of *EDUC* (respondent's education) and *SPEDUC* (spouse's education):

```
if (marital = 1 and sex = 1) hused = educ.
if (marital = 1 and sex = 2) hused = speduc.
variable labels hused "Husband's education".
```

- As each case is processed, the first IF command checks whether the respondent is married (*MARITAL* = 1) and male (*SEX* = 1). If so, the new variable *HUSED* is set equal to *EDUC*. If not, *HUSED* is undefined, or system-missing. (Every variable must have a value. When you create a new variable, SPSS/PC+ initially assigns a system-missing value. It stays system-missing unless a valid value is assigned.)

- The second IF command similarly checks whether the respondent is married and *SEX* is 2; and if so, it sets *HUSED* equal to *SPEDUC*.

- For respondents not currently married, *HUSED* remains system-missing, which is what you want. If there were people with other values for *SEX* (there aren't in the General Social Survey), they also would remain system-missing.

- Finally, the VARIABLE LABELS command assigns a label to *HUSED* for clarity.

Missing Values and IF

In the second part of an IF, which actually computes something if the condition is true, missing values work just as they do in the COMPUTE command. But missing values in the condition itself are a new problem.

Can you test whether a condition involving a missing value is true? You cannot. Missing values in a condition are simply missing. You can't test them like ordinary values. You can't say that a missing value equals something, and you can't say that it doesn't equal something. When you're writing an IF command, remember that when a missing value turns up in a condition, the computation following the condition will not be executed. This happens both with system-missing values (where there really *isn't* any value) and with user-missing values (where there is a value but you instructed SPSS/PC+ to treat it as missing).

The following commands attempt to convert the missing value 9 for the *exciting-routine-dull* variable to the value 2, *Pretty routine*:

```
get file 'gss.sys'.
missing value life (9).
variable labels life 'Is life exciting or dull?'.
value labels life 1 'Exciting' 2 'Pretty routine' 3 'Dull'
  9 'Missing data'.
if (life eq 9) life = 2.
```

What does the IF command do? It tries to catch the 9s and set *LIFE* equal to 2 for those cases. But 9 is declared as missing. If the value of *LIFE* is missing (keep reading, this isn't a philosophy class), then it is *not* true that the value of *LIFE* is equal to the number 9. So the IF command won't work. Cases with the missing value 9 will keep the missing value 9.

To recode the missing value 9 to 2, you can use the VALUE function explained above. VALUE treats user-missing values like regular values:

```
if ( value(life) eq 9 ) life = 2.
```

When IFs Multiply

The IF command is extremely flexible. Once you've learned how to use it, you'll see that you can do all sorts of things with it. Soon you'll find yourself doing things like the following, which creates an education variable with five categories:

```
compute educ = yrseduc.
if (yrscoll gt yrseduc) educ = yrscoll.
if (educ le 6)                 educ = 1.
if (educ gt 6 and educ le 9)   educ = 2.
if (educ gt 9 and educ le 12)  educ = 3.
if (educ gt 12 and educ le 16) educ = 4.
if (educ gt 16 and educ le 20) educ = 5.
if ( value(educ) eq 99 )       educ = 9.
value labels educ 1 "Elementary" 2 "Junior high"
 3 "High school" 4 "College" 5 "Graduate school"
 9 "Missing data".
missing value educ (9).
```

There are a lot of IF commands here. They work just fine, but they are tedious to type, and they waste your valuable time. They also waste the computer's valuable time. There's an easier way. When you find that you have a lot of IF commands that just use one variable, try to use the RECODE command instead (see Chapter 11). That's what RECODE is designed for. When you can use it, it's easier to type than a lot of IF commands, and it's more efficient for the computer too.

THE ORDER OF TRANSFORMATION COMMANDS

Commands are executed one at a time, in the order you enter them. This sounds obvious enough, but let's look again at the previous example of the IF command. Suppose the commands had been entered in reversed order:

```
if (educ gt 16 and educ le 20) educ = 5.
if (educ gt 12 and educ le 16) educ = 4.
if (educ gt 9 and educ le 12)  educ = 3.
if (educ gt 6 and educ le 9)   educ = 2.
if (educ le 6)                 educ = 1.
```

Look what the last IF command does. It takes all the values of 5, 4, 3, and 2 that the first four commands created, and assigns them—along with everybody else—to code 1. All the nonmissing values in the file end up coded 1 for *EDUC*. (Notice that this sort of problem doesn't arise when you use a

RECODE command. A RECODE command never changes the value of a case more than once.)

The moral here is pretty obvious. When you have a series of transformation commands, take the time to step through them to make sure you know how they're going to work. Try them with missing values, too.

LABELING NEW VARIABLES

As with RECODE (see Chapter 11), you'll often need to change the variable and value labels for variables you've altered or created with COMPUTE or IF. Simply enter VARIABLE LABELS and VALUE LABELS commands when you want them to take effect. Remember, you can't label a variable that doesn't exist. If you're *creating* a new variable on one of these transformation commands, wait until after you create it to assign labels to it.

? *Do these transformation commands permanently change the data? What if I need the original values again sometime?* You can always read your original data again, whether you used DATA LIST to read a data file or GET to read a system file. The transformation commands don't affect any of your disk files. They affect your active file, the file you're using in your current SPSS/PC+ session. Similarly, VARIABLE LABELS and VALUE LABELS commands affect only your active file.

Of course, you can always save a new system file after making transformations. If you save a file that's been transformed with RECODE, COMPUTE, or IF commands, the transformed values will be the ones saved. If you've changed the labels, the new labels will also be saved. ■■■

SELECTING AND SAMPLING CASES

Sometimes you don't want to process all of the cases that you have. There are two ways to select some of them. One is to select certain cases yourself by telling SPSS/PC+ which ones to use. The other is just to tell SPSS/PC+ how many cases you want to use and let it take a sample for you.

The SELECT IF Command

The SELECT IF command means just what says. It tells SPSS/PC+ to select cases for processing if they satisfy some condition. You specify a condition in parentheses, just like the condition for the IF command. Cases that are not selected (because the condition is not true) are discarded. They're no longer available to you during the SPSS/PC+ session. Of course, they are still in your data or system file, and you can read them again with another DATA LIST or GET command.

Here's an example of how you might use SELECT IF to process only people in their thirties:

```
select if (age ge 30 and age le 39).
```

You can also use SELECT IF with short string variables—just remember to put the values in quotes.

```
select if (city = 'Chicago ').
```

Notice that you have to specify the value of a string variable in apostrophes and *exactly* as SPSS/PC+ read it from the data file—capitalization, trailing blanks, and all.

The SAMPLE Command

With the SELECT IF command, you tell SPSS/PC+ which cases to process. Sometimes you don't want to say *which* cases to select, but you just want to cut down the number of cases. Maybe you've got a file with a thousand or more cases and you want to make a plot (see Chapter 23). Plots are more readable if they don't show too many cases.

In SPSS/PC+, it's easy to cut down the number of cases. Use the SAMPLE command and give it a decimal fraction telling it what proportion of the cases in the file to use. For example, the following command takes a random sample of about 10% (or 0.1) of the cases in your file:

```
sample .1.
```

If you know how many cases you have in all, you can also sample an exact number of them. Say you have 2,391 cases in your file, and you want to take a random sample of 100 cases. You can do it this way:

```
sample 100 from 2391.
```

Note that SAMPLE creates a temporary sample, in effect only for the next analysis command, or **procedure.** After that you'll have the whole file again. (A procedure is a command that processes the data, like FREQUENCIES or CROSSTABS. SPSS/PC+ has to read through the data file in order to produce statistical tables or results. Transformation commands don't produce any immediate results, so SPSS/PC+ saves them up and executes them before the next procedure.) If you want to use the random sample for several procedures, save it as a system file, then get that system file and run your analyses.

MORE ABOUT TRANSFORMATIONS

Although the commands in this chapter are enough for most of the situations you'll encounter, the SPSS/PC+ transformation language has many features that are more advanced. We'll discuss just a few of these: string variables, temporary case selection, and functions.

String Variables

The important things to remember about string variables are:

- Enclose the values of string variables in apostrophes or quotation marks.

- Specify quoted values *exactly* the way they appear in your data: with uppercase or lowercase letters or both, and with the same number of blanks in the same positions.

You need to specify blank spaces, even at the end of a quoted value; for example, 'A   ' is not the same as 'A'.

A string variable has a definite length—the length you specified on the DATA LIST command (see Chapter 5). You can't change that length. Also remember that *long* string variables (those with more than 8 characters) can't be used in transformation commands at all. One trick you can use, if you need to use a long string variable in transformations, is to read part of the long string variable as a *short* string, which you *can* use in transformations:

```
data list file  'city.dat' / cityname 1-20 (a)
  shortnam 1-8 (a)   revenue 21-28 typegovt 29 ...
compute bigcity = 2.
if (shortnam = 'New York' or shortnam = 'Chicago ' or
    shortnam = 'Los Ange' or shortnam = 'Philadel')
    bigcity = 1.
```

This DATA LIST command reads the full city name as a long string variable *CITYNAME* and also reads its first 8 characters as a short string variable *SHORTNAM.* You can use the short string in transformations and other commands that don't accept long strings, but you still have the long string variable for case listings, reports, and so on.

String variables are not very useful in most types of data analysis. Try to use numeric codes wherever possible.

Temporary Case Selection

We saw above how to use the SELECT IF command to select cases according to specific criteria, and the SAMPLE command to select, temporarily, a random sample of cases. And we noted that you can preserve the temporary random sample by saving it into a system file on disk. What about the other possibility: a temporary selection of cases according to specific criteria? SPSS/PC+ provides a special command, PROCESS IF, to make this possible. The PROCESS IF command is just like SELECT IF except for two things:

1 The selection is only in effect for the next procedure.

2 You can't use AND, OR, or NOT in the logical condition of the PROCESS IF command.

PROCESS IF can be used more than once if you want to perform the same analysis on different groups of cases. You can select a group of cases, perform one procedure, and then make another selection of cases (or continue with all your cases as before):

```
get file  'gss.sys'.
process if (age lt 35).
crosstabs  life by marital.
process if (age ge 35).
crosstabs  life by marital.
```

If you used SELECT IF instead of PROCESS IF in this sequence of commands, you wouldn't have any cases for the second crosstabulation. SELECT IF makes a "permanent" selection, and you wouldn't have much luck selecting people 35 or older from among the previously selected group of people younger than 35.

Functions

SPSS/PC+ provides quite a few functions you can use in transforming your data. You supply one or more arguments (in parentheses) to a function. The arguments are numbers or variable names that SPSS/PC+ uses to evaluate the function.

Here are some of the more useful functions. The term *arg* (for argument) stands for either a number or a variable name.

ABS(arg)	*Absolute value.* The value converted, if necessary, to a positive number.
RND(arg)	*Round.* The value rounded to an integer.
TRUNC(arg)	*Truncate.* The value with any fractional part stripped off.
VALUE(arg)	*Numeric value.* A variable's numeric value, even if that value is declared user-missing. System-missing if the value is system-missing.

MISSING(arg)   *Test for missing.* A true or false value telling whether or not the argument has a missing value. Use this function in the condition of an IF or SELECT IF command.

SYSMIS(arg)   *Test for system-missing.* A true or false value telling whether or not the argument has a system-missing value. Use this function in the condition of an IF or SELECT IF command.

YRMODA(yr,mo,da)   *Day number.* The number of days since October 15, 1582. The three arguments are either variables or integer constants representing year, month, and day. By subtracting two such day numbers, you can calculate time intervals in days, as shown below.

This example uses the YRMODA function to calculate the number of days between the date stored in YEAR1, MONTH1, DAY1 and the date stored in YEAR2, MONTH2, DAY2:

```
compute days = yrmoda(year2, month2, day2) -
               yrmoda(year1,month1,day1).
variable labels days 'Number of days from date 1 to date 2'.
```

WHAT'S NEXT?

You've learned a lot about using SPSS/PC+, describing your data, and transforming it when you need to. In the next chapters, you'll see how to analyze data in new ways. We'll go beyond particular sets of data and see how to make statements about people who were *not* included in your sample.

Summary

How can you use SPSS/PC+ and the computer to create new variables and to change the values of the ones you have?

You can use the COMPUTE command to create or modify variables by calculating their values. The calculation can simply involve making a copy of an existing variable.

You can use the IF command to test the values of your variables and decide whether to carry out a calculation.

Calculations involving missing values result in the system-missing value for a case.

Calculations are not carried out if they depend on a condition that involves missing values.

Transformation commands (RECODE, COMPUTE, and IF) are carried out in the order in which you enter them. You must consider the order when planning a series of related commands.

You can use the SELECT IF command to choose a group of cases for processing based on a logical decision, or the SAMPLE command to choose a group randomly.

EXERCISES

Syntax

1 Correct the syntax errors in the following commands:

   a. `score = part1 + part2 + part3.`

   b. `compute profit1 = sales1 - expense1`
       `/    profit2 = sales2 - expense2.`

   c. `if (year = 1980) compute adjusted = wage / 1.73.`

   d. `compute composit = verbal plus math.`

2 A specification on the RECODE command says, roughly, "If the value is this, set it equal to that." It's often possible, therefore, to replace a RECODE by a series of IF commands, or to replace a series of IF commands by a RECODE.

   a. Which form is shorter?

   b. Can you replace the commands

```
if (age lt 40) age = 1.
if (age ge 40) age = 2.
if (missing(age)) age = 9.
```

   with a single RECODE command? If so, show the command. If not, explain why
   this is not possible.

   c. Can you replace the commands

```
if (sex eq 1) hused = educ.
if (sex eq 2) hused = speduc.
```

   with a single RECODE command? If so, show the command. If not, explain why this
   is not possible.

Statistical Concepts

1 On a COMPUTE command that uses several operations, you can use parentheses to
   specify the order in which the operations should be performed. If you don't, SPSS/
   PC+ performs multiplication and division before it performs addition and subtraction. In a series of multiplications and divisions, SPSS/PC+ works from left to
   right. In which of these examples would the answer be different if SPSS/PC+
   worked from right to left?

   a. compute answer = a * b * c.

   b. compute answer = a / b / c.

   c. compute answer = a * b / c.

   d. compute answer = a / b * c.

   Hint: try these out. Make up values for A, B, and C (perhaps 2, 3, and 4). Work first
   from the left: 2 times 3 is 6, times 4 is 24. Now from the right: 4 times 3 is 12, times
   2, and so forth.

PART THREE
Testing Hypotheses

Means from Samples

What can you say about the mean of a population, based on the results observed in a sample?

- Will the results from a sample be identical to the results you would get if you examined the entire population?

- How does the size of your sample affect what you can say about the population?

- How does the variability in the population affect your sample results?

- Do means computed from different samples from the same population differ?

- What determines how much sample means vary from sample to sample?

- What is a statistic, and what is a parameter?

- What is the distribution of a statistic?

In previous chapters, we've tried to answer questions like: "What percentage of the sample thinks that life is exciting?" or "What is the average age of the people who said life is dull?" or "In this study, what percentage of married people and what percentage of single people think life is exciting?" The emphasis was always on reporting the results of the survey. We looked at the data and described the sample. Nothing more.

In this chapter, we'll begin to look at the problems we face when drawing conclusions about a whole population on the basis of what's observed in a sample.

FROM SAMPLE TO POPULATION

In our sample, the men were more likely than the women to find life exciting. No doubt about it: 50% of the men but only 44% of the women called life exciting. Unless an error was made somewhere in entering the data into the file, the results are crisp and clear. We can speak about the sample with confidence. We know, or can figure out, anything we want to about the sample—assuming that we asked the right questions and had the data entered correctly into the file.

But talking about a sample is usually not enough. We don't want conclusions about the 1,473 people in the General Social Survey sample. We want conclusions about the population that this sample represents. We want to be able to say things like: "American men are more excited about life than American women" or "As Americans age, their enthusiasm for life diminishes" or "People who have never been married find life more exciting than people who have." Based on the results in the sample, we want to speak about the population from which the sample was selected.

This may not seem like a big deal. Why not just assume that whatever is true for the sample is also true for the population? If the men in the sample found life more exciting than the women did, why not claim that the same must be true in the population? Let's just conclude that American men are more enthusiastic about life than American women. That would certainly be simple. But would it always be correct?

Problems in Generalizing

Suppose you had a sample of two men and two women, and you found that one of the men but neither of the women was excited by life. Would you be willing to draw the conclusion that, in general, men are more excited by life than are women? The numbers, especially if you don't think about them, suggest the headline, "Amazing new research shows that half of all men but no women at all are excited by life!" It doesn't take much statistical know-how to find fault with this headline. Generalizing from a tiny sample of two men and two women to the whole U.S. population is laughable. If you sampled another two men and two women, you'd probably get completely different results. But you couldn't generalize from those results, either. You can't conclude much at all about the whole population from a sample of four people.

What if the sample were larger, say 200 men and 200 women? Conclusions from a study with this sample size would certainly be more believable than those from a four-person study. It's easier to believe that the results observed in the larger sample hold true for the population. But if you found that 50% of all the men and 49% of all the women in the larger sample said their lives were exciting, would you be willing to conclude that in the population, men are more likely than women to find life exciting? What if the difference were larger, say 50% of the men compared to 40% of the women?

Sampling Variability

You get different results from different samples. Consequently, it takes some thought to sort out what you can reasonably say about the population based on the results from a sample. If you and I each look at samples of 400 people from the same population, we're not going to get exactly the same answers when we analyze our own data. Our samples will undoubtedly include different people, and our results will differ. With any luck, the results will be similar, but it's very unlikely that they'll be identical to the last decimal place. Even if they are, they probably won't be the values we'd obtain if we questioned the whole population.

How much the results vary from one sample to another depends not only on the size of the samples but also on how often the various responses occur in the population. (Statisticians call this the distribution of responses in the population.) If everybody in the United States plans to vote for the same candidate for President—say, the one you've been working for—any old sample will lead to the same answer to the question, "What percentage of the vote will my candidate receive?" The answers wouldn't vary from person to person, and they wouldn't vary from survey to survey. Any survey would tell you that 100% of the voters plan to vote for your candidate.

On the other hand, if only half of the voters plan to vote for your candidate, there would be more variability in the samples. One sample might show that 60% of the vote will go to your candidate, and another sample might show that your candidate will get 45% of the vote. If 1,000 researchers took random samples of 400 voters each, there would be a lot of different percentages. Some would be close to the correct figure of 50%, while others would be higher or lower.

A COMPUTER MODEL

We can use SPSS/PC+ to actually do what we've been talking about. With the proper instructions, it can set up a population in which half of the people say they'll vote for your candidate and half say they won't.

We can instruct SPSS/PC+ to conduct a hypothetical survey by randomly selecting 400 cases from this population. Then we can tell SPSS/PC+ to calculate from this sample the percentage of the cases that endorse your candidate. We can have SPSS/PC+ repeat this kind of survey as many times as we want. Each time, it will select a new random sample of 400 hypothetical people and compute the percentage planning to vote for your candidate. (This is called a simulated survey.)

Let's have the computer do the survey 1,000 times. We then have 1,000 results, one for each time the survey was simulated. We can tell how much these results vary from survey to survey, and how different the results are from the "true" value of 50%. This kind of information will help us decide what can be said about the population based on the survey.

Building 1,000 Samples

For the examples that follow, SPSS/PC+ did exactly what was just described. It set up a population in which half the people agree with the statement about planning to vote for your candidate and the other half disagree. Then it selected a random sample of 400 cases from the population and calculated the percentage that agreed with the statement. It went on to conduct 1,000 such surveys, each with 400 cases.

The results of the 1,000 simulated surveys were stored in a variable named *VOTE*. Each case corresponds to the results from a survey of 400 people. The value for the *VOTE* variable is the percentage of people who plan to vote for the candidate.

Comparing the Results

Now that we have results from 1,000 surveys, we can see how close the results come to the population value (which we know to be 50% for these simulations).

How can we summarize the data from the 1,000 surveys? We can start with a frequency table. Many different results from the surveys are possible, so the table could be large. A condensed frequency table will be easier to read, and a histogram and some descriptive statistics will also be helpful:

```
frequencies vote
 /format condense
 /histogram
 /statistics mean median mode stddev min max.
```

Figure 15.1 Responses to 1,000 hypothetical surveys

VOTE   Percent who will vote for my candidate

VALUE	FREQ	PCT	CUM PCT	VALUE	FREQ	PCT	CUM PCT	VALUE	FREQ	PCT	CUM PCT
42.50	1	0	0	48.00	27	3	22	53.25	14	1	89
42.75	2	0	0	48.25	38	4	25	53.50	18	2	90
43.00	2	0	0	48.50	36	4	29	53.75	15	1	92
43.25	1	0	1	48.75	42	4	33	54.00	9	1	93
43.50	1	0	1	49.00	33	3	36	54.25	17	2	94
43.75	2	0	1	49.25	35	3	40	54.50	10	1	95
44.00	2	0	1	49.50	46	5	45	54.75	7	1	96
44.25	1	0	1	49.75	38	4	48	55.00	9	1	97
44.75	4	0	2	50.00	46	5	53	55.25	5	0	98
45.00	6	1	2	50.25	31	3	56	55.50	4	0	98
45.25	2	0	2	50.50	28	3	59	55.75	3	0	98
45.50	5	0	3	50.75	30	3	62	56.00	2	0	98
45.75	7	1	4	51.00	33	3	65	56.50	1	0	99
46.00	14	1	5	51.25	43	4	69	56.75	2	0	99
46.25	17	2	7	51.50	32	3	73	57.00	1	0	99
46.50	16	2	8	51.75	28	3	75	57.25	4	0	99
46.75	14	1	10	52.00	30	3	78	57.50	2	0	99
47.00	22	2	12	52.25	22	2	81	57.75	3	0	100
47.25	19	2	14	52.50	25	2	83	59.25	1	0	100
47.50	27	3	16	52.75	25	2	86	59.75	1	0	100
47.75	24	2	19	53.00	15	1	87				

The frequency table is shown in Figure 15.1. The entries in the column labeled *VALUE* are the percentages obtained from 1,000 surveys. About 5% of the samples (46 out of 1,000) had the true population value of 50. The remaining 954 samples didn't. So it doesn't seem very likely that sample results are identical to the population value. However, all is not lost. Most of the values are *around* 50. Some are a little larger, some a little smaller. The smallest value is 42.50; the largest is 59.75.

Look at the histogram of the results in Figure 15.2. You can see that most of the samples have values around 50. Not very many samples are far off the mark. In fact, the farther away you move from 50 (the true value in the hypothetical population), the smaller the number of samples with those values. Of the 1,000 samples, 60% are concentrated in the range of 48 to 52.

Figure 15.2 Histogram for the hypothetical surveys

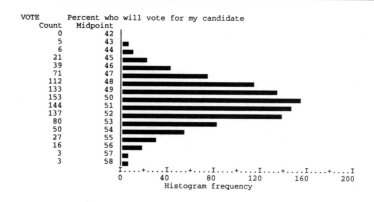

Consider the descriptive statistics in Figure 15.3. The mean, median, and mode for the cases are very similar; they are equal or close to 50. The average of all 1,000 samples is pretty much on target. The standard deviation of the sample percentages is 2.62, not a very large number. That's because most of the values are close to 50.

Figure 15.3 Statistics for the hypothetical surveys

Mean	50.129	Median	50.000	Mode	49.500
Std Dev	2.615	Minimum	42.500	Maximum	59.750
Valid Cases	1000	Missing Cases	0		

What is a statistic? A statistic is nothing more than some characteristic of a sample. The average height of the people in a sample is a statistic. So is the standard deviation or the variance of the heights. The term *statistic* is used only to describe sample values. The term *parameter* is used to describe characteristics of the population. If you could measure the height of all the people in the United States and calculate their average height, the result would be a parameter, since it would be the value for the population. Most of the time, population values, or parameters, are not known. You must estimate them based on statistics calculated from samples. ■■■

What you've seen here is true in general. It doesn't just happen in hypothetical surveys inside computers. It happens in real-life surveys and experiments. *The average value of the results from many samples is fairly close to the population value.*

The Effect of Sample Size

What if we take smaller samples, say 50 people in each survey instead of 400? Would the smaller samples differ more or less from one another? This question is simple enough to answer. We used SPSS/PC+ to run the simulations again but this time included 50 people in each survey instead of 400. Everything else was done the same way.

The histogram and descriptive statistics for the new hypothetical surveys are shown in Figure 15.4. The values still bunch around 50, but they show a lot more spread. Only 34% of the samples have results between 48 and 52. That's smaller than before. The standard deviation is 6.9, a fairly big increase from the 2.6 for the 400-case samples. Of the 1,000 50-case surveys, 15 show results in the low 30s and 4 show results in the 70s. Among the 400-case surveys, the smallest value was 42.50 and the largest was 59.75. A basic fact to remember is that *results from large samples do not vary as much as results from small samples.*

Figure 15.4 Results of 1,000 smaller hypothetical surveys

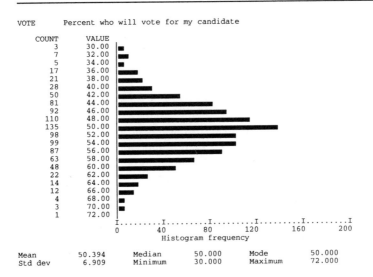

```
VOTE        Percent who will vote for my candidate

  COUNT       VALUE
      3       30.00
      7       32.00
      5       34.00
     17       36.00
     21       38.00
     28       40.00
     50       42.00
     81       44.00
     92       46.00
    110       48.00
    135       50.00
     98       52.00
     99       54.00
     87       56.00
     63       58.00
     48       60.00
     22       62.00
     14       64.00
     12       66.00
      4       68.00
      3       70.00
      1       72.00
              I.........I.........I.........I.........I.........I
              0        40        80       120       160       200
                             Histogram frequency

  Mean        50.394   Median    50.000   Mode       50.000
  Std dev      6.909   Minimum   30.000   Maximum    72.000
```

The overall average for the 400-case samples was 50.13. For the 50-case surveys, it's 50.40. Both of these values are fairly close to the true value of 50. If the number of samples were increased from 1,000 to 100,000—a lot of simulations—the overall average would be even closer to the population value.

THE EFFECT OF POPULATION VARIABILITY

In the previous examples, half of the voting population preferred the candidate you were working for. What if there is more agreement in the population? What if 90% of the voters plan to vote for your candidate? Will the results from different surveys vary as much as they do when only half of the population is in your camp?

Again, we can use SPSS/PC+ to perform 1,000 hypothetical surveys, each with 400 respondents, in which 90% of the population of voters will vote for your candidate. What do the simulations report now?

Figure 15.5 Hypothetical surveys from a more uniform population

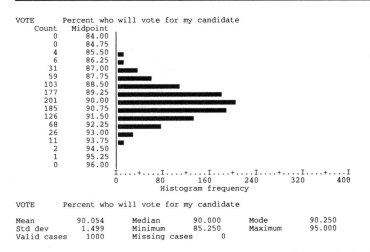

```
VOTE      Percent who will vote for my candidate
   Count   Midpoint
       0     84.00 |
       0     84.75 |
       4     85.50 |
       6     86.25 |
      31     87.00 |
      59     87.75 |
     103     88.50 |
     177     89.25 |
     201     90.00 |
     185     90.75 |
     126     91.50 |
      68     92.25 |
      26     93.00 |
      11     93.75 |
       2     94.50 |
       1     95.25 |
       0     96.00 |
                   I....+....I....+....I....+....I....+....I....+....I
                   0        80       160      240      320      400
                            Histogram frequency

VOTE      Percent who will vote for my candidate

Mean          90.054    Median    90.000    Mode       90.250
Std dev        1.499    Minimum   85.250    Maximum    95.000
Valid cases     1000    Missing cases  0
```

Figure 15.5 shows the histogram and descriptive statistics for the new simulations. As you'd expect, the average value over the 1,000 surveys, 90.05, is very close to 90%, the "true" value. Do the results vary from survey to survey as much as they did when 50% of the population was in agreement? No. The standard deviation of the sample percentages is only 1.5, as compared with 2.6 from the 50-50 samples. Again, this makes sense. If most people are in agreement with each other about an issue, it's much harder to come up with unusual samples. Most samples will result in fairly similar results. In this example, the smallest result from a sample is 85.25, and the largest is 95.00. All sample values are closer to the true value than before.

These last simulations give us another rule about variability among samples: *The less a characteristic varies in the population, the less estimates of it vary from sample to sample.*

Other Statistics

Although we examined the percentage of people planning to vote for a candidate, the same principles apply to the mean. For example, we could have looked at mean weight, mean number of pencils owned, or mean income. The procedure would have been the same. For each of the random samples from a population, we would have calculated the mean. Then we would have seen how much the mean values varied from sample to sample. The results would have been very similar to what we've seen, and the same basic rules would have applied. After all, percentages agreeing with a statement are equivalent to means.

? *How can a percentage be the same thing as a mean?* For a variable that can have only two possible values (such as *Yes* or *No, Agree* or *Disagree, Cured* or *Not cured*), you can code one of the responses as 0 and the other response as 1. If you add up the values for all of the cases, divide by the number of cases, and then multiply by 100, you'll obtain the percentage of cases giving the response coded as 1.

Let's consider a simple example. You ask five people whether they approve of the President's performance. Three say they do, and two say they don't. If you code *Approve* as 1, you have the values 1, 1, 1, 0, 0. The mean of these values is 3/5, or 0.6. To get the percentage agreeing with the statement, just multiply the mean by 100. In this survey, 60% of the people approved of the President's performance. ■■■

DISTRIBUTIONS OF STATISTICS

You can now see that both variables and statistics have distributions. Think about that. You can make a histogram of the actual ages of all the cases in a sample. This is fairly easy to visualize. You just count the number of cases that have ages within particular intervals. Using such histograms, you can answer questions like, "What percentage of the sample are older than 50?" and "What percentage of the cases are in their thirties?" The distribution of a variable like age tells you about the individual cases in the sample.

The *mean* age calculated from samples of, say, 100 cases also has a distribution. The distribution of mean age describes how often the different mean age values are expected to occur if the same survey is repeated over and over, using the same population and samples of the same size.

The distribution of a statistic (like the mean or the percentage) is used to answer questions like, "How often would I get a sample value of 60% or more with a sample size of 100 cases if the true population value is 50%?"

"How often would I get a mean income of $13,000 or more with a sample size of 100 if the mean income in the population is $12,000?" The distribution tells you about a particular statistic for *samples* of a particular number of cases, rather than about the *individual* cases.

WHAT'S NEXT?

When you conduct a survey, you calculate one mean or one percentage for each item. From this sample result, you want to draw conclusions about the population. You can figure out (with mathematics) what the distribution of sample values looks like, based on the results from just a single sample. That's how you can determine what you're able to say about your whole population. The next chapter will explain how this is done.

Summary

What can you say about the mean of a population, based on the results observed in a sample?

When you take a sample from a population and compute the sample mean, it will not be identical to the mean you would have gotten if you'd observed the entire population.

Different samples result in different means.

The distribution of all possible values of the mean, for samples of a particular size, is called the sampling distribution of the mean.

The variability of the distribution of sample means depends on how large your sample is and on how much variability there is in the population from which the samples are taken.

As the size of the sample increases, the variability of the sample means decreases.

As variability in a population increases, so does the variability of the sample means.

EXERCISES

Statistical Concepts

1 Let's assume that our population of interest consists of five creatures who were found on Mars. The number of limbs on each of the creatures is 10, 12, 14, 16, and 50.

   a. List all possible samples of size 2 from this population. (There are ten different samples you can take. The same creature cannot be included more than once in any sample.)

   b. Calculate the mean for each of the ten samples.

   c. Calculate the mean of the means in part b. How does this compare to the value that you get when you find the mean for the original five creatures?

2 Repeat question 1, taking all possible samples of size 3. Look at the variability of the means for samples of size 2 and samples of size 3. Which appears to be smaller, and why?

3 Suppose you're interested in estimating the average IQ of all people who have come to see the Wednesday matinee of *Attack of the Killer Tomatoes*. All 200 people in the theater audience at the time are your population. In the audience there are 5 brilliant college professors attempting to evade their students, 30 students attempting to avoid studying, 25 farmers who think this is an agricultural movie, and 140 average folks looking for cheap thrills.

   a. If you take a random sample of 5 people, discuss what sorts of samples it's possible to obtain. That is, describe possible mixes of people in the sample.

   b. If you take a random sample of 50 people, discuss what sorts of samples it's possible to obtain. Can you get the same types of samples as when you were taking samples of five people?

   c. Would samples of size 5 or size 50 be more variable?

4 In a large university there is a proposal to drop statistics as a requirement for graduation. Each of the 500 professors at the university commissions a survey to gauge student support for the proposal. Each survey contains a random sample of 50 students. The histogram below shows the distribution of the results of the surveys.

```
        COUNT     VALUE    ONE SYMBOL EQUALS APPROXIMATELY  1.50 OCCURRENCES

          2      24.00   *
          7      26.00   *****
         11      28.00   *******
         20      30.00   *************
         26      32.00   *****************
         36      34.00   ************************
         52      36.00   **************************************
         53      38.00   ***************************************
         62      40.00   **********************************************
         61      42.00   *****************************************
         55      44.00   **************************************
         31      46.00   *********************
         27      48.00   ******************
         26      50.00   *****************
         17      52.00   ***********
          5      54.00   ***
          5      56.00   ***
          0      58.00
          2      60.00   *
          2      62.00   *
                         I.........I.........I.........I.........I......... I
                         0        15        30        45        60       7 5
                                        HISTOGRAM FREQUENCY

    MEAN        40.484    MEDIAN     40.000    MODE      40.000
    STD DEV      6.700    MINIMUM    24.000    MAXIMUM   62.000

    VALID CASES    500    MISSING CASES    0
```

Based on the histogram and summary statistics:

a. What is your best guess for the percentage of students favoring the proposal?

b. When all 500 professors presented their results to the President, she was aghast that the results of all of the surveys were not similar. She is considering censuring the professors whose polls were far removed from the average value. She thinks that they "rigged" their polls to support their own viewpoints. How would you defend the professors at their hearing?

c. Based on the histogram, if the true percentage favoring the proposal is 40%, what's the probability that a poll will estimate the value to be 25% or greater? 55% or greater? Less than 35%?

5 Explain why you agree or disagree with each of the following statements:

a. It's better to include a small number of subjects in a study than a large number.

b. All samples from the same population give the same results.

c. How much means vary from sample to sample depends on both the size of the sample and the variability in the population.

d. Both variables and statistics have distributions.

 # Working with the Normal Distribution

What is the normal distribution, and why is it important for data analysis?

■ What does a normal distribution look like?

■ Within a normal distribution, what percentage of the observations fall where?

■ What is the relationship of the mean, median, and mode in a normal distribution?

■ What are standard scores, and how are they computed?

■ Is a sample from a normal population exactly normal?

■ What is the Central Limit Theorem, and what does it tell you about the distribution of sample means?

■ What is a confidence interval?

Y ou may have noticed that the shapes of all the histograms in Chapter 15 were bell-shaped. Most of the values were bunched in the center. As you looked farther and farther from the center, you found fewer and fewer observations.

In the general population, many variables—such as height, weight, blood pressure, and scores on IQ tests—turn out to have distributions that are bell-shaped. There is a particular type of bell-shaped distribution, called the **normal distribution**, that describes them well. The normal distribution is very important in data analysis, as you'll see throughout the rest of this book. In this chapter, you'll look more closely at some characteristics of the normal distribution.

THE NORMAL DISTRIBUTION

A mathematical equation defines the normal distribution exactly. For a particular mean and standard deviation, this equation determines what percentage of the observations fall where. Figure 16.1 is a picture of a normal distribution with a mean of 100 and a standard deviation of 15. As you can see, the distribution is symmetric. If you folded it in the center, the two sides would match; they're identical. The center of the distribution is at the mean. The mean of a normal distribution is also the most frequently occurring value (the mode), and it's the value that splits the distribution into two equal parts (the median). In any normal distribution, the mean, median, and mode all have the same value.

Figure 16.1 A normal distribution

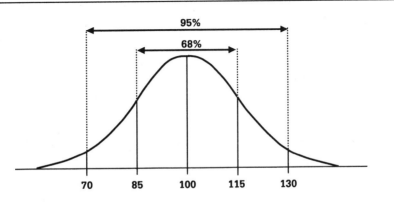

Areas in the Normal Distribution

For a normal distribution, the percentage of values falling within any interval can be calculated exactly. For example, in a normal distribution with a mean of 100 and a standard deviation of 15 (as in Figure 16.1), 68% of all values fall between 85 (one standard deviation less than the mean) and 115 (one standard deviation more than the mean). And 95% of all values fall in the range 70 to 130, within two standard deviations of the mean.

A normal distribution can have any mean and standard deviation. However, the shape of a normal distribution doesn't change. Most of the observations are near the average, and a mathematical function describes how many observations are at any given distance (measured in standard deviations) from the mean. Means and standard deviations differ from variable to variable. But the percentage of cases within a fixed number of standard deviations from the mean is always the same in a normal distribution.

It turns out that many variables you can measure have a distribution close to the mathematical ideal of a normal distribution. We say these variables are "normally distributed," even though their distributions are not exactly normal. Usually when we say this, we mean that the histograms look like Figure 16.1. For example, we say that IQ scores are normally distributed with a mean of 100 and a standard deviation of 15. Heights of adult males or females are also said to be normally distributed.

? *Serious questions have been raised about interpreting these so-called intelligence tests. Do they really tell you anything, or are they culturally biased?* That's a question for another book. The only important thing about IQ in this book is that scores from an IQ test administered to the adult population are found to follow a normal distribution with a mean of 100 and a standard deviation of 15. IQ scores are used here simply as an example of a normally distributed variable with a standard deviation that's known. ■■■

STANDARD SCORES

If I tell you that I own 250 books, you probably won't be able to make very much of this information. You won't know how my library compares to that of the average college professor. Wouldn't it be much more informative if I told you that I own the average number of books, or that I am two standard deviations above the average? Then, if you know that the number of books owned by college professors is normally distributed, you could calculate what percentage of my colleagues have more books than I do.

To describe my library in comparison to other libraries, you can calculate what's called **a standard score**. It describes the location of a particular case in a distribution: whether it's above average or below average and how much above or below. The computation is simple:

1 Take the value and subtract the mean from it. If the difference is positive, you know the case is above the mean. If it's negative, the case is below the mean.

2 Divide the difference by the standard deviation. This tells you how many standard-deviation units a score is above or below the average.

For example, if book ownership among college professors is normally distributed with a mean of 150 and a standard deviation of 50, you can calculate my standard score for the 250 books I own like this:

Step 1:

250 (my books) – 150 (average number of books)
= 100 (I own 100 more books than the average professor)

Step 2:

$$\frac{100 \text{ (difference from step 1)}}{50 \text{ (standard deviation of books)}} = 2 \text{ (standard score)}$$

My standard score is 2. Since its sign is positive, it indicates that I have more books than average. The number 2 indicates that I am two standard-deviation units above the mean. In a normal distribution, 95% of all cases are *within* two standard deviations of the mean. Therefore, you know that only 2.5% of college professors have libraries more extensive than mine. (Of course, no one has more SPSS manuals than I do!)

In a sample, the average of the standard scores for a variable is always 0, and the standard deviation is always 1. Suppose you ask 15 people on the street how many hamburgers they consume in a week. If you calculate the mean and standard deviation for the number of hamburgers eaten by these 15 people and then compute a standard score for each person, you'll get 15 standard scores. The average of the scores will be 0, and their standard deviation will be 1.

When you use standard scores, you can compare values for a case on *different* variables. For example, if you have standard scores of 2.9 for number of books, –1.2 for metabolic rate, and 0.0 for weight, then you know:

■ You have many more books than average.

■ You have a somewhat slower metabolism than average.

■ Your weight is exactly average.

You couldn't meaningfully compare the original numbers, since they all have different means and standard deviations. Owning 20 cars is much more extraordinary than owning 20 shirts.

Tables of the Standard Normal Distribution

It's also convenient to tabulate areas under the normal curve using standard scores (also known as **Z scores**). This allows you to use a single table to determine the probability of obtaining a particular value or a larger one from a normal distribution, regardless of what the means and standard deviations of the original variable are.

Consider Figure 16.1, which shows a normal distribution with a mean of 100 and a standard deviation of 15. We can replace this figure with what's called a "standard normal" distribution. A standard normal distribution has a mean of 0 and a standard deviation of 1. It shows the distribution of standard scores for IQ.

Figure 16.2 shows the areas under a standard normal curve. You see that 50% of the area in a standard normal curve is above the standard score value of 0. This means that, if values are normally distributed, 50% of the cases have standard scores (Z scores) greater than or equal to 0. Similarly, close to 31% of the population will have Z scores greater than 0.5. Only 2.5% of the population will have Z scores greater than 1.96. This means that the probability of obtaining a Z score of 1.96 or greater from a normal distribution is 0.025.

Figure 16.2 Proportion above a Z score

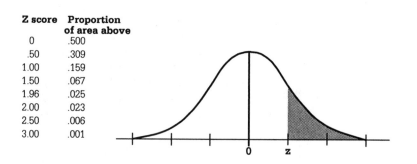

Z score	Proportion of area above
0	.500
.50	.309
1.00	.159
1.50	.067
1.96	.025
2.00	.023
2.50	.006
3.00	.001

? *What should I do about negative scores?* You've seen that the two halves of a normal distribution are identical. That is, the probability of getting a Z score of +0.5 or greater is the same as the probability of getting a Z score of -0.5 or smaller. So you can use the same table to look up areas for both positive and negative Z scores. Just remember that for a positive Z score, the table shows the probability of getting a larger Z score, while for a negative Z score, the table shows the probability of getting a smaller Z score. If you multiply the percentage value in the table by 2, you'll get the probability of getting a Z score that in absolute value is at least as large as the one you observed.

For example, if you want to find the percentage of people who have IQ scores greater than 120 (Z score of +1.96) or less than 80 (Z score of -1.96), you look up the area for a Z score of +1.96 and multiply that area by 2. Multiplying the table value of 2.5% by two, you see that 5% of the population have IQs less than 80 or greater than 120. To make your life simpler, the table in Appendix G has a column of the areas multiplied by 2. ∎∎∎

The extensive table of areas under the normal curve in Appendix G provides considerable detail on the probability of obtaining various results if the values are normally distributed.

A SAMPLE FROM THE NORMAL DISTRIBUTION

Even if a variable is normally distributed in the population, a sample from the population doesn't necessarily have a distribution that's exactly normal. Samples vary, so the distributions for individual samples vary as well. However, if a sample is reasonably large and it comes from a normal population, its distribution should look more or less normal.

Consider Figure 16.3, a histogram for a normally distributed variable, like IQ, for a sample of 400 cases. In the population, the variable has a mean of 100 and a standard deviation of 15. The histogram for the sample looks about normal. SPSS/PC+ can help you imagine what a true normal distribution for the variable would look like. If you run the command

```
frequencies yourvar
    /histogram normal.
```

you will see colons and dots showing a true normal distribution superimposed on the histogram. The colons and dots indicate how many cases would be expected in the intervals if the distribution were exactly normal, with the same mean and standard deviation as the sample. A colon appears on the output if the normal distribution falls inside the histogram. A dot appears if the normal distribution falls outside the histogram. You can see that the observed numbers of cases don't always match the numbers expected on the basis of the normal distribution. That's all right. Overall, the observed distribution doesn't differ much from the expected normal distribution.

Figure 16.3 A histogram for a normally distributed variable

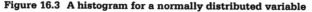

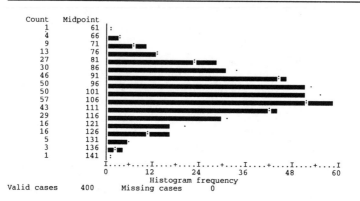

Distributions That Aren't Normal

The normal distribution is often used as a reference for describing other distributions. A distribution is called **skewed** if it isn't symmetric but has more cases, or a "tail," toward one end of the distribution than the other. If the tail is toward larger values, the distribution is called positively skewed, or skewed to the right. If the tail is toward smaller values, the distribution is negatively skewed, or skewed to the left. A variable like income has a positively skewed distribution. That's because some incomes are very much above average and make a long tail to the right. Since incomes less than 0 are impossible, the tail to the left is not so long.

If a larger proportion of cases falls into the tails of a distribution than into those of a normal distribution, the distribution has positive **kurtosis**. If fewer cases fall into the tails, the distribution has negative kurtosis.

You can compute statistics that measure how much skewness and kurtosis there is in a distribution in comparison to a normal distribution. These statistics are 0 if the observed distribution is exactly normal. Positive values for kurtosis indicate that a distribution has heavier tails than a normal distribution. Negative values indicate that a distribution has lighter tails than a normal distribution. Of course, the measures of skewness and kurtosis for samples from a normal distribution will not be exactly 0. Because of variation from sample to sample, they will fluctuate around 0.

To calculate these statistics, just run the command:

```
frequencies yourvar
  / format notable
  / statistics mean stddev skewness kurtosis.
```

Figure 16.4 gives the statistics for the distribution shown in Figure 16.3. Both the value for skewness and the value for kurtosis are small. The distribution is close to normal. Additional (and better) ways to check whether or not a sample comes from a normal population are discussed in Chapter 20.

Figure 16.4 Skewness and kurtosis

Mean	100.319	Std Dev	14.403	Kurtosis	-.169
Skewness	.004				
Valid Cases	400	Missing Cases	0		

MORE ON THE DISTRIBUTION OF THE MEANS

It's understandable that variables like height and weight have distributions that are approximately normal. We know that most of the world is pretty close to average and that the farther we move from average, the fewer people we find. But why did the distributions of sample *means* in Chapter 15 look normal?

The Central Limit Theorem

Let's look again at the histogram for samples of size 400 from a hypothetical population in which half of the people agree to vote for a candidate (see Figure 16.5).

Figure 16.5 Histogram for the hypothetical surveys

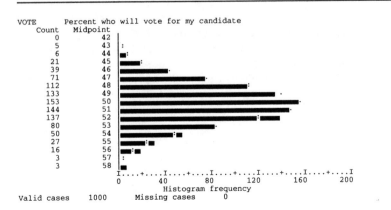

The observed frequencies are very close to those expected if the distribution is normal. That's surprising, in a way. The distribution of the sampled responses wasn't even close to normal. There were equal proportions of value 1 (agree) and value 0 (disagree).

This remarkable fact is explained by the **Central Limit Theorem**. The Central Limit Theorem says that for samples of a sufficiently large size, the real distribution of means is almost always approximately normal. The original variable can have any kind of distribution. It doesn't have to be bell-shaped in the least. (The "real" distribution is the one you'd get if you took an infinite number of random samples. The "real" distribution is a mathematical concept. You can get a pretty good idea of what the "real" distribution looks like by taking a lot of samples and examining plots of their values—as we've been doing.)

? *Sufficiently large size? What kind of language is that for a mathematical theorem?* Actually, there are several vague parts of our paraphrase of the Central Limit Theorem. You have to say what you're willing to consider "approximately normal" before you know what size sample is "sufficiently large." How large a sample you need depends on the way the variable itself is distributed. The important point is that the distribution of means gets closer and closer to normal as the sample size gets larger and larger—regardless of what the distribution of the original variable looks like. If the distribution of a variable is not too far from normal, even means from small sample sizes will be normally distributed.   ■■■

Let's suppose that the number of books that professors own ranges from 0 to 300 and that all values from 0 to 300 are equally likely, making the distribution **uniform**. Figure 16.6 shows a histogram of this uniform distribution. All of the lines representing intervals from 0 to 300 are of approximately equal length.

What happens if we take a sample of ten professors, calculate the average number of books they own, and do this sampling and calculating again and again? What will the distribution of the average values look like? To answer this question, we can use another computer model. Each simulation will compute the average of ten observations from the uniform distribution. Figure 16.7 shows the results of 1,000 such simulations.

Figure 16.6 A uniform distribution

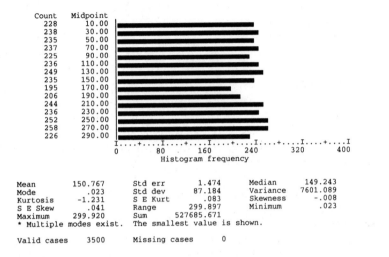

```
Count   Midpoint
228      10.00
238      30.00
235      50.00
237      70.00
225      90.00
236     110.00
249     130.00
235     150.00
195     170.00
206     190.00
244     210.00
236     230.00
252     250.00
258     270.00
226     290.00
        I....+....I....+....I....+....I....+....I....+....I
        0      80      160     240     320     400
                     Histogram frequency
```

```
Mean           150.767    Std err       1.474   Median     149.243
Mode              .023     Std dev      87.184   Variance  7601.089
Kurtosis        -1.231     S E Kurt       .083   Skewness     -.008
S E Skew          .041     Range       299.897   Minimum       .023
Maximum        299.920     Sum      527685.671
* Multiple modes exist.    The smallest value is shown.

Valid cases       3500     Missing cases      0
```

Figure 16.7 The distribution of means from the uniform distribution

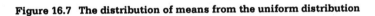

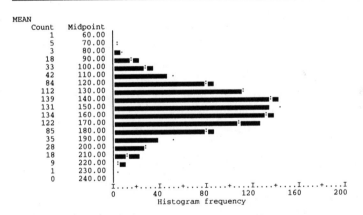

```
MEAN
    Count   Midpoint
      1      60.00
      5      70.00
      3      80.00
     18      90.00
     33     100.00
     42     110.00
     84     120.00
    112     130.00
    139     140.00
    131     150.00
    134     160.00
    122     170.00
     85     180.00
     35     190.00
     28     200.00
     18     210.00
      9     220.00
      1     230.00
      0     240.00
           I....+....I....+....I....+....I....+....I....+....I
           0      40      80      120     160     200
                        Histogram frequency
```

The means from these simulations have a distribution that's not at all like the uniform distribution of the individual observations. The distribution of means is approximately normal. *That's* why the normal distribution is so important in data analysis. Your *variable* doesn't have to be normally distributed. Means that you calculate from samples will be normally distributed if the sample size is large enough. If the variable you're studying actually does have a normal distribution, then the distribution of means will be normal for samples of any size. The further from normal your variable is, the larger the samples have to be for the distribution of the means to be approximately normal.

MORE ABOUT MEANS OF MEANS

We've seen that for a sufficiently large sample size, the distribution of means is normal. This tells us a lot about how likely different means are, but only if we know what the mean and standard deviation of the distribution are. The mean of the "real" distribution of means is the population mean.

The mean of the means is the mean? What does that mean? It means (one step at a time, now): Suppose you could take an infinite number of samples and calculate the average for each one. Suppose you then calculate the average of your averages. What you'd get is the same number as if you just went ahead and took the average of the whole population. That really isn't surprising at all. ■■■

For example, if 50% of all the people in a population agree with a statement, then

- The true population mean is 50%. (We just said that: 50% of all the people in a population agree.)
- The mean of the distribution of sample means from that population is 50%, too.

Similarly, if the average IQ in the population is 100, then the mean of the distribution of means from the population is also 100. It doesn't matter how large the samples are, whether you have 10-case samples or 10,000-case samples. Nor does it matter whether IQ itself is normally distributed. The mean of the distribution of means is the population mean.

THE STANDARD ERROR OF THE MEAN

If the mean of the distribution of sample means is the population mean, what's the standard deviation of the distribution of sample means? Is it also just the standard deviation of the population? No! In Chapter 15, you saw that the standard deviation of the means depends on two things:

1. How large a sample you take. When we looked at samples of 400 cases, most of the means were pretty close to the population value. When we looked at smaller samples of size 50, the means had more spread. Larger samples meant a smaller standard deviation for the sample means.

2 How much variability there is in the population. When only 50% of our population agreed with a statement, there was more variability in the means than when 90% of the population agreed with the statement. Less variability in the samples also meant a smaller standard deviation for the sample means.

To calculate the exact standard deviation of the distribution of sample means, you must know:

- The standard deviation in the population.
- The number of cases in the sample.

All you have to do is divide the standard deviation by the square root of the sample size. The result, the standard deviation of the distribution of sample means, is called the **standard error of the mean**. Although it has an impressive name, it's still just a standard deviation—the standard deviation of the sample means.

Think about the formula for computing the standard error of the mean: take the standard deviation of the variable and divide by the square root of the sample size. Suppose the standard deviation of number of books owned is 50 and the sample size is four cases. Then the standard error is 50 divided by the square root of 4, or 25. If the sample size is *increased* to 9, the standard error decreases to 50 divided by the square root of 9, or 16.7. If the sample size is *increased* to 100, the standard error is only 5. The larger the sample size, the less variability there is in the sample means.

CALCULATING A CONFIDENCE INTERVAL

You've spent a lot of time reading about sample means and how they vary. You've actually seen what their distribution looks like. You have to understand these things in order to use statistics for testing hypotheses about the population. If you know how much the means vary from sample to sample, you can draw conclusions about the population by looking at just a single sample.

For example, let's take a well-defined population: the audience at a matinee performance of the classic film *Attack of the Killer Tomatoes*. Suppose that you want to estimate the average IQ of the people in the audience. You go to the theater, randomly select 25 patrons, and give them an IQ test. The average IQ of these 25 lovers of the cinema turns out to be 112, and the standard deviation of their IQ scores is close to 15, the value for the population. Based on this sample, what can you conclude about *all* of the patrons in the theater?

The sample you selected is one of many possible samples. So the mean you calculated is one of many possible means. In particular, it's one of the means in the distribution of means for samples of size 25. The problem is that you don't know where your sample falls in the distribution of means. Is it close to the true population value? Is it one of the extreme means? Since you don't know the true value for the IQ of people at the movie, you can't tell if your sample value is too high, too low, or right on target. You *never* know the true value in the population, because if you did you wouldn't do the study!

You don't know the population mean, and therefore you don't know the mean of the distribution of sample means. Nevertheless, you can estimate the standard error of the mean from your observed standard deviation. Remember, the standard error of the mean is the standard deviation of the distribution of sample means. The estimated standard error is the standard deviation (15) divided by the square root of the sample size (25), which makes 15 divided by 5, or 3. Using this piece of information, you can visualize the sampling distribution of means, as shown in Figure 16.7.

Based on the Central Limit Theorem, you can assume that the distribution is normal. That's what the Central Limit Theorem says: for a sufficiently large sample size, sample means are normally distributed, whether the original variable, IQ in this case, is normally distributed or not. Since you don't know the mean IQ for the population in the theater, it's labeled with a question mark in the figure. Because the distribution is normal, you know that 95% of all sample means should fall within two standard errors of the population mean. The standard error of the mean was found to equal 3. So 95% of all sample means should fall within 6 of the question mark. The values falling outside of this interval are shaded in the figure.

Figure 16.8 The sampling distribution of means

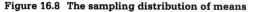

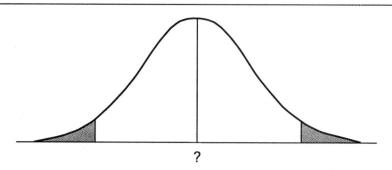

?

Where is your sample mean in this distribution? You can't figure that out. If you knew the population value (at the question mark), then you could mark the location of the mean; but of course, you don't.

Based on this picture, what can you say about the value of the population mean? Although you can't give an exact value, you can calculate a range of values—an interval—that should include the population mean

95% of the time. You calculate the lower limit of this interval by subtracting two times the standard error from your mean. The lower limit is 112 − 6 = 106. You calculate the upper limit by adding two times the standard error to your mean. This is 112 + 6 = 118. The interval is from 106 to 118. Now you have what's known as a **confidence interval**, extending from two standard errors below the sample mean to two standard errors above the sample mean.

Think of what the diagram shows. You can imagine your sample mean somewhere in the distribution and see what happens. Figure 16.9 shows the sample mean at 1.5 standard errors above the population mean (the question mark). The confidence interval is marked off. Does the interval include the unknown population value? Sure—because it reaches out 2 standard errors, and the difference between your sample mean and the population mean is only 1.5 standard errors.

Figure 16.9 The sample mean 1.5 standard errors above the population mean

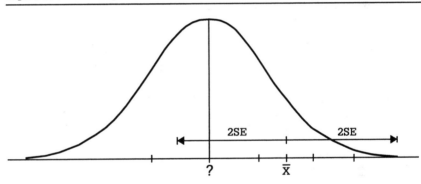

Now imagine your sample value at 1 standard-error unit below the mean, as in Figure 16.10. Does the confidence interval still include the population value? Yes. Once again, your sample mean is within 2 standard errors of the population mean, so the population mean lies within the confidence interval.

The only time your interval wouldn't include the population value is when your sample mean falls in the shaded region of Figure 16.7. The shaded region corresponds to the 5% of the distribution that is more than two standard-error units from the population mean.

You don't know the exact value for the population mean. But as shown here, you can calculate an interval around your sample mean that will include the true, unknown population mean 95% of the time. This is called a **95% confidence interval.** Of course, you can never tell whether your particular sample mean is one of the unlikely ones in the shaded region. All

Figure 16.10 The sample mean 1 standard error below the population mean

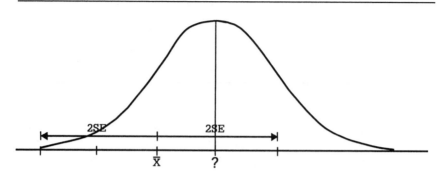

you can do is calculate the interval and hope that you have one of the 95-out-of-100 times that the interval includes the population value.

Smarter Than Average?

You calculated a mean IQ of 112 for a sample of 25 patrons at the movie. This is 12 points higher than 100, which is supposedly the average value for people in general. Is it reasonable to conclude that these moviegoers (the people in the audience at *Killer Tomatoes* that night) are different, on average, from people in general? You know that sample means vary, so you don't expect the value observed in a sample to be exactly the same as the population value.

? *Where did the population come in here? We were just looking at people in the theater, right?* Yes. In this rather improbable study, the "population" is just the people who were in the theater that night. For them, the "population value" of average IQ is the value you'd get if you gave tests to everybody in the theater and took the average. Any time you're talking about statistics, the word "population" has a special meaning. It's the people (or animals or things) you're trying to draw conclusions about. In this study, it's the movie audience. ∎∎∎

What you have to figure out from your sample of moviegoers is this: How likely is this sample mean of 112 if the mean is 100? Use a picture again. Figure 16.11 is the distribution of means for samples of size 25 when the population mean is 100 and the standard deviation is 15. It looks a lot like some of the previous diagrams. The difference is that instead of the question mark, you see the value 100, the mean for people in general. You can now locate the observed sample mean on the distribution. The value 112 is 4 standard error units above the mean, a rather unusual outcome if the population mean is 100.

Figure 16.11 The distribution of means for samples of size 25

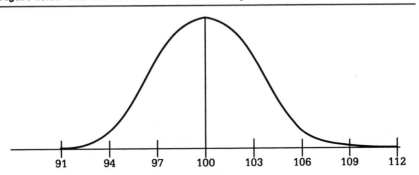

91   94   97   100   103   106   109   112

This result indicates that it's very unlikely to observe a sample mean as large as 112 in a sample of size 25 when the true population value is 100. Only about 0.006% of the cases in a normal distribution have values as much as 4 standard deviations away from the mean. (You can use the table in Appendix G to get areas for a distribution of means. Instead of using the standard deviation to calculate a standard score, use the standard error of the mean.) So it appears highly unlikely that the movie patrons have the same mean IQ as the general population. On the other hand, if you observed a mean IQ of 103 in your sample, you couldn't say with confidence that the patrons were smarter than average, since a sample mean of 103 is perfectly reasonable for a population value of 100.

WHAT'S NEXT?

In this chapter, you saw how to use distributions of the mean to calculate confidence intervals for the population mean. You also saw how to use them to evaluate hypotheses about a population mean. We'll spend the rest of the book using ideas from this chapter to evaluate hypotheses of many kinds.

Summary

What is the normal distribution, and why is it important for data analysis?

A normal distribution is bell-shaped. It is a symmetric distribution in which the mean, median, and mode all coincide. In the population, many variables, such as height and weight, have distributions that are approximately normal.

Although normal distributions can have different means and variances, the distribution of the cases about the mean is always the same.

You use standard scores to locate an observation within a distribution. The mean of standard scores is 0, and the standard deviation is 1.

The Central Limit Theorem states that for samples of a sufficiently large size, the distribution of sample means is approximately normal. (That's why the normal distribution is so important for data analysis.)

A confidence interval provides a range of values that, with a designated likelihood, contains the population mean.

EXERCISES

Statistical Concepts

1 If I tell you that in the population of adults in the United States, nostril width is normally distributed with a mean of 0.9 inches and a standard deviation of 0.2 inches, list all the facts about nostril width that you can deduce from my statement.

2 If grades on an examination are approximately normally distributed with an average of 70 and a standard deviation of 10, what percentage of the students:

a. Received grades less than 70?

b. Received grades greater than 70?

c. Received grades less than 60?

d. Received grades less than 50?

e. Received grades less than 50 or greater than 90?

f. Received grades less than the median?

3 Based on question 2, what is the standard score for a student who received a grade of

   a. 70?

   b. 75?

   c. 60?

   d. 55?

   e. 90?

4 Assume that, in the population of males in the United States, diastolic blood pressure is normally distributed with a mean of 90 and a standard deviation of 12. Use the table in Appendix G to determine what percentage of U.S. males have diastolic blood pressure

   a. Greater than 108.

   b. Less than 108.

   c. Between 108 and 114.

   d. Less than 80.

   e. Between 80 and 102.

5 Two researchers are studying the effect of positive thinking on recovery time after surgery. Both take a sample of 25 persons about to undergo surgery, teach them how to think positively, and then examine how long they stay in the hospital.

   a. The first researcher calculates the average stay to be 12 days, and the standard deviation to be 3 days. He reports these results in the *Journal of Positive Living*. The second researcher calculates the average stay to be 12.5 days. He reports the standard error of the mean to be 0.6 days. When he submits his results to the same journal, the editors question his findings. They want to know why his measure of variability is so much less than the first researcher's. Explain to the editors of the journal the difference between the two statistics. Indicate the relationship of the two statistics as well.

   b. What would be the standard error of the mean if the standard deviation remained at 3, but the sample size was increased to 50? What if it was decreased to 10?

6 You read in the newspaper that the average person watches 4 hours of television per night. The 95% confidence interval for the number of hours watched is reported as 3 hours to 5 hours. Do you agree or disagree with each of the following statements? Give your reasons:

   a. Ninety-five percent of all people watch between 3 and 5 hours of television per night.

   b. You can't tell whether this particular interval does or doesn't include the true population value for hours of television watched per night.

   c. The purpose of a confidence interval is to provide a range of values that are thought to include the sample mean.

   d. When you do a study you want your 95% confidence interval to be as wide as possible, since it will then include more values.

   e. The size of a confidence interval depends on the number of cases in the sample and the standard deviation.

7 You take a sample of 100 hamburgers and find their average weight to be 0.15 pounds. If the standard deviation of hamburger weights is known to be 0.05 pounds, calculate a 95% confidence interval for the unknown population value.

8 A macaroni manufacturer claims that the weight of 1-pound boxes of his macaroni is normally distributed with a mean of 1 and a standard deviation of 0.02 pounds. You take a random sample of 16 boxes of the macaroni and find their average weight to be 0.90 pounds. What is the probability that you would obtain a sample mean of 0.90 or less if the manufacturer's claim is correct? Do you believe the manufacturer's claim?

Testing Hypotheses about Two Independent Means

Based on the means observed in two independent samples, how can you test the hypothesis that two population means are equal?

- What does a distribution of the differences between two sample means look like?

- How can you figure out whether the difference you have observed between two sample means is unlikely or likely if the two population means are equal?

- How can you use statistical methods to test a hypothesis?

- What is the null hypothesis?

- What is the observed significance level?

- What are Type 1 and Type 2 errors, and when do you make them?

- What is a *t* test?

- What is the difference between a one-tailed and a two-tailed significance level?

- What assumptions about your data are necessary in order to use the *t* test?

A few chapters back, you looked at excitement with life and how it related to several other characteristics such as age, sex, and marital status. All that you did was to describe a sample. That was all you could do when you didn't understand very much about the relationships of samples and populations. Now you can do more.

You can look at the percentage of people who found life exciting and relate that information back to the population. You know you have one of many possible samples and that the chances are pretty slim that the value calculated from the sample is identical to the population value. However, you know that the General Social Survey sample is very large, 1,473, so the variability of the sample means is probably not very much. You can calculate the standard error for the percentage who found life exciting (it's 1.3) and use that number to calculate a 95% confidence interval for the population value. The interval is from 44.2% to 49.4%.

Although you never know if the particular interval you calculated contains the population value (it either does or it doesn't), you know that the interval will include the population value 95 times out of 100.

The confidence interval from 44.2% to 49.4% is narrow. That's good, since you want to pinpoint the population value as closely as possible. You don't know where within a confidence interval the population value might be. It's much more useful, then, to know that the 95% confidence interval is from 44 to 49 than to know that it's from 20 to 80. When you conduct a survey or experiment, look at both the mean and its confidence interval. If the interval is wide, you have only a very rough estimate of the population mean.

IS THE DIFFERENCE REAL?

Usually when you conduct a study, you have some ideas that you want to explore. These ideas, often called *hypotheses*, typically involve comparisons of several groups: "Do men and women find life equally exciting?" "Does income differ between people who find life exciting and those who don't?" "Are excited people more educated than those who find life dull?"

If you look at the results in your sample for the groups of interest, you'll probably find that they do differ. For example, people who said life is exciting had, on the average, 14.2 years of education, compared to 13.1 for people who said life is routine or dull. What can you make of this difference? You can say that the excited people in your sample had more education than those who were unexcited. But is that true for the population?

You've seen that different samples from the same population give different results. Even if the education levels are the same for the excited and the unexcited groups in the population, their sample means will differ. The real issue is, how much will they differ? How can you decide whether a difference in sample means can be attributed to their natural variability or to a real difference between groups in the population?

Review of the Distribution of Means

The question about sample means isn't terribly hard. Look at Figure 17.1, which you've seen in previous chapters. It shows the distribution of sample means for an agree/disagree item. These means are for 400-person samples from a population in which 50% agree and 50% disagree.

Figure 17.1 Means from samples of size 400

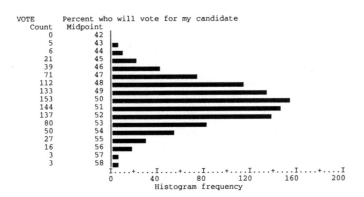

```
VOTE      Percent who will vote for my candidate
  Count   Midpoint
     0       42  |
     5       43  |
     6       44  |■
    21       45  |■■■■
    39       46  |■■■■■■■
    71       47  |■■■■■■■■■■■■
   112       48  |■■■■■■■■■■■■■■■■■■■
   133       49  |■■■■■■■■■■■■■■■■■■■■■■■
   153       50  |■■■■■■■■■■■■■■■■■■■■■■■■■■
   144       51  |■■■■■■■■■■■■■■■■■■■■■■■■
   137       52  |■■■■■■■■■■■■■■■■■■■■■■■■
    80       53  |■■■■■■■■■■■■■
    50       54  |■■■■■■■■
    27       55  |■■■■
    16       56  |■■
     3       57  |
     3       58  |■
             I....+....I....+....I....+....I....+....I....+....I
             0        40       80      120      160      200
                        Histogram frequency
```

The histogram in the figure gives you a pretty good idea of the real mathematical distribution of the sample values. What if a sample value is 52? It falls near the other cases in the distribution. This would lead you to believe that the observed sample may well be from a population in which 50% agree. You certainly wouldn't have much reason to doubt that. On the other hand, what if a sample value is 70? That's certainly far removed from the other cases. It seems unlikely that you'd get a sample value of 70 based on a sample of 400 cases if the population value is 50. It's *so* unlikely, that you'd doubt the hypothesis that the sample actually comes from a population with a value of 50.

Differences between Means

We can extend these ideas to differences between two means. Let's say we want to compare the mean IQ of students on the Dean's List to the mean IQ of students on academic probation. We have a sample of 20 students from each group. What we'll need to find out is how likely various differences in means are if the two groups have the same mean IQ in the population. We'll look at the distribution of differences between pairs of means. This will give us some idea of how much variability between means to expect when both samples are from the same population.

Let's do this by building a computer model again. We'll take two samples of 20 cases each from a normal population with a mean of 100 and a standard deviation of 15. Then we'll calculate the means for the two samples and find the difference between the two means. We'll have to keep repeating this again and again to get an idea of what the real distribution looks like. Figure 17.2 is a histogram of 1,000 such differences.

Figure 17.2 Differences between two means

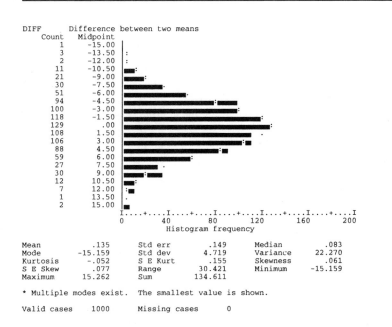

```
DIFF       Difference between two means
     Count    Midpoint
        1     -15.00
        3     -13.50  :
        2     -12.00  :
       11     -10.50  ▮:
       21      -9.00  ▮▮:
       30      -7.50  ▮▮▮.
       51      -6.00  ▮▮▮▮▮▮.
       94      -4.50  ▮▮▮▮▮▮▮▮▮:
      100      -3.00  ▮▮▮▮▮▮▮▮▮:
      118      -1.50  ▮▮▮▮▮▮▮▮▮▮▮:
      129       .00   ▮▮▮▮▮▮▮▮▮▮▮▮:
      108      1.50   ▮▮▮▮▮▮▮▮▮▮ .
      106      3.00   ▮▮▮▮▮▮▮▮▮▮:
       88      4.50   ▮▮▮▮▮▮▮▮:
       59      6.00   ▮▮▮▮▮.
       27      7.50   ▮▮ .
       30      9.00   ▮▮:▮
       12     10.50   ▮:
        7     12.00   :▮
        1     13.50   .
        2     15.00   ▮
                      I....+....I....+....I....+....I....+....I....+....I
                      0        40       80      120      160      200
                             Histogram frequency

Mean          .135      Std err       .149     Median       .083
Mode       -15.159      Std dev      4.719     Variance   22.270
Kurtosis     -.052      S E Kurt      .155     Skewness     .061
S E Skew      .077      Range       30.421     Minimum   -15.159
Maximum     15.262      Sum        134.611

* Multiple modes exist.  The smallest value is shown.

Valid cases   1000      Missing cases      0
```

The Central Limit Theorem works not just for means, but for differences of means as well, so the distribution looks normal. The mean of the distribution is close to 0. That's because the samples are from the same population. If you had taken one of the samples from a population with a mean IQ of 120 and the other sample from a population with a mean IQ of 110, the average difference for all pairs of samples would be 10. Sample means from the smarter population would be, on average, ten points higher than means from the other population—just as you'd expect.

Looking at the histogram in Figure 17.2, you see that there's quite a bit of variability among the differences. Differences greater than four points are not unusual. However, differences of more than ten points, though possible, are infrequent.

To compare the mean IQ of a sample of 20 students on the Dean's List and the mean of a sample of 20 students on academic probation, you need to see where your observed difference between the means falls in the distribution of possible differences. If you observe a difference of ten points or more, you may not be willing to believe that the difference is due to the natural variability of means from the same population. You wouldn't often see a difference this large when two population means are equal. You may think that a more likely explanation for this large a difference is that two population means really are not equal.

Evaluating a Difference between Means

How can you decide when a difference between two means is big enough for you to believe that the two samples are from a population with different means? It depends on how willing you are to be wrong.

Figure 17.3 Theoretical distribution of differences of means

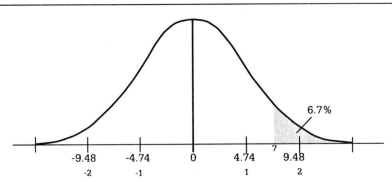

Look at Figure 17.3, which is the real distribution of differences of means for samples of size 20 from a normal distribution with a standard deviation of 15. (You can calculate the standard deviation of the distribution of differences. It's called the **standard error of the difference**.) Since the distribution is normal, you can find out what percentage of the samples falls into each of the intervals.

The scale on the distribution is marked with the actual values and with "standardized" values, which are computed by dividing the differences by the standard error. Looking at standardized distances is convenient, since the percentage of cases within a standardized distance from the mean is always the same. For example, 34% of all samples are between 0 and 1 standardized unit greater than the mean, and another 34% are between 0 and 1 standardized unit less than the mean. If you always express your distances in standardized units, you can use the standard normal distribution for evaluating the likelihood of a particular difference.

Suppose the Dean's List students in your sample had a mean IQ of 112, and the academic probation students had a mean IQ of 105. The difference is 7. For samples of size 20 from a population with a standard deviation of 15, the standard error of the difference is 4.74. (Don't worry now about the calculations.) Since you observed a difference of 7 between your two groups, the standardized difference is simply 7 divided by 4.74, or 1.48. That is, your observed difference of 7 is about one and a half standard errors above the mean.

From Figure 17.3, you can see that about 13% of the time, you'd expect to have at least a 7-point IQ difference in the sample means when two population means are equal. Why? You just found out that the 7-point difference is 1.5 standard errors. Look on the figure to see what percentage of the differences are that big. You should look at the area to the right of +1.5 and the area to the left of –1.5. Since the distribution is symmetric, the two areas are equal. Each one is about 6.7% of the total, and together they make up a little over 13% of the total. So about 13% of differences in sample means are going to be as big as 1.5 standard errors (or 7 points of IQ score) if the real difference in means is 0.

You can use the table in Appendix G to determine what percent of the values in a standard normal distribution are above 1.5. Look up the Z value of 1.5. The column labeled *Two-tailed Probability* indicates that 13.3% of the area in a standard normal distribution is above +1.5 or below –1.5.

Why the Entire Area?

You may wonder why you don't find the probability of getting a difference of just 7. Think of the following analogy. You're tired of being a poor student and have decided that the quickest (legal) way to upgrade your status is to marry rich. You settle on a definition of rich. Perhaps you need an income of $250,000 a year. Now you want to see how likely it is that you can achieve your goal. You go to the university library and ask the reference librarian to find some facts. Would you ask her to find just the number of eligible singles with incomes of $250,000? No, you'd ask for incomes of

$250,000 or more, since they all satisfy your criterion of being rich. In evaluating your chances of marrying rich, you'd include all incomes of $250,000 or more. Similarly, when you're trying to decide whether 7 is a likely outcome for a difference, your interest is not just on the number 7 but on all differences that are at least that large.

The example referred to differences that were not only larger than +7 but also less than –7—differences at both sides of the distribution in Figure 17.3. Why include the area less than –7? The reason is that when you did your study, you had no idea of which of the two groups of students should have the higher mean IQ. It's certainly possible that brighter students may goof off more than average ones and increase their chances of winding up on probation. Or, of course, it's possible that brighter students may find making the Dean's List easier, so it's more likely that you'll find them there. You had no idea of the direction in which the difference might go.

Since both outcomes were possible, when you evaluate the chances of seeing a difference at least as large as 7 points, you have to look in both directions. Both of the extreme regions of the distribution are atypical.

Sometimes, though, you can look in just one direction. It really depends on how you stated your initial hypothesis. If you hypothesized that students on the Dean's List have higher scores than students on probation, you look at only one side of the distribution in Figure 17.3. This ftype of test is called a **one-tailed** test. The only possibility that would concern you is that Dean's List students do score higher. But if their scores turn out to be lower in your sample, you're out of luck. You can't switch sides and apply the one-tailed test for a difference that's in the other direction. Use a one-tailed test only if you definitely expect one specific group to be higher. Otherwise, use a **two-tailed** test, and look at both sides of the distribution.

Drawing a Conclusion

In the previous example, you saw that when there is no difference between the two population means, you expect to see sample differences bigger than +7 or less than –7 about 13% of the time. Generally, 5% or less is considered unusual. So the observed results aren't all that unlikely. They don't make it hard to believe the hypothesis that in the population, the mean IQ values of the two groups are equal.

? *Now that I've seen how to use the standard error of a difference in means, how do I compute it?* When you have two means from independent samples, the variance of their difference equals the sum of their variances. This neat little fact would take too long to prove here, but you can see how it's used. The example above had two means from independent samples of size 20, taken from a population whose standard deviation was 15. You calculate the standard error of the difference by following these steps:

1 As explained in Chapter 16, the standard error of each mean equals 15 (the standard deviation) divided by the square root of 20 (the sample size).

2 The variance of each mean is just the square of that fraction: 15 squared divided by 20. That's 225 divided by 20, or 11.25.

3 The variance of the difference between the means is the sum of the variances of each mean. That's 11.25 plus 11.25, or 22.5.

The standard error of the difference between the means is therefore the square root of 22.5, or 4.74. ■■■

MORE ON HYPOTHESIS TESTING

In the previous example, you performed a statistical test of a hypothesis. You tested whether the population of students on the Dean's List and the population of students on academic probation have the same average IQ scores. This was the basic procedure:

1 You wanted to draw conclusions about the populations of students on the Dean's List or on probation. You couldn't include all possible students, so you had to base your conclusions about the populations on the results from a sample.

2 You randomly selected 20 students each from the Dean's List and the probation list. You found a 7-point difference in IQ scores between the two groups.

3 You calculated how likely it is that a difference as large as the one you observed would occur *if* there is no difference between the two means in the populations.

4 Since there was a 13% chance that you could see a difference as large as the one you observed when there was no difference between the population means, the evidence was insufficient to reject the hypothesis of no difference.

Why Is That So Complicated?

You're probably wondering why an admirably clear book like this has suddenly become garbled. Just listen to that last part again: "The evidence was insufficient to reject the hypothesis of no difference." Why are we going around in circles? Why do we have to assume that there's no difference between the means in the population and then figure out how likely the observed results are if there is no difference? Why not just calculate the probability that there *is* a difference? That's what we really want to know, isn't it?

Although it sounds like a good idea, in this situation there's no way that you can calculate the probability that there is a difference. There either is a difference or there isn't a difference. If we have two *sample* means, say 11 and 12, what do they tell us about whether it's true that the two means in the population are different? Not much. The probability of getting two sample means that differ by at least 1 depends on how much of a difference and how much variability there is in the population. It depends on whether the true difference is 0, 1, 2, 4, 100, or whatever. A difference of 1 may be very unlikely if the true difference is 100 but perfectly likely if the true difference is 0 or 2. But we don't know what the true difference is! We can only consider the likelihood of a value of 1 or more in relation to some hypothetical situation, such as a true difference of 0 or a true difference of 100. We can't assign the difference some overall probability.

What if you found that the two sample means were 11 and 11? Would you claim that it's certain the two means are exactly equal in the population? Would you be willing to forget the possibility that the population means might be 11 and 11.1? Of course not (I hope). You've seen that there's variability from sample to sample and that it's most unlikely for two sample means to be exactly equal even if the two means are equal in the population.

You simply can't figure out the probability that two population means are equal or unequal. You can, however, estimate the probability that you'd see a difference of at least 2 (or some other value) in the sample when there is no difference in the population (or when there is a difference of a particular size.) In the previous example, you saw the calculations for the probability that the means from two samples would differ by at least 7 when there is no difference in the population.

Steps for Hypothesis Testing

To test a hypothesis, you do the following:

1 State the hypothesis of interest. This is what you think is really true for the population. (Dean's List students and probation students differ in average IQ score. Excited people and unexcited people differ in average income and education.)

2 Determine the frame of reference you'll use to evaluate your hypothesis. This is what's true in the population if your hypothesis is wrong. This "frame of reference" is called the **null hypothesis**, since it describes the population when the hypothesis you're interested in is not true when it's null. One null hypothesis is that Dean's List students and probation students have the same average IQ. Another is that excited and unexcited people do not differ in their average income and education.

3 Calculate the probability that you'd see a difference at least as large as the one you observed in your sample if the null hypothesis is true.

4 If this probability (called the **observed significance level**) is small, say less than 0.05, reject the null hypothesis.

5 If the observed significance level is large, do not reject the null hypothesis. This doesn't mean that you have shown that the null hypothesis is true. You simply do not reject it as being quite unlikely. You remain uncertain.

You must state the null hypothesis in such a way that you can calculate the distribution of sample means when it's true. You can't use a null hypothesis that says the population means are unequal, since there's no single distribution of sample means for that statement. But you can have a null hypothesis that says the difference between two population means is 5 or some other particular number. The null hypothesis must provide the reference point for calculating the probability of the observed results. You calculate the probability of the observed results *if* the null hypothesis is true.

T TESTS

Let's consider another example of testing a hypothesis. Let's see if there's a difference in the average years of education for people who find life exciting and those who don't.

To simplify things while getting started, we'll just compare two groups. We'll combine the people who say that life is pretty routine with those who say it's dull and call them the *Not excited* group, in contrast to the *Excited* group. The SPSS/PC+ commands in the rest of this chapter will use this collapsed version of the variable LIFE.

The null hypothesis that we'll be testing is that the excited people have the same average number of years of education as the unexcited people. The hypothesis of interest (sometimes called the **alternative hypothesis**) is that excited and unexcited people differ in average years of education.

Consider a problem we may encounter when comparing years of education for the two groups. In previous chapters, we've seen that age seems to be related to the way people feel about life. If we find that excited people are better educated than unexcited people, we'll have some difficulty in interpreting the results. In the United States today, people in their thirties have more education than people in their sixties. If excited people are better educated than unexcited people, that difference may just be due to a difference in age. (In this example, age may be an **intervening variable**, since it may come between the variables we're actually interested in, education and excitement. Age may explain a difference in education between the two excitement groups.)

We can minimize this problem by restricting the comparison to people in a particular age group. We'll take people in their thirties and compare the years of education for the two excitement groups, and we'll be controlling for age. That is, age will no longer affect the comparison as much. The results will be much easier to interpret.

The top part of Figure 17.4 contains the means and standard deviations for years of education in the two groups. The commands that produce this output are

```
get file 'gss.sys'.
select if (age ge 30 and age le 39).
recode life (3 = 2).
t-test groups life(1,2) /variables educ.
```

You can see that there were 161 people in the age range 30–39 who found life exciting (labeled Group 1 in the figure). Their average education is 14.17 years. The standard deviation is 2.76. Since the sample size is fairly large, the standard error is small, 0.22. (The 95% confidence interval for average years of education in Group 1 is from 13.7 to 14.6.) For Group 2, the people who found life routine or dull, the average education is 13.1 years. (The 95% confidence interval is 12.7 to 13.5.) The difference between the two averages is 1.07 years.

Using the *t* Distribution

Now we have to answer the question, "How often would we expect to see a difference of 1.07 years in the sample when there's no difference between the two groups in the population?"

In Chapter 16, we always knew or pretended to know the standard deviation in the population. In fact, though, it usually must be estimated from the sample. When this is necessary—when we use the same sample both to test the hypothesis and to estimate the standard deviation in the population—we have to use the t distribution instead of the normal distribution to calculate the observed significance level.

The t distribution is very much like the normal distribution. It just shifts the area in the normal distribution to adjust for the fact that we don't know what the standard deviations really are. (When sample sizes are large, the t distribution looks very much like the normal distribution.)

As always, we compute the difference between the two means, find its standard error, and then calculate how improbable the observed difference is if the null hypothesis is true. For example, our difference is 1.07 years, and its standard error is .30. By dividing the difference by its standard error, we compute its standardized score, 3.55. Then we use the t distribution to calculate how often a standardized score of 3.55 (in absolute value) or greater occurs when there is no difference between the two groups in the population.

Of course, we don't actually have to do any of the computations.

Figure 17.4 A t test for the difference between two means

```
Independent samples of  LIFE      Is life exciting or dull?

Group 1:  LIFE  EQ 1         Group 2:  LIFE  EQ 2

t-test for:  EDUC      Highest year of school completed

                    Number              Standard    Standard
                    of Cases    Mean    Deviation    Error

        Group 1      161      14.1739     2.758       .217
        Group 2      171      13.1053     2.718       .208
```

		Pooled Variance Estimate			Separate Variance Estimate		
F Value	2-Tail Prob.	t Value	Degrees of Freedom	2-Tail Prob.	t Value	Degrees of Freedom	2-Tail Prob.
1.03	.851	3.55	330	.000	3.55	328.15	.000

The group statistics in the output in Figure 17.4 should be familiar; just statistics we've already seen. The numbers at the bottom, where it says Pooled Variance Estimate, contain the information we're after. In the column labeled t Value is the standardized score, 3.55, that was described above. The entry in the column labeled Degrees of Freedom is based on the number of observations in each of the two groups. (It's just the total number of observations minus two.) The degrees of freedom are used together with the <t value to determine how likely it is to get a score as big as 3.55 (or as small as –3.55) if the mean value of education for the two groups is the same in the population. You see this probability in the column labeled 2-tail Prob. (A table that shows the areas in a t distribution is provided in Appendix G.)

The probability given is 0.000. Does this show that the probability is zero? No. It means that the probability is less than 0.0005. In this procedure, SPSS/PC+ prints probabilities to only three decimal places. Anything less than 0.0005 is printed as 0.000.

This probability, the **observed significance level**, is very small. It therefore appears unlikely that the excited people in the population have the same amount of education as the unexcited people. We qualified this conclusion with "appears unlikely" not to be wishy-washy but because we can't be absolutely sure. It's possible, though very unlikely, that this sample came from a population in which there really is no difference. The probability that it did is less than 0.0005.

Two Types of Errors

There are two types of mistakes that you can make when testing a hypothesis about two means. You can claim that the two means are not equal in the population when in fact they are. Or you can fail to say that there's a difference when there really is one. Statisticians, being very methodical people, have given these two types of errors particularly descriptive, easy-to-remember names. They call the first error (claiming that two means are not equal when in fact they are) a **Type 1** error. No doubt you've deduced what to call the second type of error (not finding a difference when there is one): a **Type 2** error.

> **?** *It may be easy to remember that you call the two kinds of error Type 1 and Type 2, but how do you remember which is which?* Perhaps you can remember it this way. The Type 1 error is the error you're tempted to make. When you say, proudly, "There *is* a difference. Something is happening here. I have found a relationship," you are taking the chance of making a Type 1 error.
>
> If you can remember what the Type 1 error is, then it's pretty easy to figure out that the Type 2 error is the one you're not tempted to make, saying "Nothing is happening here" when there really is a difference in the population. ∎∎∎

Table 17.1 shows what can happen when testing a hypothesis. There may or may not be a difference in the population, and you may or may not find it. When you detect a difference that exists in the population, you're doing fine. When there is no difference in the population and you conclude, based on your sample, that there is no difference, all is well. The problems are in the remaining two cells of the table. We'll talk more about that later.

Table 17.1 What can happen when testing a hypothesis

		The real world: The null hypotheses is really..	
		True	False
Your conclusion: You say the null hypothesis is...	True	No problem	Type 2 error
	False	Type 1 error	No problem

Output from the T-TEST Procedure

The computation of the t test differs depending on whether you assume that in the population the two groups have the same variances or not. If you can assume that the two variances are equal, use the numbers in the columns labeled Pooled Variance Estimate. If you cannot assume that the two variances are equal, use the t test labeled Separate Variance Estimate.

The ratio of the variances in the two samples is shown in the column labeled F Value. In Figure 17.4, it is 1.03. If this number is close to 1, the sample variances are similar. The larger the number, the more dissimilar the sample variances.

Next to the F value of 1.03, SPSS/PC+ prints the probability that you would see a ratio of the sample variances at least as large as the one observed in the sample if the variances are equal in the population and if the distribution of the variable is normal. (The F test for equality of variances depends heavily on the assumption that the data are from normal populations, while the t test does not. If the data are not from normal populations, the observed significance level for the F statistic may be unreliable.)

A better test of the hypothesis that the population variances are equal is the Levene test, which is calculated by the EXAMINE procedure. Figure 17.5 shows the results of the Levene test. The observed significance level is 0.382. So you don't reject the hypothesis that the population variances are equal, and you can use the pooled variance t test.

If the observed significance level is small, you should use the *t* test marked
Separate Variance Estimate. In general, it's a good idea to use the separate-
variance *t* test whenever you suspect that the variances are unequal.

Figure 17.5 Levene test for equality of variances

```
EXAMINE EDUC BY LIFE /PLOT=SPREADLEVEL.

Test of homogeneity of variance          df1      df2     Significance
Levene Statistic                  .7659    1       330           .3821
```

INTERPRETING A T TEST

Now that you have an idea of what happens when you test a hypothesis
about two means, let's test one more hypothesis. Is there a difference in
the average size of the households for excited people and unexcited people? Again, since older people often live in smaller households than people
who are raising families, let's restrict the comparison to people in their
thirties. The null hypothesis is that average household size for people who
are excited by life is the same as that for people who are not. The alternative hypothesis is that average household size differs between the two
groups.

The variable name in the General Social Survey for the question that
asks how many people live in the household is *HOMPOP*. Run the command

```
t-test groups life (1,2) / variables hompop.
```

and you get the output shown in Figure 17.6.

Figure 17.6 Do excited people live in larger or smaller households?

```
Independent samples of  LIFE     Is life exciting or dull?

Group 1:  LIFE  EQ 1         Group 2:  LIFE  EQ 2

t-test for:  HOMPOP    Number of people in household

                   Number             Standard    Standard
                   of Cases    Mean    Deviation    Error

       Group 1       161      3.2298     1.530       .121
       Group 2       171      3.3801     1.519       .116


               | Pooled Variance Estimate | Separate Variance Estimate
       F   2-Tail |   t    Degrees of 2-Tail |   t    Degrees of  2-Tail
   Value  Prob.   | Value   Freedom   Prob.  | Value   Freedom    Prob.

   1.01   .926    | -.90     330       .370  | -.90    328.50      .370
```

The respondents who found life exciting (Group 1) had an average household size of 3.23 people, while the average household size for those who found life unexciting was 3.38. How likely is it to see a difference of this magnitude if, in fact, there is no difference in household size between the two groups in the population? Look at the pooled-variance t test. The observed significance level associated with a t value of -0.90 is 0.37. This says that 37% of the time a difference of at least this size would occur when the two population means are equal. There doesn't seem to be much reason to believe that the means differ in the population.

You've probably noticed the hesitancy in this and the other conclusions. This one doesn't say that the two means are equal in the population. It hedges. It says there's no reason to doubt that the means are equal. There's a reason for being conclusion-shy. It's *impossible* to prove, based on samples, that two population means are exactly equal. What if the excited people in the population have a mean household size of 3.2500, and the unexcited people have a mean household size of 3.2501? Since sample means differ, and the statistical procedures for evaluating differences between means must allow for variability from sample to sample, we'll never be able to detect such a small difference in the population.

What will happen is that we'll take two samples, compute a t test, and find a large observed significance level. Perhaps we find a probability of 0.50 that the t value could be observed in a population with no difference. This large observed significance level doesn't tell us that the means are exactly equal. It just indicates that the results would not be "far out" if the two means are equal in the population. So instead of embracing the null hypothesis and claiming that it's true, we just say that we have no evidence to believe that it's not true. We can't *prove* the null hypothesis.

An Analogy: Coin Flips

Suppose someone comes up to you, hands you a coin, and says, "Tell me if this is a fair coin—a coin in which heads and tails are equally likely." If you had nothing better to do, you'd probably start flipping the coin and counting the number of times heads and tails occur.

You're no longer naive. You know that if you flip a fair coin 10 times, it's not often that you'll get exactly 5 heads and 5 tails. All sorts of outcomes are possible. There's even a reasonable chance that with a fair coin you'll get 8 tails and 2 heads, or 8 heads and 2 tails. The first histogram in Chapter 14 gives you an idea of the probability that you'd get an unusually high proportion of heads (or tails) in 400 flips of a fair coin. If the coin is really way off (say, it has 2 heads or 2 tails), you should be able to figure that out with 10 flips. The probability that you get all heads or all tails on 10 flips of a fair coin is 2/1024. So, if it always comes up the same, you can be pretty

? *So what is a small significance level?* Most of the time, significance levels are considered small if they're less than 0.05, and sometimes if they're less than 0.01. A difference with an observed significance level of 0.05 or less is often called a "statistically significant" difference. Rather than just rejecting or not rejecting the null hypothesis, look at the actual significance level as well. An observed significance level of 0.06 is not the same as an observed significance level of 0.92, though both may not be statistically significant. When reporting your results, give the exact observed significance level. It will help the reader evaluate your results. Treat the observed significance level as a guide to whether or not the difference could be due to chance alone.   ■ ■ ■

sure that it's rigged—though it's still possible that the coin is fair.

As the coin becomes less and less unfair, it gets harder and harder for you to detect the difference. If the true probability of a head on the coin is 0.4999 instead of 0.5000, you'd never figure that out unless you're willing to spend the rest of your life coin flipping. Any combination of flips that you come up with will appear perfectly reasonable if the coin is fair or if it's minutely biased. Although you can disprove with a certain degree of confidence that a coin is fair, it's an impossible task to prove that it's exactly fair.

That's why we couldn't say we proved the average household sizes are the same in the two groups. All we could say is that there wasn't evidence to disprove it.

Observed Significance Levels

The observed significance level tells you the probability that the observed difference could be due to chance. The observed significance level is the probability that your sample could show a difference at least as large as the one that you observed, if the means are really equal. When your observed significance level is small, its interpretation is fairly straightforward: the two means seem to be unequal in the population.

If your observed significance level is too large to reject the hypothesis that the means are equal, more than one explanation is possible.

The first explanation is that there may be no difference between the two means, or it may be so small that you just can't detect it. If the true difference is very small, it may not matter that you can't find it. Who really cares about a difference in household size of 0.001 or a difference in annual income of $10? Little, if anything, is lost by your failure to establish such tiny differences.

The second explanation is more troublesome: There is an important difference, and you can't find it. This can occur if the sample size is small. If you flip a coin only twice, you'll never be able to establish whether it's fair. A fair coin has a 50% chance of coming up heads twice or tails twice in two flips and a 50% chance of coming up with one of each. Any outcome that you see is consistent with the coin's being fair. As the number of flips increases, so does your ability to detect differences.

In the previous chapters, you saw how the distribution of means has less variability as sample size increases. To detect a small difference, you need a big sample so that the difference would clearly be outside the expected amount of sample variation.

The variability of the responses (in the population) also affects your ability to detect differences. If there's a lot of variability in the observations, the sample means will vary a lot as well. Even large differences in observed means can be attributed to variability among the samples.

To summarize: if you don't find evidence to reject the hypothesis that two means are equal in the population, one of two possibilities is true:

1 The means are equal or very similar.

2 The means are unequal, but you aren't able to detect the difference because of small sample size, large variability, or both.

Tails and Significance Tests

The observed significance level printed on the SPSS/PC+ t test output is labeled 2-Tail Prob., standing for *two-tailed probability*. This value tells you the probability that you'd see a difference in *either direction* at least as large as the one you observed when there's no difference in the population. Either the first group has a mean larger than the second group by at least the observed size, or the second group has a mean larger than the first group by at least the observed size.

If you don't know which of the two groups should have the larger mean, you have to look for differences in both directions. That is, you look at the two tails of the distribution. It isn't obvious how household size, or even education, might be related to a feeling that life is exciting. There's no reason to believe that excited people should come from larger households than unexcited people. Similarly, the excited people need not be better educated than the unexcited people. It's perfectly reasonable to think that too much education may wear you down and make it harder to find life exciting. Or, of course, the opposite may be true. Differences in either direction cast doubt on the null hypothesis that in the population the two groups have the same means.

If you do know in advance which group will have the larger mean if they differ, then you can use a one-tailed significance level. Suppose you know that a new drug for insomnia will either leave the amount of time you need to fall asleep unchanged, or the drug will decrease it. You take two random samples of people and perform an experiment. One group gets the drug, and the other gets a placebo (a fake drug just to make the subjects think they're being treated). Then you find the average time it takes each group to fall asleep. You calculate the difference between the two means, along with its standard error. To find out how often you'd get a difference of this magnitude by chance when the drug and placebo are equally effective, you need only calculate the probability that you see a decrease at least as large as the one observed. You're confident that people treated with the drug won't take longer to fall asleep, so you decide in advance not even to test for that possibility.

Think back to the coin analogy. Suppose your friend tells you, as he is handing you the coin, that he suspects the coin is biased. Perhaps his wife always used it to settle disputes, and she always bet heads and won. You've got a pretty good suspicion that the coin is biased in favor of heads, and no reason at all to suspect bias in favor of tails. If you toss the coin 10 times, and it comes up all heads, you just want to know what the probability is that a fair coin comes up 10 heads out of 10 flips. You don't worry that it might have come up with 10 tails, since the only situations that will cause you to doubt your coin are excesses of heads.

If you know in advance which of two means should be larger, you can convert the two-tailed significance level to a one-tailed level. All you do is divide the two-tailed probability by two. The result tells you the percentage of the t distribution in one of the tails.

THE HYPOTHESIS-TESTING PROCESS

In the previous example, we used a statistical technique called the t test to test the hypothesis that two groups have the same mean in the population. We did the following:

1 For each of the groups, we calculated the mean of the variable we were interested in comparing.

2 We subtracted one mean from the other to determine the difference between the two.

3 We calculated a t statistic by dividing the difference of the two sample means by its standard error.

4 We calculated the observed significance level. This told us how often we'd expect to see a difference as large as the one we observed if there was no difference between the groups in the population.

5 If the observed significance level was small (less than 0.05), we rejected the hypothesis that the two means are equal in the population.

6 Otherwise, we didn't reject the null hypothesis, and we didn't accept it either. We remained undecided. That's because we didn't know whether there really was no difference in the means or whether our sample was simply too small to detect the difference.

This procedure is the same for tests of most hypotheses:

1 You formulate a null hypothesis and its alternative.

2 You calculate the probability of observing a difference of a particular magnitude in the sample when the null hypothesis is true.

3 If this probability (the observed significance level) is small enough, you reject the null hypothesis.

4 If the probability is not small enough, you remain undecided.

The only part of this process that changes for different situations is the actual statistic used to evaluate the probability of the observed difference. In the chapters that follow, we'll use different types of statistics to test these kinds of hypotheses:

■ Variables are independent.

■ Several groups have the same means.

■ There is no linear relationship between several variables.

If you make sure now that you understand the way hypothesis testing works, the rest of this book will be easy.

Assumptions Needed

To perform a statistical test of a hypothesis, you must make certain assumptions about the data. The particular assumptions you must make depend on the statistical test you are using. Some procedures require stricter assumptions than others.

The assumptions are needed so that you (or your computer) can figure out what the distribution of the statistic is. Unless you know the distribution, you can't determine the correct significance levels. For the pooled-variance t test, you need to assume that you have two random samples with the same population variance. You also need to assume that the distribution of the means is approximately normal, which can happen one of two ways. The variable itself is normally distributed, so the means will automatically be normally distributed. Or the sample size must be large enough so you can rely on the Central Limit Theorem to make sure the means are distributed normally.

Of course, some assumptions are more important than others. Moderate violation of some of them may not have very serious consequences. Therefore, it's important to know for each statistical procedure not only what assumptions are needed, but also how severely their violation may influence the results. We'll talk about these things when we discuss the different statistical procedures. For example, the F test for equality of variances is quite sensitive to departures from normality. The t test for equality of means is less so. (We talked about the F test briefly above, and it will turn up again in Chapter 20.)

You should include tests of the assumptions as part of your hypothesis-testing procedure. If your sample size is small, before doing a t test, obtain histograms or stem and leaf plots for each of your groups. If the distributions appear far from normal, you may have to reconsider using a t test. (Procedures that require very few assumptions about the data are discussed inAppendix E.)

MORE ABOUT THE T-TEST PROCEDURE

Using the SPSS/PC+ T-TEST procedure, you can test the hypothesis that in the population, two independent groups have the same mean. You obtain:

- The number of cases, the mean, the standard deviation, and the standard error for each of the two groups.

- Two t statistics for testing the hypothesis that two population means are equal, as well as their two-tailed observed significance levels. SPSS/PC+ calculates one test based on the assumption that the two population variances are equal (the pooled-variance t test) and the other test based on the assumption that the population variances are not equal (the separate-variance t test).

To calculate a t test for the hypothesis that the average age of men is the same as that of women, run the command:

```
t-test groups sex(1,2) /variables age.
```

Following the keyword GROUPS, you give the name of the variable that's used to classify the cases into the two groups. The actual codes assigned to the two groups are given in parentheses. The specification GROUPS=SEX(1,2) tells the computer that the cases are to be split into two groups according to the values of the SEX variable. Cases with values of 1 for *SEX* go into one group, while cases with values of 2 go into the other. If there are cases with other values for the *SEX* variable, they're excluded from the analysis.

You can give only two distinct codes for the variable that's used to determine the groups. The codes can be any integers. For example, in the unlikely event that you had coded males as 10 and females as 8, you would use the command:

```
t-test groups sex (8,10) /variables age.
```

After the word VARIABLES, give the name of the variable whose means are being compared. In the above example, the means of the *AGE* variable are compared for the groups coded 8 and 10 on *SEX*. If you want to compare the means of several variables, follow the word VARIABLES with a list of all of them. This variable list must follow the GROUPS subcommand.

To get the Levene test for equality of variances, you must ask for the spread against level plot in the EXAMINE procedure, as in:

```
examine educ by life /plot spreadlevel.
```

WHAT'S NEXT?

This chapter explained the logic of hypothesis testing by discussing *t* tests. But all the *t* tests we looked at involved cases that were not related in any way. They were independent. We compared the mean for one group of people against the mean for another group of people. Sometimes, though, we want to compare means that aren't independent in this way. The next chapter shows how you can use *t* tests when the two samples are related.

Summary

Based on the means observed in two independent samples, how can you test the hypothesis that two population means are equal?

To test the null hypothesis that two population means are equal, you must calculate the probability of seeing a difference at least as large as the one you've observed in your two samples, if there is no difference in the population.

The hypothesis that there is no difference between the two population means is called the *null hypothesis*.

The probability of seeing a difference at least as large as the one you've observed, when the null hypothesis is true, is called the *observed significance level*.

If the observed significance level is small, usually less than 0.05, you reject the null hypothesis.

If you reject the null hypothesis when it's true, you make a Type 1 error. If you don't reject the null hypothesis when it's false, you make a Type 2 error

The *t* test is used to test the hypothesis that two population means are equal.

EXERCISES

Syntax

1   You want to see whether there is a difference in the weight of infants whose mothers received a new type of vitamin and those whose mothers did not. Mothers who received the new vitamin have a code of 1 for *TREAT*. Mothers who received the old vitamin have a code of 0. The variable name for the infants' weight in grams is *WEIGHT*. Write the command to perform a *t* test to test the hypothesis that there is no difference in weight between the two groups.

2   What if the two groups were coded 1 and 2? How would your command change?

3   Suppose you were giving two dosages of both the old and new vitamin so that you have four codes for the variable *TREAT*: 1=*old vitamin, low dose*; 2=*old vitamin, high dose*; 3=*new vitamin, low dose*; 4=*new vitamin, high dose*. Write the commands necessary to perform a *t* test for a comparison of the new vitamin (both doses combined) to the old vitamin (both doses combined).

4   Correct the following commands if necessary:

   a. `test groups ales(0,1)/var income.`

b. `t-test groups employ(7,9)/ dep age.`

c. `t-test gr employ(7,9,8)/var children.`

d. `t-test groups sex(1,2) race (1,4)/var reslengt.`

Statistical Concepts

1 You think that Republicans earn more money than Democrats. To test this you take a random sample of 100 Democrats and 100 Republicans and record their earned income.

a. What is the null hypothesis that you want to test?

b. What is the alternative hypothesis?

2 You run a two-sample *t* test of the hypothesis in question 1 using the SPSS/PC+ T-TEST procedure. The output is shown below. Write a short paragraph summarizing your conclusions.

```
Independent samples of  PARTYID      Political party affiliation

Group 1:  PARTYID  EQ 1          Group 2:  PARTYID  EQ 2


t-test for:  EDUC      Highest year of school completed

                 Number                Standard    Standard
                of Cases     Mean      Deviation     Error

    Group 1        100      23.8300     20.396       2.040
    Group 2        100      31.2750     21.303       2.130
```

		Pooled Variance Estimate			Separate Variance Estimate		
F Value	2-Tail Prob.	t Value	Degrees of Freedom	2-Tail Prob.	t Value	Degrees of Freedom	2-Tail Prob.
1.09	.666	-2.52	198	.012	-2.52	197.63	.012

3 Answer the following questions based on the output in question 2.

a. Have you proven that, in the population, Democrats and Republicans have exactly the same income? Explain.

b. Have you proven that, in the population, Democrats and Republicans don't have the same income? Explain.

c. How often would you expect to see a difference at least as large as the one you observed if the null hypothesis is true?

4 What if you had obtained the following results? Summarize your conclusions.

```
Independent samples of  PARTYID      Political party affilitation

Group 1:  PARTYID  EQ 1          Group 2:  PARTYID  EQ 2


t-test for:  EDUC      Highest year of school completed

                 Number                Standard    Standard
                of Cases     Mean      Deviation     Error

    Group 1        100      23.8300     20.396       2.040
    Group 2        100      27.2750     21.303       2.130
```

		Pooled Variance Estimate			Separate Variance Estimate		
F Value	2-Tail Prob.	t Value	Degrees of Freedom	2-Tail Prob.	t Value	Degrees of Freedom	2-Tail Prob.
1.09	.666	-1.17	198	.244	-2.52	197.63	.244

5 Discuss whether the following statement is true or false, and why: "The observed significance level tells you the probability that the null hypothesis is true."

6 Discuss whether the following statement is true or false, and why: "The observed significance level tells you the probability that the null hypothesis is false."

7 The following table is the output from an independent samples t test. Fill in the missing information and interpret the results.

```
Independent samples of  TYPE

Group 1:  TYPE  EQ 1          Group 2:  TYPE  EQ 2


t-test for:  RECALL        Commercial recall score

                   Number              Standard    Standard
                   of Cases    Mean    Deviation    Error

          Group 1     66      17.1087    2.804       ▓▓▓▓
          Group 2     82      16.3093    ▓▓▓▓▓       .208
```

```
              | Pooled Variance Estimate | Separate Variance Estimate
              |                          |
   F   2-Tail |   t   Degrees of 2-Tail  |   t    Degrees of 2-Tail
 Value  Prob. | Value  Freedom   Prob.   | Value   Freedom    Prob.

      0.000   |  2.12   ▓▓▓▓▓    .036    |  2.02   103.96     .046
```

8 Assume that the observed significance level for the test of the null hypothesis that two groups have the same alcohol intake is 0.0005. Is there a possibility that the two population means are really equal? Explain.

9 Assume for question 8 that the observed significance level is 0.75. Is there a possibility that the two population means are really unequal? Explain.

10 A market research analyst is studying whether men and women find the same types of cars desirable. He asks 150 men and 75 women to indicate which one of the following types of cars they would be most likely to buy: two-door with trunk; two-door with hatchback; convertible; four-door with trunk; four-door with hatchback; or station wagon. Each of the possible responses is assigned a code number. The analyst runs a t test and finds that the average value for males and females appears to differ ($p=0.008$). He doesn't know how to interpret his output, so he comes to you for advice. Explain to him what his results mean.

11 You are interested in whether average family income differs for people who find life exciting and for those who don't. You take a sample of people at a local museum on Sunday afternoon and find that there is a $5,000 difference in income between the two groups. You do a t test and find the observed significance level to be 0.03.

Your friend is also studying the same problem. She takes a sample of people in a department store on Saturday afternoon. She finds a $10,000 difference in family income between the two groups. But when she does a t test, she finds an observed significance level of 0.2.

Discuss these studies, their shortcomings, and possible reasons for the contradictory results.

12 You're doing a door-to-door survey. Some people won't let you in. Others are not at home. You don't let this bother you; all you do is go to more houses to get the total sample size you want. Discuss possible problems with your approach and ways you might overcome them.

Data Analysis

Use the gss.sys system file to answer the following questions.

1 You think that people who believe in life after death have less education than people who do not.

  a. State the null hypothesis that you will be testing.

  b. Perform the appropriate statistical analysis to test the null hypothesis.

  c. Write a brief paragraph summarizing your results.

2 Make a crosstabulation of the highest degree received by a person and whether the person believes in an afterlife or not. Be sure to calculate the appropriate percentages. How do the results of this analysis compare to those you obtained in question 1?

3 Using the SELECT IF command described in Chapter 14, make histograms of years of education for people who do believe in life after death and those who don't. Compare the two distributions.

4 Test the null hypothesis that the average age in the population is the same for people who believe in life after death and for people who don't. Write a paragraph summarizing your results.

5 Test the null hypothesis that the average age at which males and females get married is the same. Summarize your results.

18 Testing Hypotheses about Two Dependent Means

Based on the means observed in two related samples, how can you test the null hypothesis that in the population there is no difference between the means?

- What are paired experimental designs, and what are their advantages?

- What types of problems can occur when you use paired designs?

- How must you arrange the data file for a paired design?

- What is a paired t test?

- What assumptions do you need to use the paired t test?

- If a difference is statistically significant, does that mean it is important?

I n Chapter 17, you looked at tests of two null hypotheses: people who find life exciting have the same amount of education on average as people who find life routine or dull, and these two groups come from households that are the same average size. Testing the hypotheses involved two distinct groups of cases: those with responses of *Exciting* and those with responses of *Pretty routine* or *Dull*. A case was a member of either one group or the other. It couldn't belong to both. In such situations, the two groups are called **independent**, and the t tests you calculate are sometimes called **independent-sample** t tests, since they are used only when there is no relationship between the cases in the two groups.

But sometimes the groups you want to compare are related in some important way. There is a special statistical technique for dealing with these situations.

PAIRED DESIGNS

Suppose you're studying whether a new treatment for insomnia is effective. You record how long it takes subjects to fall asleep when they're not taking the drug and again how long it takes the same subjects to fall asleep when they are taking the drug. Or you may be studying father-and-son pairs and want to find out whether the fathers' caloric intake differs from the sons'. Or you may want to know whether there is a difference between husbands and wives in average hours worked around the house.

All of these study designs involve *pairs* of observations. In the insomnia study, a pair consists of the same case before and after treatment. In the dietary study, a pair consists of father and son. In the comparison of hours of work, a pair consists of husband and wife.

Designs in which the same subject is observed under two different conditions or the members of two groups are matched in some way are called **paired-sample** or **correlated-sample** designs. Each subject in one group has a corresponding subject in the other group. Often, the corresponding subject is the very same person. In any event, the members of the groups form pairs.

Advantages of Comparing Pairs of Subjects

You might wonder why anyone would want to use designs like these. Why not just take two groups of subjects, give one the drug and the other the placebo, and see if the means are significantly different? Instead of studying couples, why not just take a sample of married men and married women and not worry about who's married to whom? To answer that question, think about possible explanations when the difference between two sample means is found to be "statistically significant." One obvious reason is that there is a difference between the population means. Another possible reason is that the people in the two samples are different.

For example, people suffer from insomnia in varying degrees. One person may take two hours to fall asleep without a drug, and another person may have to toss and turn for five hours before falling asleep. When you select two random samples of insomniacs with the intention of giving placebos to one group and the new drug to the other, you have no assurance that the two groups are comparable. They might differ in severity of insomnia or suggestibility. If your placebo group happens to contain the more severe sufferers, the drug may appear to have an effect even though it's actually no more effective than the placebo. Why? Because the people who received the drug were better off to start with.

How can you make your two groups as similar as possible so that observed differences are more likely due to the treatment rather than the random variation between the two groups? One possibility is to use the same individual twice. You can give each person the placebo one time and the new drug another time. That way, you eliminate some of the differences between people from your comparison. You *control* for variables such as severity of insomnia, suggestibility, sex, age, and so on. The placebo and the treatment groups are as similar as possible: they're the same people!

Consider the study comparing caloric intake in fathers and sons. Suppose you select two independent groups of men: men who are fathers of high-school students and sons who are high-school students themselves. You don't match fathers and sons, you just have a group of fathers and a group of sons. If you find differences between the two groups, there are many possible explanations. Suppose one group is richer than the other, and socioeconomic level is related to caloric intake. You'll find differences between the groups that have nothing to do with the father-son distinction you're interested in.

If you select father-son pairs, on the other hand, you can eliminate some of the differences. For example, a father and son will probably be of the same socioeconomic level. Some possible explanations for the observed differences in caloric intake will be eliminated or at least minimized.

? *When comparing two treatments in an experiment, is it always bet-*
ter to form pairs of similar subjects (or to observe the same subject
under both conditions) than to use two independent groups? No. Paired
experimental designs are only useful when you can form pairs on the basis
of a variable that's related to the one you're studying. If you pair your subjects based on shoe size when you're studying responses to a new drug, the
paired design actually makes it *less* likely that you can identify a true difference when it exists. The two members of a pair are not alike in any way
that matters. In this case, using a paired *t* test makes it more difficult, statistically, to detect true differences than just treating the two groups as independent samples.   ■■■

Some Possible Problems

A paired design is a good way to eliminate some of the differences between
subjects in two groups so you can focus on the particular difference that
you're testing. But you need to keep some things in mind:

- If the effect of a treatment does not wear off quickly, you must make
  sure that enough time passes between treatments so that one wears off
  before another begins. Otherwise, you won't know whether the first or
  the second treatment is causing the results during the second observation.

- You should also be aware of the learning effect. You encounter it when
  a subject's response improves merely by doing the same thing again.
  For example, if you give subjects the same test twice, they may do better the second time, regardless of what else has happened.

You must also pay attention to both the timing and the sequence of admin-
istering the treatments. You may want to include a control group that
doesn't receive any treatment but has measurements taken.

Paired Data and SPSS/PC+

When you have paired samples, information from both members of each
pair must be together in the data file. The case is the pair of responses, not
the individual person. For example, if you're comparing husbands' and
wives' education, you have two variables, one for the husbands and one for
the wives. The variables have different variable names, such as *HUSED* and
WIFED. If each subject gets two treatments, the two variables represent
the two treatments for each subject, say *PLACEBO* for the length of time to
fall asleep when the placebo is administered and *NEWTREAT* for the length
of time to fall asleep when the drug is administered. Your paired data
might look like this:

PLACEBO	NEWTREAT
2.4	1.0
1.8	4.6

This arrangement differs from a design using independent groups. You still have two variables for each case, but one variable contains the response and the other identifies the group to which each case belongs. Suppose you have two groups of subjects: one received the placebo and the other received the new treatment. The variable you measured might be called *TIME*, representing the length of time it took for the subject to fall asleep. You would also have a variable such as *GROUP*, which might be coded 1 if the subject received the placebo and 2 if the subject received the new treatment. Each person is represented only once in the file, because each received either the drug or the placebo, not both. The data for the independent groups design might look like this:

GROUP	TIME
1	2.4
2	1.0
1	1.8
2	4.6

? *Why do you have to set up the file differently just because your subjects are paired? Couldn't the people who designed SPSS/PC+ have let you use the same setup either way?* Actually, the way it's done makes sense. In a paired design, you have to know for each individual:

1 Which group the individual is in.

2 The other member of the pair.

3 The value of the variable or score you're comparing.

If you set up a file with each individual as a separate case, you'd need three variables to keep track of these things. By setting up a file with cases representing the pairs, you need half as many cases, and you need only two variables. There's no magic here. In a file of pairs, the two variable names tell you which value goes with which "group," and they're paired with one another simply by being part of the same case. That's just a better way of representing the same information.   ■■■

ANALYZING PAIRED DESIGNS

When you have paired data, you test hypotheses basically in the same way as when you have two independent groups. The only thing that changes is how you compute the *t* statistic. For each pair, you find the difference between the two values. Then you analyze these differences.

The Paired t Test

The General Social Survey contains information about years of education for both the person interviewed and his or her spouse. Let's test the null hypothesis that there is no difference in years of education between husbands and wives. This is a paired-samples design, since we have pairs of husbands and wives. To run a paired *t* test using this data file, we have to set up the *HUSED* and *WIFED* variables ourselves, since sometimes the husband was the respondent and sometimes he was the spouse. It wouldn't make a lot of sense to test respondent's education versus spouse's education; one of the two (husband or wife) was chosen randomly to be the respondent.

The SPSS/PC+ commands are:

```
get file 'gss.sys'.
* Now set up HUSED and WIFED according to sex of respondent.
if (sex = 1) hused = educ.
if (sex = 1) wifed = speduc.
if (sex = 2) wifed = educ.
if (sex = 2) hused = speduc.
variable labels hused "Husband's education"
 wifed "Wife's education".
t-test pairs hused wifed.
```

The GET command retrieves the file gss.sys. The second command (beginning with an asterisk) is a **comment.** The asterisk is followed by any explanation you want; it doesn't affect the analysis at all. (You do have to terminate the comment with a period.) The IF commands set up the *HUSED* and *WIFED* variables. The PAIRS subcommand on T-TEST tells SPSS/PC+ that you have a paired design. The names of the two variables that contain the information for each pair follow the keyword PAIRS.

Figure 18.1 Paired t test for years of education

```
         - - - t-tests for paired samples - - -

                   Number of        2-tail
     Variable        pairs   Corr   Sig      Mean     SD    SE of Mean
    -------------------------------------------------------------------
     HUSED                                  12.5292   3.417    .119
                       822     .641  .000
     WIFED                                  12.4197   2.679    .093


            Paired Differences
     Mean       SD     SE of Mean  |   t-value   df  2-tail Sig
    ----------------------------------------------------------------
      .1095    2.669      .093      |    1.18    821    .240
    95% CI (-.073, .292)
```

Look at Figure 18.1, which shows the output from this *t* test. You can see that the husbands had an average of 12.53 years of education while the wives had an average of 12.42. On the average, these husbands had about 0.11 more years of education than their mates. This is shown in the column labeled *Paired Differences Mean*. The standard deviation of the 822 differences is 2.669. The standard error of the mean difference is 0.093. The *t* value, printed in the last set of columns, is obtained by dividing the difference between the two means by its standard error: 0.1095 divided by 0.093 equals 1.18. The degrees of freedom used in calculating the observed significance level are just the number of *pairs* minus one.

In this example, you see that the probability of obtaining a difference as large as 0.1095 in a sample of 822 pairs from a population in which there was no difference is 0.240. Since this probability, the observed significance level, is fairly large, you don't have enough evidence to reject the null hypothesis.

The Confidence Interval for a Difference

As explained in the last few chapters, it's a good idea to calculate confidence intervals for means and differences of means. Confidence intervals give you an idea of the range of values within which the population value may fall. The 95% confidence interval for the average difference in years of education between husbands and wives is from –0.73 to +0.292.

The confidence interval includes 0. This tells you the same thing that the hypothesis test did. Namely, it's not unlikely that the true value for the difference is zero. There's a close relationship between hypothesis tests and confidence intervals:

- If you take any value within a 95% confidence interval and test the null hypothesis that it is the population value, you will not reject the null hypothesis. Your observed significance level will be greater than 0.05.

- If a value is outside of the 95% confidence interval, then your hypothesis test will find it to be an unlikely value as well. You will reject the null hypothesis that it's likely to be the population value. The observed significance level will be less than 0.05.

When you don't know the population standard deviation and your sample sizes are small (less than 30), you must use a value from the *t* distribution instead of just multiplying the standard error by 2 to get the confidence interval.

Assumptions

Remember that in the independent-samples t test output, there were two different tests. You used the pooled-variance test when it was reasonable to assume that the variances were the same for the two groups. You used the separate-variance test when you had reason to doubt that the groups had the same variances.

For the paired t test, you don't have to make any assumptions about the variances of the original variables. For each pair, you compute the difference between the husband's and wife's education. It doesn't matter what the standard deviations of the original variables are, because you analyze just the differences.

For the paired-samples t test, just as for the independent-samples t test, it's essential for the observations to be a random sample from the population. It's also a good idea to look at the distribution of the differences. If the distribution looks more or less normal, you don't have to worry about anything. However, if the sample size is small and the distribution is very far from normal, the t test may not be a good way to test the hypothesis you're interested in.

Remember, if the variables are normal, their means and the differences of their means will be normally distributed. If the variables are not normal, you have to rely on the Central Limit Theorem, and that may require larger samples. If you have a small sample *and* the distribution of the variables isn't normal, you may have to use a **nonparametric test**. That's a type of test that doesn't require assumptions about the form of the distribution. SPSS/PC+ provides several nonparametric tests; they're discussed in Appendix E.

Figure 18.2 is a histogram of the differences between husbands' and wives' average years of education. The distribution looks fairly symmetric, but it has a very large peak at 0. Why? Most men and women in the sample were high-school graduates. It's quite likely that their spouses were high-school graduates as well. There were also a lot of couples in which both the husband and the wife were college graduates. So there were a *lot* of cases in which the years of education matched perfectly. Since the sample size is large and the distribution differs from normal only in having a very high peak, you can be pretty confident that the distribution of sample means is approximately normal.

Figure 18.2 Histogram for differences in education

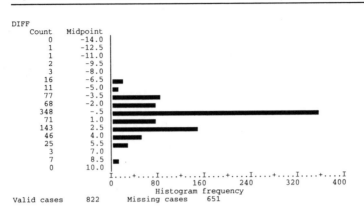

```
DIFF
    Count   Midpoint
        0    -14.0
        1    -12.5
        1    -11.0
        2     -9.5
        3     -8.0
       16     -6.5
       11     -5.0
       77     -3.5
       68     -2.0
      348      -.5
       71      1.0
      143      2.5
       46      4.0
       25      5.5
        3      7.0
        7      8.5
        0     10.0
              I....+....I....+....I....+....I....+....I....+....I
              0       80      160      240      320      400
                        Histogram frequency
Valid cases     822    Missing cases    651
```

Using EXAMINE to Test for Normality

Although a histogram gives you a good idea about the distribution of a variable, you should be familiar with some additional statistical techniques that are used to test whether a sample comes from a normal population. Testing for normality is an important consideration, since the normal distribution is very important for statistical inference. Techniques for checking on the normality assumption are available in the EXAMINE procedure.

You can use a normal probability plot instead of, or in addition to, a histogram to assess normality. A normal probability plot is constructed in such a way that, if the sample is from a normal population, the points will fall more or less on a straight line.

Look at Figure 18.3, which is a normal probability plot of a sample of 200 points from a normal distribution. Note how the points cluster around a straight line. You can also plot the distances between the observed points and a straight line. This is called a detrended normal probability plot and is shown in Figure 18.4. If your sample is from a normal population, the points should cluster around a horizontal line through 0. That is, you shouldn't see a pattern to the points. If you see a striking pattern, your sample is probably not from a normal distribution.

Figure 18.3 Normal probability plot

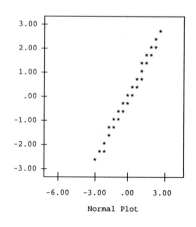

Figure 18.4 Detrended normal plot

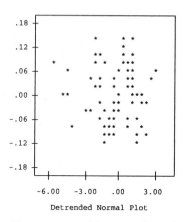

To get some idea of what these plots look like when the data are not from a normal population, look at Figure 18.5. In this case the sample came from a uniform distribution. (Remember, a uniform distribution is one in which all data values are equally likely.) You see that the points in the first plot do not fall on a straight line. Similarly, in the detrended normal plot, the points don't haphazardly fall around a horizontal line through zero. That's how you can tell that the sample is probably not from a normal distribution.

Figure 18.5 Normal plots for a uniform distribution

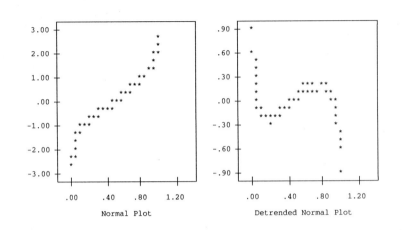

There are also statistical tests that can be used to test the null hypothesis that data come from a normal population. You can calculate two of these tests, the Shapiro-Wilks and the Lilliefors, using the EXAMINE procedure. (The Shapiro-Wilks test is only computed if the sample size is less than 50.) These tests actually tell you how often you'd expect to see a sample as "non-normal" as yours if, in fact, it's coming from a normal distribution. If this observed sigificance level is small, you can reject the hypothesis that the sample is from a normal distribution.

The Distribution of Age Differences

In Figure 18.2, you saw that the distribution of differences in years of education between husbands and wives doesn't appear to be normal. We weren't bothered by this, since the distribution is not too far from normal and we have a large sample size. We're quite confident that the distribution of means is normal. Let's see what the plots and statistics from EXAMINE would look like for the education differences.

```
compute diff = hused - wifed.
examine diff /plot npplot.
```

Figure 18.6 Normal and detrended probability plots for DIFF

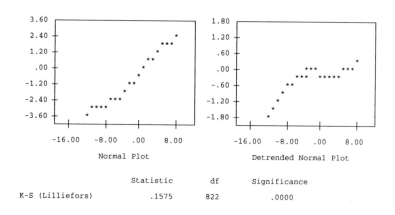

	Statistic	df	Significance
K-S (Lilliefors)	.1575	822	.0000

You can see in the normal probability plot in Figure 18.6 that the points don't fall on a straight line. The pattern in the detrended normal probability plot is certainly not random. Looking at the test for normality, you see a very small observed significance level, less than 0.00005. All of this supports what we already know: the distribution of the differences is probably not normal.

[?] *Should I not use the* t *test if the significance level for the normality tests is small?* If you have a large sample size, even small differences from normality will result in a small observed significance level for the tests of normality. This is just another example of the fact that when samples are large, even small differences may be statistically significant, though not necessarily important. So if your sample is large, and the distribution of values is somewhat normal, you don't have to worry about the fact that your data are not exactly normal. The *t* test doesn't by any means require exact normality. ■■■

Education and Excitement

Although there is no overall difference in the average years of education for husbands and wives, let's see if this is true both for people who find life exciting and for those who find life routine or dull. Perhaps unexcited people differ from their spouses in some important way.

Since men and women may differ in their responses, we'll take that into consideration as well. Let's first look at men who classify their lives as exciting and see how they compare in education to their wives. Figure 18.7 shows a test of the hypothesis that men who find life exciting have the same average number of years of education as their wives. The following commands produced the test:

```
select if (life = 1 and sex = 1).
t-test pairs wifed hused.
```

The average years of education for the husbands was 13.14, while for their wives it was 12.65. On the average, men who characterized their lives as exciting had about half a year of education more than their wives. The observed significance level for the test of the hypothesis that there is no difference is 0.012. We can reject the null hypothesis that men who find life exciting have the same average level of education as their wives. It looks as if these men are married to women with somewhat less education, although the difference is not very large.

Figure 18.7 Paired t test for men excited by life

```
            - - - t-tests for paired samples - - -

                    Number of         2-tail
    Variable          pairs    Corr   Sig      Mean      SD      SE of Mean

    WIFED  Wife's education               12.6484    2.767       .205
                         182      .704   .000
    HUSED  Husband's education            13.1429    3.693       .274


            Paired Differences
    Mean        SD      SE of Mean  |   t-value    df   2-tail Sig
    -.4945     2.627       .195     |    -2.54     181     .012
    95% CI (-.879, -.110)
```

Let's see if the same holds true for men who are not excited by life. These results are shown in Figure 18.8, and they were produced by the following commands:

```
get file 'gss.sys'.
select if (life ge 2 and sex = 1).
*  Simplify calculation, since we selected men only.
compute hused = educ.
compute wifed = speduc.
variable labels hused "Husband's education"
   wifed "Wife's education".
t-test pairs wifed hused.
```

The husbands had an average of 12.00 years of education. The wives had an average of 12.11 years of education. The observed significance level associated with this difference is 0.602, so we don't reject the null hypothesis that men who find life routine or dull have the same average level of education as their wives.

Figure 18.8 Paired t test for men not excited by life

```
              - - - t-tests for paired samples - - -

                   Number of          2-tail
   Variable          pairs    Corr    Sig       Mean      SD     SE of Mean

   WIFED  Wife's education                      12.1098   2.792    .212
                        173     .605   .000
   HUSED  Husband's education                   12.0000   3.331    .253


            Paired Differences
    Mean        SD      SE of Mean  |    t-value    df   2-tail Sig
                                    |
    .1098      2.763      .210      |     .52      172     .602
   95% CI (-.305, .525)            |
```

Looking at the means in the previous analyses, you see what you've seen before. The biggest difference between any of the means is the actual years of education of married men who found life exciting compared to those who didn't. Married men who found life exciting had an average of 13.14 years of education, while married men who found life unexciting had an average of 12.00.

SIGNIFICANCE VERSUS IMPORTANCE

What does it mean if you reject the null hypothesis that two population means are equal? Does it mean that there's an important difference between the two groups? Not necessarily. Whether a difference of half a year of education between two groups is found to be statistically significant or not depends on several factors. It depends on the variability in the two groups, and it depends on the sample sizes.

A difference can be statistically significant with a sample size of 100, while the same difference would not be significant with a sample size of 50. The difference between the two sample means is the same, half a year, but its statistical interpretation differs. For large sample sizes, small differences between groups may be statistically significant, while for small sample sizes, even large differences may not be.

What can you make of this? Finding that a difference is *statistically significant* does not mean that the difference is *large*, nor does it mean that the difference is *important* from a research point of view.

For sufficiently large sample sizes, you might find that a difference of even a month in education between excited men and unexcited men is statistically significant. That doesn't mean that the difference is of any practical importance. We all know that on the average, an extra month of education won't do much for you. It's unlikely to alter your perception of the world. It doesn't explain why some people find life exciting and others don't.

On the other hand, if the sample sizes in the two groups are small, even a difference of four years of education may not appear to be statistically significant. In this case, you don't want to rule out education as an important variable. Instead, you must worry about the fact that with small sample sizes you can miss important differences. You must allow yourself the possibility that there might be a big difference, because your ability to find it is poor.

(The probability of detecting a difference of a particular magnitude when it exists is called the **power** of a test. You can estimate in advance how big a sample you need to detect a difference that you consider really important. Discussion of how that's done is a little beyond this book.)

In summary, remember that even though two groups are statistically different, their difference is not necessarily of practical importance. Evaluate the difference on its own merits.

MORE ABOUT PAIRED T TESTS

You can use T-TEST to compare two means from:

- Independent groups, as discussed in Chapter 17.
- Paired data, as discussed in this chapter.

A typical application of a paired-samples test is the comparison of scores before and after an experimental procedure. To obtain a paired-samples *t* test, use the PAIRS subcommand to indicate the two variables being compared, as in:

```
t-test pairs before after.
```

More than Two Variables

If you list more than two variables on the PAIRS subcommand, each variable is compared with every other variable. For example, if you specify

```
t-test pairs son dad mom.
```

the following are compared: *SON* with *DAD*, *SON* with *MOM*, and *DAD* with *MOM*.

If you have several variables that you've measured at two times, for example before and after a treatment, you can use the keyword WITH and the (PAIRED) keyword to compare each variable before WITH with the corresponding variable after WITH. The command

```
t-test pairs wgt1 bp1 anxiety1
   with wgt2 bp2 anxiety2 (paired).
```

compares *WGT1* with *WGT2*, *BP1* with *BP2*, and *ANXIETY1* with *ANXIETY2*. If you use WITH without (PAIRED), each variable before WITH is compared with each variable after WITH. In the previous example, this would produce nine comparisons in all.

WHAT'S NEXT?

In this chapter and in Chapter 17, we discussed ways to test the null hypothesis that two population means are equal. In the next chapter, we'll look at variables that have a limited number of categories, and we'll consider how to test whether the two variables are independent.

Summary

Based on the means observed in two related samples, how can you test the null hypothesis that in the population there is no difference between the means?

In a paired design, the same subject is observed under two conditions, or data are obtained from a pair of subjects that are matched on some basis.

Paired designs help to make the two groups being compared more similar. Some of the differences between subjects are eliminated.

If you observe the same subject under two conditions, you must make sure that the effect of one treatment has worn off before the other one is given.

In your data file, you must record the values for both members of a pair in the same case.

You can compare two related means using a paired-sample *t* test.

A statistically significant difference need not be large or important.

EXERCISES

Syntax

1 You've done a study in which you measured learning time in rats before and after administration of a memory improvement drug. Each of the rats ran through the maze twice: before and after the drug was administered. How would you arrange your data in the file? What values would you record for each case?

a. Write the DATA LIST command for your file.

b. Write the appropriate T-TEST command for the test of the hypothesis that there is no difference in learning times.

2 Suppose that instead of studying the same rats under two conditions, you had two groups of rats. One received the agent and the other did not. How would you arrange your data file? How does this arrangement differ from that in question 1? Write the appropriate T-TEST command to test the null hypothesis that the new agent has no effect.

3 To perform a paired *t* test you run the command

```
t-test  variables before after.
```

and receive the following error message:

```
ERROR   11821
The VARIABLES subcommand must follow a GROUPS subcommand.
This command not executed.
```

Identify and correct the problem.

4 Where necessary, correct the following commands:

a. `ttest groups  before after.`

b. `ttest pairs   before.`

c. `t-test groups  sex(0,1) / pairs  before after.`

Statistical Concepts

1 For the following experimental designs, indicate whether an independent-samples or paired-samples *t* test is appropriate:

a. Weight is obtained for each subject before and after Dr. Nogani's new treatment. The hypothesis to be tested is that the treatment has no effect on weight loss.

b. The Jenkins Activity Survey is administered to 20 couples. The hypothesis to be tested is that husbands' and wives' scores do not differ.

c. Elephants are randomly selected from a jungle. Trunkgro1 is administered to one group of elephants and Trunkgro2 to the other. The hypothesis to be tested is that both agents are equally effective in promoting trunk growth.

d. Subjects are asked their height and then a measurement of height is obtained. The hypothesis to be tested is that self-reported and actual heights do not differ.

e. Two sleeping pills (Drugs A and B) are given to a sample of insomniacs. The subjects take Drug A during the first week of the study and Drug B during the second week. The total amount of time before falling asleep is recorded for each subject for each week.

2 Assume that the following output is obtained from the study of the memory drug (see question 1 in Syntax exercises):

```
        - - - t-tests for paired samples - - -

                      Number of          2-tail
Variable                pairs    Corr    Sig       Mean      SD     SE of Mean

BEFORE  Learning time without memory d             12.4986   6.103     .323
                        356      .867   .000
AFTER   Learning time with memory drug             12.6488   6.666     .353
```

```
         Paired Differences
Mean        SD        SE of Mean    |    t-value    df    2-tail Sig
                                    |
 -.1502     3.332       .177        |     -.85      355      .396
95% CI (-.498, .197)
```

a. State your null hypothesis.

b. State the alternate hypothesis.

c. What can you conclude on the basis of the t test?

d. Interpret the observed significance level.

3 For the memory problem, when would you be justified in doing a one-tailed t test instead of a two-tailed t test?

4 How can you calculate the one-tailed observed significance level based on the two-tailed level printed on the output?

5 An investigator wishes to test the hypothesis that children who drink orange juice before class will be more attentive than children who drink milk. He selects a classroom of children and obtains an alphabetic list of the students. He assigns the first child to orange juice therapy, the next to milk therapy, and so on down the list. He wants to analyze the experiment using the paired t test, since he has formed pairs of children based on the alphabetic list. Suggest to him how he might analyze his data. Do you think this is a paired experiment? If not, give an example of a paired design for this question.

6 Studies sometimes use twins who have been raised separately in order to investigate questions like, "What are the roles of parental influence and genetic heritage on children's intellectual development?" Discuss the advantages and disadvantages that you see in using twins for studies of this nature.

7 Discuss any problems you see in the following experiments:

a. Anxiety often affects performance on tests. A psychologist has formulated a new method for reducing stress during statistics exams. To evaluate the new method he tests each of 50 students under two conditions. He gives each student the final exam before administration of the stress reduction training, and then again after the training. He wishes to compare the two scores.

b. A market researcher wishes to study consumer preferences for five brands of pizza. He invites 250 people to a "pizza party." Each person is instructed to make sure that throughout the course of the evening he or she eats a piece of all five brands. As they are leaving, each participant fills out a questionnaire evaluating the five brands of pizza.

c. A drug company is interested in studying the effectiveness of a new drug for headache relief. They advertise in the newspaper for "headache sufferers" who wish to participate in their study. At the beginning of the study they question each participant about the frequency and duration of headaches. Then they send the sufferers home with a week's supply of the new medicine. Upon returning a week later, each participant is again asked the same questions about headaches.

d. You wish to compare two methods for weight reduction. You recruit 123 people who are interested in losing weight. You instruct everyone to use the first method until they have lost ten pounds, and then the second method until they have lost ten more. You then compare the length of time it takes to lose the first 10 pounds to the length of time it takes to lose the next 10 pounds.

Data Analysis

Use the gss.sys system file to answer the following questions.

1 Test the null hypothesis that the average years of education are the same for a person's mother and father. Summarize your results.

2 Using COMPUTE, calculate a new variable that is the difference between mother's and father's years of education. Using the FREQUENCIES procedure, calculate descriptive statistics for the difference variable. How can you calculate the paired t test based on the FREQUENCIES output?

3 Test the null hypothesis that there is no difference between the average years of education for respondents in the survey and their fathers. Write a paragraph summarizing your results.

19 Testing Hypotheses about Independence

How can you test the null hypothesis that two percentages are equal in the population? How can you test the null hypothesis that two variables are independent?

- What are observed and expected frequencies, and how are they calculated?

- What is the chi-square statistic, and how is it used to compare two proportions?

- What does it mean to say that two variables are independent?

- What are the degrees of freedom of a crosstabulation?

- How can you use the chi-square test to test the null hypothesis that two variables are independent?

- How does sample size affect the value of the chi-square test for independence?

I n the previous chapters, you saw how to test hypotheses about two population means. This works fine for variables such as age, education, and income, since the mean is a good descriptive measure for them. But how about variables that aren't measured on an interval or ratio scale? If you want to test whether people's marital status or health or belief in an afterlife is related to whether or not they perceive life as exciting, you can't use a *t* test. The mean is not an appropriate summary measure for variables like these. In fact, anytime you're using a variable that is a nominal, calculating its mean doesn't make sense, and therefore performing a *t* test doesn't make sense. For example, it's not reasonable to test whether the mean marital status is the same for those who find life exciting and those who don't. What's a "mean" marital status?

All is not lost. To deal with variables like these, you can calculate chi-square tests. That's what this chapter is all about.

CROSSTABULATION AGAIN

In Chapter 10, we saw that 50.3% of all the men and 44.4% of all the women in the General Social Survey sample described life as exciting. Is this sufficient evidence for us to believe that the percentages of men and women who find life exciting differ in the population? Or can the observed difference just be attributed to variability among samples?

Figure 19.1 is a table from the CROSSTABS procedure. It was produced by the following commands:

```
get file 'gss.sys'.
* Combine Pretty routine (3) and Dull (2) into
single category.
recode life (3 = 2).
value labels life 1 'Excited' 2 'Not excited'.
crosstabs life by sex /cells count column.
```

The table tells us how many men and how many women in the sample found life exciting and how many did not. It contains column percentages, showing that 50.3% of all the men and 44.4% of all the women found life exciting. The row totals tell us that overall, 46.8% of the sample found life exciting. How can we use these numbers to test whether there are differences in the population between men's and women's outlooks?

Figure 19.1 Crosstabulation of SEX and LIFE

```
LIFE  Is life exciting or dull?  by  SEX  Respondent's sex

                      SEX           Page 1 of 1
              Count
              Col Pct |Male    Female
                      |                Row
                      |   1       2    Total
   LIFE         ──────┼────────────────
                  1   |  300     384    684
        Excited       | 50.3    44.4   46.8

                  2   |  296     481    777
    Not excited       | 49.7    55.6   53.2

              Column     596     865   1461
               Total    40.8    59.2  100.0

Number of Missing Observations:  12
```

First of all, let's consider the hypotheses:

- The null hypothesis is that men and women are equally likely to find life exciting.

- The alternative hypothesis is that they are *not* equally likely to find life exciting.

Another way of phrasing the null hypothesis is to say that excitement and sex are **independent,** meaning there's no relationship between a person's sex and whether the person finds life exciting. We'll talk more about independence later.

THE NULL HYPOTHESIS FOR A CROSSTABULATION

As with the *t* test, we must first figure out what results to expect if the null hypothesis is true. In Chapter 17, we followed these steps:

1 Assume that the null hypothesis is true.

2 Figure out what the distribution of means would look like on the basis of that assumption.

3 Estimate how often we'd expect to see a difference as large as the one observed if the null hypothesis is true.

Would we expect similar numbers of men and women in the sample to find life exciting if the null hypothesis is true? No, because there were different numbers of men and women in the sample. Instead, we'd expect that similar *percentages* of men and women would find life exciting, and similar *percentages* of both sexes would find life unexciting.

We need estimates of what these percentages might be. The only information we have is from the sample. Reasonable estimates based on the null hypothesis are the percentage of people in the sample who found life exciting and the percentage who did not. These are the row percentages given in the right margin of Figure 19.1. If the null hypothesis is true, we'd expect that 46.8% of the men and 46.8% of the women would have said that they find life exciting. Similarly, we'd expect that 53.2% of both the men and the women would have described life as unexciting.

Expected Frequencies

Let's convert these percentages to the actual number of cases we expect to find in each of the cells of the table if the null hypothesis is true. In the sample, there were 596 men, so we'd expect

$$596 \times 46.8\% = 279 \text{ men}$$

to find life exciting. The number who find life routine or dull should be

$$596 \times 53.2\% = 317 \text{ men}$$

Similarly, if the null hypothesis is true, we'd expect

$$865 \times 46.8\% = 405 \text{ women}$$

to find life exciting, and we'd expect the remaining 460 to find life unexciting. Notice that the expected frequencies for men add up to the total number of men in the sample, and the expected frequencies for women add up to the total number of women. The expected frequencies for excited people also add up to the total number of excited people, and the expected frequencies for the unexcited add up to the number of unexcited people.

Comparing Observed and Expected Frequencies

Now we must compare the observed number of cases in each of the cells to the number that would be expected if the null hypothesis is true. These two sets of numbers are called the **observed frequencies** and the **expected frequencies**. Based on differences between the observed and expected frequencies, we'll be able to estimate the likelihood of seeing a difference at least as large as the one observed in the sample if the null hypothesis is true. As in the *t* test, we know that even if there's no difference between the sexes in the population, the sample percentages won't be exactly equal. We expect to see variability from sample to sample.

THE CHI-SQUARE STATISTIC

When comparing two sample means, you use the t distribution to figure how likely the observed difference between the means would be if the null hypothesis is true. You use a similar procedure with crosstabulations.

When you want to evaluate the discrepancy between a set of observed frequencies and a set of expected frequencies, you use the **chi-square statistic**. It's simple to compute. For each cell,

1 Find the difference between the observed frequency and the expected frequency.

2 Square this difference.

3 Then divide the squared difference by the expected frequency.

Repeat this three-step procedure for each of the cells in your table. Then add up all of these numbers. The sum is the Pearson chi-square statistic for the table.

Think of our current example. Figure 19.2 shows a table that contains in each cell the observed frequency, the expected frequency, and the difference between the two. (The directory in the upper left-hand corner always explains the numbers in a table.) Each difference between the observed and expected frequency is called a **residual**, and it is obtained in step 1 in the above procedure. Look at the first cell. It shows that 300 men found life exciting. If the null hypothesis is true, we'd expect 279 men in this cell. The residual, 21, is the difference between these two numbers. A residual with a positive sign indicates that more cases were observed than are expected if the null hypothesis is true. A negative residual indicates that fewer cases were observed than expected.

Figure 19.2 Expected frequencies and residuals

```
LIFE   Is life exciting or dull?  by  SEX  Respondent's sex

                          SEX              Page 1 of 1
                Count
                Exp Val  Male    Female
                Residual                   Row
                           1        2      Total
    LIFE        ─────────
                   1      300      384      684
       Excited          279.0    405.0     46.8%
                         21.0    -21.0

                   2      296      481      777
    Not excited          317.0    460.0     53.2%
                        -21.0     21.0

                Column   596      865      1461
                Total    40.8%    59.2%    100.0%

Number of Missing Observations:  12
```

This is how you calculate the chi-square statistic for the table:

1 For each cell, subtract the expected frequency from the observed frequency. The differences are the residuals: 21, –21, –21, and 21. (Don't be distracted by the fact that these numbers are all plus or minus the same value. This always happens when both variables have just two categories, but not when either variable has more than two.)

2 Square the differences. Each of the squared residuals equals 441.

3 Divide by the expected frequencies. For cell 1, 441 divided by 279 equals 1.58. For cell 2, 441 divided by 405 equals 1.09. For cell 3, 441 divided by 317 equals 1.39. For cell 4, 441 divided by 460 equals 0.96.

4 Now add up the parts: 1.58 + 1.09 + 1.39 + 0.96 = 5.0.

If in the population there's no difference between men's and women's descriptions of life, the observed and expected frequencies should be fairly close. When this is true, the chi-square statistic is not very large. On the other hand, if the discrepancies between the observed and expected frequencies are big, the chi-square statistic will also be big. In general, large chi-square values occur when the sample results differ from those predicted by the null hypothesis.

Just as with the t statistic, you can calculate how often you would obtain a value of the chi-square statistic at least as large as the one you observed for your table if the null hypothesis is true. If the null hypothesis is true, the observed significance level for the chi-square statistic can be obtained from the **chi-square distribution**. You can use the chi-square distribution to find out how often you'd expect to observe various values of the chi-square statistic in samples when the null hypothesis is true.

USING SPSS/PC+ TO CALCULATE CHI-SQUARE

To calculate the chi-square statistic in SPSS/PC+, run the following command:

```
crosstabs life by sex
 /cells count expected resid
  /statistics chisq.
```

The EXPECTED and RESID keywords on the CELLS subcommand tell SPSS/PC+ to calculate the expected cell frequencies and the residuals. The keyword CHISQ on the STATISTICS subcommand tells SPSS/PC+ to compute the chi-square test. You can request several statistics on the STATISTICS subcommand. The others are discussed in Chapter 21. At the end of that chapter is a list of all the statistics available in CROSSTABS.

Results of the Test

The results are shown in Figure 19.3. SPSS/PC+ prints two versions of the chi-square statistic, which you can see below the crosstabulation. The one labeled *Pearson* equals 5.005. (We'll consider the other version below.) The observed significance level for a chi-square of 5.005 for a table that has two rows and two columns is 0.025. A discrepancy this large between the observed and expected frequencies would occur only 2.5% of the time if, in the population, men and women are equally excited with their lives. Since the observed significance level is quite small, we reject the null hypothesis that men and women find life equally exciting.

Figure 19.3 A chi-square test

```
LIFE   Is life exciting or dull?   by  SEX   Respondent's sex

                   SEX              Page 1 of 1
            Count
            Exp Val |Male    Female
            Residual|                  Row
                    |   1   |   2   | Total
LIFE        --------
              1     |  300  |  384  |  684
  Excited           | 279.0 | 405.0 | 46.8%
                    |  21.0 | -21.0 |
                    --------
              2     |  296  |  481  |  777
  Not excited       | 317.0 | 460.0 | 53.2%
                    | -21.0 |  21.0 |
                    --------
            Column     596     865    1461
            Total     40.8%   59.2%  100.0%

        Chi-Square            Value      DF    Significance
    --------------------    ----------  ----  ------------

    Pearson                   5.00467     1       .02528
    Continuity Correction     4.76884     1       .02898
    Likelihood Ratio          5.00327     1       .02530
    Mantel-Haenszel test for  5.00124     1       .02533
        linear association

    Minimum Expected Frequency -  279.031

    Number of Missing Observations:  12
```

If some of the *expected* frequencies in a table are less than 5, the observed significance level based on the chi-square distribution may not be correct. On the output, the smallest expected frequency for the table is printed after the statistics. In this example, the minimum expected frequency is 279, so you have nothing to worry about. If there are cells with expected frequencies less than 5, the number and percent of such cells is also displayed. In general, you should not use the chi-square test if more than 20% of the cells have expected values less than 5. You should also make sure that none of the expected values are less than 1.

If any of the expected values in a table with just two rows and two columns is less than 5, SPSS/PC+ automatically performs an additional test, called **Fisher's exact test**. Fisher's exact test evaluates the same hypothesis as the chi-square test, and it's suitable for tables having two rows and two columns with small expected frequencies.

Continuity Correction

For a table with two rows and two columns, an adjustment to the chi-square statistic is sometimes made. The adjustment.is intended to improve the estimate of the observed significance level. It's called the **continuity correction.** As shown in Figure 19.3, the continuity corrected chi-square for this table is 4.769. Statisticians aren't in agreement as to whether this correction is really necessary. Continuity correction always makes the observed chi-square value smaller. (The last two statistics in the column labeled *Chi-Square* are beyond the scope of this book.)

RELATIONSHIPS BETWEEN VARIABLES

The chi-square test helps us decide whether two variables are related in the population. In the previous examples, the two variables were *LIFE* (*Excited* versus *Not excited*) and *SEX* (*Male* versus *Female*). What do we mean when we say that the two variables forming the rows and columns of a crosstabulation are related?

Let's first consider what it means to say that variables are *not* related. Sex is not related to voting preference if men and women have the same preferences among the candidates. Hair color is not related to having fun if the same percentage of people with each hair color have fun. If these variables are unrelated, then knowing your hair color tells me nothing about the likelihood of your having fun, and knowing that you're enjoying yourself tells me nothing about your hair color. When this is true, hair color and fun are described as statistically *independent,* which is a statistical way of saying *unrelated.*

Two values are **independent** whenever knowing the value of one variable tells you nothing about the value of the other variable. If you toss a die while your friend flips a coin, getting a 1 on the die has no effect on whether the coin comes up heads or tails. The two events are completely unrelated, or independent.

What Is a Relationship?

It is commonly believed that the number of hours you study for a class is related to your final grade. Or that your eating habits are related to your weight. Or that your anxiety level is related to your ability to perform well on a test. In all of these situations, the word *related* means that the two variables have something in common. They are in some way connected to each other. Up to a point, the more hours you study, the better your grade should be. The more between-meal snacks and high-calorie foods you consume, the heavier you should be. Anxiety and performance are thought to be related in a more complex way. Moderate anxiety levels can be helpful for doing well on an exam. Very severe anxiety—or no anxiety at all—can get in the way.

When two variables are related, knowing the value of one variable is helpful in predicting the value of the other variable. If you tell me that you got an *A* on the statistics exam, I would predict that you studied a lot. I may well be wrong; perhaps you understand statistics without much effort at all. But on the average, I expect that students who studied hard did well, and students who did well studied hard. (Those two statements are not the same. Think of how either one of them could be true and the other one false.)

The existence of a relationship between two variables does *not* mean that one causes the other. A famous study found that the number of storks in an area was related to the local birth rate. Areas with many storks had a high birth rate, while areas with few storks had a lower birth rate. Well, storks don't bring babies. It turns out that storks live mostly in rural areas and that rural areas have higher birth rates than the storkless urban areas.

We'll discuss this more in Chapter 23.

Testing Independence

So how do we test whether two variables are independent? We've already done it! The chi-square test we used to see whether men and women find life equally exciting can also be used to test whether sex is independent of perception of life. That's because the expected values we used in calculating the chi-square are the values that would be expected if the two variables are independent.

CHI-SQUARE IN LARGER TABLES

The procedure described for the previous example can be extended to test whether any two variables in a crosstabulation are independent. For example, you can test whether hair color is related to education, or whether the size of the car people drive is related to belief in life after death, or whether health is related to perception of life as exciting. Look at Figure 19.4, a crosstabulation of health and perception of life. It was produced by these commands:

```
get file 'gss.sys'.
crosstabs life by health
   /cells count column.
```

From the column percentages, you can see that almost 58% of the people who claimed to be in excellent health found life exciting, 46% of those in good health, 37% of those in fair health, and only 23% of those in poor health. These percentages tell us that in the sample, there is a relationship between health and finding life exciting.

Figure 19.4 Health and excitement with life

```
LIFE   Is life exciting or dull?  by  HEALTH  Condition of health

                      HEALTH                          Page 1 of 1
             Count
             Col Pct |Excellen Good     Fair    Poor
                     |t                                  Row
                     |   1       2       3       4     Total
LIFE
               1     |   249     320     95      16      680
     Exciting        |  57.6    46.0    37.3    23.2    46.9

               2     |   175     350     137     36      698
 Pretty routine      |  40.5    50.4    53.7    52.2    48.1

               3     |    8       25      23      17      73
     Dull            |   1.9     3.6     9.0    24.6     5.0

            Column       432     695     255     69     1451
            Total       29.8    47.9    17.6     4.8    100.0

Number of Missing Observations:  22
```

As before, however, our primary interest is in the population that the sample represents. Do we have sufficient evidence to suggest that there's a relationship between the two variables—health and excitement—in the population? How often would you expect to see differences as large as the ones observed in the sample if the two variables aren't related in the population (that is, if the two variables are independent)?

Chi-Square Test of a Relationship

We'll use the chi-square statistic to compare the observed frequencies to those that would be expected if the two variables are independent.

First, let's consider how to calculate the expected frequencies. Look at Figure 19.4 again. From the row totals (at the right-hand side of the table), you see that 46.9% of the sample found life exciting, 48.1% found life routine, and 5.0% found life dull. If health and excitement are independent, you'd expect that the same percentages of people in each health category would have found life exciting, routine, or dull. That's what it means for variables to be independent.

Thus, 46.9% of the 432 people in excellent health should have found life exciting, 48.1% should have found it routine, and 5% should have found it dull. Exactly the same should have been true for the people in the other health categories.

Expected Frequencies and Chi-Square

For the chi-square test, we must convert the expected percentages to actual numbers. This is simple enough. Just multiply the expected percentages by the number of people in each of the categories. There were 432 people in excellent health, so we would expect 46.9% of 432, or 202.5, to be excited by life. In exactly the same way, we would expect 48.1% of 432, or 207.8, to find life routine, and we would expect 5% of 432, or 21.7, to find life dull. You calculate the chi-square statistic exactly as before. For each cell:

1 Compute the difference between the observed number of cases and the number expected if the two variables are independent.

2 Square the difference.

3 Divide by the expected count.

Then add up the results of this process for all the cells.

You can have SPSS/PC+ do these calculations by running the following command:

```
crosstabs life by health
  /cells count expected resid /statistics chisq.
```

Figure 19.5 contains the observed frequencies, the expected frequencies, and the residuals (the differences between the observed and expected frequencies), as well as the chi-square statistic. Remember: *expected* values are what you'd expect if the two variables are independent. If the variables are independent, the observed and expected frequencies should be close to each other, and the value of the chi-square statistic should be small.

The residual for the first cell in Figure 19.5 is 46.5. This means that there were many more people in excellent health who found life exciting than you would expect if the two variables are independent. For the rest of the *Exciting* row, the residuals are negative. This means that there were fewer excited people than you'd expect. You can also see that more people than expected in the fair and poor health categories found life to be dull. They have positive residuals for the *Dull* cell. For any particular row or column, the sum of the residuals is 0. For this table, the value of the Pearson chi-square statistic is 104.213. The observed significance level is less than 0.000005.

Figure 19.5 Chi-square test for health and excitement

```
LIFE  Is life exciting or dull?  by  HEALTH  Condition of health
                      HEALTH                       Page 1 of 1
           Count
           Exp Val |Excellen Good     Fair     Poor
           Residual|t                                    Row
                   |   1        2        3        4     Total
    LIFE       ----+----------------------------------+
               1   |   249      320       95       16  |  680
    Exciting       | 202.5    325.7    119.5     32.3  | 46.9%
                   |  46.5     -5.7    -24.5    -16.3   |
                   +----------------------------------+
               2   |   175      350      137       36  |  698
    Pretty routine | 207.8    334.3    122.7     33.2  | 48.1%
                   | -32.8     15.7     14.3      2.8   |
                   +----------------------------------+
               3   |     8       25       23       17  |   73
    Dull           |  21.7     35.0     12.8      3.5   |  5.0%
                   | -13.7    -10.0     10.2     13.5   |
                   +----------------------------------+
           Column     432      695      255       69     1451
           Total     29.8%    47.9%    17.6%     4.8%   100.0%

Chi-Square                     Value           DF         Significance
--------------------         -----------       ----       ------------
Pearson                      104.21250          6            .00000
Likelihood Ratio              81.77819          6            .00000
Mantel-Haenszel test for      72.26830          1            .00000
linear association
Minimum Expected Frequency -   3.471

Cells with Expected Frequency < 5 -    1 OF    12 (  8.3%)

Number of Missing Observations:  22
```

Degrees of Freedom

It may occur to you that a big table (one with lots of rows and columns) is likely to produce a big chi-square statistic. You do the three-step calculation for each cell in the table and then add up all the results. It seems that the bigger your table, the more likely you are to get a big chi-square value.

In fact this is true—so we account for it. To calculate the observed significance level, we also use the number of degrees of freedom in the table. The number of degrees of freedom in a table is a way of accounting for how many different cells can contribute independent pieces of information to the chi-square. To calculate the degrees of freedom:

1 Subtract 1 from the number of rows.

2 Subtract 1 from the number of columns.

3 Multiply these two numbers together.

The product is the number of degrees of freedom. As you can see, the degrees of freedom are based on the number of observed and expected frequencies being compared and their arrangement in a table.

In the example above, we had three rows and four columns. The number of rows minus one is two, and the number of columns minus one is three. Multiply two times three, and you find that the table has six degrees of freedom.

Interpreting the Chi-Square Test

The observed significance depends both on the degrees of freedom and on the value of the chi-square statistic. For this table, the observed significance level is less than 0.000005.

> **?** *Where did this 0.000005 come from? The output says the probability is zero.* As with *t* tests, the probability isn't really zero. It's less than 0.000005, and SPSS/PC+ prints it as zero. If it weren't less than 0.000005, it would have been rounded to some number other than zero. ■■■

The very low probability indicates that it's quite unlikely the two variables are independent in the population. The chances are less than 5 in 1,000,000 that we'd get sample results like the ones we've seen if the variables are independent in the population. That's sufficient for us to reject the null hypothesis of independence. From Figure 19.5, you can see that one cell has an expected value of less than 5. However, the expected value, 3.5, is bigger than 1, and only one cell out of 12 has this problem. So you can be pretty confident about using the chi-square statistic in this situation.

SAMPLE SIZE AND THE CHI-SQUARE STATISTIC

In previous chapters, we considered how the number of cases included in a study affects whether or not you can reject the null hypothesis. If the sample is too small, you won't be able to detect even large differences. On the other hand, if the sample size is very large, even small differences can be statistically significant. Let's consider another example so we can observe the effect of sample size on the chi-square test.

We've identified several variables that are related to whether life is perceived as exciting—age, sex, and condition of health. How about race? Is there any reason to believe that members of minorities respond to life differently? Let's crosstabulate *RACE* with *LIFE*. To keep the cell sizes from getting too small, we'll collapse the races coded 2 (*Black*) and 3 (*Other*) into a new code 2 (*Black & Other*):

```
recode race (3 = 2).
value labels race 1 'White' 2 'Black & Other'.
crosstabs life by race
   /cells count expected resid /statistics chisq.
```

Figure 19.6 is a crosstabulation of race and perception of life. Look at the residuals. All are close to zero. This suggests that there's not much rela-

tionship between race and excitement with life. As expected, the value of
the Pearson chi-square statistic is small, 1.081, and the observed significance level is large, 0.582. What can we conclude from this? We can conclude it's unlikely that race and excitement are related in the population.
We can't reject the null hypothesis that the two variables are independent.

Figure 19.6 Race and excitement about life

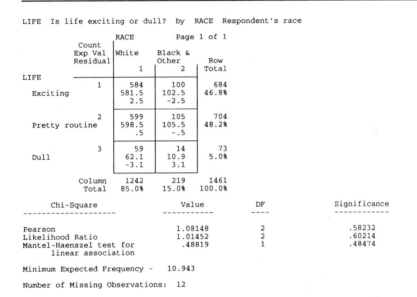

```
LIFE   Is life exciting or dull?  by  RACE  Respondent's race

                    RACE           Page 1 of 1
            Count
            Exp Val  White   Black &
            Residual         Other     Row
                       1        2     Total
LIFE
             1        584      100      684
   Exciting         581.5    102.5    46.8%
                      2.5     -2.5

             2        599      105      704
 Pretty routine     598.5    105.5    48.2%
                       .5      -.5

             3         59       14       73
   Dull              62.1     10.9     5.0%
                     -3.1      3.1

            Column   1242      219     1461
            Total   85.0%    15.0%   100.0%

    Chi-Square              Value       DF      Significance
-------------------------  -----------  ----    ------------

Pearson                      1.08148     2        .58232
Likelihood Ratio             1.01452     2        .60214
Mantel-Haenszel test for      .48819     1        .48474
   linear association

Minimum Expected Frequency -   10.943

Number of Missing Observations:  12
```

But what would happen if we multiplied all the observed counts in Figure 19.6 by 10. That is, we increase our sample size tenfold, but we don't
change the pattern of the data. The percentage of cases in each of the cells
remains exactly the same. The new table is shown in Figure 19.7.

As a result of multiplying the sample size by a factor of 10, we've multiplied all of the entries in the table by 10. That is, for each cell, the observed
frequency is now 10 times as large as before. Therefore, the expected frequency is 10 times as large, and so is the residual. Since everything we use
in calculating the chi-square statistic is 10 times as large, the value of the
chi-square statistic for the table also is multiplied by 10. The Pearson chi-
square value is now 10.81.

The observed significance level associated with this chi-square value,
0.0045, is very small. The conclusion we'd now draw is that there *is* a relationship between the variables. That's completely different from before.
We haven't changed the relationship in the data. We've just increased the
sample size. There's no mystery in this. It happens for the same reasons

Figure 19.7 Race and excitement with cases multiplied by 10

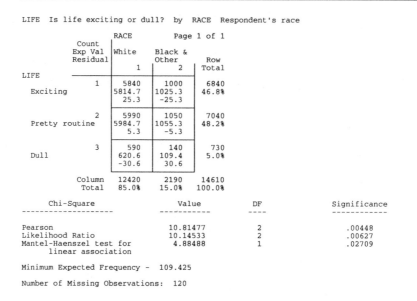

```
LIFE  Is life exciting or dull?  by  RACE  Respondent's race

                      RACE            Page 1 of 1
              Count
              Exp Val  White    Black &
              Residual           Other    Row
                          1          2    Total
       LIFE
                    1    5840     1000     6840
         Exciting        5814.7   1025.3   46.8%
                         25.3     -25.3

                    2    5990     1050     7040
         Pretty routine  5984.7   1055.3   48.2%
                         5.3      -5.3

                    3    590      140      730
         Dull            620.6    109.4    5.0%
                         -30.6    30.6

             Column      12420    2190     14610
             Total       85.0%    15.0%    100.0%

       Chi-Square              Value       DF       Significance
    --------------------      ---------    ----     ------------

    Pearson                    10.81477     2         .00448
    Likelihood Ratio           10.14533     2         .00627
    Mantel-Haenszel test for    4.88488     1         .02709
       linear association

    Minimum Expected Frequency -  109.425

    Number of Missing Observations:  120
```

we've discussed earlier. If you've got a large sample size, even a very small difference between two groups (or a very small departure from independence between two variables) may turn out to be statistically significant. You must look at the actual percentages in the table to determine whether the observed differences are of any practical importance.

MORE ABOUT HYPOTHESIS TESTING IN CROSSTABS

The CELLS subcommand in CROSSTABS was discussed at the end of Chapter 10 as a way of displaying percentages in the table, but you can also use it to display the expected frequencies, residuals, and standardized residuals. The standardized residuals are the residuals divided by the square root of the expected values. If you square the standardized residual for a cell, you get the "contribution" of that cell to the value of chi-square for the table. Large standardized residuals indicate cells with either considerably more or considerably fewer observations than you would expect if the variables were independent.

Use keyword EXPECTED on the CELLS subcommand to get expected frequencies, keyword RESID to get residuals, and keyword SRESID to get standardized residuals. Use keyword CHISQ on the STATISTICS subcommand to get the value of chi-square for the table as a whole.

WHAT'S NEXT?

In the last few chapters, you've tested several types of statistical hypotheses: equality of means from independent groups, equality of means from paired samples, and independence of the two variables in a crosstabulation. The next chapter will expand our discussion of hypothesis testing with a test for equality of several means. The technique will build on what we've already discussed. When it comes to hypothesis testing, the basic approach is always the same.

Summary

How can you test the null hypothesis that two percentages are equal in the population? How can you test the null hypothesis that two variables are independent?

Observed frequencies are simply the numbers of cases with specific combinations of values.

Expected frequencies are the numbers of cases that would have specific combinations of values if the null hypothesis were true.

The chi-square statistic is based on a comparison of observed frequencies with expected frequencies. From it, you can obtain an observed significance level for the hypothesis that two proportions are equal.

Two variables are independent if knowing the value of one variable tells you nothing about the value of the other.

The degrees of freedom of a crosstabulation reflect the number of cells in the table that are free to vary. You compute them by taking the number of rows minus one and multiplying that by the number of columns minus one.

From the chi-square statistic and the degrees of freedom in a crosstabulation, you can calculate the observed significance level for the null hypothesis that the two variables are unrelated.

Chi-square increases in direct proportion to sample size, if the strength of the relationship stays the same. If you double the number of cases in each cell of a crosstabulation, chi-square is doubled.

EXERCISES

Syntax

1 You want to study whether there is a relationship between the highest degree a person's father received (*PADEG*) and the highest degree the person received (*DEGREE*). Write out the SPSS/PC+ command to make a crosstabulation with the father's degree as the column variable and the child's degree as the row variable. Make sure the command will produce the appropriate percentages and calculate the chi-square test of independence.

2 You run the command

```
crosstabs  eyecolor  carcolor /statistic chisq.
```

and receive the following error message:

```
ERROR   10317
Syntax error in CROSSTABS command, a table request specified only one
dimension.  Perhaps the BY keyword was left out of a tables request.  The
form should be VARA BY VARB.
This command not executed.
```

Correct the command.

3 Correct the errors in the following commands:

a. `crosstabs rowvar colvar.`

b. `crosstabs a by b.`
   `cells row.`

c. `crosstabs a by c  /print statistics=chisq.`

d. `crosstabs rowvar by colvar /sadistic chisp.`

4 You are studying the relationship between obesity in children and obesity in parents. For each child in your study you have the actual weight and height of the child (*WEIGHT, HEIGHT*) and of the parents (*PAWEIGHT, PAHEIGHT, MAWEIGHT, MAHEIGHT*). Using a special formula that relates height and sex to ideal body weight, you have created additional variables that contain the ideal body weight for the child and both parents (*IDEAL, PAIDEAL, MAIDEAL*). Write out the SPSS/PC+ commands to

a. Compute the ratio of actual weight to ideal weight for the child and each parent. Make up any names you like for these ratios.

b. Create a new set of variables (*OBESE, PAOBESE, MAOBESE*) that have the value 1 if the ratio of actual weight to ideal weight is greater than or equal to 1.3 (indicating that actual weight exceeds ideal weight by more than 30%) and 0 if it is not.

c. Crosstabulate *OBESE* with *PAOBESE* and *MAOBESE*. Also calculate the chi-square test of independence.

Statistical Concepts

1 Which pairs of variables do you think are independent, and which are dependent?

a. Zodiac sign and number of hamburgers consumed per week

b. Severity of a disease and prognosis

c. Shoe size and glove size

d. Color of car and highest degree received

e. Husband's highest degree and wife's highest degree

2 Consider the following table:

SATJOB Satisfaction with job or housework by AGE Age of respondent

Count	AGE				Page 1 of 1
	18 - 29	30 - 45	46 - 59	60 and over	Row
SATJOB	1	2	3	4	Total
1 Very satisfied	131	202	116	106	555 45.9
2 Moderately satis	126	172	68	57	423 35.0
3 Dissatisfied	86	87	41	16	230 19.0
Column Total	343 28.4	461 38.2	225 18.6	179 14.8	1208 100.0

Number of Missing Observations: 265

a. Calculate the number of cases you would expect in each cell if the two variables are independent.

b. For each cell, calculate the difference between the observed and the expected number of cases.

c. Calculate the chi-square statistic for the table.

d. What are the degrees of freedom for the table?

e. What null hypothesis are you testing with the chi-square statistic you computed?

3 The observed significance level for a chi-square value of 7.83753 with 3 degrees of freedom is 0.0495.

a. What conclusion would you draw about the relationship between the two variables based on the observed significance level?

b. How often would you expect to see a chi-square value at least as large as the one you observed if the two variables are independent?

c. If you reject the null hypothesis that the two variables are independent, can you conclude that one of the variables causes the other?

4 The following table is a crosstabulation of respondent's sex and satisfaction with family life:

SEX by SATFAM FAMILY LIFE

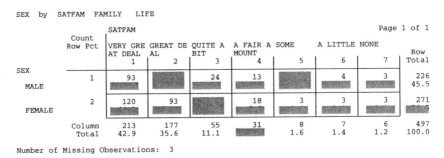

Number of Missing Observations: 3

a. Fill in the missing entries. Be sure to fill in the appropriate percentages.

b. Write a few sentences summarizing the table. What can you conclude about the relationship between the two variables?

5 Suppose a random sample of size 100 resulted in Table 1 below, while another random sample of size 500 resulted in Table 2. If you know that the chi-square value for Table 1 is 9.09, can you find the chi-square value for Table 2 without doing any chi-square calculations involving the data in Table 2?

Table 1

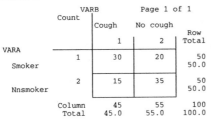

Table 2

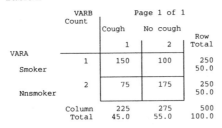

6 The following table is a crosstabulation of belief in life after death and excitement with life.

```
POSTLIFE  Belief in life after death  by  LIFE  Is life exciting or dull?
```

	LIFE			Page 1 of 1
Count	Exciting	Pretty r outine	Dull	
	1	2	3	Row Total
POSTLIFE				
1 Yes	531	▓▓▓	50	1070 79.5
2 No	▓▓▓	157	▓▓▓	276
Column Total	635 ▓▓▓	646 ▓▓▓	65 4.8	1346 100.0

```
Number of Missing Observations:  127
```

a. Fill in the missing entries in the table.

b. Calculate the value of the chi-square statistic.

c. Summarize your results.

7 You are studying the relationship between severity of a disease at diagnosis and whether someone lives for five years. (Severity of a disease is objectively coded as 1=*mild*; 2=*moderate*; and 3=*severe*.) You compute a chi-square test of independence and find the observed significance level to be 0.35. Another investigator does a similar study using the same criteria for determining severity of a disease. He calculates a chi-square test of independence and obtains an observed significance level of 0.002. You examine his results and notice that the percentage of cases in each of the severity categories that survive five years is almost identical to the percentages that you observed. You conclude that he doesn't know how to correctly calculate a chi-square value. Give another explanation for why his chi-square could differ from yours.

8 The residuals—the differences between the observed and expected frequencies—are helpful in locating which cells don't fit the independence model well.

a. What does a negative residual mean?

b. What does a positive residual mean?

c. What does a zero residual mean?

d. What is the sum of the residuals for any row of a table?

e. What is the sum of the residuals for any column of a table?

f. Is it possible for a table to have only positive or negative residuals?

g. If all of the residuals for a table are zero, what is the value of the chi-square statistic?

Data Analysis

Use the gss.sys system file to answer the following questions.

1 You wonder whether the percentages of men and women believe in life after death are the same.

a. Make a crosstabulation of *POSTLIFE* and *SEX*. Be sure to include the appropriate percentages.

b. State the null hypothesis that you are testing.

c. Obtain the appropriate statistical test to test the null hypothesis.

d. Write a short paragraph summarizing your results.

2 Test the null hypothesis that perception of life as exciting, routine, or dull is independent of one's views on afterlife. Summarize the results of your analysis.

3 Look at the variables that are available in your copy of the gss.sys file. Select two pairs of categorical variables and test the two null hypotheses that the variables in each pair are independent. Write a summary of your results.

20 Comparing Several Means

How can you test the null hypothesis that several population means are equal?

- What is analysis of variance?
- What assumptions about the data are needed to use analysis of variance techniques?
- How can you test hypotheses about means by looking at the variability of the observations?
- What is within-groups variability?
- What is between-groups variability?
- How is an F test computed, and how is it interpreted?
- What are multiple comparison procedures, and why do you need them?

To compare two means, you can use the two-sample *t* test described in Chapter 17. But what if you have more than two groups? For example, what if you want to compare the average years of education for people who find life exciting, those who find it routine, and those who find it dull? This chapter will discuss a special class of statistical techniques called **analysis of variance** that allow you to compare means for more than two groups.

DESCRIBING THE GROUPS

Before you proceed with any type of statistical analysis, you should always look at the data first. Look at the means and standard deviations for each of the groups. You'll find out how different the observed means are and how much the observations in the groups vary. This is important information, since you know that even large differences between observed means are not statistically significant if there's a lot of variability in the groups. If you find that the differences are statistically significant, it's important to know how large they are.

The basic descriptive statistics for years of education for the three excitement groups are shown in Figure 20.1. (These statistics come from the SPSS/PC+ ONEWAY command. The command is given later in this chapter.) The excited people have the highest average years of education (13.0), while the bored people have the smallest (9.5). The people who found life routine fall in the middle, with an average of 12.0 years. The standard deviations in the first two groups are fairly similar, around 3. The last group has a somewhat higher standard deviation of 3.5.

The minimum value is zero for all three groups. It's interesting that at least one person in each group claimed to have no formal education. From the maximum values, you can see that at least one person in each group reported more than four years of college.

Figure 20.1 also has a column for standard error of the mean. (Remember that this is a measure of how much the sample means vary in repeated samples from the same population.) Since the first two groups in Figure 20.1 contain about 700 cases each, the standard error of the mean for each of these groups is fairly small: it is 0.12 for people who find life exciting and 0.11 for people who find life routine.

Figure 20.1 Descriptive statistics for years of education

Group	Count	Mean	Standard Deviation	Standard Error	95 Pct Conf Int for Mean		
Grp 1	684	13.0365	3.1789	.1215	12.7979	To	13.2752
Grp 2	702	11.9929	2.9385	.1109	11.7751	To	12.2106
Grp 3	73	9.5479	3.5002	.4097	8.7313	To	10.3646
Total	1459	12.3598	3.1884	.0835	12.1961	To	12.5236

Group	Minimum	Maximum
Grp 1	.0000	20.0000
Grp 2	.0000	20.0000
Grp 3	.0000	18.0000
Total	.0000	20.0000

The confidence intervals are shown in the columns after the standard error. Recall what a confidence interval is. It's the range of values that, with a designated likelihood, contains the true population value. If you take repeated samples from the same population and calculate 95% confidence intervals, 95% of them should include the unknown population value. Because the standard errors for the first two groups in Figure 20.1 are fairly small, the 95% confidence intervals for these groups are fairly narrow. You can be 95% confident that, in the population, the average years of education for people who find life exciting is somewhere between 12.8 and 13.3; and for people who find life routine, between 11.8 and 12.2.

Only 73 people found life dull. There are fewer cases in this group than in the others and the observed standard deviation is larger, so the standard error of the mean is also larger. Since confidence intervals depend on the standard error of the mean, the confidence interval for the bored people is wider than for the other two groups. You can be 95% confident that the true mean for the bored group is somewhere between 8.7 and 10.4, a range of almost two years.

After the statistics for the individual groups, SPSS/PC+ prints statistics for all cases combined in the row labeled *Total*. From these statistics, you can see that the overall average years of education is 12.4 with a standard deviation of 3.2.

The Distribution of the Responses

The means, standard deviations, and confidence intervals give you some idea about the years of education in each of the three groups. If you look at a histogram for the years of education, you can see even more detail. You can also see whether the distribution looks approximately normal. This is important in many situations, since statistical hypothesis testing is often based on the assumption of normality. If the population from which you're taking a sample has a distribution that's approximately normal, even for small sample sizes the distribution of sample means will be normal. The three excitement groups may have different distributions, so it's important to look at them individually.

Figure 20.2 shows the histogram for people who found life exciting. This distribution has a very sharp peak at 12 years, the year of high-school graduation. It has smaller peaks at 14 and 16 years. The majority of cases have 12 to 16 years of education. For people who found life routine (Figure 20.3) there's a single peak at 12 years, or high-school graduation. The distribution is fairly symmetric about this peak.

For people who found life dull (Figure 20.4) the distribution of the sample is different. Although there's a peak at 12 years, it's not as marked as for the other two groups. Smaller peaks are at 8 and 10 years of education. Very few cases have more than 12 years of education.

Figure 20.2 Education: people who found life exciting

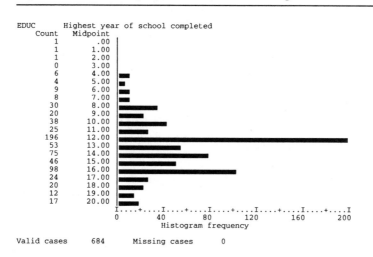

```
EDUC        Highest year of school completed
   Count     Midpoint
      1         .00 |
      1        1.00 |
      1        2.00 |
      0        3.00 |
      6        4.00 |
      4        5.00 |
      9        6.00 |
      8        7.00 |
     30        8.00 |
     20        9.00 |
     38       10.00 |
     25       11.00 |
    196       12.00 |
     53       13.00 |
     75       14.00 |
     46       15.00 |
     98       16.00 |
     24       17.00 |
     20       18.00 |
     12       19.00 |
     17       20.00 |
              I....+....I....+....I....+....I....+....I....+....I
              0       40      80     120     160     200
                        Histogram frequency

Valid cases      684      Missing cases      0
```

Are the Means Really Different?

The descriptive statistics and histograms suggest that there are differences in years of education among the three excitement groups. Now we need to figure out whether the observed differences in the samples can be attributed to just the natural variability among sample means or whether there's reason to believe that the three groups have different means in the population.

The null hypothesis says that in the population, the means of the three groups are equal. That is, there's no difference in the average years of education for people who find life exciting, routine, or dull. The alternative

Figure 20.3 Education: people who found life routine

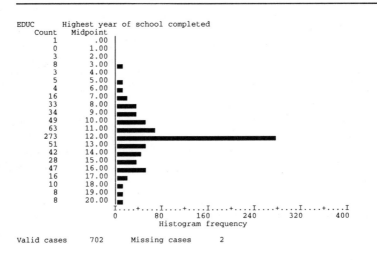

```
EDUC       Highest year of school completed
    Count    Midpoint
       1       .00  |
       0      1.00  |
       3      2.00  |
       8      3.00  |■
       3      4.00  |
       5      5.00  |■
       4      6.00  |■
      16      7.00  |■
      33      8.00  |▬▬
      34      9.00  |▬▬
      49     10.00  |▬▬▬
      63     11.00  |▬▬▬▬
     273     12.00  |▬▬▬▬▬▬▬▬▬▬▬▬▬▬▬▬▬▬▬▬▬▬▬
      51     13.00  |▬▬▬
      42     14.00  |▬▬▬
      28     15.00  |▬▬
      47     16.00  |▬▬▬
      16     17.00  |■
      10     18.00  |■
       8     19.00  |■
       8     20.00  |■
                    I....+....I....+....I....+....I....+....I....+....I
                    0        80       160      240      320      400
                              Histogram frequency

Valid cases     702     Missing cases     2
```

Figure 20.4 Education: people who found life dull

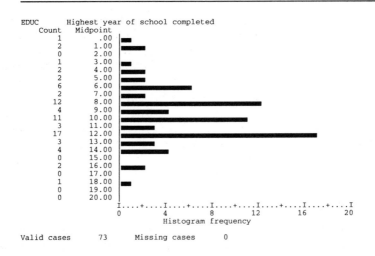

```
EDUC       Highest year of school completed
    Count    Midpoint
       1       .00  |■
       2      1.00  |▬▬
       0      2.00  |
       1      3.00  |■
       2      4.00  |▬▬
       2      5.00  |▬▬
       6      6.00  |▬▬▬▬▬
       2      7.00  |▬▬
      12      8.00  |▬▬▬▬▬▬▬▬▬▬
       4      9.00  |▬▬▬
      11     10.00  |▬▬▬▬▬▬▬▬
       3     11.00  |▬▬
      17     12.00  |▬▬▬▬▬▬▬▬▬▬▬▬▬▬
       3     13.00  |▬▬
       4     14.00  |▬▬▬
       0     15.00  |
       2     16.00  |▬▬
       0     17.00  |
       1     18.00  |■
       0     19.00  |
       0     20.00  |
                    I....+....I....+....I....+....I....+....I....+....I
                    0        4        8        12       16       20
                              Histogram frequency

Valid cases     73     Missing cases     0
```

hypothesis is that there is a difference. The alternative hypothesis doesn't say which groups differ from one another. It just says that the groups are not all the same; at least one of the groups differs from the others.

ANALYSIS OF VARIANCE

The statistical technique used to test the null hypothesis that several population means are equal is **analysis of variance**. It's called that because it examines the variability in the sample and, based on the variability, determines whether there's reason to believe the population means are unequal. We'll be drawing conclusions about means by looking at variability.

SPSS/PC+ contains several different procedures that can perform analysis of variance. In this chapter, we'll use the ONEWAY procedure. It's called **one-way analysis of variance** because cases fall into different groups based on their values for one variable. In our example, that variable is perception of life.

Necessary Assumptions

The data must meet two conditions for you to use analysis of variance:

1 Each of the groups must be a random sample from a normal population.

2 In the population, the variances in all groups must be equal.

You can visually check these conditions by making a histogram of the data for each group and seeing whether the data are approximately normal. You can also use the EXAMINE procedure to test for normality. To check whether the groups have the same variance in the population, you can examine the histograms and compute the Levene test (use keyword SPREADLEVEL on the PLOT subcommand in EXAMINE).

In practice, analysis of variance gives good results even if the normality assumption doesn't quite hold. If the number of observations in each of the groups is fairly similar, the equal-variance assumption is also not too important. The assumption of random samples, however, is always important and cannot be relaxed.

Partitioning the Variability

In analysis of variance, the observed variability in the sample is divided, or **partitioned**, into two parts: variability of the observations *within* a group (around the group mean), and variability *between* the group means themselves.

> ? *Why are we talking about variability? Aren't we testing hypotheses about means?* In Chapter 16, we considered the relationship between the variability of the observations and the variability of sample means. If you know the standard deviation of the observations, you can estimate how much the sample means should vary. In this example, you have three different groups—people who find life exciting, people who find it routine, and people who find it dull. If the null hypothesis is true (that is, if in the population all three groups have the same mean), you can estimate how much the observed means should vary due to sampling variation alone. If the means you actually observe vary more than you'd expect, you have reason to believe that this extra variability is due to the fact that some of the groups don't have the same mean in the population.   ■■■

Within-Groups Variability

Let's look a little more closely now at the two types of variability we need to consider. **Within-groups variability** is a measure of how much the observations within a group vary. It's simply the variance of the observations within a group in your sample, and it's used to estimate the variance within a group in the population. (Remember, analysis of variance requires the assumption that all of the groups have the same variance in the population.) Since you don't know if all of the groups have the same mean, you can't just calculate the variance for all of the cases together. You must calculate the variance for each of the groups individually and then combine these into an "average" variance.

For example, suppose you have three groups of 20 cases each. All 20 cases in the first group have a value of 100, all 20 cases in the second group have a value of 50, and all 20 cases in the third group have a value of 0. Your best guess for the population variance within a group is 0. It appears from your sample that the values of the cases in any particular group don't vary at all. But if you'd computed the variance for all of the cases together, it wouldn't even be close to zero. You'd calculate the overall mean as 50, and cases in the first and third groups would all vary from this overall mean by 50. There would be plenty of variation.

Between-Groups Variability

Remember the discussion in Chapter 15. There's a relationship between the variability of the observations in a population and the variability of sample means from that population. If you divide the standard deviation of the observations by the square root of the number of observations, you have an estimate of the standard deviation of the sample means, also known as the standard error. So if you know what the standard error of the mean is, you can estimate what the standard deviation of the original observations must be. You just multiply the standard error by the square root of the number of cases to get an estimate of the standard deviation of the observations. You square this to get an estimate of the variance.

Let's see how this insight can give you an estimate of the variance based on **between-groups variability**. You have a sample mean for each of the groups, and you can compute how much these means vary. If the population mean is the same in all three groups, you can use the variability among the sample means and the number of cases in each sample to estimate the variability of the original observations. Of course, this estimate depends on whether the population means really are the same in all three groups. If the null hypothesis is true, the estimate of variability based on the group means is correct. However, if the groups have different means in the population, then the between-groups estimate will be too large.

Back to the Examples

Consider again the example of three groups with sample means of 100, 50, and 0. Since they vary quite a bit, if the null hypothesis is true, you'd expect the observations within the groups to vary even more. They don't. In fact, all 20 observations in each group were equal. Your within-groups and between-groups estimates of variability would therefore be quite different. This suggests that the differences you saw in the sample group means aren't attributable to natural variability from sample to sample. The groups almost certainly do come from populations with different means.

How does this apply to the question about education in the General Social Survey? If the means of the three groups vary a lot but the amount of education doesn't vary much for individuals within each excitement group (for example, most of the people who found life routine had no more than high-school educations), you will have reason to suspect that the population means are not equal for all three groups.

In summary, with analysis of variance you compare the within-groups and between-groups estimates of variability. The within-groups estimate is always a good estimate of the variability of observations in the population. The between-groups estimate is a measure of the variability of the observations only if the null hypothesis is true. If the two estimates are substantially different, you can reject the null hypothesis that the population means are equal.

Analysis of Variance in SPSS/PC+ ONEWAY

The commands for getting an analysis of variance from the SPSS/PC+ ONEWAY procedure are:

```
get file 'gss.sys'.
oneway educ by life(1,3) /statistic 1.
```

The variable named before BY is the one whose means you want to test. The variable after BY defines the different groups and the numbers following it in parentheses are the highest and lowest values for the grouping variable. The output from this analysis of variance is shown in Figure 20.5. Figure 20.1 shows the descriptive statistics produced by Statistic 1 in ONE-WAY.

Figure 20.5 Analysis of variance

```
          - - - - - - - - - - O N E W A Y - - - - - - - - - -

       Variable  EDUC      Highest year of school completed
     By Variable  LIFE      Is life exciting or dull?

                          Analysis of Variance

                              Sum of          Mean         F       F
          Source      D.F.    Squares        Squares      Ratio   Prob.

Between Groups          2     984.9535       492.4768    51.8204   .0000

Within Groups        1456    13837.1328        9.5035

Total                1458    14822.0864
```

Computing Within-Groups Variability

Now let's see how the numbers in Figure 20.5 are computed. We use three steps to compute the estimate of how much the observations within a group vary. First, we calculate the **within-groups sum of squares**. Just take the variance in each of the groups (the square of the standard deviation), multiply it by one less than the number of cases in the group, and add all the results together.

For our example, the within-groups sum of squares is:

$$3.1789^2 \times 683 + 2.9385^2 \times 701 + 3.5002^2 \times 72 = 13,837$$

This number is shown in the second row of numbers in Figure 20.5 in the column labeled *Sum of Squares*.

The second step of estimating the variability in the individual groups is to divide the previously computed sum of squares by its **degrees of freedom**. The degrees of freedom are easy to obtain. For each group, find the number of cases minus one, and add the results together for all of the groups. In our example, the degrees of freedom are

$$(684 - 1) + (702 - 1) + (73 - 1) = 1,456$$

This number is shown on the *Within Groups* line of Figure 20.5 in the column labeled *D.F.* (for degrees of freedom).

The third and final step is to divide the sum of squares by its degrees of freedom to get what's called a **mean square**. This is an estimate of the average variability in the groups. It's really nothing more than an average of the variances in each of the groups, adjusted for the fact that the numbers of observations in the groups are unequal. As you can see in Figure 20.5, the within-groups mean square is 13,837 divided by 1,456, or 9.50.

Computing Between-Groups Variability

Now we must calculate another estimate of the variance based on how much the means differ among themselves. Again the computations involve three steps. First we calculate the between-groups sum of squares, then the degrees of freedom, and finally the between-groups mean square.

To calculate the between-groups sum of squares, start by subtracting the overall mean (the mean of all the observations) from each group mean. Then square each difference and multiply the square by the number of observations in that group. Finally, add all the results together.

For our example, the between-groups sum of squares is:

$$684 \times (13.04 - 12.36)^2 + 702 \times (11.99 - 12.36)^2 + 73 \times (9.55 - 12.36)^2 = 984.95$$

To find the degrees of freedom for the between-groups sum of squares, subtract one from the number of groups. In this example, there are 3 groups, so there are 2 degrees of freedom.

The between-groups mean square is calculated just like the within-groups mean square. Divide the sum of squares by its degrees of freedom:

$$984.95 / 2 = 492.5$$

This number is found in the column labeled *Mean Squares* in Figure 20.5.

Calculating the *F* Ratio

You now have two estimates of the variability in the population: the *within-groups* mean square and the *between-groups* mean square. The within-groups mean square is based on how much the observations within each of the groups vary. The between-groups mean square is based on how much the group means vary among themselves. If the null hypothesis is true, the two numbers should be close to each other. If we divide one by the other, the ratio should be close to 1.

The statistical test of the null hypothesis that all of the groups have the same mean in the population is based on computing such a ratio. It's called an F statistic. You take the between-groups mean square and divide it by the within-groups mean square as shown in the following formula:

$$F = \frac{\text{between-groups mean square}}{\text{within-groups mean square}}$$

For our example,

$$F = \frac{492.5}{9.5} = 51.8$$

This number appears in Figure 20.5 below the label *F Ratio*. It certainly doesn't appear to be close to 1. What we need to do now is obtain the observed significance level. We want to know how often we'd expect to see a ratio of 51.8 or larger if the null hypothesis is true.

The observed significance level is obtained by comparing the calculated F value to the F distribution, the distribution of the F statistic when the null hypothesis is true. (Like the normal distribution, the F distribution is defined mathematically. SPSS/PC+ can calculate it and compare your F value to it automatically.) The significance level is based on both the actual value of F you obtain and on the degrees of freedom for the two mean squares.

The observed significance level is shown in the column labeled *F Prob* in Figure 20.5. Since a value of 0.0000 is printed, you know that the observed significance level is less than 0.00005. In other words, it's very unlikely that you'd see such a large F ratio when the null hypothesis is true. You reject the null hypothesis that, in the population, people who find life exciting, routine, or dull have the same number of years of education.

MULTIPLE COMPARISON PROCEDURES

A significant F value only tells you that the population means are probably not all equal. It doesn't tell you *which* pairs of groups appear to have different means. For example, people who find life exciting may differ in education from people who find life dull but not from people who find life routine. Or people who find life exciting may differ from both other groups. In most situations, you want to pinpoint exactly where the differences are. To do this, you must use **multiple comparison procedures**.

> **?** *Why do you need yet another statistical technique? Why not just calculate t tests for all possible pairs of means?* The reason for not using many *t* tests is that when you make a lot of comparisons involving the same means, the probability that one will turn out to be statistically significant increases.

For example, if you have 5 groups and compare all pairs of means, you're making 10 comparisons. When the null hypothesis is true (that is, all of the means are equal in the population), the probability that at least one of the 10 observed significance levels will be less than 0.05 is about 0.29. If you make many comparisons, it is likely that you will observe some "unlikely" results. The more comparisons you make, the more likely it is that you'll find one or more pairs to be statistically different, even if all means are equal in the population.

Multiple comparison procedures protect you from calling too many differences significant by adjusting for the number of comparisons you're making. The more comparisons you're making, the larger the difference between pairs of means must be for a multiple comparison procedure to report a significant difference. So differences that multiple *t* tests find significant may not be significant based on multiple comparison procedures. When you use a multiple comparison procedure, you can be more confident that you're finding true differences. ■ ■ ■

There are several different procedures that can be used when making multiple comparisons. The procedures differ in how they adjust the observed significance level for the fact that many comparisons are being made. Some require larger differences between pairs of means than others. For further discussion of multiple comparisons, see R. Kirk's *Experimental Design* (1968).

Multiple Comparisons in ONEWAY

Multiple comparisons are simple to do in SPSS/PC+. A number of different methods are available. One of the most widely used is the **Tukey-b** multiple comparison test. To calculate the Tukey-b test, type:

```
oneway educ by life(1,3) / ranges=btukey.
```

Figure 20.6 shows the output. At the bottom of the output, all of the group means are ordered from smallest to largest in rows and columns. Pairs of means that are different at the 0.05 level are marked with an asterisk in the lower half of the table. You can see that all of the groups differ from one another. In other words, people who find life routine differ in education from people who find life dull, and people who find life exciting differ from both of the other groups.

Figure 20.6 Multiple comparisons from ONEWAY

```
        - - - - - - - - - O N E W A Y - - - - - - - - - -

        Variable  EDUC     Highest year of school completed
     By Variable  LIFE     Is life exciting or dull?

Multiple Range Test

Tukey-B Procedure
Ranges for the   .050 level -

          3.07   3.33

The ranges above are table ranges.
The value actually compared with Mean(J)-Mean(I) is..
        2.1799 * Range * Sqrt(1/N(I) + 1/N(J))

(*) Denotes pairs of groups significantly different at the  .050 level

                          G G G
                          r r r
                          p p p
        Mean      Group   3 2 1

        9.5479    Grp 3
       11.9929    Grp 2    *
       13.0365    Grp 1    * *
```

Differences are marked only once, in the lower half of the table. If the significance level is not less than 0.05, an asterisk is not printed; the space is left blank. The line above the table indicates how large an observed difference must be for the comparison procedure to call it significant. If no pairs are found to be significantly different, the table is not printed at all. Instead, a message saying that the differences are significant is printed.

MORE COMPLICATED ANALYSIS OF VARIANCE DESIGNS

In this chapter, we've considered analysis of variance when only one variable determines the groups. Our three groups were formed according to one variable, *LIFE*, whose values indicate whether a person finds life exciting, routine, or dull. But you can use analysis of variance techniques for more complicated designs as well.

Suppose you're interested in testing hypotheses about the relationship between income and both marital status (married or not) and race (white or black). You would classify cases based on both marital status and race. Since each of these variables has two values, together they classify a case into one of four groups (called **cells**, analogous to the cells in a crosstabulation). Using analysis of variance techniques, you can test whether whites and blacks differ in average income, whether married people and single people differ in average income, and whether the relationship between being married and income is the same for whites and blacks. All of these tests would be included in a **two-way analysis of variance**. It's called that because it's based on two classification variables, in this example *MARITAL* and *RACE*.

Interactions

Analysis of variance allows you to test not only for the effects of individual variables but also for their combinations. This is an important concern. As you've seen in previous chapters, combinations of variables sometimes have a different effect than you'd expect from each of the variables alone.

Think back to the crosstabulation relating excitement, marital status, and sex in Chapter 10. You saw that the relationship between marital status and excitement was different for men and women. Single women were much more likely to find life exciting than single men. The relationship between marital status and excitement differed for the two sexes. In statistical terms, we say that there was an **interaction effect** between sex and marital status. It's important to identify interaction effects, since it doesn't make sense to talk about the effect of marital status alone if the effect is different for men and women. If there is an interaction effect, you must talk about the effect of marital status separately for men and women.

Cases can also be classified on the basis of more than two variables. Then analysis of variance provides tests for the effects of the individual variables and all possible interactions of the variables. A discussion of interaction effects and of the many complicated relationships that analysis of variance can test for is beyond the scope of this book. If you're interested in knowing more, a good place to start is Kirk's *Experimental Design*.

Analysis of Variance in SPSS/PC+ ANOVA

You use the ANOVA command to perform analysis of variance with more than one classification variable, or **factor.** ANOVA doesn't include the multiple-comparison procedures that ONEWAY offers, but it does allow you to analyze the effects and interactions of several factors at once.

For example, to analyze the effect of marital status and race on family income, specify the dependent variable, the keyword BY, and the factors *MARITAL* and *RACE*. After each factor, enter the range of categories that should be used in the analysis. Here we only want categories 1 and 2 of each of the factors.

```
* Recode all "not married" codes into one code, and
  recode income categories to thousands of dollars.
recode marital (3 thru 5 = 2)
 /income (1=.5)(2=2) (3=3.5)(4=4.5)(5=5.5)(6=6.5)(7=7.5)
  (8=9) (9=11.25)(10=13.75)(11=16.25)(12=18.75)(13=21.25)
  (14=23.75) (15=30)(16=42.5)(17=60).
anova income by marital (1,2) race(1,2)
 /option 9.
```

This ANOVA command produces the analysis of variance table in Figure 20.7.

Figure 20.7 Two-way analysis of variance

```
            * * *   A N A L Y S I S   O F   V A R I A N C E   * * *

              INCOME    Total family income
         by   MARITAL   Marital status
              RACE      Respondent's race

                            Sum of              Mean              Sig
Source of Variation         Squares     DF      Square      F     of F

Main Effects              26591.260      2    13295.630  57.561   .000
    MARITAL               14555.412      1    14555.412  63.015   .000
    RACE                   8623.144      1     8623.144  37.333   .000

2-Way Interactions           34.839      1        34.839   .151   .698
    MARITAL  RACE            34.839      1        34.839   .151   .698

Explained                 50547.135      3    16849.045  72.945   .000

Residual                 297504.609   1288       230.982

Total                    348051.744   1291       269.599
```

1473 Cases were processed.
181 Cases (12.3 PCT) were missing.

This analysis of variance table is simply a more elaborate version of the one shown in Figure 20.5. As before, the table has columns for sums of squares, degrees of freedom, mean squares, the *F* ratio, and the significance of *F*. Under *Main Effects* are the statistics for *MARITAL* and *RACE* considered separately. (The statistics across from *Main Effects* let you evaluate the significance of all the single-variable effects considered together, if you want to do that.) Under these statistics are the statistics for the interaction between *MARITAL* and *RACE*. The row labeled *Residual* contains the within-cell sum of squares and mean square.

For each effect in the table, the *F* statistic is calculated as the ratio of the mean square for that effect to the mean square for the residual. Thus for *MARITAL*, *F* equals 14555.41 divided by 230.98, or 63.02. For the interaction, *F* equals 34.84 divided by 230.98, or 0.15.

When you interpret an analysis of variance table, start by checking the statistical significance of the interactions. The interaction between *MARITAL* and *RACE* has a large significance level of 0.698, so you don't reject the null hypothesis that there is no interaction effect. The effect of race on income, if any, seems to be the same among married people as among single people. Looking at it the other way, any effect of marriage on income is the same among whites and blacks. It makes sense, therefore, to look at the main effects individually.

The F statistics for both *MARITAL* and *RACE* are both highly significant: the probability of seeing F values this large if the null hypothesis is true is less than 0.0005. Thus you can reject the null hypothesis for the main effects. Married people do not have the same average family income as unmarried people, and whites do not have the same average family income as blacks.

MORE ABOUT THE ONEWAY PROCEDURE

To test the null hypothesis that several population means are equal, you can use the ONEWAY analysis of variance procedure. For example, to test that there is no difference in average age for people who find life exciting, routine, and dull, specify

```
oneway age by life(1,3).
```

The variable whose means are being compared is named before the BY keyword. The variable used to form the groups is indicated after BY. Give the lowest and highest values for the variable that forms the groups in parentheses, separated by a comma. These values must be integers. You can use only one variable to designate the groups in ONEWAY.

If you have several variables you want to compare, list them all before the keyword BY, separated by commas or blanks. For example,

```
oneway age educ by life(1,3).
```

produces separate analyses for age and education.

Obtaining Multiple Comparisons

To obtain multiple comparison tests, enter a slash, the RANGES subcommand, and the name of the test:

```
oneway age by life(1,3) /ranges=btukey.
```

The following keywords for multiple comparison tests are available:

LSD   *Least-significant difference.*

DUNCAN   *Duncan's multiple range test.*

SNK   *Student-Newman-Keuls test.*

BTUKEY   *Tukey's alternate procedure.*

> **TUKEY**   *Tukey's honestly significant difference.*
>
> **MODLSD**   *Modified least-significant difference (Bonferroni test).*
>
> **SCHEFFE**   *Scheffe's test.*

For a description of these tests, see Winer (1971).

Available Options

These options can be specified on the OPTIONS subcommand on ONEWAY:

1   Include cases with user-missing values.
2   Exclude cases with missing values listwise.
3   Don't print variable labels.
6   Use value labels as group labels.

Available Statistics

On the STATISTICS subcommand, you can request descriptive statistics using Statistic 1. These include the number of cases, mean, standard deviation, standard error, minimum, maximum, and 95% confidence interval for each group.

MORE ABOUT THE ANOVA PROCEDURE

The ANOVA command is based on a variables specification much like that for ONEWAY. To test whether mean education level is the same among the groups defined by sex, race, and life satisfaction, type

```
anova educ by sex (1,2) race life (1,3).
```

The grouping variables, or factors, are followed by a range of values to be used in the analysis. When two factors have the same value range (like *RACE* and *LIFE* in this example), you can specify the range once, after both of them.

The factors should be coded as consecutive integers. If your factor is coded 10, 20, or 30, use the RECODE command to reassign the codes to consecutive integers such as 1, 2, 3.

Cases for which the factors have values outside the specified range are not analyzed. For instance, in Figure 20.7 the range for *RACE* was specified as (1,2). Cases coded 3 (the "other" races) were omitted from that analysis.

Estimation Method

ANOVA uses the **classical experimental approach** in calculating the sums of squares, unless you tell it differently. This means that it calculates the sums of squares for main effects before calculating them for interactions. If you specify Option 9 on the OPTIONS subcommand, ANOVA uses the alternative **regression approach**, in which all sums of squares are evaluated simultaneously. Option 9 usually results in an analysis that is easier to interpret. It was used in Figure 20.7.

Suppressing High-Order Interactions

You can specify up to five factors on the ANOVA command. Thus in theory you can estimate the significance of interactions among five factors. It is very difficult, however, to interpret interactions involving more than two or three factors. Sometimes you may want to use one of the following options (on the OPTIONS subcommand) to suppress the estimation of high-order interactions.

3   Suppress all interactions terms.
4   Suppress 3-way (and higher) terms.
5   Suppress 4-way (and higher) terms.
6   Suppress 5-way terms.

Displaying Cell Means

An analysis of variance table such as Figure 20.7 tells you which groups have significantly different means, but it doesn't show you what those means are. Request Statistic 3 on the STATISTICS subcommand to get a display of the mean and number of cases in each cell.

Because of the computational method used, you can't specify Statistic 3 along with Option 9. If you want to use Option 9, you can see the cell means by using the MEANS procedure.

WHAT'S NEXT?

In this part of the book, we have considered how to draw conclusions about the population based on results observed in a sample. We have also looked at several commonly used procedures for testing hypotheses about group means. In the next part of the book we'll continue to test various hypotheses, but the emphasis will change from studying whether groups differ to studying the relationships between pairs of variables. We'll consider how to describe the strength and nature of the relationships between variables. In Chapter 21 we look at how to describe a relationship between the variables in a crosstabulation.

Summary

How can you test the null hypothesis that several population means are equal?

Analysis of variance can be used to test the null hypothesis that several population means are equal.

To use analysis of variance, your groups must be random samples from normal populations with the same variance.

In analysis of variance, the observed variability in the samples is subdivided into two parts—variability of the observations within a group about the group mean (within-groups variation), and variability of the group means (between-groups variation).

The F statistic is calculated as the ratio of the between-groups estimate of variance to the within-groups estimate of variance.

The analysis of variance F test does not pinpoint which means are significantly different from each other.

Multiple comparison procedures are used to identify pairs of means that appear to be different from each other.

EXERCISES

Syntax

1 You run the command

```
oneway weight by income.
```

and get the following error message:

```
ERROR   11404,  (End of command)
Missing MIN/MAX range on ONEWAY command.
This command not executed.
```

Fix the command.

2 Correct the following commands (if necessary):

a. oneway income by race(4).

b. oneway temperature by region(1,4).

c. oneway educ by zodiac(1,12).

d. oneway educ by zodiac(1,12) /options = ranges btukey.

3 You wish to investigate the relationship between cholesterol levels (*CHOL*) and years of education (*EDUC*). You have education recorded in actual years. Write out the command you would use to create four categories of people (8 or fewer years of education; 9–12 years; 13–16 years; and more than 16 years). Then write the ONE-WAY command to test the hypothesis that there is no difference in average cholesterol levels for the different education categories.

4 Modify your previous commands to obtain multiple comparisons using the BTUKEY procedure.

5 Correct the following commands (if necessary):

a. oneway analysis=blp by disease(1,3).

b. oneway var1 by var2(1,3) var3(1,2).

c. oneway var by var2(2,9).

d. oneway weight height temp by region(1,4).

Statistical Concepts

1 You are interested in comparing four methods of teaching. You randomly assign 20 students to each of the four methods and then administer a standardized test at the end of the study.

a. What null hypothesis are you interested in testing?

b. What statistical procedure might you use to test the hypothesis?

c. What assumptions are necessary for the statistical procedure you have selected?

2 You wish to test the null hypothesis that, in the population, there is no difference in the average age at marriage for people who find life exciting, routine, or dull. You run an analysis of variance and obtain the following table:

```
- - - - - - - - - - O N E W A Y - - - - - - - - - -

    Variable  AGEWED     Age of first marriage

    By Variable  LIFE     Is life exciting or dull?

                         Analysis of Variance
```

Source	D.F.	Sum of Squares	Mean Squares	F Ratio	F Prob.
Between Groups	2	46.6433	23.3216	1.0832	.3388
Within Groups	1164	25060.5461	21.5297		
Total	1166	25107.1894			

a. Is there sufficient evidence to reject the null hypothesis?

b. What conclusion can you draw from the table?

c. If you compute the average ages at marriage for each of the groups, would you expect the sample means to be similar or quite different?

d. Since people who have never been married are assigned a "missing" code for the *AGEWED* variable, do you think they are included in this analysis or not?

3 We've seen that there is a statistically significant difference in average years of education for people who find life exciting, routine, or dull. Now let's see whether there is a difference in their mothers' education levels.

a. The variable name for mother's education is *MAEDUC*. Write out the SPSS/PC+ command to obtain an analysis of variance table and Tukey's alternate multiple comparison test (BTUKEY).

b. What is the null hypothesis that you're testing?

c. The following table is the analysis of variance. What can you conclude from it?

```
- - - - - - - - - O N E W A Y - - - - - - - - -

Variable   MAEDUC     Mother's highest year of school

By Variable  LIFE     Is life exciting or dull?


                         Analysis of Variance

                              Sum of        Mean          F      F
          Source      D.F.    Squares       Squares     Ratio  Prob.

Between Groups           2    503.2386      251.6193   21.8666  .0000

Within Groups         1228  14130.5989       11.5070

Total                 1230  14633.8375
```

d. The results of Tukey's multiple comparison procedure is shown below. Which groups are significantly different from each other?

```
Multiple Range Test


Tukey-B Procedure
Ranges for the 0.050 level -

      3.07   3.33

The ranges above are table ranges.
The value actually compared with MEAN(J)-MEAN(I) is..
      2.3986 * Range * Sqrt(1/N(I) + 1/N(J))

   (*) Denotes pairs of groups significantly different at the 0.050 level


                          G G G
                          r r r
                          p p p
     Mean      Group      3 2 1

    8.0204     Grp 3
    9.9537     Grp 2      *
   10.8464     Grp 1      * *
```

4 A market researcher wants to see whether people in four regions of a city buy the same brand of dishwashing detergent. He takes a random sample of people in the different areas and asks them which of 10 brands (coded from 1 to 10) they purchase most often. He enters the data into SPSS/PC+ and runs the ONEWAY procedure. The observed significance level for his F value is 0.00001.

a. Explain his results to him. What can he conclude?

b. How would you analyze these data?

Data Analysis

Use the gss.sys system file to answer the following questions.

1 Using the RECODE command, modify the marital status variable (*MARITAL*) so it has three categories: 1=*married*; 2=*widowed, divorced,* or *separated*; and 3=*never married*.

a. Test the null hypothesis that the average number of years of education is the same in all three groups. Be sure to test the required assumptions using EXAMINE.

b. Using a multiple comparison procedure, identify which groups are significantly different from each other.

c. Summarize your results.

d. Explain why you agree or disagree with the statement that people who are well educated tend not to marry. Perform whatever analysis you may think is helpful to support your position. Consider other possible explanations for the results you obtain.

2 You're interested in seeing whether the number of siblings a person has (*SIBS*) is related to perception of life.

a. State the null hypothesis.

b. Perform the appropriate statistical analysis to test the hypothesis.

c. Which groups have significantly different means?

d. What explanations can you offer for the observed results?

3 We've seen that there is a relationship between education and perception of life. Investigate whether there is a relationship between the education of a person's parents and his or her perception of life. Write a paragraph summarizing your results.

4 For the GSS data, formulate four hypotheses that can be tested using analysis of variance procedures. Explore two of these hypotheses with ONEWAY and write a short paper summarizing your results.

PART FOUR
Examining Relationships

21 Measuring Association

How can you measure the strength of the relationship between two categorical variables?

■ What are measures of association, and why are they useful?

■ Is there a single best measure of association?

■ Why is the chi-square statistic not a good measure of association?

■ How can the chi-square statistic be modified so it could be used to express the strength of the association between two variables?

■ What is proportional reduction in error?

■ When a measure of association equals zero, does that always mean the two variables are unrelated?

■ For variables measured on an ordinal scale, how can the additional information about order be incorporated into a measure of association?

■ What are concordant and discordant pairs, and how are they used in various measures of association?

One of the most frequently asked questions in any study is, "Are these two variables related?" Is education related to voting behavior? Is marital status related to happiness? Is ability to close a sale related to the experience of the salesperson? You usually want to know more than just *whether* the two variables are related. You also want to know the strength and nature of the relationship. If job satisfaction is related to perceiving life as exciting, how strongly is it related? And does the likelihood of perceiving life as exciting increase or decrease as job satisfaction increases?

THE STRENGTH OF A RELATIONSHIP

Many different statistical techniques are used to study the relationships among variables. We'll consider some of them in the chapters that follow. In this chapter, we'll look at techniques that are useful for measuring the strength and nature of relationships between two categorical variables. These variables have a limited number of possible values, and their distribution can be examined with a crosstabulation table.

Why Not Chi-Square?

In Chapter 19, we used the chi-square test to test the null hypothesis that two categorical variables are independent. If you reject the null hypothesis of independence, what can you say about the two variables? Can you conclude anything about the strength or nature of their association on the basis of the chi-square value? Do large chi-square values indicate strong associations and small values indicate weak ones?

The value of the chi-square statistic provides little information about the strength and type of association between two variables. In Chapter 19, you saw how sample size influences the value of chi-square. If you take a particular crosstabulation and multiply all cell frequencies by 10, you also increase the value of the chi-square by 10 even though you're not in any way changing the nature or strength of the association.

Since the value of the chi-square statistic depends on sample size as well as the amount of departure from independence for the two variables, you can't compare chi-square values from several studies with different sample sizes. This is one reason why the chi-square statistic isn't very useful as a measure of association.

Furthermore, since chi-square is based only on expected and observed frequencies, it's possible for many different types of tables to have the same value for the chi-square statistic. Different types of relationships between two variables can result in the same chi-square value. Knowing the chi-square tells you nothing about the nature of the association.

Measures of Association

Statistics that are used to quantify the strength and nature of the relationship between two variables in a crosstabulation are called **measures of association**. There are many different measures of association, since there are many different ways to define "association." The measures differ in how they can be interpreted and in how they define perfect and intermediate levels of association. They also differ in the level of measurement required for the variables. For example, if two variables are measured on an ordinal scale, it makes sense to talk about their values increasing or decreasing together. Such a statement is meaningless for variables measured on a nominal scale.

No single measure of association is best for all situations. To choose the best one for a particular situation, you must consider the type of data and the way you want to define association. If a certain measure has a low value for a table, this doesn't necessarily mean that the two variables are unrelated. It can also mean that they're not related in the way that the measure can detect. But you shouldn't calculate a lot of measures and then report only the largest. Select the appropriate measures in advance. If you look at enough different measures, you increase your chance of finding significant associations in the sample that do not exist in the population.

MEASURES OF ASSOCIATION FOR NOMINAL VARIABLES

When you have variables that are measured on a nominal scale, you're limited in what you can say about their relationship. You can't say that marital status increases as religious affiliation increases, or that automobile color decreases with increasing state of residence. You can't say anything about the direction of the association. If the categories of the variables don't have a meaningful order, it doesn't make sense to say they're associated in one direction or another. All you can do is try to measure the strength of the association. Two types of measures of association are useful for nominal variables: measures based on chi-square and measures of proportional reduction in error (called PRE measures). Let's look at each of these in turn.

Measures Based on Chi-Square

We just finished discussing why the chi-square statistic is not a good measure of association. And it isn't. However, since its use is common in tests of independence, people have tried to construct measures of association based on it. The measures based on chi-square attempt to modify it so it isn't influenced by sample size and so it falls in the range of 0 to 1. Without such adjustments, you can't compare chi-square values from tables with different sample sizes and different dimensions. In the range from 0 to 1, a value of 0 corresponds to no association and a value of 1 to perfect association. Coefficients are often **normalized** to fall in this range.

The Phi Coefficient

The phi coefficient is one of the simplest modifications of the chi-square statistic. To calculate a phi coefficient, just divide the chi-square value by the sample size and then take the square root. The formula is

$$\phi = \sqrt{\frac{\chi^2}{N}}$$

The maximum value of phi depends on the size of the table. If a table has more than two rows or two columns, the phi coefficient can be greater than 1—an undesirable feature.

The Coefficient of Contingency

The coefficient of contingency is always less than or equal to 1. It's often abbreviated with the letter C. It's calculated from the chi-square statistic using the following formula:

$$C = \sqrt{\frac{\chi^2}{\chi^2 + N}}$$

Although the value of C is always between 0 and 1, it can never get as high as 1, even for a table showing what seems to be a perfect relationship. The largest value it can have depends on the number of rows and columns in the table. For example, if you have a four-by-four table, the largest possible value of C is 0.87.

Cramér's V

Cramér's V is a chi-square-based measure of association that *can* attain the value of 1 for tables of any dimension. Its formula is:

$$V = \sqrt{\frac{\chi^2}{N(k-1)}}$$

where k is the smaller of the number of rows and columns. If the number of rows or columns is 2, Cramér's V is identical in value to phi.

Calculating Chi-Square-Based Measures

To make our discussion a little more concrete, let's compute phi, Cramér's V, and the contingency coefficient C for the variables in Figure 21.1. (This figure is the crosstabulation of marital status and excitement. It's from Chapter 10, with added statistics.) The commands for the crosstabulation and the statistics are:

```
get file 'gss.sys'.
crosstabs life by marital
  /cells count column /statistics chisq phi cc.
```

Keyword CHISQ on the STATISTICS subcommand gives us chi-square, keyword PHI gives both phi and Cramér's V, and keyword CC gives the contingency coefficient.

Look at the Pearson chi-square value and its associated significance level printed below the table. From these, you'd reject the null hypothesis that the two variables are independent. Now look at the three chi-square-based measures to see how strongly marital status and excitement are related. Since marital status is a nominal variable, all you can do is measure the strength of the association between the two variables.

The value for phi is 0.146. It is obtained by dividing 31.04 by 1,461 and then taking the square root. The value for Cramér's V is 0.103. It's the square root of the chi-square value divided by twice the sample size. You divide by twice the sample size because k, the smaller of the number of rows and columns, is 3, so $k-1$ is 2. The contingency coefficient is 0.144. It's the square root of the chi-square value divided by the sum of chi-square and the sample size.

Although the three measures of association aren't equal, they're of the same magnitude. On a scale of 0 to 1, none of the numbers is particularly large, even though the observed significance level for the chi-square statistic is quite small. That's because for large sample sizes, even small departures from independence are statistically significant.

The "not particularly large" interpretation of these statistics isn't very satisfying. It would be helpful to have a more concrete interpretation, some way of putting into words what it means for two variables to have a Cramér's V of 0.103. Unfortunately, there is none. Chi-square-based measures are difficult to interpret. They can be used to compare the strength

Figure 21.1 Chi-square-based measures of association

```
LIFE   Is life exciting or dull?  by  MARITAL  Marital status

             MARITAL                                    Page 1 of 1
        Count
        Col Pct |Married Widowed  Divorced Separate Never ma
                                          d        rried
                |  1       2        3        4       5    | Row
    LIFE        |                                         | Total
                +------------------------------------------
              1 |  392      51       77       18     146  | 684
    Exciting    | 47.6    33.8     46.7     42.9    52.3  | 46.8

              2 |  401      82       77       20     124  | 704
    Pretty routine| 48.7  54.3     46.7     47.6    44.4  | 48.2

              3 |   31      18       11        4       9  | 73
    Dull        |  3.8    11.9      6.7      9.5     3.2  | 5.0

        Column     824     151      165       42     279   1461
        Total     56.4    10.3     11.3      2.9    19.1  100.0

        Chi-Square                Value        DF           Significance
    --------------------        ----------     ----         ------------

    Pearson                      31.04002       8              .00014
    Likelihood Ratio             27.48840       8              .00058
    Mantel-Haenszel test for       .95311       1              .32893
        linear association
    Minimum Expected Frequency -  2.099
    Cells with Expected Frequency < 5 -    1 OF    15 (  6.7%)

                                                              Approximate
        Statistic                Value    ASE1    T-value    Significance
    --------------------        ---------  --------  -------  ------------

    Phi                          .14576                        .00014 *1
    Cramer's V                   .10307                        .00014 *1
    Contingency Coefficient      .14424                        .00014 *1

    * 1 Pearson chi-square probability
```

of association in different tables. However, the "strength of association" being compared isn't easily related to an intuitive concept of association.

Proportional Reduction in Error

Commonly used alternatives to the measures based on chi-square are coefficients based on the idea of **proportional reduction in error**, or PRE. Unlike chi-square-based measures, PRE coefficients have a clear interpretation. These measures are based on how well you can predict the value of a dependent variable when you know the value of the independent variable. The measures compare the errors in two different situations: one where you don't use the independent variable for prediction and one where you do.

Suppose you have a sample of married people. The dependent variable is whether life is seen as exciting, routine, or dull, and the independent variable is the happiness of a person's marriage.

■ In the first situation, you try to predict how a person feels about life, knowing only what percentage of the sample falls into each of the excitement categories.

■ In the second situation, you have an additional piece of information available—the happiness of the person's marriage.

If the two variables are related, the additional piece of information in the second situation improves your ability to predict correctly. If all happily married people find life exciting, all moderately happy people find life routine, and all unhappily married people find life boring, then knowing the condition of a person's marriage lets you predict perfectly whether they find life exciting, routine, or dull. There is a perfect relationship between the variables. If you know one, you know the other. Most of the time, though, a relationship is less than perfect.

Let's consider how you can compute the error rates in these two situations and calculate lambda, a commonly used PRE measure.

Calculating Lambda

Figure 21.2 is a crosstabulation of the happiness of people's marriages with the excitement they find in life. The entry in each cell is just the number of cases in that cell. The following commands produced the crosstabulation as well as lambda statistics, which are shown in Figure 21.3:

```
get file 'gss.sys'.
crosstabs life by hapmar
 /statistics lambda.
```

Figure 21.2 Excitement by marital happiness

```
LIFE  Is life exciting or dull?  by  HAPMAR  Happiness of marriage

                          HAPMAR                    Page 1 of 1
                  Count
                         Very hap Pretty h Not too
                         py       appy     happy     Row
                           1        2        3      Total
       LIFE       ────────────────────────────────
                    1      302       83        6      391
        Exciting                                     47.6

                    2      225      161       14      400
      Pretty routine                                 48.7

                    3       11       14        5       30
        Dull                                          3.7

                 Column    538      258       25      821
                 Total    65.5     31.4      3.0    100.0
```

If you had no information about how happy a person's marriage is, what would you predict that the person would say about how exciting life is? Since you're interested in making as few errors as possible, you should predict the excitement category that occurs most often in the sample. In this case, you should predict that the person finds life routine. More people said they find life routine than any other response, so that's the best guess when you don't know anything about a person. Now count the number of cases in the table that you'd misclassify if you guessed "routine" for everyone. Your prediction would be wrong for the 391 people who said life is exciting and for the 30 people who said life is dull. The total number of misclassified people is the sum of these two numbers, 421. This is the error for the first situation, when you know nothing except the distribution of the dependent variable in the sample.

Let's take a look at the second situation. The rule is straightforward: for each category of the *independent* variable, predict the category of the *dependent* variable that occurs most frequently. If you know that someone is very happily married, the best guess for the excitement category is *Exciting*, because that's the most frequent choice of people who were very happily married. Using this rule, you'd incorrectly classify 236 people who said they're very happily married: 225 who found life routine and 11 who found life dull.

Applying the same rule, you'd predict *Pretty routine* for people who said their marriages are pretty happy. You'd be wrong in 97 cases. For people whose marriages are not too happy, you'd also predict *Pretty routine*. You'd be wrong for 11 of these people.

Now let's compare the errors. In the first situation, you incorrectly classified 421 people. In the second situation, you incorrectly classified 344 people. The **lambda** statistic tells you the proportion by which you can reduce your error in predicting the dependent variable if you know the independent variable. That's why it's called a **proportional reduction in error** measure. Lambda (λ) is calculated as:

$$\lambda = \frac{\text{Misclassified in situation 1} - \text{Misclassified in situation 2}}{\text{Misclassified in situation 1}}$$

For this table,

$$\lambda = \frac{421 - 344}{421} = \frac{77}{421} = 0.183$$

By knowing how happy a person's marriage was, you reduced your error by 18%.

The largest value that lambda can be is 1. Figure 21.3 shows a table in which lambda is 1. For each category of the independent variable, there is one cell with all of the cases. If you guess that value for all cases, you make no errors. The introduction of the independent variable lets you predict perfectly, and it results in a 100% reduction in error rate.

A value of zero for lambda means the independent variable is of no help in predicting the dependent variable. When two variables are statistically independent, lambda is zero; but a lambda of zero does not necessarily imply statistical independence. As with all measures of association, lambda

Figure 21.3 A table in which lambda equals 1

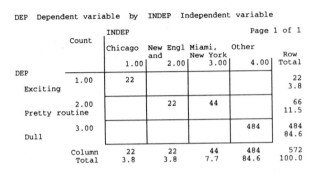

DEP Dependent variable by INDEP Independent variable

		INDEP				Page 1 of 1	
	Count	Chicago	New Engl and	Miami, New York	Other		Row
		1.00	2.00	3.00	4.00		Total
DEP	1.00	22					22
Exciting							3.8
	2.00		22	44			66
Pretty routine							11.5
	3.00				484		484
Dull							84.6
	Column	22	22	44	484		572
	Total	3.8	3.8	7.7	84.6		100.0

measures association in a very specific way—reduction in error when values of one variable are used to predict values of the other. If this particular type of association is absent, lambda is zero. Even when lambda is zero, other measures of association may find association of a different kind. No measure of association is sensitive to every type of association imaginable.

Two Different Lambdas

Lambda is not a symmetric measure. Its value depends on which variable you predict from which. Suppose that instead of predicting the excitement category based on marital happiness, you tried to predict the reverse— how happy a person's marriage was based on how exciting the person found life to be. You'd get a different value for lambda. You'd get a value of 0.011. Both of these values are shown in Figure 21.3. The first is in the line labeled *With LIFE Dependent,* and the second is in the line labeled *With HAPMAR Dependent.*

Figure 21.4 Different versions of lambda

Statistic		Value	ASE1	T-value	Approximate Significance
Lambda :					
symmetric		.11364	.03149	3.42933	
with LIFE	dependent	.18290	.04929	3.37739	
with HAPMAR	dependent	.01060	.01757	.60013	

Number of Missing Observations: 652

The number in the column labeled *ASE1* is an estimate of the standard error of the lambdas. It tells you how much you would expect the value of lambda to vary from sample to sample. The ratio of the coefficient to its standard error is in the column labeled *T value.* (The standard error used to compute the *t* value is somewhat different than ASE1. It's based on the assumption that the population coefficient is zero.) The larger the *t* value, the less likely it is that, in the population, the value of lambda is zero. (The column labeled *Approximate Significance* is left blank because, especially for small samples, it is difficult to mathematically estimate.)

The statistics in Figure 21.3 were produced by the CROSSTABS command that produced the table in Figure 21.2. The LAMBDA keyword on the STATISTICS subcommand provides both lambdas, as well as another one we're about to discuss.

?   *Why can't I get the* t *value when I divide the coefficient by ASE1?*
There are two slightly different estimates of the standard error for a coefficient. One of them assumes that the value of the coefficient is zero. The other, labeled *ASE1*, does not make any assumptions about the value of the coefficient. The standard error used by SPSS/PC+ to calculate the *t* value is not ASE1, but the other one. That's why you can't obtain the *t* value from the other two numbers.   ■■■

Symmetric Lambda

In the previous example, we considered view of life as the dependent variable and happiness of the marriage as the independent variable. But this need not be the case. It's certainly possible that a good marriage makes life exciting or that an exciting life makes for a happy marriage. If you have no reason to consider one of the variables dependent and the other independent, you can compute a **symmetric** lambda coefficient. You predict the first variable from the second and then the second variable from the first.

For example, if marital status is predicted without knowledge of the excitement category, you misclassify 283 people. With the addition of the excitement variable, you misclassify 280 people, not a big difference. From the calculation of lambda with excitement as dependent, you found that inclusion of marital status decreased the number misclassified from 421 to 344. The symmetric lambda is calculated as the sum of the two differences divided by the total number misclassified without additional information. In other words, you just add up the numerators for the two lambdas, then add up the denominators, then divide:

$$\text{Symmetric } \lambda = \frac{(421 - 344) + (283 - 280)}{421 + 283} = \frac{77 + 3}{704} = 0.114$$

This number is the symmetric lambda in Figure 21.3.

Figure 21.5 A table in which lambda equals zero

```
DEP  Dependent variable  by  INDEP  Independent variable
                    INDEP                    Page 1 of 1
              Count
                                                 Row
                         1.00|   2.00|   3.00  Total
      DEP     ────────
              1.00       19      10       1        30
                                                 25.0

              2.00       20      20      20        60
                                                 50.0

              3.00        1      10      19        30
                                                 25.0

              Column     40      40      40       120
               Total    33.3    33.3    33.3    100.0
```

```
                                                        Approximate
          Statistic                Value    ASE1   T-value  Significance
     ─────────────────────        ───────  ───────  ──────  ───────────

     Lambda :
         symmetric                 .12857   .02684  4.32762
         with DEP    dependent     .00000   .00000
         with INDEP  dependent     .22500   .04921  4.32762
```

Is it really possible for variables to be related and still have a lambda of zero? That doesn't sound right. Actually, this can happen easily, depending on the distribution of the dependent variable. For example, consider Figure 21.5. The two variables are clearly associated, but value 2 of the dependent variable occurs most often in each category of the independent variable. You'd predict that value whether or not you knew the independent variable. Since knowing the independent variable doesn't help at all, lambda equals zero. You can see that SPSS/PC+ reports a lambda of zero when *DEP* is the dependent variable. Remember: a measure of association is sensitive to a particular kind of association. ∎∎∎

MEASURES OF ASSOCIATION FOR ORDINAL VARIABLES

Lambda can be used as a measure of association for variables measured on ordinal scales as well as for variables measured on nominal scales. In fact, both variables we used in the previous example, happiness of marriage and degree of excitement with life, are ordinal variables. The computation of lambda, however, didn't use the order information. We could have interchanged the order of the rows and columns in any way we wanted (for example, we could have put *Not too happy* before *Very happy*, or *Pretty routine* before *Excited*) and not changed the value of lambda.

There are measures of association that make use of the additional information available for ordinal variables. They tell us not only about the strength of the association but the direction as well. If the degree of excitement with life increases as the degree of happiness of marriage increases, we can say that the two variables have a **positive relationship**. If, on the other hand, the values of one variable increase while those of the other decrease, we can say the variables have a **negative relationship**. We can't make statements like these about nominal variables, since there's no order to the categories of the variables. Values can't increase or decrease unless they have an order.

Concordant and Discordant Pairs

Many ordinal measures of association are based on comparing pairs of cases. For example, look at Table 21.1, which contains a listing of the values of *LIFE*, the excitement variable, and *HAPMAR*, the marriage variable, for three cases.

Table 21.1   Values of LIFE and HAPMAR

	LIFE	HAPMAR
Case 1	1	2
Case 2	2	3
Case 3	3	2

Consider the pair of cases Case 1 and Case 2. Both Case 2 values are larger than the corresponding values for Case 1. That is, the value for *LIFE* is larger for Case 2 than for Case 1, and the value for *HAPMAR* is larger for Case 2 than for Case 1. Such a pair of cases is called **concordant**. A pair of cases is concordant if the value of each variable is larger (or each is smaller) for one case than for the other case.

A pair of cases is **discordant** if the value of one variable for a case is larger than the value for the other case, but the direction is reversed for the second variable. For example, Case 2 and Case 3 are a discordant pair, since the value of *LIFE* for Case 3 is larger than for Case 2, but the value of *HAPMAR* is larger for Case 2 than for Case 3.

When two cases have identical values on one or both variables, they are said to be **tied**.

There are five possible outcomes when you compare two cases. They can be concordant, discordant, tied on the first variable, tied on the second variable, or tied on both variables. When data are arranged in a crosstabulation, it's easy to compute the number of concordant, discordant, and tied pairs just by looking at the table and adding up cell frequencies.

If most of the pairs are concordant, the association is said to be positive. As values of one variable increase (or decrease), so do the values of the other variable. If most of the pairs are discordant, the association is negative. As values of one variable increase, those of the other tend to decrease. If concordant and discordant pairs are equally likely, we say there is no association.

Measures Based on Concordant and Discordant Pairs

The ordinal measures of association that we'll consider are all based on the difference between the number of concordant pairs (P) and the number of discordant pairs (Q), calculated for all *distinct* pairs of observations. Since we want our measures of association to fall within a known range for all tables, we must standardize the difference, P-Q, so that it falls between -1 and 1, where -1 indicates a perfect negative relationship, +1 indicates a perfect positive relationship, and 0 indicates no relationship. The various measures differ in the way they attempt to standardize P-Q.

Goodman and Kruskal's Gamma

One way of standardizing the difference between the number of concordant and discordant pairs is to use Goodman and Kruskal's **gamma**. You calculate the difference between the number of concordant and discordant pairs (P-Q) and then divide this difference by the sum of the number of concordant and discordant pairs (P+Q).

Look at Figure 21.6, which contains the value of gamma for the *LIFE* by *HAPMAR* table. Commands for producing the table and gamma are:

```
get file 'gss.sys'.
crosstabs life by hapmar
  /statistics=gamma.
```

Keyword GAMMA on the STATISTICS subcommand requests the value of gamma for the table.

Figure 21.6 Goodman and Kruskal's gamma

Statistic	Value	ASE1	T-value	Approximate Significance
Gamma	.45929	.05592	7.27564	

Number of Missing Observations: 652

For this table, gamma is 0.459. What does this mean? A positive gamma tells you that there are more "like" (concordant) pairs of cases than "unlike" pairs. There is a positive relationship between happiness of marriage and degree of excitement. As happiness of marriage increases, so does excitement with life. A negative gamma would mean that as happiness in marriage increases, excitement with life decreases.

The absolute value of gamma has a proportional reduction in error interpretation. You are trying to predict whether a pair of cases is concordant or discordant. In the first situation, you classify pairs as like or unlike based on the flip of a fair coin. In the second situation, you base your decision rule on whether there are more concordant or discordant pairs. If most of the pairs are concordant you predict "like" for all pairs. If most of the pairs are discordant you predict "unlike." The absolute value of gamma (the numerical value, ignoring a minus sign if there is one) is the proportional reduction in error when the second rule is used instead of the first.

For example, if half of the pairs of cases are concordant and half are discordant, guessing randomly and classifying all cases as concordant leads to the same number of misclassified cases—one half. The value of gamma is then zero. If all the pairs are concordant, guessing "like" will result in correct classification of all pairs. Guessing randomly will classify only half of the pairs correctly. In this situation, the value of gamma is 1.

If two variables are independent, the value of gamma is zero. However, a gamma of zero does not necessarily mean independence. (If the table is two by two, though, a gamma of zero *does* mean that the variables are independent.)

Kendall's Tau-*b*

Gamma ignores all pairs of cases that involve ties. A measure that attempts to normalize P-Q by considering ties on each variable in a pair separately (but not ties on both variables) is **tau-b**. It's computed as

$$\tau_b = \frac{P - Q}{\sqrt{(P + Q + T_X) \times (P + Q + T_Y)}}$$

where T_X is the number of ties involving only the first variable and T_Y is the number of ties involving only the second variable. Tau-*b* can have the value of +1 and –1 only for square tables. Since the denominator is complicated, there's no simple explanation in terms of proportional reduction of error. However, tau-*b* is a commonly used measure.

Tau-*c*

A measure that can attain, or nearly attain, the values of +1 and –1 for a table of any size is **tau-c**. It's computed as

$$\tau_c = \frac{2m(P - Q)}{N^2(m - 1)}$$

where m is the smaller of the number of rows and columns. Unfortunately, there is no simple proportional reduction of error interpretation of tau-c either.

Somers' d

Gamma, tau-b, and tau-c are all symmetric measures. It doesn't matter whether one of the variables is considered dependent. The value of the statistic is the same. Somers proposed an extension of gamma in which one of the variables is considered dependent. It differs from gamma only in that the denominator is the sum of all pairs of cases that are not tied on the independent variable. (In gamma, *all* cases involving ties are excluded from the denominator.)

MEASURES INVOLVING INTERVAL DATA

If the two variables are measured on an interval scale, you can calculate coefficients that make use of this additional information. The Pearson correlation coefficient, which we will discuss in Chapter 23, measures the strength of what's called a **linear** association. The eta coefficient can be used when a dependent variable is measured on an interval scale and the independent variable on a nominal or ordinal scale. When eta is squared, it can be interpreted as the proportion of the total variance in the dependent variable that can be accounted for by knowing the values of the independent variable.

TESTING HYPOTHESES

In addition to assessing the strength and nature of a relationship, you may want to test hypotheses about the various measures of association. For example, you may want to test the null hypothesis that the value of a measure is zero in the population. This doesn't involve anything new. You just have to calculate the probability that you'd obtain a value as large (in absolute value) as the one you observed if the value is zero in the population. SPSS/PC+ prints the approximate significance levels for some of the measures of association we've discussed in this chapter.

MORE ABOUT STATISTICS FOR CROSSTABS

The STATISTICS subcommand requests summary statistics. You can specify the STATISTICS subcommand by itself or with one or more keywords. If you specify STATISTICS by itself, CROSSTABS calculates CHISQ. If you include a keyword or keywords on the STATISTICS subcommand, CROSSTABS calculates all the statistics you request.

The following keywords can be specified on the STATISTICS subcommand:

CHISQ *Chi-square.* The output includes the Pearson chi-square, likelihood-ratio chi-square, and Mantel-Haenszel linear association chi-square. For 2×2 tables, Fisher's exact test is computed when a table that does not result from missing rows or columns in a larger table has a cell with an expected frequency less than 5; Yates' corrected chi-square is computed for all other 2×2 tables.

PHI *Phi and Cramér's* V.

CC *Contingency coefficient.*

LAMBDA *Lambda (symmetric and asymmetric) and Goodman and Kruskal's tau.*

UC *Uncertainty coefficient (symmetric and asymmetric).*

BTAU *Kendall's tau*-b.

CTAU *Kendall's tau*-c.

GAMMA *Gamma.* Zero-order gammas are displayed for 2-way tables and conditional gammas are displayed for 3-way to 10-way tables.

D *Somers'* d *(symmetric and asymmetric).*

ETA *Eta.* Available for numeric data only.

CORR *Pearson's* r *and Spearman's correlation coefficient.* Available for numeric data only.

KAPPA *Kappa coefficient.* Kappa can only be computed for square tables in which the row and column values are identical. (Kraemer, 1982.)

RISK *Relative risk.* Relative risk can be calculated only for 2×2 tables. (Kleinbaum et al., 1982.)

ALL *All available statistics.*

NONE *No summary statistics.* This is the default if the STATISTICS subcommand is omitted.

WHAT'S NEXT?

In this chapter, we considered how to measure the strength and nature of the relationship between two variables that have a limited number of distinct categories. What if we want to examine the relationship between two variables that are measured on an interval or ratio scale? That's what the remainder of the book is about.

Summary

How can you measure the strength of the relationship between two categorical variables?

Many measures of association can be used to measure the strength of the relationship between two categorical variables.

Measures of association differ in the way they define association.

You should select a measure of association based on the characteristics of the data and how you want to define association.

The chi-square statistic is not a good measure of association. Its value doesn't tell you anything about the strength of the relationship between two variables.

Measures of proportional reduction in error (PRE) compare the error you make when you predict values of one variable based on values of another with the error when you predict them without information about the other variable.

Special measures of association are available for ordinal variables. They are based on counting the number of concordant pairs (as one variable increases, so does the other) and the number of discordant pairs (as one variable increases, the other decreases).

EXERCISES

Syntax

1 Write the commands to recode the *AGE* variable into decades and to obtain a crosstabulation of age in decades and satisfaction with job or housework (*SATJOB*). Include the appropriate percentages and measures of association.

2 Correct the errors in the following commands:

```
recode satjob (1= 1,2) (2=3) (3=4).
value labels satjob 1 Very or moderately satisfied
    /2 A little dissatisfied/ 3 Very dissatisfied.
crosstabs satjob by life / all statistics.
```

3 Write the appropriate commands to obtain a crosstabulation of condition of health and belief in life after death. Obtain appropriate percentages and measures of association.

Statistical Concepts

1 Indicate whether you agree or disagree with each of the following statements, and why.

   a. If one of the measures of association provided by CROSSTABS has a very small value, it is safe to assume that the other measures of association will also have small values.

   b. Chi-square-based measures of association are easier to interpret than PRE-based measures.

   c. A good measure of association for nominal variables indicates the strength of the association as well as the direction.

   d. Large values for the chi-square statistic indicate strong association between two variables.

2 For each of the following measures of association, indicate whether its value depends on which variable is specified as the row variable and which is specified as the column variable.

   a. Lambda

   b. Symmetric lambda

   c. Gamma

   d. Somers' d

   e. Cramér's V

   f. Tau-b

   g. Tau-c

3 Which of the measures of association calculated by CROSSTABS are sensitive to all types of association?

4 What is the reason for normalizing measures of association to make their values fall within the range from –1 to +1 or from 0 to 1?

5 The following is a crosstabulation of condition of health and perception of life as exciting, routine, or dull:

```
LIFE   Is life exciting or dull?  by  HEALTH  Condition of health

                    HEALTH                              Page 1 of 1
            Count
            Exp Val  Excellen Good     Fair     Poor
            Col Pct  t                                    Row
                       1        2        3        4       Total
    LIFE
               1     249      320       95       16       680
    Exciting           202.5    325.7    119.5    32.3    46.9%
                     57.6%    46.0%    37.3%    23.2%

               2     175      350      137       36       698
    Pretty routine     207.8    334.3    122.7    33.2    48.1%
                     40.5%    50.4%    53.7%    52.2%

               3       8       25       23       17        73
    Dull              21.7     35.0     12.8      3.5      5.0%
                      1.9%     3.6%     9.0%    24.6%

            Column   432      695      255       69      1451
            Total   29.8%    47.9%    17.6%     4.8%    100.0%


      Chi-Square              Value         DF       Significance
------------------------      -----------   ----     ------------

Pearson                       104.21250      6         .00000
Likelihood Ratio               81.77819      6         .00000
Mantel-Haenszel test for       72.26830      1         .00000
   linear association

Minimum Expected Frequency -    3.471
Cells with Expected Frequency < 5 -   1 OF   12 (  8.3%)


                                                    Approximate
    Statistic           Value      ASE1    T-value  Significance
--------------------    ---------  ------- -------   ------------

Phi                      .26799                        .00000 *1
Cramer's V               .18950                        .00000 *1


Lambda :
    symmetric            .04904    .01322  3.60986
    with LIFE   dependent .09827   .02597  3.60986
    with HEALTH dependent .00000   .00000
Goodman & Kruskal Tau :
    with LIFE   dependent .02357   .00646            .00000 *2
    with HEALTH dependent .01549   .00396            .00000 *2


Gamma                    .30264    .03825  7.55347


*1 Pearson chi-square probability
*2 Based on chi-square approximation
```

a. Interpret all of the statistics printed.

b. Discuss the advantages and disadvantages of the various measures.

c. Show how lambda was computed.

6 The following table shows the relationship between depth of hypnosis and success in treatment of migraine headaches (Cedercreutz, 1978). Calculate the appropriate lambda statistic. How can you interpret this value?

```
Crosstabulation:    HYPNOSIS  by  MIGRAINE

                    MIGRAINE                    Page 1 of 1
              Count
              Tot Pct  Cured    Better   No chang
                                          e          Row
                         1        2        3      Total
HYPNOSIS      ─────────────────────────────────
              1        13        5                   18
  Deep                13.0      5.0                 18.0

              2        10       26       17          53
  Medium             10.0      26.0     17.0        53.0

              3                  1       28          29
  Light                         1.0     28.0        29.0

            Column     23       32       45         100
            Total     23.0     32.0     45.0       100.0
```

Number of Missing Observations: 0

7 Discuss the difference you would see in the gamma statistic if you coded job satisfaction from low to high and condition of health from good to poor, as compared to
   the value you would get if both job satisfaction and condition of health are coded in
   the same direction.

Data Analysis

Use the gss.sys system file to answer the following questions.

1 We've seen that there is a relationship between perception of life and marital status. Compute the appropriate statistics to measure the strength of the association.
   Discuss why you selected those particular measures.

2 To see whether the strength of the association of marital status and perception of
   life is similar for males and for females, make two separate tables. Compute the
   measures of association you chose in the previous question for each of the two tables. What do you conclude about the strength of the relationship? Give some possible explanations for it.

3 Select four pairs of variables in the gss.sys file for which the gamma statistic would
   be an appropriate measure of association. Write and run the SPSS/PC+ commands
   to compute it. Describe your results.

4 Select two nominal variables from the data file and compute appropriate measures
   of association. What can you conclude about the *direction* of the association?

 **Plotting Data**

How can you display the relationship between two variables
that are measured on an interval or ratio scale?

- What is a plot and why is it useful?

- What happens if several cases have the same or similar values for the
  variables you're plotting?

- How can a plot of two variables be modified to include information about an
  additional variable?

- How can a plot be used to identify unusual observations?

In Chapter 21, you saw how to use various statistics to measure the strength of a relationship between two variables. If you're interested in variables that have a limited number of categories—such as race, sex, or excitement with life—crosstabulations and measures of association are effective ways to look at relationships.

However, you may want to study the relationship between two variables that are measured on an interval or ratio scale. If so, then counting the number of cases for each of the possible combinations of values may be awkward, and it may not tell you much. Think of all the possible combinations of salary and age if salary is measured in dollars and age in years. A crosstabulation of these variables would have a very large number of cells. Of course, you could group the values into smaller numbers of categories, such as salary ranges of $5,000 or $10,000. It's easy then to construct tables based on these grouped values, and this is often a convenient way to examine the patterns in the data. But the grouping ignores some of the available information.

PLOTTING YOUR VARIABLES

A better way to display the data is to **plot** the values of the variables for all the cases. Look at Figure 23.1, a plot of father's education by mother's education for about 10% of the respondents in the General Social Survey. The commands that produce this plot are:

```
get file 'gss.sys'.
set seed 100000000.
sample .1.
variable labels paeduc "Dad's education"
 maeduc "Mom's education".
plot symbols default /plot paeduc with maeduc.
```

The SET SEED command determines the starting point for the random number generator which is used to select the random sample of cases. It is included here so you can reproduce the results shown in the book.

The SAMPLE command (discussed in Chapter 14) takes a 10% sample of the General Social Survey respondents because it is easier to read plots that use a modest number of observations. The VARIABLE LABELS command supplies variable labels that are short enough to fit on the plot, where SPSS/PC+ puts them automatically.

The SYMBOLS subcommand requests the default plotting symbols and the PLOT subcommand specifies the variables to be plotted. The variable before WITH is displayed on the vertical axis and the variable after WITH is displayed on the horizontal axis.

Figure 22.1 Plot of father's and mother's education

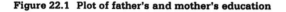
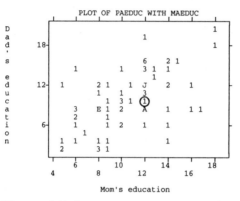

112 cases plotted.

Each person in the survey was asked about the education of both parents. The plot displays the pairs of values—father's education and mother's education. The number of years of education for the mother is shown on the horizontal axis (also called the **X axis**), and the number of years of education for the father is shown on the vertical axis (the **Y axis**).

Look at the circled point in Figure 23.1. Its value on the horizontal axis is 12 and on the vertical axis 10. This point represents a person whose mother had 12 years of education and whose father had 10.

You might wonder why the father's education is on the vertical axis and the mother's is on the horizontal axis. In this plot, there's no particular reason. These two variables could be interchanged. However, if one of the variables is considered a dependent variable and the other an independent variable, it's customary to plot the dependent variable on the vertical axis and the independent variable on the horizontal axis. For example, if salary is thought to depend on age, then it's customary to put salary on the vertical axis and age on the horizontal axis.

Interpreting a Plot

Looking at the plot in Figure 23.1, you see that a variety of different symbols are used to represent points. The number 1 is shown at the circled point, while the letter A appears below it. The symbol chosen by SPSS/

PC+ to represent a point depends on the number of cases in the data that have the particular combination of values. Since there is only one case plotted for which the mother has 12 years of education and the father has 10, the symbol 1 is used. When there are two cases with a certain combination of values (for example, 8 years of mother's education and 12 years of father's education), the symbol 2 is used.

Figure 22.2 Default symbols used in PLOT

```
Frequencies and symbols used (not applicable for control or overlay plots)

        1 - 1      11 - B     21 - L     31 - V
        2 - 2      12 - C     22 - M     32 - W
        3 - 3      13 - D     23 - N     33 - X
        4 - 4      14 - E     24 - O     34 - Y
        5 - 5      15 - F     25 - P     35 - Z
        6 - 6      16 - G     26 - Q     36 - *
        7 - 7      17 - H     27 - R
        8 - 8      18 - I     28 - S
        9 - 9      19 - J     29 - T
       10 - A      20 - K     30 - U
```

Figure 23.2 explains the meaning of each of the symbols. (SPSS/PC+ prints this table when you use the SYMBOLS subcommand on PLOT.) The number to the left of each dash indicates the number of cases that each symbol following the dash represents. For example, you can see that the numerals *1* to *9* represent 1 to 9 cases. The symbol *J* is used to represent 19 cases. Looking at Figure 23.1 again, you can see that for 19 cases, both parents have twelve years of education.

What does the plot show? The points seem to be arranged in a band running from the bottom left to the top right. You can see the pattern: as one variable increases, so does the other. Most of the cases with low values for *MAEDUC* also have low values for *PAEDUC*. Similarly, most of the cases with high values of one variable also have high values of the other. Looking at a plot is one of the best ways to examine relationships.

Cases with Similar Values

SPSS/PC+ normally produces a plot that will fit on the PC screen. The one shown above is 16 lines (from top to bottom) by 38 columns (from left to right). The two variables plotted are measured in whole years from 0 through 20, so each possible response has a different position horizontally—with some space in between—but not enough lines are available to put each different value of *PAEDUC* on a different line. This often happens in plots. What if both variables were salaries measured in dollars from $0 through $50,000? With just 16 lines available, SPSS/PC+ would have to lump cases within each $3125 range into a single line. Therefore, when you plot variables with many values and find a symbol indicating two or more cases at the same position, it's possible that those cases have close, but not identical, values.

USING A CONTROL VARIABLE ON A PLOT

Suppose you also want to know if father's and mother's education seem to make any difference in how the respondent perceives life. You could make three separate plots of mother's and father's education: one for people who found life exciting, one for people who found life routine, and one for people who found life dull. You could then compare the three plots and see whether the relationship between parents' education differs for the three groups. Another way to approach the problem, though, is to make a single plot in which individual points are identified as belonging to the different excitement categories. This **control plot** is easy to produce with SPSS/PC+:

```
set seed 100000000.
sample .1.
value labels life 1 'Exciting' 2 'Routine' 3 'Dull'.
plot plot paeduc with maeduc by life.
```

We have to repeat the SAMPLE command before each plot, since its effect is temporary and lasts only for a single procedure. The PLOT command looks much like the one used before. We dropped the SYMBOLS subcommand and added the keyword BY and the variable *LIFE*. The keyword BY indicates that the points are to be identified by their values for the following variable, in this case *LIFE*.

Interpreting a Control Plot

Look at the plot in Figure 23.3. The symbols that represent the points no longer indicate the number of cases. Instead, they tell you whether the person found life *exciting (E)*, *routine (R)*, or *dull (D)*. If cases with more than one excitement level overlap at the same point on the plot, a dollar sign is printed. The explanation of the symbols appears below the plot.

? *How does SPSS/PC+ know what symbols to print for people who found life exciting, routine, or dull?* It just takes the first character in each value label. If a control variable doesn't have value labels, the first character of the actual value is used. This is the only way SPSS/PC+ can guess what symbol you want. Often, you'll want to supply new value labels before making a control plot—as we did here. You'll certainly need to do this if the value labels for more than one category begin with the same letter, so you can easily tell the categories apart. ■■■

Figure 22.4 shows the control plot again, this time with a line drawn in to separate people whose mothers had more education from people whose fa-

Figure 22.3   Control plot

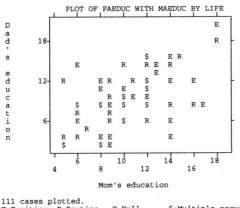

111 cases plotted.
E:Exciting   R:Routine   D:Dull $:Multiple occurrence

Figure 22.4   Which parent was better educated?

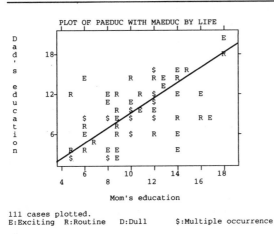

111 cases plotted.
E:Exciting   R:Routine   D:Dull $:Multiple occurrence

thers had more education. The people represented below the line are those whose mothers were better educated than their fathers. If people with better-educated mothers were more excited by life than people with better-educated fathers, you'd expect to find a higher proportion of *E*s below the line than above it.

USING REFERENCE LINES

In Figure 22.4, the diagonal line was drawn in by hand. If you want a vertical or horizontal line on a plot, SPSS/PC+ can print it for you. These lines are called **reference lines,** and they can make it easier to see patterns that indicate relationships in the data.

For example, if you want to separate cases whose parents were high-school graduates from cases whose parents were not, you can instruct SPSS/PC+ to draw reference lines at the value 12 for both of the axes. Just modify the PLOT command like this:

```
set seed 100000000.
sample .1.
plot horizontal reference(12) /vertical reference(12)
   /plot=paeduc with maeduc by life.
```

Two additional instructions are included in this PLOT command. The instruction HORIZONTAL REFERENCE(12) tells SPSS/PC+ to draw a line at the value 12 on the horizontal axis. The instruction VERTICAL REFERENCE(12) does the same for the vertical axis.

Figure 22.5 Plot with reference lines

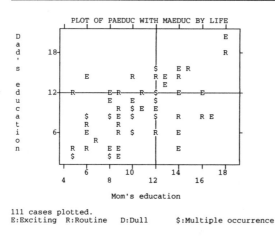

You can see the plot produced by the above command in Figure 22.5. It differs from Figure 23.3 only in that two lines have been added. This makes it easier to judge, for example, whether people with both parents well educated (in the upper right part of the plot) were more or less likely to be excited by life than people with less-educated parents (in the lower left part).

WHY PLOT?

Plotting data is one of the best ways to look for relationships and patterns. A plot is simple to understand and conveys a lot of information about the data. In other chapters, we discuss methods of summarizing and describing relationships, but those methods are no substitute for plots. Whenever possible, you should plot the data *first* and then think about appropriate methods for describing the plots.

A plot can also alert you to possible problems in the data. For example, if you're plotting salary and age and you find a 22-year-old with a salary of $100,000, you have reason to be suspicious. Although there's a chance that the values are correct, it's much more likely that either the age or the salary was recorded or entered incorrectly. You wouldn't have been able to pick out this point as suspicious if you examined the variables individually. A salary of $100,000 is high but possible. An age of 22 is not unusual. It's the combination of the values that leads you to suspect the point may be a mistake. Even if the point is correct, it's important to identify it early, since it may need special treatment in later analyses.

MORE ABOUT THE PLOT PROCEDURE

The minimum specification to obtain a plot is simply the PLOT subcommand:

```
plot plot paeduc with maeduc.
```

The first variable named (before WITH) goes on the vertical axis; the second goes on the horizontal axis. The PLOT procedure labels the axes according to the ranges of values it finds in the data and according to the size of the plot. You can change the size of the plot, either for a more convenient size or for more convenient labels, by using the HSIZE (horizontal size) and VSIZE (vertical size) keywords. All additional specifications such as these must *precede* the PLOT subcommand:

```
plot  hsize 32 /vsize 14
  /plot paeduc with maeduc.
```

The default plot size on a standard 25-line display is 38 horizontal spaces by 16 vertical spaces.

Multiple Plots

You can get multiple plots from the same command simply by naming more than one variable for either axis. The command

```
plot plot educ with paeduc maeduc.
```

produces a plot of *EDUC* with *PAEDUC* and another plot of *EDUC* with *MAE-DUC*.

If you name more than one variable on each side of WITH, you get a plot of each variable on the left with each variable on the right. By adding the keyword (PAIR), you can instead match up the variables one to one. The command

```
plot plot = age, paeduc with agewed maeduc (pair).
```

produces two plots, one of *AGE* with *AGEWED* and one of *PAEDUC* with *MAEDUC*.

Reference Lines

You can supply one or more reference lines crossing either the horizontal or the vertical axis. For reference lines at 12 and 16 years of mother's education on the horizontal axis, specify:

```
plot  horizontal reference(12,16)
  /plot paeduc with maeduc.
```

Note that reference lines crossing the horizontal axis are themselves vertical.

Control Plots

To get a control plot, where each plotted point is labeled by the first letter of the value label from a control variable, specify:

```
plot plot paeduc with maeduc by life.
```

Overlay Plots

If you request multiple plots, as discussed above, you can combine them into a single plot by specifying FORMAT OVERLAY before the PLOT subcommand. The command

```
plot format overlay /plot = educ with paeduc, maeduc.
```

places the two plots *EDUC* with *PAEDUC* and *EDUC* with *MAEDUC* in the same plotting frame, using a different symbol to represent the points for each plot.

Regression Plots

The specification FORMAT REGRESSION places the letter R in the margins of the plot to show where the "best" line through the data points would fall. This line is discussed in more detail in Chapter 24.

Remember that you can use the SAMPLE or SELECT IF command to limit the number of cases. Always place the required PLOT subcommand last:

```
plot  hsize 32 /vsize 14
 /horizontal reference(12,16) /vertical reference(12,16)
 /format regression
 /plot paeduc with maeduc by life.
```

WHAT'S NEXT?

Many important relationships look much like Figure 23.1. The values cluster around a straight line running through the plot. If the cases cluster tightly around a straight line, there is a strong relationship between the two variables. You can measure the strength of a linear relationship of this kind with a statistic, the correlation coefficient. We'll look at correlations in the next chapter.

Summary

How can you display the relationship between two variables that are measured on an interval or ratio scale?

A plot displays the values of two variables for each case.

By examining a plot, you can see what sort of relationship, if any, there is between two variables.

The points on a plot may be identified by their values for an additional variable (called a control variable). This lets you see whether the relationship between the two variables differs for the different categories of the control variable.

Points that have unusual combinations of values can be easily identified from a plot since they are far removed from the other points.

EXERCISES

Syntax

1 Write the appropriate command to obtain a plot of *INCOME* and *AGE*. Put values of *INCOME* on the vertical axis.

2 How would you change the command in question 1 so that *INCOME* would be on the horizontal axis?

3 Write the command to identify each of the points on the *INCOME* and *AGE* plot as males or females (variable *SEX*).

4 Correct the errors in the following PLOT commands:

a. `plot sbp by age.`

b. `plot spb with age.`

c. `plot plot sbp with age by sex(1,2).`

d. `plot plot age by sex with sbp.`

5 You run a simple PLOT command and obtain the following error messages. Explain the error messages and indicate how you would correct the mistake.

```
ERROR   14104, Text: EDUC
Valid subcommands on the PLOT command are: MISSING, HSIZE, VSIZE,
CUTPOINT, SYMBOL, TITLE, HORIZONTAL, VERTICAL, FORMAT and PLOT.
This command not executed.
```

```
ERROR   14102
The PLOT subcommand must come last on the PLOT command.
This command not executed.
```

Statistical Concepts

1 Indicate whether you would use the CROSSTABS procedure, the MEANS procedure, or the PLOT procedure to display the relationship between the following pairs of variables:

a. Job satisfaction and income measured in dollars

b. Race and marital status

c. Systolic blood pressure and age

d. Husband's highest degree and wife's highest degree

e. Hours studied for an examination and letter grade on the exam

f. Miles per gallon that a car gets and its weight in pounds

2 Describe the relationships between the variables in the following plots::

a.

b.

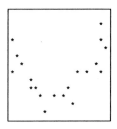

c.

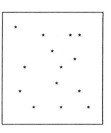

d.

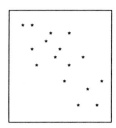

3 The following table contains the age at first marriage, years of education, and sex for five people. Plot these values, identifying whether each is for a male or female.

AGEWED	EDUC	SEX
18	12	Male
22	13	Female
30	16	Male
16	10	Male
25	18	Female

PLOT OF EDUC WITH AGEWED BY SEX

Age of first marriage

Data Analysis

Use the gss.sys system file to answer the following questions.

1 Obtain a plot of the age at which a person first marries (*AGEWED*) and his or her years of education (*EDUC*). (To make the plot easier to read, take a random sample of 10% of the cases.) Describe the relationship that you see.

2 Repeat the plot in question 1, this time drawing reference axes corresponding to grammar school, high school, and college. Also identify the points corresponding to males or females.

3 Suggest four pairs of variables in the gss.sys file for which it makes sense to obtain plots. Draw plots for two of these pairs and describe any relationship that you see.

4 For men and women separately, obtain a plot of the age at which they were first married and the years of education of their mothers (*MAEDUC*). Describe the relationships that you see. Do they differ for the two sexes? Repeat the analysis using father's education (*PAEDUC*). Are the relationships similar?

23 Interpreting Correlation Coefficients

How can you summarize the strength of the linear relationship between two variables?

- What is a linear relationship?

- What is a positive linear relationship, and what is a negative linear relationship?

- What is the Pearson correlation coefficient?

- What does a correlation coefficient of +1 or −1 indicate?

- Is it possible that two variables are related if the correlation coefficient is zero?

- How can you test the hypothesis that, in the population, two variables have a correlation coefficient of zero?

- Does correlation imply causation?

- When should you use a one-tailed significance level?

- What can happen when you test whether a large number of correlation coefficients are zero?

- What should you do if you have cases with missing information in your data file?

F rom a plot of the values of two variables, we can see if they appear to be related. What do we mean by "related"? Nothing complicated. Two variables are **related** if knowing the value of one variable tells us something about the value of the other variable. Neither of the variables has to be considered dependent or independent; all we're interested in is how they behave together. In Chapter 23, we saw that father's education and mother's education appear to be related. As years of education for one parent increase, so do the years for the other.

In this chapter, we'll consider some different types of relationships between variables and how we can statistically measure the strength of the relationships. Our primary interest will be in **linear** relationships—those in which the values of the two variables cluster about a straight line on a plot.

TYPES OF RELATIONSHIPS

To get some idea of the types of relationships among variables, let's consider relationships between the educational level of the GSS respondents and that of their parents. We'll also include the age at which the respondents married.

Relationships can be very complicated and can require many different complex analyses. However, a good place to start is by looking at the plots of the variables. Let's first look at a plot in which there doesn't appear to be any relationship. It will serve as a good reference point for determining whether relationships are present.

Figure 23.1 is a plot of the age at which a respondent first married and the years of education of the respondent's mother for a random sample of cases from the GSS. The SPSS/PC+ commands that produced the plot are:

```
get file 'gss.sys'.
set seed = 100000000.
sample .1.
plot plot maeduc with agewed.
```

The SET SEED command determines the starting point for the random number generator which is used for selecting a random sample of cases.

Figure 23.1 Mother's education with age at marriage

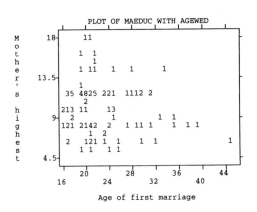

PLOT OF MAEDUC WITH AGEWED

Age of first marriage

How would you characterize the relationship between the two variables? There doesn't appear to be any. The points are scattered all over the plot. Knowing the age at which a person was married tells you nothing about the education of the person's mother. Or if you're told the mother's education, you know nothing about the age at which the person was married. There seems to be no association, or relationship, between the two variables.

Perfect Relationships

When there's no relationship between two variables, you can't see any kind of pattern on a plot. Points appear to be randomly distributed. If there's a perfect relationship between two variables, you should be able to see a distinct pattern. There are no perfect relationships in the General Social Survey, so we'll create one. Let's pretend that every father is twice as old as his child. If we know the father's age, we know the child's age, and vice versa. We can use the following commands to create the fathers' ages we want and to plot the results:

```
process if (age < 50).
set seed 100000000.
sample .1.
compute dadsage = 2 * age.
variable labels dadsage "Father's age".
plot plot dadsage with age.
```

As explained in Chapter 23, we have to repeat the SAMPLE command, since its effect is only temporary.

The plot of these variables is in Figure 23.2. The relationship is perfectly linear, since the points fall exactly on a straight line. The relationship is also positive, since as *DADSAGE* increases, so does *AGE*.

Figure 23.2 Perfect linear positive relationship

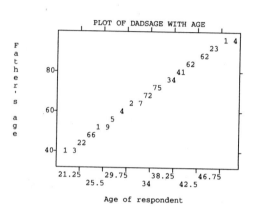

Now let's look at a perfect negative linear relationship. We need a variable that *decreases* as age increases. If everyone lived to a spry 100 years, we could calculate the remaining years of life for each case using:

```
set seed 100000000.
sample .1.
compute timeleft = 100 - age.
variable labels timeleft "Years remaining".
plot plot = timeleft with age.
```

Figure 23.3 is a plot of actual age and remaining years. Again the points fall exactly on a straight line, but as the values of one variable increase, the values of the other variable decrease.

More about Linear Relationships

In real life, linear relationships look more like the plot of parental education in the last chapter. The plot is shown again in Figure 23.4, with a straight line drawn through the center of the points. The points are clustered around the line, but most of them don't fall exactly on it. To find out the best place to draw the line, put the subcommand FORMAT REGRESSION on the PLOT command. SPSS/PC+ puts the letter *R* at two positions on the frame of the plot, and the best line connects those positions. (In Chapter 24, we'll find out how this is selected.)

Figure 23.3 Perfect linear negative relationship

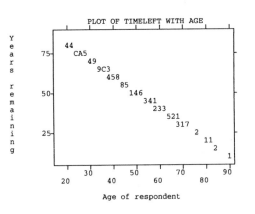

```
set seed 100000000.
sample .1.
plot format = regression /plot = paeduc with maeduc.
```

You can see that the points don't fall exactly on the line. Instead, they are distributed around it. There's quite a bit of variability around the line, but most points are not too far removed. You can see that the relationship is *positive*, since as the mother's education increases, so does the father's.

Another Linear Relationship

Although the relationship between father's and mother's education is not perfect, there's a fairly strong tendency for the points to cluster around a straight line. Figure 23.5 shows an example of another linear relationship. It's a plot of the respondents' age and their fathers' education.

```
set seed 100000000.
sample .1.
plot format regression /plot age with paeduc.
```

We know that people's average education has increased substantially over the last several decades, so we would expect that older people have less education than young people. They would also have parents with less education than the parents of younger people. The plot supports this notion. A line through the *R*s that SPSS/PC+ puts in the border of the plot indicates that there is a negative relationship between age and father's education. As age increases, father's education decreases.

Figure 23.4 Father's education with mother's education

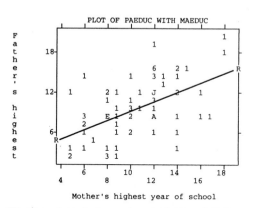

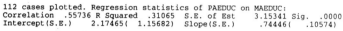

112 cases plotted. Regression statistics of PAEDUC on MAEDUC:
Correlation .55736 R Squared .31065 S.E. of Est   3.15341 Sig.   .0000
Intercept(S.E.)   2.17465(1.15682) Slope(S.E.)   .74446(.10574)

Figure 23.5 Age with father's education

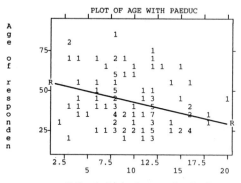

118 cases plotted. Regression statistics of AGE on PAEDUC:
Correlation -.29279 R Squared .08572 S.E. of Est   15.22549 Sig. .0013
Intercept(S.E.)   54.49684(4.08603) Slope(S.E.)   -1.25938(.38187)

CORRELATION

Although plots give you a pretty good idea of the strength of a linear association, they don't provide an objective summary measure that you could use to compare and summarize the relationships between pairs of variables. On the basis of the previous plots you could say that the relationship between parents' education *appears* to be stronger than the relationship between father's education and respondent's age. You can't really say how much stronger unless you have a summary measure that quantifies your visual impressions.

The Pearson Correlation Coefficient

The most commonly used measure is the **Pearson correlation coefficient,** which is abbreviated as **r.** (The statistic is named after Karl Pearson, an eminent statistician of the early twentieth century.) Let's consider some of its characteristics:

- If there is no linear relationship between two variables, the value of the coefficient is 0.
- If there is a *perfect positive linear* relationship, the value is +1.
- If there is a *perfect negative linear* relationship, the value is –1.

To summarize, the values of the coefficient can range from –1 to +1, with a value of 0 indicating no linear relationship. Positive values mean that there's a positive relationship between the variables. Negative values mean that there's a negative relationship. If one pair of variables has a correlation coefficient of +0.8 while another pair has a coefficient of –0.8, the strength of the relationship is the same for both. It's just the direction of the relationship that differs.

Let's find out what the correlation coefficients are for some of the plots that we've considered previously. (These coefficients are printed by the SPSS/PC+ PLOT procedure if you use the FORMAT REGRESSION subcommand shown above.) The correlation coefficient for age at marriage and mother's education is –0.156. This supports what we've said before, that there doesn't appear to be much of a relationship between the two variables. For mother's and father's education, the correlation coefficient is 0.557. This is a fairly large positive value, as you would expect. How about father's education and age of the respondent? From the plot, we saw that the relationship is negative, so the sign of the correlation coefficient should also be negative. The relationship was not a very strong one, so the coefficient shouldn't be very large. In fact, it's –0.293.

> **?** *Does a correlation coefficient of zero mean that there is no relationship between two variables.* No! The Pearson correlation coefficient only measures the strength of a *linear* relationship. Two variables can have a correlation coefficient close to zero and yet have a very strong *nonlinear* relationship. Look at Figure 23.6, which is a plot of two hypothetical variables. You'll note that there is a strong relationship between the two variables. The value of the correlation coefficient, however, is close to zero. It's very important to always plot the values of the variables before you compute a correlation coefficient. This will allow you to detect nonlinear relationships, for which the Pearson correlation coefficient is not a good summary measure. The Pearson correlation coefficient should only be used for linear relationships. ■■■

Figure 23.6 Strong relationship but very low correlation

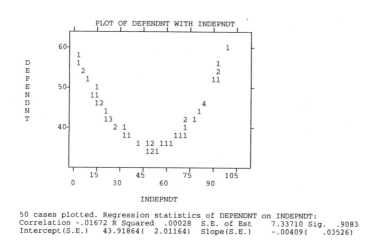

```
             PLOT OF DEPENDNT WITH INDEPNDT
          60-                           1
    D        1
    E        1                          1
    P        2                          2
    E        1                          11
    N    50-  1
    D        11
    N        12                    4
    T        1               1
             13            2 1
          40-  2 1            1
               11           111
               1 12 111
               121

           |    |    |    |    |    |
             15   45   75   105
          0    30   60   90
```

INDEPNDT

```
50 cases plotted. Regression statistics of DEPENDNT on INDEPNDT:
Correlation -.01672 R Squared  .00028  S.E. of Est    7.33710 Sig.   .9083
Intercept(S.E.)   43.91864(  2.01164)  Slope(S.E.)   -.00409(   .03526)
```

CALCULATING THE CORRELATION COEFFICIENT

The following mathematical formula defines the correlation coefficient for a pair of variables:

$$r = \frac{\sum_{i=1}^{N} (X_i - \overline{X})(Y_i - \overline{Y})}{(N-1)S_x S_y}$$

where X and Y are the values of the two variables for a case, N is the number of cases, and S_X and S_Y are the standard deviations of the two variables. It doesn't matter which variable is X and which is Y in the formula, since the correlation coefficient will be the same.

The correlation coefficient is not expressed in any unit of measurement. The correlation coefficient between two variables will be the same regardless of how you measure them. For example, you'll get the same answer if you convert education from years to months. The correlation is an absolute number.

The SPSS/PC+ PLOT procedure calculates Pearson's correlation coefficient, but SPSS/PC+ also has a procedure called CORRELATION specifically dedicated to computing correlations. To obtain correlations for all cases for the variables we've been discussing, run the command:

```
correlation educ paeduc maeduc age agewed
    /options 3 5.
```

The names of the variables for which you want coefficients follow the command name. We'll talk about the options later. The output from this command is shown in Figure 23.7.

Figure 23.7 Pearson correlation coefficients

```
Correlations:   EDUC        PAEDUC      MAEDUC      AGE         AGEWED

    EDUC        1.0000       .4661       .4698      -.2139       .2156
              (  798)      (  798)     (  798)     (  798)     (  798)
               P=  .       P= .000     P= .000     P= .000     P= .000

    PAEDUC       .4661      1.0000       .6280      -.3841       .0023
              (  798)      (  798)     (  798)     (  798)     (  798)
               P= .000      P=  .       P= .000     P= .000     P= .949

    MAEDUC       .4698       .6280      1.0000      -.3880      -.0180
              (  798)      (  798)     (  798)     (  798)     (  798)
               P= .000      P= .000      P=  .       P= .000     P= .611

    AGE         -.2139      -.3841      -.3880      1.0000       .1793
              (  798)      (  798)     (  798)     (  798)     (  798)
               P= .000      P= .000     P= .000      P=  .       P= .000

    AGEWED       .2156       .0023      -.0180       .1793      1.0000
              (  798)      (  798)     (  798)     (  798)     (  798)
               P= .000      P= .949     P= .611     P= .000      P=  .
```

(Coefficient / (Cases) / 2-tailed Significance)

" . " is printed if a coefficient cannot be computed

Each row and column of the table represents one of the variables. In each cell of the table you have three numbers. The first is the value of the coefficient. The second is the number of cases used to calculate it. The third number is the observed significance level—the next topic to be covered in this chapter. (The numbers of cases and significance levels are produced by the OPTION 5 specification.)

Testing Hypotheses about the Correlation Coefficient

Sometimes the correlation coefficient is used simply to summarize the strength of a linear relationship between two variables. In other situations you may want to do more than that; you may want to test hypotheses about the population correlation coefficient. For example, you may want to test the null hypothesis that there is no linear relationship between mother's and father's education in the population.

Remember, if your data are a random sample from a population, you want to be able to draw conclusions about the population based on the results you observe in your sample. As was the case with other descriptive measures such as the mean, you know that the value of the correlation coefficient you calculate for your sample will not exactly equal the value that you would obtain if you had values for the entire population. You know that if you took many samples from the same population and calculated the correlation coefficients, their values would vary. That is, there is a distribution of possible values of the correlation coefficient, just as there was a distribution of possible values for sample means. If you know what the distribution is, you can calculate observed significance levels. For example, you can calculate how often you would expect to find, in samples of a particular size, a coefficient of 0.3 or greater when the population value is zero.

Look again at Figure 23.7. The value of the correlation coefficient for education and age at marriage is 0.2156. It is based on 798 cases. The probability is less than 0.0005 that you would observe, in such a sample, a correlation coefficient larger than 0.2156 or smaller than –0.2156, when the value in the population is zero. Since the observed significance level is less than 0.05, you reject the null hypothesis that there is no linear association between the two variables in the population.

Does Significant Mean Important?

If you reject the null hypothesis, does that mean there is an important relationship between the two variables? No. It simply means that it is unlikely that the value of the correlation coefficient is 0 in the population. For large sample sizes, even very small correlation coefficients have small observed significance levels. You can have a correlation coefficient of 0.1 and have it be "statistically" significant. It indicates that there is a very small, but nonzero, linear relationship between the variables. You should look at both the value of the coefficient and its associated significance level when evaluating the relationships among variables.

One-Tailed and Two-Tailed Significance Probabilities

If you don't know before looking at your data whether a pair of variables should be positively or negatively correlated, you must use a two-tailed significance level. You reject the null hypothesis for either large positive or large negative values of the correlation coefficient.

If you know in advance whether your variables should be positively or negatively correlated, you can use a one-tailed significance test. For example, if you're studying the relationship between total yearly income and value of housing, you know that if there is a relationship, it will be positive. Poor people can't own expensive houses.

For a one-tailed test, you reject the null hypothesis only if the value of the correlation coefficient is large and in the direction you specified. For a one-tailed test, the observed significance level is one-half the two-tailed value. That's because you only calculate the probability that you would obtain a more extreme value in one direction, not two.

If you don't specify what kind of test you want when you use the SPSS/PC+ CORRELATION command, you get a one-tailed test. In order to get two-tailed tests, we specified OPTION 3 in the command that produced Figure 23.7.

Assumptions about the Data

In order to test hypotheses about the Pearson correlation coefficient, you have to assume that your data are a random sample from a population in which the distribution of the two variables together is normal. If it seems unreasonable to assume that the variables are from normal distributions, you may have to use other statistical procedures that don't require the normality assumption. These are nonparametric procedures and are described in Appendix E.

Examining Many Coefficients

If your study involves many variables, you may be tempted to compute all possible correlation coefficients among them. If you're interested in exploring possible associations among the variables, you may find the coefficients helpful in identifying possible relationships. However, you must be careful when examining the significance levels from large tables. If you have enough coefficients, you expect some of them to be statistically significant even if there is no relationship between the variables in the population. If you compute 100 coefficients, you expect somewhere around 5 of them to have observed significance levels less than 0.05 even when there is no relationship among the variables in the population.

Missing Values

If you look at Figure 23.7, you'll see that the number of cases used for calculating the coefficients is less than the total number of cases in the file. The reason for this is that not all of the respondents in the General Social Survey answered all of the questions. Some may not have known how many years of education their mothers and fathers had. Those who had never married did not have a value for age at first marriage.

In Figure 23.7, the coefficient for each pair of variables was calculated from all the cases that had valid data for all the variables in the list. This is called **listwise deletion** of missing data. There is another way that uses as much available information as possible. For example, if a case had values for age and age at first marriage but not for any of the education variables, the case would be used in the computation of the coefficient for age and age at first marriage, but not for any of the other coefficients. This method of calculation, where the correlation coefficient for two variables is based on all cases that had valid data for those two variables, is called **pairwise deletion** of missing data. OPTION 2 on the CORRELATION command requests pairwise deletion of missing data. If you do not specify pairwise deletion, SPSS/PC+ uses listwise deletion.

Analysis of data when some of the cases have missing information can be troublesome, especially if you have reason to believe that the missing values are related to values of one of the variables you're analyzing. For example, people with low incomes may be less willing to report their financial status than more affluent people. People who are highly educated and poor may be even less likely to reveal their income than poor people in general. If this is the case, it may be very difficult to draw correct conclusions about income and education from the data.

If there are missing values in the data, you should see whether there is a pattern to the missing values. For example, you can calculate the average education for people who reported their income and those who did not. If these values are quite different, you have reason to suspect that the income values are not randomly missing. When values are not randomly missing, you must use great caution in attempting to analyze the data. In fact, you may not be able to analyze some of it. (With pairwise deletion of missing data, you could even end up with correlation coefficients that were based on entirely different groups of cases!)

> **?** *If two variables are correlated, does that mean one of them causes*
> **!** *the other?* Not at all. You can never assume that just because two
> variables are correlated, one of them causes the other. If you find a large
> correlation coefficient between the ounces of coffee consumed in a day and
> number of auto accidents in a year, you can't conclude that coffee consump-
> tion causes auto accidents. It may well be that coffee drinkers also con-
> sume more alcohol, or are older, or more poorly coordinated than non-
> coffee drinkers. You can't easily tell which of the factors may influence the
> occurrence of accidents.   ■■■

MORE ABOUT THE CORRELATION PROCEDURE

To compute all possible correlation coefficients between several variables,
specify all the variables, as in:

```
correlation educ paeduc maeduc.
```

This command will print correlation coefficients for all three possible pairs
of the variables. All coefficients will be based on the same set of cases—
those with valid data for all three variables (listwise deletion). In the correlation matrix that results from this command, correlation coefficients
whose one-tailed significance levels are less than 0.01 will be marked with
an asterisk, and those whose one-tailed significance levels are less than
0.001 will be marked with two asterisks.

When you simply list the variable names on the CORRELATION command, as shown above, you get a square correlation matrix: each variable
is correlated with each other. You can request a rectangular matrix by using the keyword WITH in the list of variables. Specify the variables defining the rows of the matrix, then the keyword WITH, then the variables
defining the columns. For a matrix with ten rows (*VAR1* through *VAR10*)
and three columns (*SCORE1*, *SCORE2*, *SCORE3*), you would use the command

```
correlation var1 to var10 with score1 score2 score3.
```

If you specify more than one list of variables, separated by slashes, SPSS/
PC+ processes them independently. The following command produces a
square matrix followed by a rectangular matrix:

```
correlation var1 to var10 /
 var1 to var10 with score1 score2 score3.
```

Options and Statistics

To modify the output, specify one or more of the following option numbers on an OPTIONS subcommand after the variables on the CORRELA-
TION command:

1   Include user-missing values.
2   Exclude missing values pairwise.
3   Two-tailed test of significance.
5   Display count and significance level.

We used Option 3 in this chapter to get two-tailed significance tests. Option 5 expands the output by printing correlation coefficients, case counts and significance levels. The significance levels displayed by Option 5 are more helpful than the asterisks that are used by default to indicate statistical significance.

If you request the subcommand STATISTIC 1 on the CORRELATION command, you will get the mean, standard deviation, and count of valid cases for each variable.

WHAT'S NEXT?

The correlation coefficient measures the strength of a linear relationship—how tightly the points are clustered around a straight line. In Chapter 24 we'll learn more about that line itself. We'll find out how to choose the best line and how to use it.

Summary

How can you summarize the strength of the linear relationship between two variables?

The Pearson correlation coefficient measures the strength of the linear relationship between variables.

Two variables have a positive relationship if, as the values of one variable increase, so do the values of the other.

Two variables have a negative relationship if, as the values of one variable increase, the values of the other decrease.

A correlation coefficient of +1 means that there is a perfect positive linear relationship between two variables. A value of −1 means that there is a perfect negative linear relationship.

A correlation coefficient measures only the strength of a linear relationship. If there is a strong nonlinear relationship between two variables, the correlation coefficient can be zero.

A correlation between two variables doesn't mean that one causes the other.

To test the null hypothesis that the correlation coefficient is zero in the population, you can calculate the observed significance level for the coefficient.

You can use a one-tailed test if you know in advance whether the relationship between two variables is positive or negative.

If you have missing values in your data, you should see whether there is a pattern to the cases for which information is missing.

EXERCISES

Syntax

1 Write the SPSS/PC+ command to obtain correlation coefficients and two-tailed significance levels for all pairs of the following variables: *MONEY, INVEST, SALARY,* and *WEALTH.*

2 Correct the errors in the following commands:

a. correlations a b c d

b. correlations age.

c. correlations one two many / significance = 2.

Statistical Concepts

1   For the following pairs of variables, would you expect the correlation coefficient to be positive, negative, or zero?

   a. A person's total family income and his neighbor's total family income
   b. Number of registered voters in a district and the number voting on election day
   c. Number of cigarettes smoked and lung function
   d. Calories consumed and weight
   e. Altitude and mean temperature
   f. Gross national product and infant mortality rate
   g. Age at first marriage and years of education
   h. Number of cars in a household and total family income

2   A medical researcher studying the relationship between two variables finds a correlation coefficient of 0.02. She concludes that there is no relationship between the two variables. Do you agree or disagree with her conclusion? Why?

3   A mail-order house is interested in studying the relationship between income and type of product purchased. They take a random sample of orders, and then they call people to determine family income. They then calculate the correlation coefficient between income and product code. The value is 0.76, and the two-tailed observed significance level is 0.03. Based on this study, what can you conclude about the relationship between income and type of product purchased? Explain.

4   A dental association is studying the relationship between ounces of orange juice consumed per week and yearly family dental bill. They find a large positive coefficient with an observed significance level of less than 0.01. What do you think of their conclusion that orange juice causes tooth decay? Discuss other possible explanations for their findings.

5   A friend of yours is analyzing the relationships among a large number of variables. He's decided that the best strategy is to compute correlation coefficients among all of them and see which relationships appear to be significant. Advise him on issues he must consider when using the correlation coefficient to describe the relationships between variables.

6   The correlation coefficient between variables A and B is 0.62. For variables C and D it is −0.62. Which pair of variables is more strongly related?

7   An educator wishes to study the relationship between father's and son's education. Five hundred randomly selected fathers of sons are interviewed and the years of education are recorded for both fathers and sons. Since a fairly high proportion of "Unknown" responses was obtained, the educator divides the education variables into two groups and obtains the following table:

```
PAEDUC  Father's education  by  EDUCSON  Son's education

                   EDUCSON                    Page 1 of 1
           Count
                   Low      High     Missing
                                              Row
                    1        2        3       Total
  PAEDUC    ───────────────────────────────
            1      120      120       10       250
  Low                                          50.0

            2       40      130       80       250
  High                                         50.0

          Column   160      250       90       500
          Total    32.0     50.0      18.0     100.0
```

Number of Missing Observations: 0

a. Is there reason to suspect that there is a relationship between father's education and non-response to son's education level? What may be going on?

b. Is there a satisfactory way to deal with the missing values when estimating the correlation coefficient between father's and son's education?

Data Analysis

Use the gss.sys system file to answer the following questions.

1 In Chapter 23 you were asked to identify four pairs of variables for which a plot was an appropriate means of displaying their relationship. Compute a correlation matrix for all possible pairs of these variables.

2 What null hypothesis are you testing when you compute the observed significance level for the correlation coefficient?

3 Compute the correlation coefficient between mother's education (*MAEDUC*) and father's education (*PAEDUC*) for males and females separately. Discuss your findings.

4 Compute the correlation coefficient for age at first marriage (*AGEWED*) and education (*EDUC*) for males and females separately. Does there appear to be a relationship between these two variables? Does it differ for the two sexes?

24 Calculating Simple Regression Lines

How can you determine the line that best summarizes the linear relationship between two variables?

- How do you choose among the many lines that can be drawn through the data points?

- What does the slope tell you? The intercept?

- What is a least-squares line?

- How can you predict values for one variable based on the values of another variable?

- How can you tell how well a line fits the data?

- How can you tell what proportion of the variability in one variable is "explained" by the other?

A correlation coefficient provides you with a measure of the strength of the linear association between two variables. All it measures, though, is how *closely* the points cluster about a straight line. It doesn't tell you anything about the line itself.

In many situations it's useful to obtain information about the actual line which is drawn through the data points. If there's a linear relationship between two variables and you know the equation for the line that describes their relationship, you can use one variable to predict values of the other. For example, if there's a linear relationship between the amount of money a company spends on advertising and its sales volume for the year, you can use the line to predict sales volume based on advertising. That's what this chapter is about. You'll learn how to calculate what's called a **regression line** and what it means.

CHOOSING THE BEST LINE

Thinking back to Chapter 23, you'll remember that the correlation coefficient was based on how closely points cluster about "a line." We didn't say anything about how we selected the line which was shown on the plots. We'll consider that now.

When the correlation coefficient is +1 or –1, all the data points fall exactly on a straight line. All you have to do is connect the points and you have a line. You don't have to worry about choosing a line. When the observations are not perfectly correlated, many different lines can be drawn through the data. How do we select among them? Since we want a line that describes the data, it should be as close as possible to the points. There are different ways to define "as close as possible." The most commonly used method for determining the line is called the method of least squares. The **least-squares line** is the line that has the smallest sum of squared vertical distances from the observed points to the line.

To understand what this means, look at Figure 24.1, which is a plot of the education of respondents and that of their fathers for a sample of cases. We took a sample of the cases in the gss.sys so that the plot would be easier to read and interpret.

Figure 24.1 Least-squares line

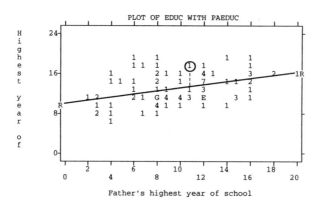

The least-squares line has been drawn on the plot. For any point on the plot you can find the vertical distance from the point to the line. The dotted line on the plot shows such a vertical distance for the circled point. If you find the vertical distances to the line for all points, square them, and then add them up, you'll have the **sum of the squared distances.** If you draw any other line on the plot, it would have a larger sum of squared distances than the least-squares line. That's why this line is called the least-squares line.

The Equation of a Line

Before we talk any more about lines, let's consider the equation for a straight line. Take two variables, say X and Y. Call the variable we plot on the vertical axis Y, and the variable we plot on the horizontal axis X. Then the equation for a straight line is

$$Y = A + BX$$

The value A is called the **intercept,** and the value B is called the **slope.** To understand what the slope and intercept are (and why they're called slope and intercept), look at Figure 24.2, which is a plot of the line

$$EDUC = 10 + 0.3 \times PAEDUC$$

The intercept, 10, is the value for the respondent's education when father's education is 0. It is the point at which the line hits the vertical axis. The slope tells you how much increase there is in a respondent's education for every year of his or her father's education. In this case it's 0.3. If a father has 10 years of education, the respondent should have 13 years: 10 to start off with (the intercept) and 3 more because of the father's 10 years of education (10 years × 0.3, the slope, makes 3 years). If a father has 11 years of education, the respondent should have 13.3 years (10 years for the intercept + 11 years × 0.3). The additional year of education for a father results in an additional 0.3 years for the respondent.

Figure 24.2 Plot of a line with intercept 10 and slope 0.3

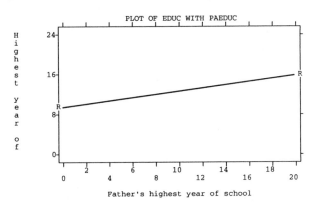

If the value for the slope is positive, it tells you that as one variable increases, so does the other variable. If the slope is negative, it tells you that as one variable increases, the other decreases. If the slope is large, the line is steep, indicating that a small change in the father's education would lead to a large change in the respondent's education. If the slope is small, there is a gradual increase or decrease. If the slope is *zero*, it means that changes in the X variable have no linear effect on the Y variable. For example, if fathers' education and respondents' education were not related, the line would look something like that in Figure 24.3. This line is completely flat. Its equation is

$$EDUC = 12 + 0.0 \times PAEDUC$$

Predicting Values from the Regression Line

The equation for the least-squares regression line in Figure 24.1 is

Predicted $EDUC = 10.24 + 0.27 \times PAEDUC$

The line is drawn on the plot by connecting the two Rs that appear on the edges of the plot. The values for the slope and intercept are obtained from Figure 24.4, which contains the regression statistics from the PLOT procedure.

Figure 24.3 Plot of a line for unrelated variables

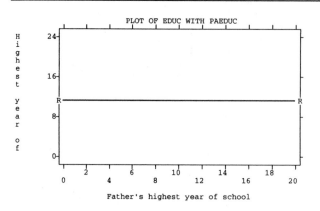

So the intercept is where the R appears along the left border of the plot? The R on the border of the plot tells you where the line crosses the left border. The intercept is where the line crosses *zero*, that is, where the independent variable (plotted on the X axis) equals zero. On this plot they're the same, because the border is at zero years of father's education. You can't count on that, though. ■■■

From the last line in Figure 24.4, you can see that the value for the intercept is 10.24, while the value for the slope is 0.27. The standard errors for the slope and the intercept are in parentheses. (The standard errors of the slope and intercept are indicators of how much variability is associated with them. These standard errors are discussed further in Chapter 25.)

Figure 24.4 Regression statistics from PLOT

```
118 cases plotted. Regression statistics of EDUC on PAEDUC:
Correlation  .37775 R Squared  .14270  S.E. of Est   2.48863 Sig.  .0000
Intercept(S.E.)   10.24339(  .66787) Slope(S.E.)    .27427(  .06242)
```

Calculating the Predicted Values

Once you have a regression equation, it's easy to obtain predicted values. All you have to do is substitute the value of the independent variable into the equation. To predict respondent's education when the father has eight years of education, use

$$\begin{aligned} \text{Predicted } EDUC &= 10.24 + 0.27 \times PAEDUC \\ &= 10.24 + 0.27 \times 8 \\ &= 10.24 + 2.16 \\ &= 12.4 \end{aligned}$$

We used the word "predicted" in front of *EDUC* because the relationship between the two variables is not perfect. For a particular value of father's education we cannot exactly say what the respondent's education is. From the regression line we can only predict what the value would be if all of the points fell exactly on the regression line.

Choosing the Dependent Variable

When we are computing correlation coefficients it doesn't matter which variable we plot on the horizontal axis and which we plot on the vertical. The correlation coefficient is exactly the same. That's not usually true for regression. The slope and the intercept will differ depending on which variable is the *Y* variable in the equation and which is the *X* variable. Since regression analysis is used to predict values of a dependent variable from values of an independent variable, *Y* is taken to be the dependent variable and *X* the independent.

In this example, it's natural to consider the respondent's education as the dependent variable and father's education as the independent variable. We know that the respondent's education is not likely to influence the father's education. However, it is possible that the father's education may influence the respondent's. Respondent's education is *dependent* on father's education.

To calculate the regression line with respondent's education as the dependent variable, it must be plotted on the vertical axis in the PLOT procedure. As described in Chapter 23, the first variable named, the one before WITH, goes on the vertical axis—so we name *EDUC* first:

```
get file = 'gss.sys'.
set seed 100000000.
sample .1.
plot format = regression / plot = educ with paeduc.
```

These commands produce the plot shown in Figure 24.1 and the statistics shown in Figure 24.4.

DETERMINING HOW WELL THE LINE FITS

Before you use a regression line, you want to know how well it fits the data. The values of the slope and intercept alone don't indicate how well the line actually fits the data. We need some measure of **goodness of fit.** We know that if the regression line fits the data perfectly, the observed values for the dependent variable equal the predicted values. They all fall exactly on the line. The poorer the line fits, the more discrepancy we would expect between the line and the actual values. Our measure of goodness of fit is based on these discrepancies.

Predicted and Observed Values

One way to measure how well the line fits is to calculate a correlation coefficient (as in Chapter 23) between the observed values of the dependent variable and those predicted from the regression equation. The value will be 1 if there is a perfect fit and close to 0 if the fit is poor.

Let's use SPSS/PC+ to do this. To calculate the predicted values for each case we will use the COMPUTE command. Run the following commands:

```
get file = 'gss.sys'.
sample .1.
compute prededuc = 10.243  +  .274 * paeduc.
variable labels
    prededuc 'Predicted values of EDUC from PAEDUC'.
correlation educ prededuc.
```

Figure 24.5 contains the output from these commands.

Figure 24.5 Correlation of education with predicted education

```
Correlations:  EDUC       PREDEDUC

    EDUC       1.0000      .3778**
    PREDEDUC    .3778**    1.0000

N of cases:    118         1-tailed Signif:  * - .01  ** - .001

" . " is printed if a coefficient cannot be computed
```

The correlation coefficient between the observed and predicted values is 0.3778, exactly the same value we obtained for the correlation of father's and respondent's education in Figure 24.4. Thus we have yet another interpretation of the correlation coefficient. It is a measure of the strength of the linear relationship between the *observed* values of the dependent variable and those *predicted* by the regression line. The correlation coefficient tells us how well the least-squares line fits the data.

This interpretation applies only to the *absolute value* of the correlation coefficient (its value if you disregard the sign). That's because even if the relationship between two variables is negative, the relationship between the observed and predicted values will be positive.

Explaining Variability

If you square the value of the correlation coefficient, you obtain yet another useful statistic. The square of the correlation coefficient tells you *what proportion of the variability* in the dependent variable is "explained" by the regression.

What do we mean when we say that the regression "explains" variability? Consider father's and respondent's education again. We know that there is variability in the education of the respondents. All respondents do not have the same amount of education. If there is a relationship between father's education and respondent's education, we can attribute some of the observed variability in respondents' education to differences in their fathers' education.

Consider the situation where the regression line fits the data points exactly. In this case there is still variability in respondent's education. However, the regression line perfectly explains the differences. Different amounts of father's education result in different amounts of respondent's education. All respondents with fathers of the same education have exactly the same amount of education. In this situation we would say that father's education explains all of the variation in respondent's education. The data points all lie exactly on the regression line when the line perfectly explains the data.

In general, the distance between a point and the regression line is a measure of how much variability we *can't* explain with the regression line. If you compare the sum of the squared distances from the data points to the regression line with the total variability in the dependent variable, you can calculate what percentage of the total variability is *not* explained by the regression. The remainder of the variability is explained.

This is what the square of the correlation coefficient tells you. It is the proportion of the total variability in the dependent variable that can be accounted for by the independent variable. In our example, the square of the correlation coefficient is about 0.38^2, or 0.14. (SPSS/PC+ reported this among the regression statistics in Figure 24.4.) This means that 14% of the variability in respondents' education can be explained by fathers' education.

MORE ABOUT REGRESSION WITH THE PLOT PROCEDURE

When you enter the command

```
plot  format = regression /plot = educ with paeduc.
```

SPSS/PC+ calculates the regression line, prints the regression statistics shown in Figure 24.4, and places the letter R at the two places where the regression line crosses the borders of the plot. You must enter the dependent variable in the regression *first* on the PLOT subcommand, so that it will be plotted on the vertical axis.

You can specify a control variable (after the keyword BY) on a regression plot. If you do so, SPSS/PC+ uses the first character of the control variable's value label as a plotting symbol, just as on a regular control plot (see Chapter 23). Regression statistics are calculated for the whole sample, however.

That's all you can do with regression in the PLOT procedure. However, SPSS/PC+ does have a more powerful REGRESSION procedure, as we're about to see.

WHAT'S NEXT?

In this chapter we considered only the very basics of calculating a regression line. In Chapter 25 we'll use the REGRESSION procedure to consider the problem of drawing conclusions about the population line from the sample line. We'll also consider other methods for establishing how well a linear regression model fits the data.

Summary

How can you determine the line that best summarizes the linear relationship between two variables?

In the equation for a straight line, $Y = A + BX$, the intercept A is the value of Y when X is zero. It is the point at which the line crosses the vertical axis.

The slope B tells you how much Y increases or decreases for a one-unit change in X.

The least-squares line has, of all possible lines, the smallest sum of squared distances from the points to the line.

By using the least-squares line, you can predict values for the dependent variable based on values of the independent variables.

You can find the correlation coefficient between the observed values and the predicted values by taking the absolute value of the Pearson correlation coefficient between the two variables.

The square of the Pearson correlation coefficient tells you what proportion of the variability in the dependent variable is explained by the independent variable.

EXERCISES

Syntax

1 Correct the errors in the following commands:

a. `plot plot dep with indep / format regression.`

b. `plot format regression / dep with indep.`

c. `plot format regression /fatigue by homework.`

d. `plot plot format noregression / plot grade with effort.`

2 Write the SPSS/PC+ commands to obtain a plot of *AGEDEATH* and *EDUCATION*. Obtain the regression statistics, with age at death being the dependent variable and years of education the independent variable.

3 Repeat the analysis in question 2 with education as the dependent variable and age at death as the independent variable.

4 Describe what output the following job produces:

```
get file 'physique.sys'.
process if (sex = 1).
plot format regression /plot weight with height.
process if (sex = 2).
plot format regression /plot height with weight.
```

Statistical Concepts

1 Plot the following two points and write the equation of the straight line that passes through them:

Point 1: age = 20, income = 20,000
Point 2: age = 30, income = 25,000

2 In question 1, what is the value for the intercept? For the slope? If the line you've calculated predicts income exactly, what would be the income for a 40-year-old?

3 Consider the following plot and statistics obtained from procedure PLOT:

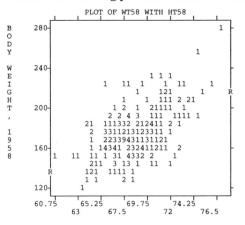

```
                    PLOT OF WT58 WITH HT58
 B      280-                                          1
 O
 D
 Y                                              1

 W      240-
 E                                    1 1 1
 I                     1    11  1    1   11        1
 G                            1     121        1
 H                            1    1 111 2 21       R
 T      200-              1 2  1   21111  1
 ,                          2 2 4 3   111   1111 1
                     21  111332 212411 2 1
 1                    2  3311213123311 1
 9                    1  22339431131121
 5      160-          1 14341 232411211   2
 8             1   11  11 1 31 4332 2      1
                     211   3 13 1   11   1
              R      121  1111 1
                     1 1      2 1
        120-         1

         60.75    65.25    69.75    74.25
              63        67.5      72       76.5
```

        STATURE, 1958 -- TO NEAREST 0.1 INCH

240 cases plotted. Regression statistics of WT58 on HT58:
Correlation .53553 R Squared .28679 S.E. of Est   20.92697 Sig.   .0000
Intercept(S.E.) -166.51879(34.77567) Slope(S.E.)   4.96169(.50719)

a. Write the equation predicting *WT58* from *HT58* and draw the line on the plot.

b. For a case with an observed value of 68 for *HT58* and 200 for *WT58*, calculate the predicted value for *WT58* and the residual.

c. Draw a line that represents the residual on the plot.

4 Consider the following plot:

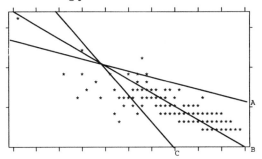

   a. Of the three lines drawn on the plot, which one is most likely to be the regression line?

   b. Is the correlation between the two variables positive, negative, or can you not tell from the plot? Why?

5 Here are the equations for two regression lines:

   Predicted weight =   100 + 5 (Adjusted height)
   Predicted weight =   105 + 50 (Ring size)

   Is the correlation coefficient larger for weight and adjusted height or for weight and ring size? How can you tell?

Data Analysis

   Use the gss.sys system file to answer the following questions.

   1 Obtain regression statistics for the pairs of variables you were analyzing in Chapter 23. Write out each of the regression equations.

   2 For which pairs of variables do you think the regression line provides a good summary of the data?

   3 Show how you would use each of the previous regression lines to predict values for new cases. Under what conditions would you expect the prediction to be good?

   4 Take one of the previous pairs of variables and reverse the regression. That is, interchange the dependent and independent variables. How do the results of this analysis compare to the one you obtained previously? Which statistics change and which remain the same? Why?

25 Testing Regression Hypotheses

How can you test hypotheses about the population
regression line based on the values you obtain in a sample?

- What is the population regression line?

- What assumptions do you have to make about the data to test
  hypotheses about the population regression line?

- How do you test the null hypothesis that the slope is zero in the
  population?

- What is the meaning of the confidence interval for the slope?

- What does the analysis of variance table for the regression analysis tell
  you?

A regression line is a good way to describe and summarize the linear relationship between two variables. Often, however, you want to do more than that. You want to draw conclusions about the relationship of the two variables in the population from which the sample was selected. You want to draw conclusions, for example, about the relationship between a person's education and their father's education for all people in the United States—not just those included in the General Social Survey. In this chapter you'll learn what's involved in testing hypotheses about the population regression line.

THE POPULATION REGRESSION LINE

When you want to calculate a regression line that is to be used only to describe an observed relationship between two variables, you have two concerns. Are the variables measured on an interval or ratio scale, and does their relationship appear to be linear? It makes no sense to calculate a regression line relating religious preference to the region in which someone lives. There is no order to the categories of either of these variables, and a statistic like the slope is meaningless. Even if the two variables are measured on an interval scale, but their relationship is not linear, it makes no sense to calculate a regression line. You may need to fit some other mathematical function besides a straight line, or perhaps change the scale on which the variables are measured. Those topics are mostly beyond the scope of this book, but we'll talk a little about them in Chapter 26.

When you're interested in drawing conclusions about the *population* regression line, you need additional assumptions. First, let's clarify what we mean by a "population regression line." In all of our previous discussions about hypothesis testing, we considered our data to be a random sample from some underlying population. We thought of the people included in the General Social Survey as a sample of the population of adults in the United States. We wanted to draw conclusions about the *population* based on what we saw in our *sample*. When we computed a sample mean, we considered it to be our best guess of the population mean. When we computed a sample correlation coefficient, we considered it our best guess for the value of the correlation coefficient in the population.

What we'll be doing now is very similar. We'll try to draw conclusions about the relationship of two variables in the population based on the results we see in our sample. If we had been able to include our entire population in the study, we could calculate a regression line that describes the relationship between the two variables in the population. This would be the "true" or **population regression line**. However, we don't know what the true line is, since all we have is a sample from the population. We don't know the true slope or the true intercept. We do have some evidence about what they might be, however. Our best guess for the population line is the results observed in our sample.

Additional Assumptions

To be able to test hypotheses about the population line statistically, we must make some assumptions about the population. We need these assumptions so we'll know that the sampling distributions of the slope and intercept will be normal. (The sampling distribution of the slope is the distribution of the values of the slope that you would get if you took all possible samples of a particular size from a population. The sampling distribution of the intercept is defined similarly.) As before, our computations of the observed significance level will be based on these sampling distributions.

Normality and Equal Variances

If I tell you that a person's father has four years of college, would you expect to be able to predict exactly how many years of education the person has? Probably not. Even if there is a strong relationship between two variables, it is unlikely to be perfect. Look at Figure 25.1, which is a histogram of years of education for only those people whose fathers have exactly four years of college. The most frequent value of education is exactly four years of college, but some people did not even finish high school. Others have several years of graduate education. There is a distribution of the values of education for each value of father's education.

Figure 25.1 Education when father's education equals 16

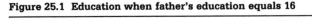

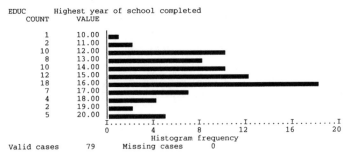

For hypothesis testing, we'll have to make the assumptions that, in the population

- For each year of father's education, the distribution of people's education is normal.

- All of these distributions have the same variance. That is, the variance in education is the same for people whose fathers had eight years of education, twelve years of education, or twenty years of education.

Linearity

We've just stated that to test hypotheses about the population line, we need to assume that the distributions of the dependent variable must be normal for each value of the independent variable and that the variances of those distributions must be equal. Now, what about the means of the distributions?

If there is a linear relationship in the population between a person's education and their father's education, then *the means of all of the population distributions must fall on a straight line.* To test regression hypotheses, we must assume that this is true.

Look at Figure 25.1, which schematically shows the assumptions we've been talking about. In the population there is a *true* regression line that specifies the relationship between a person's education and their father's education. This line is drawn in on the plot. For each value of the independent variable there is a distribution of the values of the dependent variable. These distributions are all normal and have the same variance. The means of all of these distributions fall on a straight line.

Figure 25.2 Regression assumptions

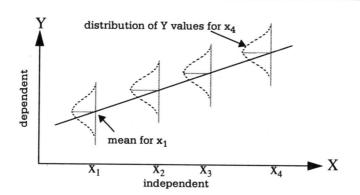

Independence

The last assumption that we need for linear regression analysis is that *all observations are selected independently*. That is, including one person in the sample should not in any way alter the chance of any other person being included. For example, if we're studying the relationship between a person's education and their father's education and we include all brothers and sisters from the same family in the sample, the observations are not independent. The same father could be included several times.

SOME HYPOTHESES OF INTEREST

We'll return in Chapter 26 to the question of how you can examine your data to see if they violate any of these assumptions. Meanwhile, suppose that the data do satisfy all of the assumptions outlined above. What sorts of hypotheses can we now test? We can test hypotheses about the values of the population slope and the population intercept, and hypotheses about how well the regression model fits the population.

Testing Hypotheses with the REGRESSION Command

The PLOT command is convenient for displaying the data and fitting a simple regression line. The REGRESSION command lets you test hypotheses about regression models and fit more complicated models. To obtain hypothesis tests for whether the population slope and intercept are zero, run the commands

```
get file 'gss.sys'.
regression dependent educ
   /enter paeduc.
```

The DEPENDENT subcommand identifies the dependent variable. Since we only have one independent variable in our model (the variable *PAEDUC*, or father's education), we simply "enter" that variable in the model, as specified by the ENTER subcommand. Other methods can be used for regression equations with more than one independent variable.

Regression Coefficients

The regression coefficients and associated statistics are shown in Figure 25.3. The values of the regression coefficients are in the column labeled *B*. You should recognize the values in this figure as quite close to the values on the PLOT output in Chapter 24. The slope is 0.35, and the intercept, sometimes called the **constant,** is 9.45. Instead of thinking of these values as descriptions of the sample, we will now treat them as our best guesses, or **estimates,** of the unknown population values of the slope and intercept.

Figure 25.3 Output from the REGRESSION command

```
        * * * *   M U L T I P L E   R E G R E S S I O N   * * * *

Listwise Deletion of Missing Data

Equation Number 1    Dependent Variable..   EDUC   Highest year of school comple

Block Number  1.  Method:  Enter


Variable(s) Entered on Step Number
   1..    PAEDUC    Father's highest year of school


Multiple R           .48221
R Square             .23253
Adjusted R Square    .23181
Standard Error       2.56857

Analysis of Variance
                    DF     Sum of Squares     Mean Square
Regression           1         2126.84923      2126.84923
Residual          1064         7019.77366         6.59753

F =      322.37045      Signif F =  .0000


------------------ Variables in the Equation ------------------

Variable             B         SE B       Beta        T  Sig T

PAEDUC          .347027     .019328    .482212    17.955  .0000
(Constant)     9.451633     .209802               45.050  .0000


End Block Number   1   All requested variables entered.
```

> **?** *But why aren't the values from* REGRESSION *exactly the same as the values from* PLOT? *They're the same variables, aren't they?* Yes, but they're not all the same cases. In Chapter 24 we took a smaller sample so there wouldn't be too many cases to plot. We'd expect the slope and intercept in Figure 25.3 to be better estimates of the population values than the values in Chapter 24, since these are now based on more cases. ∎∎∎

The next column in Figure 25.3, labeled *SE B*, contains the standard errors of the slope and intercept. The standard errors are estimates of the standard deviation of the sampling distributions of the slope and the intercept. Remember, the slope and intercept we have calculated are based on one sample from a population. If you took another sample and calculated values for the slope and intercept, they would differ. The values of the slope and intercept from repeated samples from the same population have a distribution. The standard deviation of this distribution is called the standard error. It's just like the standard error of the mean back in Chapter 16

Are the Population Values Zero?

If there is no linear relationship between two variables in the population, the true slope is zero. All of the means of the distributions are the same. The predicted value for a person's education is the same, regardless of their father's education. Even if the population value is zero, of course, you wouldn't expect the sample value for the slope to be *exactly* zero. You hope that it wouldn't be too far from zero. To test the null hypothesis that the value of the slope is zero in the population, we can calculate the probability of obtaining a slope at least as large as the one we've observed, when the null hypothesis is true. As usual, if this probability is small, we will reject the null hypothesis that the slope is zero.

The observed significance level is based on the *t* statistic shown in Figure 25.3 in the column labeled *T*. This *t* statistic is calculated (like any *t* statistic) by dividing a sample value by its standard error. In this case, the *t* values are the sample slope and the sample intercept, divided by their standard errors.

In the column labeled *Sig T* are the two-tailed significance levels for the tests of the hypotheses that the slope and intercept are zero in the population. In this example, the values 0.0000 are printed. This indicates that the probability is less than 0.00005 that a sample slope at least as large (in absolute value) as the one we've observed would occur if the true slope is zero. The same interpretation holds for the significance of the intercept.

When testing whether there is a linear relationship between two variables, the important test is the test of the *slope*. The intercept is simply the value of the dependent variable when the independent variable is zero. All that the test of the intercept tells us is whether the regression line goes through the **origin**. (The origin is the point at the intersection of the two axes. It is the point where both variables are zero.) In this example, you wouldn't predict zero years of education for a person whose parents had zero years of education. You would predict 9.45 years, because that's the intercept.

Confidence Intervals for Regression Coefficients

The sample values for the slope and intercept are our best guesses for the population values. However, we know it's unlikely that they are exactly on target. As we've discussed before, it's possible to calculate a confidence interval for the population value. A confidence interval is a range of values which, with a designated likelihood, contains the unknown population value. To obtain 95% confidence intervals for the slope and intercept using SPSS/PC+ REGRESSION, we must add an additional specification to the command. It's called the STATISTICS subcommand, and it tells the system what values we want:

```
regression statistics default ci
  /dependent educ
  /enter paeduc.
```

The keyword DEFAULT on the STATISTICS subcommand tells the system to print the usual regression output. The keyword CI tells it to print the confidence intervals also. The regression statistics and their confidence intervals are shown in Figure 25.4. The 95% confidence interval for the slope ranges from 0.309 to 0.385.

Figure 25.4 Confidence intervals for regression coefficients

```
-------------------- Variables in the Equation ----------------------

Variable              B       SE B      95% Confdnce Intrvl B       Beta

PAEDUC            .347027   .019328      .309102     .384952      .482212
(Constant)       9.451633   .209802     9.039960    9.863306


----------- in ------------

Variable          T   Sig T

PAEDUC        17.955  .0000
(Constant)    45.050  .0000


End Block Number   1   All requested variables entered.
```

Remember what *95% confidence* means: if we draw repeated samples from a population, under the same conditions, and compute 95% confidence intervals for the slope and intercept, 95% of these intervals should include the unknown *population* values for the slope and intercept. Of course, since the true population values are not known, it isn't possible to tell whether any particular interval contains the population values. Notice that in this example, neither the confidence interval for the slope nor the one for the intercept contains the value zero. An interval will include zero only if you *can't* reject the null hypothesis that the slope or intercept is zero at an observed significance level of 0.05 or less.

GOODNESS OF FIT OF THE MODEL

In Chapter 24 we discussed the importance of assessing how well the regression model actually fits the data. The REGRESSION command prints several statistics that describe the "goodness of fit." Look at the first part of Figure 25.5, which is part of the output from the same command that produced Figure 25.4. The entry labeled *Multiple R* is just the absolute value of the correlation coefficient between the dependent variable and the independent variable. It's also the correlation coefficient between the values *predicted* by the regression model and the actual *observed* values. If the value is close to 1, the regression model fits the data well. If the value is close to zero, the regression model does not fit well.

Figure 25.5 Goodness-of-fit statistics

```
            * * * *   M U L T I P L E   R E G R E S S I O N   * * * *

Listwise Deletion of Missing Data

Equation Number 1    Dependent Variable..    EDUC   Highest year of school comple

Block Number  1.  Method:  Enter

Variable(s) Entered on Step Number
    1..    PAEDUC    Father's highest year of school

Multiple R            .48221
R Square              .23253
Adjusted R Square     .23181
Standard Error       2.56857

Analysis of Variance
                     DF     Sum of Squares     Mean Square
Regression            1         2126.84923      2126.84923
Residual           1064         7019.77366         6.59753

F =     322.37045      Signif F =  .0000
```

Another way of looking at how well the regression model fits is to see what proportion of the total variability (or variance) in the dependent variable can be "explained" by the independent variable. The variability in the dependent variable is divided into two components: variability explained by the regression and variability not explained by the regression. Because of the way they're calculated, these two components are termed **sums of squares**. They are conceptually very similar to the sums of squares we discussed in Chapter 20.

The two sums of squares are displayed in the analysis of variance table at the bottom of Figure 25.5. The sums of squares explained by the regression equation are labeled REGRESSION, while the unexplained variability is labeled RESIDUAL. You can obtain the total variability in the dependent variable by adding up these two sums of squares.

To calculate what proportion of the total variability is explained by the regression, all you have to do is divide the regression sum of squares by the total sum of squares. For this example, the value is

$$\text{Variance explained} = \frac{2127}{2127 + 7020} = 0.23$$

There's an easier way to calculate this proportion. All you have to do is square the correlation coefficient. This value is shown in Figure 25.5 next to the label *R Square*. From R^2 we see that in our sample we can explain 23% of the variability in people's education by knowing their fathers' education.

Another Test for a Linear Relationship

The analysis of variance table in Figure 25.5 can also be used to test the null hypothesis that there is no linear relationship between the two variables. Below the analysis of variance table you see the label F. This is for the same kind of F statistic we discussed in Chapter 20: F is the ratio of the mean square for regression to the mean square for the residual, and the mean squares are the sums of squares divided by their respective degrees of freedom.

   You can find these mean squares in the column labeled *Mean Square*. If there is *no* linear relationship between the two variables, each of these mean squares provides an estimate of the variance, or variability, of the dependent variable. If there *is* a linear relationship, then the variability estimate based on the regression mean square will be much larger than the variability estimate based on the residuals. Large F values suggest that there is a linear relationship between the two variables. In this example, the F value is 322 and the observed significance level associated with it is less than 0.00005. We reject the null hypothesis that there is no linear relationship between the two variables.

> **?** *Is there any relationship of this* F *statistic to the test that the slope is zero? It seems like we're testing the same hypothesis in both situations.* Yes, the two tests are evaluating exactly the same hypothesis when there's only one independent variable. In fact, there's a relationship between the two statistics. If you square the t value for the test that the slope is zero, you will come up with the F value in the analysis of variance table. (Try it.) For a simple equation like this, you don't learn anything from the analysis of variance table that you didn't already know from the test of the slope. ∎

Other Regression Statistics

There are several statistics in Figure 25.5 that we haven't discussed yet. The number labeled *Standard Error* is an estimate of the standard deviation of the distributions of the dependent variable. Remember, we assumed that for each value of the independent variable there is a distribution of values of the dependent variable. All of these distributions are normal and have the same standard deviation. Our estimate of the standard deviation is the standard error.

The number labeled *Adjusted R Square* is most useful when you have a model with several independent variables. This statistic adjusts the value of R^2 to take into account the fact that a regression model always fits the particular data on which it was developed better than it will fit the population. When there is only one independent variable and a reasonably large number of cases, adjusted R^2 will be very close to the unadjusted value.

MORE ABOUT THE REGRESSION PROCEDURE

To obtain regression coefficients and goodness-of-fit statistics for the dependent variable *DEP* as predicted by the independent variable *INDEP*, run the command:

```
regression dependent dep
 /enter indep.
```

You must specify the DEPENDENT subcommand before the ENTER (or other method) subcommand. To get confidence intervals in addition to the default statistics, run the command:

```
regression statistics default ci
 /dependent dep
 /enter indep.
```

If you also want descriptive statistics for the variables you are using, run the command:

```
regression dep indep
 /descriptives all
 /statistics default ci
 /dependent dep
 /method enter.
```

Note that the DESCRIPTIVES and STATISTICS subcommands must be specified before the DEPENDENT subcommand.

Multiple Regression

The REGRESSION command can use more than one independent variable in the same equation. This is known as **multiple regression**. To use multiple independent variables, just name them all after one of the following subcommands:

ENTER (list)   *Enter a group of variables all at once.* This is the method we've been using throughout the chapter. Specify the names of the independent variables after the keyword ENTER.

REMOVE (list) *Remove a group of variables all at once.* These must be variables that entered the equation on a previous METHOD subcommand. You *must* specify the names of specific variables after the keyword REMOVE.

FORWARD (list) *Enter the variables one at a time.* List the variables after the subcommand.

BACKWARD (list) *Remove the variables one at a time.* If some variables are already in the equation from a previous METHOD subcommand, they are removed one at a time. Otherwise, all listed variables are entered and then removed one at a time.

STEPWISE (list) *Enter and remove variables one at a time.* The process continues until the F statistics do not indicate that any variables in the equation should be removed nor that any variables that are not in the equation need to be entered.

You can specify several METHOD subcommands after a single DEPENDENT subcommand. The methods are applied one after the other:

```
regression dependent y
/enter x1
/stepwise x2 x3 x4.
```

Additional features and subcommands of REGRESSION are discussed in Chapter 26.

WHAT'S NEXT?

Regression is a powerful technique, but you must make a number of assumptions in order to use it. The REGRESSION procedure provides several plots and statistics that make it easy to determine whether your data satisfy these assumptions and help you decide what to do if they don't. That's what we'll talk about next.

Summary

How can you test hypotheses about the population regression line based on the values you obtain in a sample?

To draw conclusions about the population regression line, you must assume that, for each value of the independent variable, the distribution of values of the dependent variable is normal with the same variance. The means of these distributions must all fall on a straight line.

The test of the null hypothesis that the slope is zero is a test of whether there is a linear relationship between the two variables.

The confidence interval for the population slope provides you with a range of values that, with a designated likelihood, includes the population value.

When there is a single independent variable, the analysis of variance table for the regression is equivalent to the test that the slope is zero.

EXERCISES

Syntax

1 Correct the errors in the following commands:

 a. `regression dep gpa / enter iq.`

 b. `regression enter iq /dep gpa.`

 c. `regression popiq/enter miq.`

 d. `regression dep gpa enter gpa.`

2 Write the SPSS/PC+ commands to calculate a regression equation where *SBPRES* is the dependent variable and *AGE* is the independent variable. Obtain the default regression statistics and the confidence interval for the regression coefficient.

3 When you run the command

 `regression dep gpa /enter iq /statistics def ci.`

 you obtain the following error message:

 ```
 ERROR   10595, (End of command)
 The CRITERIA, STATISTICS, ORIGIN OR NOORIGIN subcommands must be placed
 directly before the DEPENDENT subcommand for the equation to which they
 apply.
 This command not executed.
 ```

 Identify the error and correct the command.

Statistical Concepts

1 A personnel manager is interested in studying the relationship between salary and years on the job for rodent exterminators. She also wants to see whether males and females are similarly reimbursed. She has obtained salary and experience data from a sample of 1000 exterminators.

a. Outline the steps you would recommend for analyzing the data.

b. The three variables are named *SALARY, EXPER,* and *SEX* (coded 0=*male*; 1=*female*). Write the SPSS/PC+ commands to produce the analysis you recommended in part a.

2 Assume that in question 1 the personnel manager did find a a fairly good linear relationship for salaries and experience in the 1- to 5-year range. She did not include people with less than 1 year of experience or with more than 5 years of experience in the study. Discuss some of the problems she may encounter if she attempts to use her regression equation to determine compensation for people with more than 5 years of experience or less than 1.

3 Here's a hypothetical plot of salary and work experience:

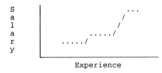

```
S
a
l
a
r
y
        Experience
```

a. Discuss the possible use of regression analysis for this problem.

b. What ways can you think of for summarizing the relationship between the two variables?

4 Based on the following statistics

```
----------------- VARIABLES IN THE EQUATION -----------------

Variable            B        SE B       BETA        T   Sig T

X                1.70000    .82260     .76642    2.067   .1307
(Constant)       4.30000   2.72825              1.576   .2131
```

a. Would you reject the null hypothesis that there is no linear relationship between *X* and the dependent variable?

b. On what do you base your conclusion?

c. What is the two-tailed observed significance level for the test of the null hypothesis that the correlation coefficient is 0?

d. What would be the value of the *F* statistic and its associated observed significance level in the analysis of variance table for this regression?

5 You are reading an article about the relationship between college GPA and IQ. The authors present the following equation:

GPA = 3.54 + 0.001 × IQ

The observed significance level for the slope is reported as 0.03.

a. Is it possible to have both a small slope and a small observed significance level for the test that the slope is zero?

b. How does the intercept affect the test of the null hypothesis that the slope is zero?

c. Is it possible to reject the null hypothesis that the slope is zero and not reject the null hypothesis that there is no linear relationship between the two variables?

d. From the value of the slope, can you tell how well the model fits the data?

e. Interpret the observed significance level reported for the equation.

Data Analysis

Use the gss.sys system file to answer the following questions.

1   In this chapter we looked at the relationship between a person's education and their father's education.

a. Perform a regression analysis to examine the relationship between a person's education and their mother's education.

b. Summarize the results.

c. Discuss the similarities and differences between the results of the two analyses (*PAEDUC* and *EDUC*, *MAEDUC* and *EDUC*). Is there a stronger linear relationship between father's education and a person's education, or between mother's education and a person's education?

2   Using the SELECT IF command, repeat the analyses in question 1 for males and for females separately. Summarize your results. Comment on whether father's education is a better predictor of son's education than of daughter's education.

3   Develop a regression equation for predicting husband's education from wife's education. Perform any other analyses that you think would be helpful in studying the relationship between two variables. Write a short paper presenting the results of all of your analyses. Be sure to include discussion of the hypotheses you are testing and the statistics you are using.

4   Is there a relationship between the age at which a woman first marries and her mother's educational attainment? Analyze this question and summarize your results.

Analyzing Residuals

How can you tell whether the assumptions necessary for a regression analysis appear to be violated?

- What is a residual and what does it tell you?

- How can you use residuals to check whether the assumption of normality appears to be violated?

- How can you use residuals to check whether the assumption of constant variance appears to be violated?

- How can you use residuals to check whether the assumption of linearity appears to be violated?

- What can you do if you suspect that some of the assumptions are being violated?

- What are transformations and how can they help you?

When you begin studying the relationship between two variables you usually don't know whether the assumptions needed for regression analysis are satisfied. You don't know whether there is a linear relationship between the two variables, much less whether the distribution of the dependent variable is normal and has the same variance for all values of the independent variable. One of the goals of regression analysis is to check whether the required assumptions of linearity, normality, and constant variance are met. In this chapter we'll discuss several procedures for looking for violations of the assumptions.

RESIDUALS

A quantity called the **residual** plays a very important role when you're fitting models to data. You can think of a residual as what's left over after a model is fit. In linear regression the residual is the difference between the observed and predicted values of the dependent variable. If a person has 12 years of education and your model predicts 9, the residual for the case is 12 - 9 = 3. You have three years of education left over or not explained by the model.

Looking at Residuals

By looking at the residual for each case you can see how well a model fits. If a model fits the data perfectly, all of the residuals are zero. Cases for which the model doesn't fit well have large residuals.

You can use the REGRESSION procedure to calculate the residuals for all cases. Run the following command:

```
get file 'gss.sys'.
regression dependent educ
 /enter paeduc
 /casewise all dependent pred resid zresid.
```

This is the same command we used in Chapter 25, except that the CASE-WISE subcommand has been added. This subcommand prints information about residuals for each case ("casewise"). Keyword ALL instructs SPSS/PC+ to print residual values for all of the cases. (If you don't want to see all the residual values, look at a few screens' worth and then press

Ctrl Break. This will stop the display and leave SPSS/PC+ ready for another command.) The other keywords tell SPSS/PC+ what to print. The keyword DEPENDENT stands for the observed dependent value, PRED for the predicted value, RESID for the residual, and ZRESID for the standardized residual. See the end of this chapter for additional keywords available on the CASEWISE subcommand.

Figure 26.1 Casewise plot and residuals from REGRESSION

```
          * * *   M U L T I P L E   R E G R E S S I O N   * * * *
Equation Number 1    Dependent Variable..   EDUC   Highest year of school compl

Casewise Plot of Standardized Residual
*: Selected    M: Missing
           -3.0      0.0      3.0
         O:........:........:O   EDUC    *PRED     *RESID    *ZRESID
Case #
  1      .         .         .    12      .          .          .
  2      .        .*         .    16    15.0041    .9959      .3877
  3      .         .         .    15      .          .          .
  4      .         .  *      .    16    12.5749   3.4251     1.3335
  5      .        .*         .    16    15.0041    .9959      .3877
  6      .         .  *      .    17    13.6160   3.3840     1.3175
  7      .         .     *   .    18    12.2278   5.7722     2.2472
  8      .    *    .         .    12    15.0041  -3.0041    -1.1695
  9      .         .         .    10      .          .          .
 10      .    *    .         .    12    15.0041  -3.0041    -1.1695
 11      .         .         .    12      .          .          .
 12      .       * .         .    12    12.2278   -.2278     -.0887
 13      .         .        ·11      .          .          .
 14      .         .         .     9      .          .          .
 15      .    *    .         .    13    16.3922  -3.3922    -1.3206
  . . .
```

Reading the Casewise Results

Figure 26.1 shows part of the CASEWISE output. The column labeled *Case #* tells you the number of the case for which the results are printed. The first column to the right of the plot shows the actual value of *EDUC* for each case. You want to see this because *EDUC* is the dependent variable, so it's the "target" for the predictions. *PRED* is the predicted value for the dependent variable based on the regression equation. *RESID* is the difference between the two, or the residual.

For example, case 2 has 16 years of education. The predicted value of education, based on the regression equation using father's education, is 15.0041. The residual is therefore 16 - 15.0041 = 0.9959. (When father's education is missing for a case, there is no prediction. For such cases, SPSS/PC+ prints periods instead of predictions and residuals.)

Judging the Size of the Residuals

How can you tell whether a residual is big or small? If I tell you that a case has a residual of 500, can you say whether the model gives a reasonably good prediction for the case? On first thought, 500 seems like a pretty large number, an indication that a model doesn't fit that case. However, if you're predicting income in dollars, a residual of 500 may not be all that large. Predicting a person's income to the nearest 500 dollars is pretty good. On the other hand, if you're predicting years of education, a residual of 500 should send you searching for a new and improved model.

One way to modify the residuals so that they are easier to interpret is to standardize them. That is, divide each residual by an estimate of its standard deviation. (This is the standard error printed on the REGRESSION output.)

> **?** *How come you're only dividing the residual by its standard deviation? Why aren't you first subtracting off the mean, like you did before when computing standardized values?* There's no need to subtract the mean of the residuals before dividing by the standard deviation, because the mean of the residuals is zero. If you add up all of the residuals you'll find that their sum, and therefore their mean, is zero. That's always true for a regression model that includes a constant.   ■■■

The standardized residuals are shown in the column labeled *ZRESID*. For most cases they range in value from –2 to +2. (Remember that in a normal distribution with a mean of 0 and a standard deviation of 1, about 95% of the cases fall within +2 and –2.) Whenever you see a standardized residual larger than +2 or smaller than –2, you should examine the case to see if there's some explanation for why the model doesn't fit. The standardized residuals are plotted on the casewise plot on the left side of Figure 26.1. Whenever a value is larger than 3, it is plotted in the border.

Looking for Outliers

If you have a large number of cases, as in the GSS, you may not want to look at the values of the residuals for all cases. Instead, you may want to look only at the cases with "large" residuals. Such cases are called **outliers**. This is easy to do with the REGRESSION procedure. Just omit the keyword ALL on the CASEWISE subcommand:

```
regression dependent educ
  /enter paeduc
  /casewise dependent pred resid zresid.
```

If you don't tell SPSS/PC+ to print all cases, it prints only those whose standardized residuals are greater than 3 or less than –3.

The output from this command is shown in Figure 26.2. You see that there are seven cases with large standardized residuals. It's interesting that four of the cases have very little education (four years or fewer), while the other three have a lot of education (twenty years). You can tell that the model predicts too little education for the people with a lot of education. Their residuals are positive, meaning that they have more education than the model predicts. The model predicts too much education for the people with little education: their residuals are negative. By looking at the characteristics of the outliers, you can see situations where the model doesn't work well.

Figure 26.2 Residuals for outliers only

```
          * * * *   M U L T I P L E   R E G R E S S I O N   * * * *
Equation Number 1    Dependent Variable..   EDUC   Highest year of school compl

Casewise Plot of Standardized Residual

Outliers = 3.    *: Selected   M: Missing

           -6.     -3.  3.     6.
   Case #   O:......:  :.......:O   EDUC      *PRED       *RESID      *ZRESID
      78    .       *  ..        .     2     10.8397     -8.8397     -3.4415
     100    .       *..         .     3     11.5338     -8.5338     -3.3224
     188    .          ..*      .    20     12.2278      7.7722      3.0259
     361    .       *..         .     4     12.2278     -8.2278     -3.2033
     836    .     *  ..         .     4     13.9630     -9.9630     -3.8788
    1188    .          ..*      .    20     12.2278      7.7722      3.0259
    1444    .          ..*      .    20     12.2278      7.7722      3.0259

        7 Outliers found.
```

CHECKING ASSUMPTIONS WITH RESIDUALS

Residuals are the primary tools for checking whether the assumptions necessary for linear regression appear to be violated. We can draw histograms of the residuals, plot them against the observed and predicted values, recompute them excluding certain cases, and manipulate them in other ways. By examining the resulting plots and statistics, we can learn much about how appropriate the regression model is for a particular data set. Let's consider how to check each of the assumptions in turn.

Normality

If in the population the relationship is linear and the dependent variable is normally distributed for each value of the independent variable, the distribution of the residuals should also be approximately normal. Figure 26.3 is a histogram of the residuals for the education example. The figure was produced by this command:

```
regression dependent educ
 /enter paeduc
 /residuals histogram.
```

The distribution of the residuals appears to be fairly normal, though it is a bit more "peaked" than you would expect. Remember, the periods and colons on the histogram indicate what a normal distribution with the same mean and variance would look like.

Figure 26.3 Histogram of standardized residuals

```
Histogram - Standardized Residual

    N    Exp N        (* = 3 Cases,      . : = Normal Curve)
    0     .82    Out
    4    1.63    3.00 :
    0    4.16    2.67 .
   23    9.51    2.33 **:*****
   30   19.45    2.00 *****:****
   21   35.64    1.67 *******
   49   58.49    1.33 ****************  .
   80   85.98    1.00 ***************************** .
   90  113.22     .67 *********************************  .
  110  133.55     .33 *************************************
  186  141.10     .00 ***********************************************:***************
  140  133.55    -.33 **********************************************:**
  162  113.22    -.67 *********************************************:*****************
   73   85.98   -1.00 ************************   .
   38   58.49   -1.33 *************  .
   26   35.64   -1.67 ********* .
   11   19.45   -2.00 **** .
   10    9.51   -2.33 **:
    6    4.16   -2.67 :*
    3    1.63   -3.00 :
    4     .82    Out *
```

When the distribution of residuals doesn't appear to be normal, you can sometimes transform the data to make it appear more normal. When you **transform** a variable, you change its values by taking square roots, logarithms, or some other mathematical function. If the distribution of residuals is not symmetric but has a tail in the positive direction, it's sometimes helpful to take logs of the dependent variable. If the tail is in the negative direction and all data values are positive, taking the square root of the data may be helpful. Figure 26.4 and Figure 26.5 show histograms for a different data set of the residuals before and after a log transformation.

The distribution of your residuals may not appear to be normal for several reasons. One is that they are from a population in which the distributions are not normal. But the distribution of the residuals may also appear to be non-normal if the variance of the dependent variable is not constant for different values of the independent variable, or if you simply have a small number of residuals. It's possible that after you've remedied some of these problems the distribution of residuals may look more normal.

Figure 26.4 Before log transformation

```
Histogram - Studentized Residual

  N   Exp N          (* = 2 Cases,     . : = Normal Curve)
  7    .37    Out ****
  2    .73   3.00 *
  4   1.85   2.67 :*
  2   4.23   2.33 *.
  6   8.65   2.00 ***.
 12  15.85   1.67 ****** .
  7  26.01   1.33 ****        .
 18  38.23   1.00 ********         .
 35  50.34    .67 *****************   .
 63  59.38    .33 *******************************:**
 87  62.74    .00 *****************************:*************
114  59.38   -.33 ***********************************:*******************************
 64  50.34   -.67 ************************:*******
 32  38.23  -1.00 ****************  .
  9  26.01  -1.33 *****  .
  6  15.85  -1.67 ***     .
  1   8.65  -2.00 *   .
  1   4.23  -2.33 *.
  2   1.85  -2.67 :
  0    .73  -3.00
  2    .37    Out *
```

Figure 26.5 After log transformation

```
Histogram - Studentized Residual

  N Exp N          (* = 1 Cases,     . : = Normal Curve)
  3   .37    Out ***
  1   .73   3.00 :
  3  1.85   2.67 *:*
  4  4.23   2.33 ***:
 10  8.65   2.00 ********:*
 14 15.85   1.67 **************  .
 21 26.01   1.33 *********************  .
 31 38.23   1.00 *******************************      .
 48 50.34    .67 ************************************************ .
 55 59.38    .33 *******************************************************:
 63 62.74    .00 **********************************************************:
 64 59.38   -.33 **********************************************************:*****
 62 50.34   -.67 *******************************************************:************
 44 38.23  -1.00 ******:********************************:******
 28 26.01  -1.33 ***************************:**
 14 15.85  -1.67 **************  .
  7  8.65  -2.00 *******  .
  1  4.23  -2.33 *  .
  1  1.85  -2.67 *.
  0   .73  -3.00 .
  0   .37    Out
```

Constant Variance

To check whether the variance appears to be constant, you can plot the residuals against the predicted values and also against the values of the independent variable. This is done in SPSS/PC+ with a simple addition to the usual REGRESSION command. Run the following command:

```
regression dependent educ
 /enter paeduc
 /scatterplot  (*resid, *pred) (*resid, paeduc).
```

The SCATTERPLOT subcommand plots the residuals against the predicted values and the residuals against the independent variable.

> *What are all those words beginning with asterisks on the SCATTER-PLOT subcommand?* Those are just the names of the temporary variables you can use to analyze residuals in REGRESSION. You saw some of them in Figure 26.1 and Figure 26.2. There's a list of them at the end of this chapter. You have to put asterisks in front of their names when you use them on the SCATTERPLOT subcommand to distinguish them from regular variables like *PAEDUC*.   ■■■

The plots produced by this command are shown in Figure 26.6. If the spread of the residuals increases or decreases either with the values of the independent variable or with the predicted values, you have reason to suspect that the variance is not constant. In both of our plots there doesn't appear to be any pattern to the residuals. They form a horizontal band.

Figure 26.6   Scatterplots of residuals

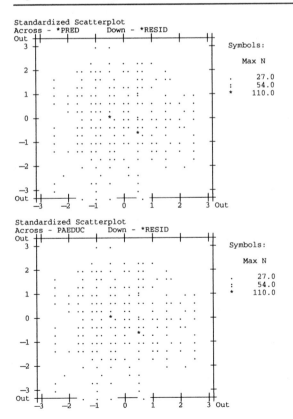

This won't always be the case. In Figure 26.7 the spread of the residuals increases with increasing values of the independent variable. The residuals form a funnel pattern. This suggests that the variance of the dependent variable increases over the values of the independent variable. This is a common occurrence. If you're studying the relationship between children's weights and ages, you would expect that there is more variability in the weights of twelve-year-olds than in the weights of one-year-olds. As age increases, so does the variability of the weights.

Figure 26.7 Variance increasing with independent variable

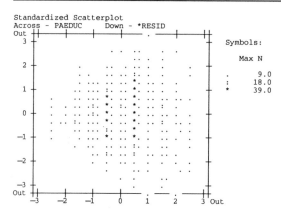

There are some common transformations that may help when the variance does not appear to be constant. If the variance increases linearly with the values of the independent variable and all values of the dependent variable are positive, take the square root of the dependent variable. If the standard deviation is increasing linearly with values of the independent variable, try taking logs of the data.

Linearity

To see whether it's appropriate to assume a linear relationship, you should always plot the dependent variable against the independent variable (see Chapter 23). If the points don't cluster around a straight line, you shouldn't fit a linear regression model.

Another way to see whether a relationship is linear is to look at the plots of the residuals against the predicted values and the residuals against the values of the independent variable. (These are the plots shown in Figure 26.6.) If you see any type of pattern to the residuals—that is, if they don't fall in a horizontal band—you have reason to suspect that the relationship is not linear. Figure 26.8 contains plots of the residuals against the predicted values when the relationships are not linear. Two of the plots show the original data and the other two show the residuals and predicted values.

Figure 26.8 Residuals from nonlinear relationships

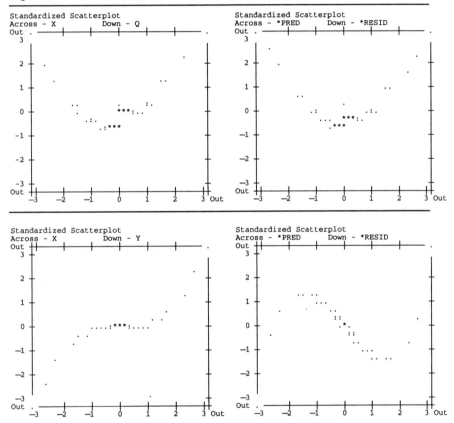

Sometimes when the relationship between two variables doesn't apear to be linear, it's possible to transform the variables and make it linear. Then you can study the relationship between the transformed variables using linear regression. For example, look at Figure 26.9. The relationship between the two variables doesn't look quite linear. However, if you take the log of the dependent variable you get the relationship shown in Figure 26.10. The relationship between the X and the log of Y appears to be fairly linear.

Figure 26.9   Nonlinear relationship

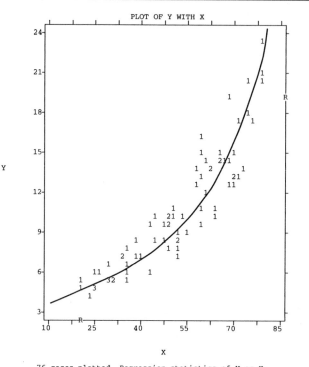

```
                    PLOT OF Y WITH X
    24-                                        1

    21-                                    1
                                         1 1
                                   1      R
    18-                              1
                                   1/ 1
                              1
    15-                    1   1 /1
    Y                      1  2)1
                         1 2    1
                         1     21
                         1     11
    12-                 1
                     1   1 1
               1 21 1    1 1
    9-         1 12   1 1
           1   1 1/ 2
           1 1 )  1 1
         2 11     1
    6-   11   1        1
       1  32  1
       1  3
       1
    3-
      -R-
       10    25     40     55     70     85

                    X
```

```
       76 cases plotted. Regression statistics of Y on X:
Correlation  .90704 R Squared  .82272  S.E. of Est   1.91524 Sig.   .0000
Intercept(S.E.)   -2.02728(   .71714)  Slope(S.E.)      .24644(   .01330)
```

> **?** *Isn't transforming the data more or less cheating, or at least distorting the true picture?* No. All that transforming a variable does is change the scale on which it's measured. Instead of saying that there is a linear relationship between work experience and salary, you say that there is a linear relationship between work experience and the log of salary. It's much easier to build models for relationships that are linear than those that are not. That's why transforming variables is often a convenient tactic. ■ ■ ■

Choosing a Transformation

How do you decide what transformation to use? Sometimes you might know what mathematical formula relates two variables. In that case you can use mathematics to figure out what transformation you need. This situation happens more often in the physical or biological sciences than in the social sciences.

Figure 26.10 After log transformation

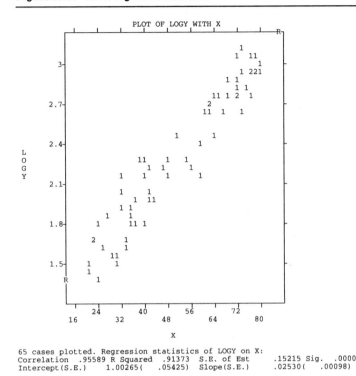

65 cases plotted. Regression statistics of LOGY on X:
Correlation   .95589 R Squared   .91373 S.E. of Est   .15215 Sig.   .0000
Intercept(S.E.)   1.00265(.05425) Slope(S.E.)   .02530(.00098)

If the true model isn't known, you choose a transformation by looking at the plot of the data. Often, a relationship appears to be nearly linear for part of the data but is curved for the rest. The log transformation is useful for "straightening out" such a relationship. Taking the square root of the dependent variable may also straighten a curved relationship. These are two of the most common transformations, but others can be used.

When you try to make a relationship linear, you can transform either the independent variable, the dependent variable, or both. If you transform only the independent variable you're not changing the distribution of the dependent variable. If it was normally distributed with a constant variance for each value of the independent variable, that remains unchanged. However, if you transform the dependent variable you change its distribution. For example, if you take logs of the dependent variable, then the log of the dependent variable—not the original dependent variable—must be normally distributed with a constant variance. In other words, the regression assumptions must hold for the variables you actually use in the regression equation.

Independence

Another assumption that we made was that all observations are independent. (The same person isn't included in the data twice on separate occasions. One person's values don't influence the others'.) When data are collected in sequence, it's possible to check this assumption. You should plot the residuals against the sequence variable. If you see any kind of pattern, such as in Figure 26.11, you should be concerned. (This plot was obtained from different data using the CASEWISE subcommand.)

Figure 26.11 Residuals that are not independent

```
Casewise Plot of Studentized Residual

               -3.0      0.0      3.0      LIFE    *PRED    *RESID   *SRESID
  SEQNUM   TIME   0:.........:.........:0
       1  78012     . *    .        .     15.0000  19.5624  -4.5624  -2.2598
       2  78055     . *    .        .     13.5000  17.8974  -4.3974  -2.1856
       3  78122     .  *   .        .      9.9000  13.8390  -3.9390  -1.9871
       4  78134     .    * .        .     15.5000  18.5218  -3.0218  -1.4997
       5  78233     .   * .         .     35.0000  38.2933  -3.2933  -1.7466
       6  78298     .      * .      .     14.7000  16.6487  -1.9487   -.9720
       7  78344     .       * .     .     34.8000  36.0040  -1.2040   -.6258
       8  79002     .        *.     .     20.8000  20.8111   -.0111   -.0055
       9  79008     .        . *    .     15.9000  14.8796   1.0204    .5123
      10  79039     .        *      .     22.0000  21.6436    .3564    .1762
      11  79101     .        .  *   .     13.7000  11.7578   1.9422    .9910
      12  79129     .        . *    .     14.2000  11.4456   2.7544   1.4082
      13  79178     .        .   *  .     33.2000  30.3847   2.8153   1.4144
      14  79188     .        .   *  .     26.2000  22.4761   3.7239   1.8401
      15  79189     .        .    * .     37.4000  33.2984   4.1016   2.0920
     ...
```

In this figure the value of the residual is related to the order in which the experiment was conducted. Early subjects had large negative residuals, while later subjects had large positive residuals. This might occur, for example, when you give a test of facts to subjects one at a time and word of its contents spreads. The first people taking the test will do worse than later people who know the questions and answers.

A Final Comment on Assumptions

It's important to examine the data for violations of the assumptions, since significance levels, confidence intervals, and other regression tests are sensitive to certain types of violations and cannot be interpreted in the usual fashion if serious departures exist. If you carefully examine the residuals, you'll have an idea of what sorts of problems might exist in your data. Transformations provide you with an opportunity to try to remedy some of the problems. You can then be more confident that the regression model is appropriate for your data.

MORE ABOUT THE REGRESSION PROCEDURE

REGRESSION provides a variety of plots and statistics for analyzing residuals.

Casewise Plots and Temporary Variables

The CASEWISE subcommand provides a listing and plot of cases and temporary variables. To obtain listings of cases whose standardized residuals are greater than +3 or less than –3, run the following command:

```
regression dependent dep
  /enter indep
  /casewise dependent pred resid zresid.
```

This displays a listing of the dependent variable (*DEP* in this example) and three of the temporary variables that SPSS/PC+ calculates automatically. To produce a listing of residuals for all cases, specify ALL on the CASEWISE subcommand:

```
regression dependent dep
 /enter indep
 /casewise all dependent pred resid zresid.
```

Twelve temporary variables are available:

PRED	*Unstandardized predicted values.*
RESID	*Unstandardized residuals.*
DRESID	*Deleted residuals.*
ADJPRED	*Adjusted predicted values.*
ZPRED	*Standardized predicted values.*
ZRESID	*Standardized residuals.*
SRESID	*Studentized residuals.*
SDRESID	*Studentized deleted residuals.*
SEPRED	*Standard errors of the predicted values.*
MAHAL	*Mahalanobis' distances.*
COOK	*Cook's distances.*
LEVER	*Leverage values.*

You can use any of the twelve temporary variables and the keywords DEPENDENT and ALL on the CASEWISE subcommand.

Histograms

To obtain histograms of standardized residuals, run the following command:

```
regression dependent dep
  /enter indep
  /residuals histogram.
```

You can specify PRED, RESID, ZPRED, ZRESID, DRESID, ADJPRED, SRESID, or SDRESID in parentheses after the HISTOGRAM keyword to get histograms of those temporary variables. All histograms will show the standardized versions of the temporary variables.

Scatterplots

To produce scatterplots of the temporary residual variables with one another or with the variables in your regression, use the SCATTERPLOT subcommand. Give the variable names in parentheses after the subcommand. Since this subcommand accepts ordinary variable names as well as temporary variables, you must place an asterisk before the names of the temporary variables:

```
regression dependent dep
 /enter indep
 /scatterplot (*resid, *pred) (*resid, indep).
```

This command prints scatterplots of the residuals (*RESID) with both the predicted values (*PRED) and the independent variable, which is named *INDEP* in this example. Scatterplots, like histograms, always use the standardized versions of the temporary variables.

Splitting the Sample

Sometimes you want to use part of your sample to find the regression coefficients and then apply those coefficients to the entire sample. The SELECT subcommand lets you do this. After SELECT specify a variable name, then one of the six relational operators (EQ, NE, GT, GE, LT, LE) and then a constants:

```
regression select group ne 1
 /dependent dep
 /enter indep
 /residuals
 /scatterplot (*resid, *pred) (*resid, indep).
```

The regression equation is calculated only from those cases for which the variable *GROUP* does not equal 1. When you request residual analysis along with the SELECT subcommand, SPSS/PC+ performs it separately for cases that are selected and cases that are not selected. Here the output produced by the RESIDUALS and SCATTERPLOT subcommands will appear twice: first for the selected cases and then for the cases not selected (where *GROUP* equals 1).

WHAT'S NEXT?

You've reached the end of the book. However, it's by no means the end of what you can learn about data analysis. To whet your appetite for more, Chapter 27 briefly describes some of the more advanced methods you can use. They're all based on the material you've studied in this book. If you understand these fundamentals, you're well on your way to understanding the more powerful techniques. As you learn to use them, though, always remember: start simply.

> ### Summary
>
> **How can you tell whether the assumptions necessary for a regression analysis appear to be violated?**
>
> A residual is the difference between the observed value of the dependent variable and the value predicted by the regression model.
>
> To check the assumption of normality, make a histogram of the residuals. It should look approximately normal.
>
> To check the assumption of constant variance, plot the residuals against the predicted values and against the values of the independent variable. There should be no relationship between the residuals and either of these two variables. If you note a pattern in the plots, you have reason to suspect that the assumption of constant variance is violated.
>
> To check whether the relationship between the two variables is linear, plot the two variables. If the points do not cluster about a straight line, you have reason to believe that the relationship is not linear.
>
> If any of the assumptions appear to be violated, transforming the data may help. The choice of the transformation depends on which assumption is violated and in what way.

EXERCISES

Syntax

1 You want to predict husband's education from wife's education using the data in

the gss.sys file. You also want to obtain a histogram of the residuals and a casewise plot of residuals that are greater than 3 in absolute value. Write *all* the SPSS/PC+ commands required to perform this analysis.

2 You run the command

```
regression statistics def ci
     /dependent gpa /casewise.
```

and obtain the following error message:

```
ERROR   10508,  Text: CASEWISE
Only the METHOD subcommand can follow a DEPENDENT subcommand.
This command not executed.
```

```
*WARNING* - REGRESSION syntax scan continues.
            Further diagnostics may be misleading - interpret with care.
```

Correct the command.

3 Correct the errors in the following commands:

a. regression casewise /dep indep /dependent dep.

b. regression statistics def ci /casewise /histogram.

c. regression dep y /casewise residuals.

d. regression dep wt /casewise /scat(*res age).

4 Write the SPSS/PC+ commands for a regression analysis in which *MAWEIGHT* is the independent variable and *MYWEIGHT* is the dependent variable. Obtain as many diagnostic plots as you can.

Statistical Concepts

1 The regression equation used to predict salary from work experience is

Salary = 10,000 + 1000(Experience)

a. What is the predicted salary for a person who has 10 years of experience?

b. If a person with 10 years of experience earns $20,000, what is the residual for the case?

c. What does a negative residual mean?

d. What does a positive residual mean?

Below are regression statistics and values of the independent and dependent variables for five cases. Fill in the missing information in the casewise plot.

```
----------------- Variables in the Equation -----------------

Variable            B        SE B      Beta       T   SIG T

X               1.70000     .82260   .76642    2.067   .1307
(Constant)      4.30000    2.72825             1.576   .2131
```

```
Casewise Plot of Standardized Residual

*: Selected   M: Missing

          -3.0          0.0         3.0
Case # X  O:.............:.............:O   Y      *PRED      *RESID
  1 1    .              . *          .    7      6.0000     1.0000
  2 2    .              .  *         .    9      ▓▓▓▓       ▓▓▓▓
  3 3    .         *    .            .    6      ▓▓▓▓       ▓▓▓▓
  4 4    .            * .            .   ▓▓     11.1000    -1.1000
  5 5    .              .   *        .   15      ▓▓▓▓       2.2000
Case # X  O:.............:.............:O   Y      *PRED      *RESID
          -3.0          0.0         3.0
```

2 What violations of assumptions, if any, are suggested by the following plots?

a.

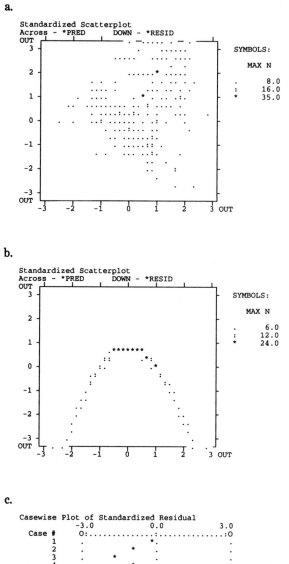

b.

c.

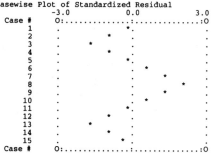

d.

```
HISTOGRAM - STANDARDIZED RESIDUAL
 N EXP N      (* = 1 CASES,     . : = NORMAL CURVE)
 0    .33   OUT
 0    .17   3.00
 0    .24   2.88
 0    .34   2.75
 0    .48   2.63
 0    .66   2.50 .
 0    .89   2.38 .
 0   1.19   2.25 .
 0   1.57   2.13  .
 0   2.03   2.00  .
 0   2.58   1.88   .
 0   3.24   1.75    .
 2   4.00   1.63 ** .
16   4.86   1.50 ****:**********
18   5.82   1.38 *****:************
 9   6.85   1.25 ******:**
12   7.95   1.13 *******:****
12   9.07   1.00 ********:***
 8  10.20    .88 ******** .
16  11.29    .75 *********:*****
21  12.30    .63 ***********:*********
 6  13.20    .50 ******      .
 6  13.94    .38 ******       .
 8  14.49    .25 ********      .
 6  14.83    .13 ******         .
17  14.95    .00 **************:**
 9  14.83   -.13 *********       .
15  14.49   -.25 *************:*
10  13.94   -.38 **********    .
11  13.20   -.50 **********  .
 7  12.30   -.63 *******     .
 8  11.29   -.75 ********   .
13  10.20   -.88 *********:***
10   9.07  -1.00 ********:*
 8   7.95  -1.13 *******:
11   6.85  -1.25 ******:****
15   5.82  -1.38 *****:*********
10   4.86  -1.50 ****:*****
12   4.00  -1.63 ***:********
 4   3.24  -1.75 **:*
 0   2.58  -1.88    .
 0   2.03  -2.00   .
 0   1.57  -2.13  .
 0   1.19  -2.25 .
 0    .89  -2.38 .
 0    .66  -2.50 .
 0    .48  -2.63
 0    .34  -2.75
 0    .24  -2.88
 0    .17  -3.00
 0    .33   OUT
```

3 a. What can you learn from a histogram of the residuals?

   b. A casewise plot of the residuals?

   c. A plot of the independent variable and the dependent variable?

   d. A plot of the residuals against the independent variable?

4 You find that cases with large values of the independent variable all have large positive residuals. Otherwise there appears to be no relationship between the residuals and the independent variable. Sketch a plot illustrating when this may happen.

Data Analysis

1 Rerun all of the regression equations you developed in Chapter 25. For each one, examine how well the data seem to fit the regression assumptions. Indicate which plots suggest that the regression model may be inappropriate. Consider strategies for dealing with violations of the assumptions.

 # Looking Beyond

What are some other commonly used statistical procedures for analyzing data?

- How can you study the relationship between a dependent variable and several independent variables?

- How can you predict what group a case falls into based on a set of variables?

- How can you look for underlying factors which explain the observed correlations in a set of variables?

- What procedures are useful for analyzing crosstabulations which have many variables?

- What if you want to test the null hypothesis that the means of *several* variables are equal in different groups?

In this book we've analyzed the General Social Survey data in many different ways. We've described and summarized, tested hypotheses, and looked for associations among the variables. We've computed means and standard deviations, t tests, and chi-square statistics. We've looked at measures of association and built regression equations.

There are many additional statistical techniques for analyzing the data in still other ways. You can test more complicated hypotheses and build more complex models. This chapter gives a brief overview of some of these other frequently used statistical procedures. Your goal for this chapter should not be to try to master these techniques but simply to be aware of how much more you can learn about your data with additional statistical methods. For more detail about these methods and the SPSS/PC+ procedures you can use to calculate them, see the *SPSS/PC+ Statistics* and *SPSS/PC+ Advanced Statistics* manuals.

MULTIVARIATE STATISTICAL TECHNIQUES

In the previous chapters we studied the relationship between a person's education and that of their father using linear regression. There was a single dependent variable, the person's education, and a single independent variable, father's education. Even the most unenlightened of researchers would realize that father's education is but one of many variables that influence a person's educational achievements. Mother's education, size of the family, socioeconomic status, intelligence, and a myriad of other variables may affect how many years of education a person endures. What you really want to do is determine which of the many possible variables are important predictors of education and then build a model that shows the relationship between education and these important predictor variables.

Variables such as mother's education, family size, and intelligence of offspring are not independent of one another. You can't just calculate separate regression models for each of the possible predictor variables and then "put them together" to assess the overall situation. You must use a statistical procedure that allows you to examine the variables *together*, a technique that takes into account the correlations among the variables.

A special class of statistical techniques called **multivariate methods** is used for studying the relationships among several interrelated variables. The goals of such multivariate analyses may be quite different, but they share many common features. Let's look at some of the most popular ones.

Multiple Linear Regression

You can use **multiple linear regression analysis** to study the relationship between a single dependent variable and several independent variables. You can build a linear model in which a person's education is the dependent variable and variables such as mother's and father's education and number of siblings are the independent variables. For example, if *PAEDUC*, *MAEDUC*, and *SIBS* are the independent variables, you can examine the model

$$EDUC = \text{Constant} + B_1 \times PAEDUC + B_2 \times MAEDUC + B_3 \times SIBS$$

The model looks like the regression model in Chapter 24. The difference is that there are now several variables on the independent variable side of the model. In addition to father's education, the model includes mother's education and number of siblings.

As before, the method of least squares can be used to estimate the coefficients. The coefficients for this model are shown in Figure 27.1. The coefficients for mother's and father's education are both positive, indicating that the more educated the parents, the more educated the person. The coefficient for *SIBS* (the number of brothers and sisters) is negative. This suggests that children from large families are less likely to continue their education than children from smaller families.

As shown at the end of Chapter 25, you can perform multiple regression analysis by simply naming all the variables after the REGRESSION command:

```
get file 'gss.sys'.
regression dependent educ
 /enter paeduc maeduc sibs.
```

Since the variables are measured in different units, you can't just compare the magnitudes of the coefficients to each other. You must standardize the variables in some fashion. The column labeled *Beta* contains the regression coefficients when all variables are standardized to a mean of 0 and a standard deviation of 1. The column labeled *Sig T* is the observed significance level for the test of the null hypothesis that the value of a coefficient is zero in the population. You can see that the null hypothesis can be rejected for all of the variables.

When you build a model with several independent variables that are interrelated, it's not easy to determine how much each variable contributes to the model. You can't just look at the coefficients and say *this* is an im-

Figure 27.1 Multiple linear regression coefficients

```
           * * * *   M U L T I P L E   R E G R E S S I O N   * * * *

Listwise Deletion of Missing Data

Equation Number 1   Dependent Variable..   EDUC   Highest year of school compl

Beginning Block Number  1.  Method:  Enter

Variable(s) Entered on Step Number
     1..    SIBS     Number of siblings
     2..    PAEDUC   Father's highest year of school
     3..    MAEDUC   Mother's highest year of school

----------------- Variables in the Equation -----------------

Variable           B         SE B        Beta        T   Sig T

SIBS         -.201871     .026952    -.210018    -7.490   .0000
PAEDUC        .207500     .024992     .290028     8.303   .0000
MAEDUC        .176143     .030834     .203262     5.713   .0000
(Constant)   9.858697     .320956                30.717   .0000


End Block Number   1   All requested variables entered.
```

portant variable for predicting the dependent variable and *this* one is not. The contributions of the variables are "shared."

The goodness-of-fit statistics we considered for a regression model with one independent variable can easily be extended to a model with multiple independent variables. They are shown in Figure 27.2. You see that a regression model with these three independent variables explains about 31 percent of the observed variability in years of education.

Figure 27.2 Multiple linear regression statistics

```
Multiple R            .55697
R Square              .31021
Adjusted R Square     .30814
Standard Error       2.42935

Analysis of Variance
                   DF     Sum of Squares     Mean Square
Regression          3        2648.83529       882.94510
Residual          998        5889.94016         5.90174

F =     149.60750      Signif F =   .0000
```

Selecting Independent Variables

Often you don't know which independent variables together are good predictors of the dependent variable. You want to eliminate variables that are of little use from your equation so you will have a simple, easy-to-interpret model. You can do this with the assistance of what are called **variable-selection methods**. Based on statistical considerations, such as the percent of variance explained by one variable that is *not* explained by any other variables, SPSS/PC+ selects a set of variables for inclusion in a regression model. (The syntax for specifying a variable-selection method is described at the end of Chapter 25.) Although such procedures often result in a useful model, the selected model is not necessarily best in any absolute sense.

Discriminant Analysis

You can use regression analysis to predict values of the dependent variable based on a set of independent variables. The dependent and independent variables are all measured on an interval or ratio scale. What if the dependent variable is not measured on an interval or ratio scale? Suppose you want to predict whether people find life exciting, routine, or dull, based on a set of variables such as education, age, income, and hours worked per week? You can't use regression analysis, since the dependent variable is ordinal. What you might want to use is a procedure called **discriminant analysis**.

In discriminant analysis, you compute "discriminant scores" for each case to predict what group it is in. These scores are obtained by finding linear combinations of the independent variables. A linear combination is formed by multiplying each variable by some constant and then adding up the products. For example, you might compute an individual's score by taking 2 times income in thousands, plus 1.5 times age, plus 1.1 times education.

Discriminant analysis uses mathematical techniques to determine the way of computing scores that results in the best *separation* among the groups (in other words, the most accurate prediction of what group each case is in). The DISCRIMINANT procedure in SPSS/PC+ Advanced Statistics does all the computations for you, including selection of the best coefficients. The results of a discriminant analysis include a table like that shown in Figure 27.3. It tells you how well you are able to predict what case a groups falls into based on the values of the independent variables.

In this example, we're able to correctly classify only 57 percent of the cases, so the independent variables don't seem to be very good predictors of whether life is viewed as exciting, routine, or dull.

Log-Linear Models

Using a crosstabulation and the chi-square statistic, you were able to test whether two variables that have a small number of distinct values are independent. For example, you were able to test whether marital status and degree of excitement are related. What if you wanted to know the effect of additional variables, such as sex, race, job satisfaction, and happiness of a marriage, on the relationships that you are examining? You could always make a crosstabulation of all of the variables, but this would be very difficult to interpret. You would have hundreds or thousands of cells and most of them would contain few cases, if any.

Figure 27.3 Classification results from discriminant analysis

```
Classification Results -

                        No. of  Predicted Group Membership
     Actual Group       Cases      1         2         3
--------------------    ------  --------  --------  --------

Group      1             652      379       270        3
Exciting                         58.1%     41.4%     0.5%

Group      2             663      253       405        5
Pretty routine                   38.2%     61.1%     0.8%

Group      3              64       11        51        2
Dull                             17.2%     79.7%     3.1%

Ungrouped Cases            9        3         6        0
                                 33.3%     66.7%     0.0%
```

Percent of "grouped" cases correctly classified: 57.00%

One way to study the relationships among a set of variables that are
categorical is with **log-linear** models. With a log-linear model you try to
predict the number of cases in a cell of a crosstabulation based on the values of the individual variables and their combinations. You see whether
certain combinations of values are more likely or less likely to occur than
others. This tells you about the relationships among the variables.

Factor Analysis

If you give a group of students 100 different aptitude tests, their scores on
the different tests will no doubt be correlated. The tests probably measure
some of the same characteristics, such as verbal skills, mathematical aptitude, reasoning ability, and perceptual speed. Characteristics such as
"verbal skill," "mathematical aptitude," and "reasoning ability" are not
well-defined, easily measured variables like weight or age. Instead, they
can be thought of as unifying concepts or labels that characterize responses to related groups of variables. A person with strong mathematical abil-
ities would score well on all of the tests that are related to mathematical
skills. In fact, that's how the definition of mathematical aptitude was ar-
rived at. **Factor analysis** is a statistical technique that attempts to measure
such concepts.

In some research situations you have a set of interrelated variables
such as consumer ratings of products. You think that the ratings are correlated because people are rating the products on similar dimensions such
as product quality and utility. But you don't know what these underlying
dimensions, or factors, are. You can use factor analysis to help you identify
these underlying concepts by using a number of variables that you can directly measure.

Cluster Analysis

If you question sick patients about their symptoms, you will undoubtedly have a very long list of complaints. You may think that there are as many combinations of symptoms as there are patients. However, if you study the types of symptoms that frequently occur together, you'll probably be able to put the patients into groups—those who have respiratory disturbances, those who have gastric problems, those who have cardiac difficulties. Classifying the patients into groups of similar individuals may be helpful both for determining treatment strategies and for understanding how the body malfunctions.

In statistics, the search for similar groups of objects or people is called **cluster analysis**. By forming clusters of objects and then studying the characteristics the objects share, as well as those in which they differ, you can gain useful insights. For example, cluster analysis has been used to cluster skulls from various archeological digs into the civilizations from which they originated. Cluster analysis is also frequently used in market research to identify groups of people for whom various marketing pitches may be particularly attractive.

Testing Hypotheses about Many Means

In the two-sample t test we tested hypotheses about the equality of two population means. We wanted to know whether people who find life exciting live in households of the same size as people who find life routine or dull. We used the analysis of variance procedure to test hypotheses that more than two population means are equal. We tested whether there was a difference in education among the three excitement groups.

What if we want to test hypotheses about several interrelated dependent variables, such as education and income? Is there a way to test the hypothesis that *both* education and income do not differ among the three excitement groups in the population? **Multivariate analysis of variance**, or MANOVA, is used to test such hypotheses. Using MANOVA, you can compare four instructional methods based on student achievement levels, satisfaction, anxiety, and long-term retention of the material. Or you compare five new ice-cream flavors based on the amount consumed, a preference rating, and the price people say they would pay.

If the same variable is measured on several different occasions, there are special "repeated measures" analysis of variance techniques that can be used to test hypotheses. These can be thought of as extensions of the simple paired t test.

THERE'S MORE

In the previous chapters we explained some of the more widely used statistical techniques, and in this chapter we've attempted to give an idea of the more sophisticated methods available. There are still others. There are nonparametric procedures that don't require such stringent assumptions about the distributions of variables (see Appendix E). There are procedures for analyzing specialized types of data such as test scores or survival times. There are often many different ways to look at the same problem. No one way is best for every problem; each view tells you something new.

Summary

What are some other commonly used statistical procedures for analyzing data?

You can study the relationship between a dependent variable and a set of independent variables using multiple regression analysis.

Discriminant analysis is used to classify cases into groups based on values of predictor variables.

With factor analysis you can explain the observed correlations among variables by identifying shared "factors."

Log-linear models are often used to study the relationships among several variables in a crosstabulation.

Multivariate analysis of variance is used to test hypotheses about several dependent variables simultaneously.

PART FIVE
Appendixes

Appendix A
Error Messages

Errors are nearly inevitable, no matter how well you know SPSS/PC+. Even the best data analysts occasionally need to run programs several times before they correct all their errors. You may not get the SPSS/PC+ commands right the first time. Always allow more time for the job than you think you need, especially if you are just learning SPSS/PC+.

MAKING ERRORS

Several kinds of errors cause programs to run improperly or to terminate. The most common ones are errors in command syntax, in the order of commands, or in the data. Syntax errors occur if you do something like forget a slash, misspell a command, or specify a subcommand out of order. Data errors stem from a number of problems, such as blanks within values and stray codes.

Whenever SPSS/PC+ encounters problems, it issues a message explaining what you did wrong and what action the system is taking. Normally, the message appears in the output immediately after the place where SPSS/PC+ detected the error.

CORRECTING ERRORS

Whenever you get an error, check the statement where it occurred and previous statements (if necessary) to see if you specified the commands correctly. Some common mistakes you might make are:

- Using variable names that don't conform to SPSS/PC+ naming conventions.

- Omitting required slashes.

- Leaving pairs of parentheses, apostrophes, or quotation marks unmatched.

- Using subcommands out of order.

Since one mistake often triggers others, you should always correct the first problem identified before you correct any others.

TYPES OF MESSAGES

SPSS/PC+ issues notes, warnings, and three types of error messages of different severity. The following sections give some common messages you might encounter and their possible causes and solutions. If the causes and solutions don't fit your problem or you get a message that isn't on the list, start out by reading the message carefully and checking your command syntax.

Notes

Notes are the least serious of all SPSS/PC+ messages. Their purpose is simply to call attention to peculiarities in the commands that won't affect the results of later commands but may alert you to things you don't know about. For example, the following note lets you know that SORT CASES was used to sort a file with only one case:

Note 5802
TOO FEW CASES TO SORT.

Since presumably you expected more than one case, the note may mean that earlier in your job you somehow deleted every case but one. Try re-examining all prior transformation statements that refer to the variable to see how the mistake was made.

Warnings

Warnings identify problems that will affect the results of later commands. If you get too many warnings (normally 80), SPSS/PC+ will stop processing your commands. For example, here's a warning message that tells you the program found a non-numeric value in a field read with a numeric format, and that it changed the contents to the system-missing value:

Warning 153, TEXT: A
INVALID DIGIT READ WITH F FORMAT—Check your data.

This warning could mean you're using the wrong format to read your data. However, it could also mean the data have some errors that you can correct with an editor. In this case, it probably means that you typed an A instead of a numeral.

Common Warning Messages

Some warning messages you may encounter are:

Warning 255 Text JOB.
Invalid symbol on VALUE LABELS command—The VALUE LABELS command contains an unrecognized symbol where a value is expected. All labels up to the next slash are ignored.

Cause: There is probably no slash between two sets of value labels. In the following example, the slash was omitted after the labels for the variable *SES*:

```
value labels ses 1 'Average Plus'
                 2 'Average'
                 3 'Average Minus'
             job 1 'White Collar'
                 2 'Blue Collar'
                 3 'Farmer'
                 4 'Other,None'.
```

Solution: Insert slashes where necessary to separate the value labels of different variables.

Warning 415. Missing closing quote—A string must be enclosed in quotes. Strings cannot be continued across command lines

Cause: All strings (alphanumerics) in SPSS/PC+ must be enclosed within apostrophes or quotation marks. These include all values of string variables and all titles, variable labels, and value labels. You cannot continue strings across command lines.

Solution: Supply all missing apostrophes or quotation marks around strings where necessary.

Warning 420, Text VAR1.
Undefined variable name—Check for a misspelled variable name.

Cause: A variable name on the VARIABLE LABELS command is misspelled or doesn't exist.

Solution: Correct the variable name.

Warning 311 Title too long—Only the first 58 characters are used.

Cause: The page title you typed has more than 58 characters, which is the limit.

Solution: Edit the title.

Errors

Error messages indicate serious problems in your job. In SPSS/PC+, there are three different kinds of error messages.

- The first kind forces the program to skip a command but continues processing subsequent commands. Normally, these involve procedures like MEANS or CROSSTABS, which the program can skip without affecting subsequent commands.

- The second kind of error forces SPSS/PC+ to stop processing commands but allows the program to continue checking for errors. SPSS/PC+ issues this kind of error message for problems that will probably make later processing meaningless. Errors on COMPUTE statements are treated this way.

- The third kind of message causes SPSS/PC+ to stop processing immediately. This happens when SPSS/PC+ encounters a "catastrophic" error, such as a damaged data file. This kind of error also occurs when SPSS/PC+ reaches the maximum number of errors or warnings allowed, or it can't access a file. No further error checking is done when SPSS/PC+ encounters these kinds of errors.

MEMORY PROBLEMS

Building tables or calculating statistics requires a certain amount of working memory, or RAM. If you receive an error message saying that insufficient memory was available, you should do one of the following:

- Split up the task. Memory requirements generally depend on the number of variables involved, so two procedures using ten variables each will use less memory (but will take longer) than one procedure using twenty variables.

- Remove memory-resident software from your machine and reboot.

COMMON ERROR MESSAGES AND WARNINGS

Following are some of the error messages produced by SPSS/PC+. Messages that are either obvious, quite unlikely to occur, or duplicates of messages attached to adjacent numbers have been omitted. (If you can't find the error number you're looking for, see if a nearby number says the same thing.) Each message is followed by a cause indicating the most likely source of the problem and a solution indicating possible action you can take.

Error 4. Invalid symbol on N command. Something else follows the integer value. Check for a missing command terminator.

Cause: Probably there is no period at the end of the N command. SPSS/PC+ thinks your next command is a continuation of this one.

Solution: Insert the period after the N command.

Error 7. Invalid sampling fraction on SAMPLE command. The number is not greater than 0 and less than or equal to 1.

Cause: A sampling fraction can be specified as any number greater than 0 and less than or equal to 1. For instance, to take a sample of 50 from 100 cases, you can specify either SAMPLE .5 or SAMPLE 50 FROM 100.

Solution: Enter a valid sampling fraction and rerun the command.

Error 8. Missing keyword BY for WEIGHT command. The next symbol is used as the weighting variable.

Cause: WEIGHT must be followed by either the keyword OFF or the keyword BY and the name of a numeric variable from the active file.

Solution: Add either OFF or BY to the WEIGHT command, plus the name of a numeric variable.

Error 13. No cases to process. Due to weighting, sampling, or a PROCESS IF command, no cases are available to this procedure.

Cause: Unfortunately, a transformation transformed the whole data set out of existence.

Solution: If it was a temporary transformation such as PROCESS IF, you're still OK. If it was a permanent transformation, you'll have to redefine your data—by getting the file again, translating a file, or running a DATA LIST command.

Error 15. Device full. Cannot continue.

Cause: There is no more room on the disk for files.

Solution: Erase any unnecessary files. You will need more space on the data disk in order to run this SPSS/PC+ analysis.

   Be careful. If the filename begins with SPSS, it's a work file and may be currently in use. The safest files to delete are data files or system files that you created, provided that you have back-up copies.

Error 20. Not enough memory for SPSS/PC+ command.

Cause: There is not enough memory to carry out the procedure.

Solution: See "Memory Problems" near the beginning of this appendix.

Error 34. This command is not permitted until a file is defined via DATA LIST or GET.

Cause: SPSS/PC+ doesn't yet have any cases or variables to work with.

Solution: You have to define your data before you can transform or analyze them. Run a DATA LIST, GET, or TRANSLATE command.

Error 37. PROCESS IF expression compares a numeric variable to a string value.

Cause: Probably the numeric value specified on PROCESS IF is in quotes.

Solution: Remove the quotes.

Error 38. PROCESS IF expression compares a string variable to a numeric value.

Cause: On one side of the equals sign is a string variable and on the other a numeric value or a variable name.

Solution: Do put string values in quotes. You may also be trying to use a conditional argument that involves more than one variable, such as PROCESS IF TIME1 = TIME2. PROCESS IF can only compare a variable to a constant.

Error 39. A long string variable cannot be specified on PROCESS IF.

Cause: PROCESS IF can accept only numeric and short string variables. A long string variable is one whose values are longer than 8 characters.

Solution: Use AUTORECODE to recode the long string variable to a numeric variable. Then use the new variable on PROCESS IF.

Error 40. Invalid symbols on PROCESS IF command. Something appears after the variable=value expression and is ignored. Check for a missing command terminator.

Cause: Possibly a period is missing at the end of the command. If you omit the period, SPSS/PC+ thinks your next command is a continuation of this one. This message also occurs when you try to specify a compound condition on a PROCESS IF command. Only one condition is allowed on PROCESS IF.

Solution: Supply the period or supply a simple condition.

Error 51. Invalid keyword on DATA LIST command. Keywords FILE, FIXED, FREE, and TABLE are valid.

Cause: You may have omitted a keyword and the slash and immediately followed your DATA LIST command with your list of variables.

Solution: If the DATA LIST is not FIXED (the default), enter the keyword FREE.

Error 53. Missing filename on DATA LIST command.

Cause: The keyword FILE has no filename after it.

Solution: Specify the filename or delete the FILE keyword.

Error 55. No variables defined on DATA LIST command.

Cause: A period appears after the DATA LIST command before the variables that you want to read.

Solution: Add the variable names to the DATA LIST command before the period.

Error 57. Duplicate variable name on DATA LIST command.

Cause: A variable name is repeated on DATA LIST.

Solution: If you meant only one variable, delete one of them. If they're not supposed to be the same, give them different names.

Error 58. More than 500 variables defined on DATA LIST command.

Cause: SPSS/PC+ can handle a maximum of 500 variables.

Solution: Reduce the number of variables, choosing the ones you want to analyze together.

Error 60. Missing format specifications on DATA LIST command.

Cause: The DATA LIST format is FIXED and there are no column locations.

Solution: Unless you specify the keyword FREE, you must provide column locations for each variable named.

Error 65. No variables defined on DATA LIST command.

Cause: There are no variables named before the period on DATA LIST.

Solution: Enter the names of the variables before the period.

Error 67. The number of columns specified on DATA LIST is not evenly divisible by the number of variables specified.

Cause: With DATA LIST FIXED, the entire range of a line of data can be specified with dashes separating the beginning and end columns only if the number of columns specified is evenly divisible by the number of variables. The variables must be in adjacent columns and each must occupy the same number of columns.

Solution: Check the column numbers. If you list YOURVAR1 YOURVAR2 YOURVAR3 15-20, each of the three variables will get two columns, 15-16, 17-18, and 19-20.

Error 70. Missing column location on DATA LIST command.

Cause: When DATA LIST is in FIXED format, the column locations must be specified for each variable.

Solution: Unless you specify the keyword FREE, you must provide column locations for each variable named.

Error 75. Variable too long. The limit for a numeric variable is 20; for a string is 160.

Cause: Strings longer than 8 characters can be listed but cannot be used in any other way.

Solution: Specify short string or numeric variables, and use the VALUE LABELS command.

Error 77. The number of records in the data file is not a multiple of the number of records in a case. The last (incomplete) case has been dropped. Examine your data.

Cause: The lines in the file didn't divide up evenly into cases. There may be duplicate or missing lines in your data file.

Solution: Review your data file to see if each case has the same number of records (lines).

Error 78. You cannot enter data from the keyboard past column 80. Specify FILE on the DATA LIST command if you want to read data from an external file.

Cause: Typed data was more than 80 columns long.

Solution: Reduce the length of the data lines or save the data into a file and use the FILE subcommand on DATA LIST. You can read data records as long as 1024 columns from a file specified on the FILE subcommand on DATA LIST.

Error 84. You cannot change the format of a string variable.

Cause: Once you have defined a string variable, you cannot change its length.

Solution: If you are specifying a COMPUTE command, be sure to use a value of the correct length, either by shortening the value or by padding with spaces.

Error 101. Misplaced procedure command. The BEGIN DATA command is expected here, since keyword FILE was not specified on the DATA LIST command.

Cause: A DATA LIST command was specified with no FILE subcommand. SPSS/PC+ expects data next.

Solution: If you mean to enter data from the keyboard, use the BEGIN DATA command and enter the data now. If not, repeat the DATA LIST command, using the keyword FILE to name the data file.

Error 140. The end of the file has been encountered in the middle of reading a case. The partial case is dropped. Use LIST to examine your cases.

Cause: The lines in the file didn't divide up evenly into cases. There may be duplicate or missing lines in your data file.

Solution: Check your data file to see if each case has the same number of records (lines).

Error 153. Invalid digit read with F format. Check your data.

Cause: This means that something other than a numeric value occurred where you said to read a numeric variable.

Solution: Check your data file for a stray character. You may have to define that variable as a string variable. String variables are much less convenient to work with.

Error 155. Embedded blank within field read with F format. Check your data.

Cause: A blank space was found in the middle of a numeric value.

Solution: Look in your data file for a numeric value containing a space.

Error 203. Too many variables defined.

Cause: SPSS/PC+ can have a maximum of 500 variables.

Solution: Limit the number of variables to 500. You can save a system file using the KEEP or DROP subcommand.

Error 204. Run a procedure to execute the current transformations before entering any more transformation commands.

Cause: There is not enough memory to hold any more transformations.

Solution: Run a procedure such as LIST CASES =1.

Error 209. No variable assignment occurs before the equals sign on the COMPUTE or IF command.

Cause: COMPUTE requires a target variable to be named before the equals sign.

Solution: Enter the name of a target variable to the left of the equals sign.

Error 212. No variable or expression is found following the "=" in an assignment on an IF or COMPUTE command.

Cause: The COMPUTE command requires some kind of instruction after the equals sign.

Solution: Type instructions to the right of the equals sign.

Error 216. The name of a function appears with no arguments in parentheses. It is not the name of a defined variable.

Cause: Since it's not a variable, it must be a function.

Solution: Specify arguments for the function, in parentheses.

Error 218. No variable or value lists are specified for COUNT or RECODE.

Cause: COUNT or RECODE requires a variable or value list.

Solution: Specify an appropriate variable or value list.

Error 219. No more memory is available to store transformations before the next procedure. Run a procedure to execute these transformations, then enter the remaining ones.

Cause: There is not enough memory for more transformations.

Solution: Run any procedure, for example, LIST CASES = 1.

Error 225. A numeric operation is specified on a string variable.

Cause: Arithmetic doesn't work with string variables.

Solution: Rethink your analysis and select numeric variables for arithmetic operations.

Error 226. Too many transformations specified between procedures. Run a procedure to execute current transformations.

Cause: The computer cannot hold all the transformations in memory.

Solution: Run any procedure, for example, LIST CASES = 1. Then you can enter more transformation commands.

Error 228. Invalid keyword on RECODE or COUNT command. The indicated keyword is invalid. Perhaps it has been used with a string variable to which it does not apply.

Cause: The keyword named may call for an arithmetic operation on a string variable.

Solution: Check your analysis and specify appropriate variables.

Error 230. Strings cannot be assigned to numeric variables.

Cause: A quoted value was assigned to a numeric variable.

Solution: If the value inside the quotes is numeric, remove the quotation marks. If it is not numeric, supply a numeric value.

Error 231. Only short string variables and literals can be specified in transformations.

Cause: A transformation was specified for a long string variable (longer than 8 characters.

Solution: Specify a short string variable or a numeric variable. You may want to use AUTORECODE to transform the long string variable to numeric.

Error 237. A single value must appear after "=" on the RECODE command.

Cause: There is more than one value after the equals sign. You may have misplaced a right parenthesis.

Solution: After the equals sign, enter one value into which you want to recode the value(s) that you entered before the equals sign.

Error 239. No output values are allowed in the value list of a COUNT command.

Cause: A RECODE appears on a COUNT command.

Solution: Respecify the value list with only input values.

Error 245. Long string variables cannot be specified in transformations.

Cause: A long string variable (one longer than 8 characters) appears on a transformation command.

Solution: Rethink your analysis and specify a short string variable or a numeric variable on the transformation command.

Error 246. Too many lag variables. The limit is 10. Run a procedure to execute current transformations to free space for more lag transformations.

Cause: More than 10 lag transformations were specified.

Solution: Run any procedure, for example, LIST CASES = 1.

Error 247. Invalid string length. One string is being compared to another and the lengths are different; or a different length string is being assigned to an existing string variable.

Cause: String variables of unequal lengths are being compared or a new value of the wrong length is being specified for a string variable.

Solution: When you write conditional arguments and transformations involving string variables, you need to "pad" the string values with extra blanks to match the defined length of the variable.

Error 256. Value labels cannot be assigned to long string variables.

Cause: A long string variable (one longer than 8 characters) cannot have value labels.

Solution: Do not use the VALUE LABELS command for this variable.

Error 259. You have mixed string and numeric variables in a variable list for the VALUE LABELS command. The string variables are ignored.

Cause: A VALUE LABELS command can handle only one type of variable.

Solution: Specify a separate VALUE LABELS command for string variables.

Error 306. Missing values cannot be defined for long string variables.

Cause: A long string variable (one longer than 8 characters) cannot have missing values specified.

Solution: Remove the long string variable from the MISSING VALUE command.

Error 313. Unexpected symbol after the closing apostrophe on the TITLE command. Check for a missing command terminator.

Cause: If you omit the period, SPSS/PC+ thinks your next command is a continuation of this one.

Solution: Enter the period after the TITLE command.

Error 314. Unexpected symbol after the closing apostrophe on the SUBTITLE command. Check for a missing command terminator.

Cause: If you omit the period, SPSS/PC+ thinks your next command is a continuation of this one.

Solution: Enter a period after the SUBTITLE command.

Warning 343. SET COLOR requires one of the keywords OR ON, or OFF, or a set of three numbers for foreground, background, and border in parentheses. SET RCOLOR accepts only three numbers for main window, second window, and border.

Cause: The specification on SET COLOR is not valid.

Solution: The manual for your monitor lists the number for each color.

Error 354. Duplicate filename on INCLUDE command. A file already open cannot be included.

Cause: The INCLUDE command has an invalid filename.

Solution: Use the INCLUDE command to process a group of commands in another file. Don't use INCLUDE for a system file or a data file.

Error 355. File cannot be opened. Check spelling and directory name.

Cause: The filename may be misspelled, or it is in another directory or on another drive.

Solution: Check spelling, drive, and directory. You can specify a drive and directory in quotes. It can also mean that you need to add FILES = to your config.sys file on the DOS disk you use to start the system. See the Installation instructions.

Error 387. File cannot be created. Check for a valid filename.

Cause: In DOS, filenames must start with an alphabetic character and cannot exceed 8 characters. A filename extension cannot exceed 3 characters and must be separated from the rest of the filename with a period.

Solution: Type a filename of no more than 8 characters plus a 3-character extension.

Error 395. You cannot specify a path for this filename.

Cause: An invalid path was specified for a file. The results file, used by the WRITE command, is always placed on your default drive in the current directory.

Solution: Do not try to specify a path. You can move the file to another directory later in DOS.

Error 601. Cannot open file specified on SET LISTING. Check for invalid filename or no disk space.

Cause: There may be no space available. If you have a floppy-based system, this drive must contain a data diskette.

Solution: Is there any space free on your default drive? If you go to the DOS prompt and execute a DIR command, you can see how many bytes are free. You may need to insert a data diskette in the floppy drive.

Error 701. Not a system file. The file named on the GET command does not appear to be an SPSS/PC+ system file.

Cause: GET can only read system files, which are files created by the SAVE command.

Solution: Specify an SPSS/PC+ system file on the GET command, or use IMPORT or TRANSLATE as appropriate.

Error 702. Damaged system file. The system file named on the GET command is damaged and cannot be read by SPSS/PC+.

Cause: A system file has been damaged. If you try to edit a system file, you will probably damage it.

Solution: Recreate the system file by running a SAVE command after you have read the data.

Error 716. I/O error while attempting to save a file. Perhaps the disk is full or damaged. The integrity of the file is not guaranteed.

Cause: The file was not saved correctly.

Solution: Try saving the file again on another diskette.

Error 10003. Not enough memory for FREQUENCIES.

Cause: FREQUENCIES needs more memory to run the analysis.

Solution: See "Memory Problems" near the beginning of this appendix.

Error 10040. Syntax error on FREQUENCIES command. A subcommand or variable name is expected. Valid subcommands are VARIABLES, FORMAT, MISSING, HISTOGRAM, HBAR, BARCHART, STATISTICS, NTILES, and PERCENTILES.

Cause: Probably either a subcommand or a variable name is misspelled.

Solution: Correct the spelling.

Error 10055. Valid keywords on the FREQUENCIES STATISTICS subcommand are MEAN, STDDEV, MINIMUM, MAXIMUM, SEMEAN, VARIANCE, SKEWNESS, SESKEW, KURTOSIS, SEKURT, RANGE, MODE, MEDIAN, SUM, ALL, NONE.

Cause: Perhaps the slash is missing before the next subcommand, or a keyword is misspelled.

Solution: Add the slash or correct the spelling.

Error 10057. Missing variable list on FREQUENCIES command.

Cause: FREQUENCIES has no variables named.

Solution: List the variables you want to analyze.

Error 10103. Not enough memory for MEANS.

Cause: The computer needs more memory to carry out this MEANS procedure.

Solution: See "Memory Problems" near the beginning of this appendix.

Error 10350. Not enough memory for CROSSTABS.

Cause: The computer needs more memory to carry out this CROSSTABS procedure.

Solution: See "Memory Problems" near the beginning of this appendix.

Error 10501. Not enough memory for REGRESSION.

Cause: The computer needs more memory to carry out this REGRESSION procedure.

Solution: See "Memory Problems" near the beginning of this appendix.

Error 10508. Only the METHOD subcommand can follow a DEPENDENT subcommand.

Cause: Some command other than METHOD, ENTER, FORWARD, BACKWARD, or STEPWISE follows the DEPENDENT subcommand.

Solution: You must specify a method after the DEPENDENT subcommand.

Error 10518. A variable cannot be named on both the DEPENDENT and METHOD subcommands.

Cause: The METHOD subcommand (ENTER, FORWARD, BACKWARD, STEP) lists a variable already named on the DEPENDENT subcommand.

Solution: Remove the variable from one of the two subcommands.

Error 10548. The keyword for the temporary variable to be saved must be followed by the name chosen for the new variable in parentheses.

Cause: SAVE was specified with no variable name in parentheses following the name of the temporary variable.

Solution: Specify a name in parentheses, for example, SAVE RESID (ERROR).

Warning 10558. REGRESSION has inserted ENTER as the first method; REMOVE is now the second method.

Cause: Independent variables have to be entered into the equation before they can be removed. SPSS/PC+ has entered the variables before removing them.

Solution: Check to see if this is what you intended.

Error 10563. REGRESSION RESIDUALS variable cannot be saved. The active file contains the maximum number of variables.

Cause: SPSS/PC+ can handle up to 500 variables. The variable created by the RESIDUALS subcommand would put the total over 500.

Solution: You can save a new system file with the subcommand KEEP. On the KEEP subcommand specify only the variables you need for this analysis.

Error 10569. Invalid variable name on REGRESSION SCATTERPLOT or PARTIALPLOT subcommand. The variable is not named on the VARIABLES subcommand.

Cause: REGRESSION plots only variables used in the regression analysis.

Solution: Specify another variable for the plot, or specify the variable on one of the subcommands VARIABLES, DEPENDENT, or METHOD.

Warning 10572. For the no-intercept model, R-square measures the proportion of variability in the y's about the origin explained by regression. This *cannot* be compared to R-square for models which include an intercept.

Cause: You have specified a no-intercept model.

Solution: Be sure you know how to interpret regression through the origin.

Error 10582. Valid METHOD keywords are STEPWISE, FORWARD, BACKWARD, ENTER, and REMOVE.

Cause: A METHOD subcommand was specified without an appropriate keyword.

Solution: There is no default METHOD. Specify one of the keywords listed.

Error 10593. No REGRESSION equation is specified. You need something like DEPENDENT varname /METHOD =method varlist.

Cause: REGRESSION requires DEPENDENT and METHOD.

Solution: You must provide SPSS/PC+ with a list of variables and indicate which of those variables is the dependent variable and how the independent variables are to be entered into the equation.

Error 10605. Not enough memory for CORRELATIONS. Split the task up.

Cause: There is not enough memory to perform the specified correlations.

Solution: See "Memory Problems" near the beginning of this appendix.

Error 10702. The syntax for a range on a factor in ANOVA requires a pair of integers enclosed in parentheses.

Cause: The range was not specified.

Solution: The first value is the minimum value for the factor and the second is the maximum value for the factor. A group is included in the analysis for the minimum value, the maximum value, and for each integer value in between.

Error 10713. Missing MIN/MAX range for factors on ANOVA command.

Cause: Same as for Error 10702.

Solution: Same as for Error 10702.

Error 10717. Not enough memory for ANOVA. Memory requirements are roughly proportional to the square of the product of the numbers of values of the independent variables.

Cause: There is not enough memory to carry out the procedure.

Solution: See "Memory Problems" near the beginning of this appendix.

Error 11404. Missing MIN/MAX range on ONEWAY command.

Cause: The independent variable does not have values specified.

Solution: You must specify a minimum value and maximum value for the factor (independent variable) in ONEWAY.

Error 11607. Not enough memory for NPAR TESTS command. Break up the request or use Option 4.

Cause: SPSS/PC+ does not have enough memory for this procedure.

Solution: See "Memory Problems" near the beginning of this appendix.

Error 11619. The CHI-SQUARE subcommand must precede the EXPECTED subcommand. EXPECTED applies to the preceding CHI-SQUARE test.

Cause: CROSSTABS has the EXPECTED subcommand misplaced.

Solution: Place the EXPECTED subcommand after the STATISTICS subcommand.

Warning 11633. The variable list before the keyword WITH is not the same length as the variable list following. Since you are using Option 5, some variables are not tested.

Cause: Option 5 pairs each variable before WITH to the corresponding variable after WITH. The number of variables on each side of WITH is not the same, and the extra variables will not be tested.

Solution: Specify equal numbers of variables on both sides of WITH.

Error 11805. Not enough memory for T-TEST.

Cause: You may have specified too many variables.

Solution: See "Memory Problems" near the beginning of this appendix.

Error 11821. The VARIABLES subcommand must follow a GROUPS subcommand.

Cause: Variables were specified on T-TEST before GROUPS.

Solution: Specify GROUPS first, then VARIABLES.

Warning 11881. No variance for independent sample T-TEST. One or more samples has no variance.

Cause: A variable was specified for which all cases have the same value in at least one of the groups.

Solution: Make sure you have specified the variable you wanted.

Warning 11882. No variance for paired sample T-TEST. Both samples have no variance.

Cause: The difference for the variables specified is constant.

Solution: Be sure you specified the correct variables.

Error 13001. Not enough memory for LIST.

Cause: Not enough memory is available to create the lists specified.

Solution: See "Memory Problems" near the beginning of this appendix.

Error 13012. Not enough memory for LIST or WRITE.

Cause: Not enough memory is available to process the command.

Solution: See "Memory Problems" near the beginning of this appendix.

Error 14101. Not enough memory for PLOT.

Cause: Not enough memory is available to process the command.

Solution: See "Memory Problems" near the beginning of this appendix.

Error 14102. The PLOT subcommand must come last on the PLOT command.

Cause: Other subcommands are after the PLOT subcommand.

Solution: You must specify the PLOT subcommand at the end of your PLOT command, after other subcommands.

Error 14123. A control variable is not valid on an overlay plot. The control variable is ignored.

Cause: FORMAT OVERLAY is specified along with a control variable after BY.

Solution: FORMAT CONTOUR may provide what you need.

Error 17002. Insufficient memory to process the command. Break up the request.

Cause: AUTORECODE requires more memory than is available for sorting and recoding the variables named.

Solution: Run more than one AUTORECODE command with fewer variables on each one.

Error 17002. An already existing variable name was used on the INTO subcommand.

Cause: On AUTORECODE, at least one of the names after INTO is the name of a variable that already exists.

Solution: Specify a unique name for the new variable. For example, specify *ARBANK* for an automatically recoded bank variable.

Error 17407. Insufficient free workspace was available to store EXAMINE's internal design table. Rerun with more memory.

Cause: There is not enough memory available to create all of the tables or plots requested on EXAMINE. If many cells are specified, large amounts of output can be produced.

Solution: Try reducing the number of factors or recode so that a factor has fewer values. Also, see "Memory Problems" near the beginning of this appendix.

Appendix B
Answers to Selected Exercises

CHAPTER 6

2　The second plan provides a more effective sample, because respondents are selected independently. In the first plan, family members are likely to give similar responses to many questions. (Of course, this must be balanced against costs, which may be lower for the first plan.)

4　None of the procedures is perfect. Procedure a is most likely to give a random sample of the entire adult population, although it misses people without telephones.

5　The major problem in the *Literary Digest* poll was probably non-response. Less than a quarter of the surveys were returned, and there is evidence that those who returned the surveys differed systematically from those who did not. For many years it was believed that the *Digest* failed by taking its lists of possible respondents from telephone books, and that in 1936 these were biased toward the well-to-do. We now know that respondents were taken from many sources other than phone books—including voting rolls—and that non-response among those to whom the surveys were mailed was a greater problem than selection of the sample.

CHAPTER 7

2　Assign identification numbers to individual voters (respondents). Record age numerically, and assign numeric codes to sex, candidate, registration, and employment status. Allow for missing values, and allow an "other" category for candidate.

6　The codes for question a overlap at 1, while omitting responses of 4 and 7. There is no reason not to enter the number itself, instead of a code. Question *b* should allow a yes-or-no response for each price category and should explain what the categories mean. Question *c* is remarkably confusing and should be written as three questions about cost, food, and service. Question *d* should use a more sensible scale, such as 1 to 10. Question *e* should be translated into simple English, perhaps as "Do you have any suggestions?"

CHAPTER 8

Syntax

1 SPSS/PC+ interpreted the word FOR as an abbreviation for FORMAT. Omit it.

2 `frequencies life marital sex race.`

Statistical Concepts

1 a. No; b. Yes; c. Yes; d. No; e. Yes; f. No.

4 a. Yes; b. No; c. No; d. Yes.

CHAPTER 9

Syntax

1 ```
data list free / loss.
begin data.
0 2 1 5 3
end data.
frequencies loss /statistics all.
```

**4**  a. FORMAT NOTABLE; b. HISTOGRAM is a separate subcommand, not a part of the FORMAT subcommand; c. AND is not part of the syntax.

### Statistical Concepts

**1**  a. Yes (1); b. Yes (1); c. No; d. No.

**3**  a. Yes (1); b. Yes (1); c. Yes (1.14).

**5**  The mean equals the proportion coded 1.

**12**  a. Histogram; b. Bar chart; c. Bar chart; d. Histogram; e. Bar chart; f. Histogram.
```

CHAPTER 10

Syntax

1   a. CROSSTABS RACE BY SATJOB. c. Add the subcommand CELLS COUNT ROW.

2   c. CELLS is a subcommand, so it must be separated from the table specification by a slash.

Statistical Concepts

1   c. 40%; d. 60%; e. 25%, 83%.

2   The independent variable is: a. race; b. sex; c. astrological sign; d. mother's degree; e. either one.

4   *GPA* is the independent variable. Use row percentages.

8   Crosstabulation would be appropriate for *b*.

CHAPTER 11

Syntax

1   b. RECODE LIFE (1 =3) (3=1). c. A hyphen cannot be used instead of the keyword THRU.

2   The second set of commands is not equivalent to the first command.

CHAPTER 12

Syntax

1   means age by satjob.

3   means systbp by smoke by drink.

5   All four commands are syntactically correct. However, *d* will produce reams of useless output if age is recorded in years. The "means" for sex can be interpreted, but you should probably obtain this information with a crosstabulation.

Statistical Concepts

1   a. MEANS; b. CROSSTABS; c. FREQUENCIES; d. MEANS; e. CROSSTABS.

2   The table is meaningless.

CHAPTER 13

Syntax

1   a. `examine income iq`
       `/plot histogram stemleaf.`

    b. `examine attnspan by tvhours.`

Statistical Concepts

3   The stem-and-leaf plot provides more information about the actual values than the histogram does.

4   a. 8; b. 10; c. 22; d. 2.

6   a. No—you can only determine salary in $100 increments.

CHAPTER 14

Syntax

1   a. The command name is missing; b. Each computation requires a separate COMPUTE command. (SPSS/PC+ would interpret the slash as the "divide" operator, would try to interpret PROFIT2 as an existing variable, and would be unable to interpret the second equals sign.) d. Use the symbol + to add.

2   b. Yes: RECODE AGE (LOWEST THRU 39=1) (40 THRU HIGHEST=2) (MISSING=9); c. No.

CHAPTER 15

Statistical Concepts

1   a. (10,12) (10,14) (10,16) (10,50) (12,14) (12,16) (12,50) (14,16) (14,50) (16,50); c. Both means equal 20.4.

4   a. 40; b. The survey responses differ because of sampling variation. Some values are low and some are high, as one expects in sample results. This variation does not indicate that the deans rigged their polls; c. Probability over 0.99 that a poll will show more than 25%; probability about 0.02 that a poll will show more than 55%; probability about 0.20 that a poll will show less than 35%.

CHAPTER 16

Statistical Concepts

2 a. 50%; c. 16%; e. 5%.

3 b. +0.5; d. -1.5.

5 b. 3 divided by the square root of 50, or about 0.42, for samples of 50; about 0.95 for samples of 10.

7 From 0.14 to 0.16.

CHAPTER 17

Syntax

2 `t-test groups treat(0,1) / var weight.`

3 RECODE TREAT (1,2=1) (3,4=2), followed by the command in question 2. Other commands will achieve the same results.

Statistical Concepts

1 a. On average, Republicans and Democrats earn the same income; b. On average, Republicans earn more than Democrats (this is a one-tailed test).

3 a. No; b. No; c. 0.006 of the time (this is a one-tailed test).

5 False. The observed significance level tells the probability of observing a value of t as large or larger than yours, *if* the null hypothesis is true.

8 Yes, this is possible (although quite unlikely).

9 In fact, it's quite likely that the two population means are unequal. Nevertheless, you can't reject the null hypothesis that they are equal.

10 The results are meaningless.

CHAPTER 18

Syntax

1 Each rat is a case. Variables are the time without the drug and the time with the drug; a. DATA LIST FREE / DRUG NODRUG. b. T-TEST PAIRS DRUG NODRUG.

2 Again each rat is a case, but in this arrangement the variables are the time and the group. The command would be something like T-TEST GROUPS AGENT(0,1) / VARIABLES TIME.

Statistical Concepts

1 a. Paired; b. Paired; c. Independent; d. Paired; e. Paired.

4 The one-tailed significance level is half the two-tailed significance level.

7 a. On the second exam, students will remember their answers from the first; b. The experiment is not controlled. The order in which pizzas are eaten and the amounts consumed are likely to be affected by such things as the location of the pizza in the room. Popular or persuasive people may convince others to prefer a particular brand; c. Respondents come forward because they have been suffering; if their headaches abate for any reason they will attribute this to the treatment. The "placebo effect" may persuade them that they must feel better if they have been given treatment. They may report improvement to avoid hurting the feelings of those conducting the study; d. Almost anybody can lose the first ten pounds easier than another ten pounds.

CHAPTER 19

Syntax

1
```
crosstabs degree by paeduc
  /cells count column
  /statistics chisq.
```

2
```
crosstabs eyecolor by carcolor
  /statistics chisq.
```

4   One set of commands that would work is:

```
get file 'wtstudy.sys'.
compute ratio=weight/ideal.
compute paratio=paweight/paideal.
compute maratio=maweight/maideal.
compute obese=ratio.
compute paobese=paratio.
compute maobese=maratio.
recode obese paobese maobese (lowest thru 1.3=0)
  (1.3 thru highest=1).
crosstabs obese by paobese maobese
   /cells count column
   /statistics chisq.
```

Statistical Concepts

1   *a* and *d* are probably independent; the others are probably dependent.

3   a. The variables are probably related in the population; b. Slightly less than 5% of the time; c. No.

5   Chi-square for the second table is 45.45.

7   The other investigator has more cases.

CHAPTER 20

Syntax

2   a. Needs a range of values for *RACE*. b. OK; c. OK; d. RANGES BTUKEY is a subcommand itself, not a part of the OPTIONS subcommand.

3
```
recode educ (missing = sysmis) (0 thru 8=1)
   (9 thru 12=2) (13 thru 16=3) (16 thru highest=4).
oneway chol by educ (1,4).
```

Statistical Concepts

2   a. No; b. There is no evidence that age of first marriage differs among the categories of whether life is exciting; c. Similar; d. No.

3   a. ONEWAY MAEDUC BY LIFE (1,3) / RANGES=BTUKEY. b. The average years of mother's education are the same for all three excitement groups in the population; c. Mother's education differs among the excitement groups. You can reject the null hypothesis; d. Each group differs from both of the other two.

CHAPTER 21

Syntax

1   ```
recode age (low thru 19=1)(20 thru 29=2)(30 thru 39=3)
  (40 thru 49=4)(50 thru 59=5)(60 thru 69=6)
  (70 thru 79=7) (80 thru 89=8)(else=sysmis).
crosstabs age by satjob
  /cells count row
  /statistics btau ctau gamma d.
```

### Statistical Concepts

1   All four statements are false.

4   It's easier to interpret values in these ranges. In particular, it's easier to compare coefficients from different tables when you know the coefficients are restricted to these ranges.

6   Lambda = 0.40, with *MIGRAINE* dependent. The two variables are strongly related.

7   This would simply reverse the sign of gamma.

# CHAPTER 23

### Syntax

1   ```plot plot income with age.```

3   ```plot plot income with age by sex.```

5   The PLOT subcommand was omitted, as in Question 4b.

### Statistical Concepts

1   a. MEANS; b. CROSSTABS; c. PLOT; d. CROSSTABS; e. MEANS; f. PLOT.

2   a. Unrelated;  d. Nonlinear (curvilinear) relationship.

# CHAPTER 23

### Syntax

1   ```correlations money invest salary wealth /option 3.```
```

Statistical Concepts

1 a. Positive; c. Negative; e. Negative; g. Positive.

3 The correlation coefficient is meaningless, since product code does not measure anything at the interval level.

5 The correlation coefficient is appropriate only when variables are measured at the interval or ratio level and when the relationship between them is linear. When he computes a large number of correlation coefficients, some of them will be large enough to be statistically significant because of sampling variation alone.

CHAPTER 24

Syntax

1 a. PLOT must be the last subcommand; b. The keyword PLOT is omitted from the specifications; c. Use WITH instead of BY. d. The second of the three PLOT keywords in this command is not needed.

Statistical Concepts

2 The intercept is 10,000 and the slope is 500. The predicted income for a 40-year-old is $30,000.

5 You can't tell which correlation is larger.

CHAPTER 25

Syntax

1 a. OK; b. DEP must precede ENTER. c. DEP is missing. d. *GPA* is named as both dependent and independent variable and the slash is missing.

3 `regression statistics def ci /dep gpa /enter iq.`

Statistical Concepts

5 a. Yes; b. It is unrelated; c. No; d. No; e. If there is no linear relationship between the two variables, there is only a 0.03 probability that the authors could have obtained a slope as large as the one they obtained.

CHAPTER 26

Syntax

2   ENTER (which is a shortened form of the METHOD ENTER subcommand) should be used after the DEPENDENT subcommand.

4
```
regression dependent myweight
   /enter maweight /residuals histogram
   /casewise all dependent pred resid zresid
   /scatterplot (*resid, *pred) (*resid, maweight).
```

Statistical Concepts

1   a. $20,000; b. Zero; c. The observed value is less than the predicted value.

3   a. The variance of the residuals is not constant; b. The relationship is not linear; c. The observations are not independent of one another; d. The residuals are not normally distributed, so the dependent variable is probably not normally distributed.

Appendix C

More Advice on Using the System

T his appendix contains information about using SPSS/PC+ that may be of interest to some users. Topics covered include:

- Possible problems getting SPSS/PC+ to run.
- Changing system behavior with the SET command.
- Editing a text (ASCII) file in SPSS/PC+.
- Printing recommendations.
- Running from the prompt.
- Finding commands in SPSS/PC+.

POSSIBLE PROBLEMS

SPSS/PC+ is quite simple to run. And once you're running the program, it will display error messages to notify you of any problems that occur. Most error messages are self-explanatory; refer to Appendix A if you need help.

If any problems arise when you are getting into the program, they are likely to be the result of the system's failure to find the program files that make up SPSS/PC+ on the hard disk. The following sections apply to situations where you can't even get into SPSS/PC+.

The CONFIG.SYS File

To run SPSS/PC+, you must have a file named config.sys on the floppy disk or hard disk from which you start your system. This file should contain a line that reads:

```
files=20
```

If you do not have a suitable config.sys file, SPSS/PC+ will stop immediately with a message:

```
ERROR - not enough file handles.
Increase your FILES in CONFIG.SYS to 20, then reboot your system.
```

When creating or modifying the config.sys file, you shouls keep in mind the following:

- The file config.sys has to be on the disk from which you boot (start) your system, and it has to be in the root directory of that disk—not in a subdirectory.

- If the computer you are using starts up from the hard disk, it is likely to have a config.sys file already. Edit the file using any text file editor.

- After editing config.sys, reboot (restart) your computer by pressing [Ctrl] [Alt] [Del].

Setting the Path

You can't run SPSS/PC+ from DOS unless DOS can find the SPSS/PC+ program files. You can set the DOS path so DOS will know where to find the files.

The PATH Command. When you run SPSS/PC+, we recommend that you do *not* make the \spss directory your current directory. Instead, put a PATH command specifying the \spss directory in your autoexec.bat file. By putting the \spss directory on your path, you can run SPSS/PC+ from another directory where you keep your own files for data, commands, and results. The Installation program automatically creates a subdirectory \spss\data, where it copies the data files used in this book. You may want to run the program from this subdirectory.

The PATH command should look like this:

```
path c:\;c:\dos;c:\spss
```

(If you installed SPSS/PC+ in a directory other than \spss, use the name of that directory.)

The autoexec.bat file should be in the root directory of the disk from which you boot DOS. You can also include directories for your other software on the PATH command; use semicolons (but not blank spaces) to separate directory names. Remember to run the updated autoexec.bat file either by rebooting your computer or by typing autoexec at the DOS prompt and pressing [↵Enter].

Rebooting. If the installation process created or modified your config.sys file, you will see a message warning you to reboot your machine after installation. To do this, hold down [Ctrl] and [Alt] and press [Del].

After you've set the path, you can run SPSS/PC+ by typing

```
spsspc
```

without having to change into any particular directory. We recommend that you run SPSS/PC+ this way, from a directory where you keep the relevant files. If the SPSS/PC+ path is not set, it is possible to change into the SPSS/PC+ directory with the command

```
cd \spss
```

and then run SPSS/PC+ by typing

```
spsspc.
```

If you run SPSS/PC+ from this directory, you should be careful to designate the correct path when you retrieve or save data files or command files. For example, to save a plot from a listing file to a diskette in the A: drive (from within SPSS/PC+), highlight the plot using F7. Then press F9, choose write Marked area, and type a:myfile.plt. When you press ◄┘Enter, myfile.plt will be saved.

THE SET COMMAND

The SET command lets you change SPSS/PC+'s "default" behavior in many ways. You can use the Menu system to learn about all of the different specifications that can be set. Turn off the menus with AltM, in the scratch pad, type

```
set
```

and press AltM again.

To find out about the color settings available, highlight operations in the SET menu and press ↵. Highlight /COLOR on the Operations menu and read about this subcommand. Then press ↵ again to read specific information about the settings available.

Some of the more useful specifications available for the SET command are:

LISTING   Lets you specify a name (in quotes) for the listing file or suppress the listing file. The listing file contains a copy of the statistical output from your session. Unless you use SET LISTING to specify something else, the file is named spss.lis and is written to your current directory. Each time you start SPSS/PC+, the old spss.lis file is erased and a new file is started.

LOG   Lets you specify a name (in quotes) for the log file or suppress the log file. The log file contains a copy of the commands executed during your session. Unless you use SET LOG to specify something else, the file is named spss.log and is written to your current directory. Each time you start SPSS/PC+, the old spss.log file is erased and a new file is started.

COLOR   Controls the colors used by SPSS/PC+ or turns color off.

SEED   Controls the random-number generator used by the SAMPLE command and by the NORMAL and UNIFORM functions that are a part of the transformation language. You can reproduce these "random" numbers by setting the seed to some number before executing a command and then setting it to the same number before repeating the command.

VIEWLENGTH   Lets you display more than 25 lines on a screen if you have an EGA or VGA graphics adapter.

SCREEN   Changes the defaults for displaying box characters, histograms, and bar charts. Some printers will not print the extended ASCII box characters. In this case, specify SET SCREEN OFF and SPSS/PC+ will use regular keyboard characters for such displays.

Running the SHOW command displays the current settings of everything controlled by SET. You can find out more about the SET and SHOW commands in the menus.

The Initialization Profile

If you create a file of SPSS/PC+ commands and name it spssprof.ini, SPSS/PC+ will execute the commands in that file every time you start up the program. SPSS/PC+ looks for spssprof.ini either in your current directory or in the directory where you installed SPSS/PC+. If both places have a file with this name, the one in your current directory is used. This file is typically used to supply a SET command that changes SPSS/PC+'s default settings to those you prefer.

If you primarily want to use SPSS/PC+ V2.0 (or higher) by typing commands in the scratch pad, you should include the command SET AUTOMENU OFF in the initialization profile. With the automatic Menu system turned off, you can still access the menus by pressing (Alt)(M).

EDITING A TEXT FILE IN SPSS/PC+

You may want to edit command files or data files in SPSS/PC+. You can edit any "text" (ASCII) file either in the scratch pad or in the listing window. To edit a file, you

- Insert it into an SPSS/PC+ window.
- Use the editing features described in Chapter 4.
- Save all or part of the file.

The following sections show you how to create a new file and edit an existing file.

Creating a New File

First start an SPSS/PC+ session by changing to the directory \spss\data, typing

```
spsspc
```

and pressing ⏎Enter. Turn off the menus by pressing AltM. The cursor is in the scratch pad. To create a new file, just start typing. When you are finished, save the file (press F9).

Loading an Existing Text File

To edit an existing text file, you must first load it into SPSS/PC+.

1. Turn off the menus, press F3 and then I (the letter I). SPSS/PC+ asks for the File to insert. Type the filename, for example,

```
educ.job
```

and press ⏎Enter. The file is inserted into the scratch pad.

Editing the File

Suppose you want to change the state of residence for the fifth person, to Rhode Island, and also add data for another person.

2. Move the cursor to the end of the New Mexico line, using the arrow keys.

3. Backspace over "New Mexico" and type "Rhode Island".

4. Use ↓ to move down two lines and press ⏎Enter. The cursor is now on a blank line below Massachusetts.

5. Type

```
35 1 18 12 12 "Utah"
```

You can put in enough spaces to make the file easier to read, although only one space is actually required between values.

Saving the File (Whole or Part)

To save the whole file, follow these steps:

1 Press [F9] and then [↵Enter].

2 Type the new name of the file (such as educ2.job) right over the words scratch.pad and press [↵Enter].

The file is saved in the current directory. If you want it in another directory or on a diskette in the A: drive, type the complete path for the filename, (such as a:educ2.job) and press [↵Enter].

You may also want to save a part of the file. To save only the *data* in this file, follow these steps:

1 Move the cursor to the Illinois line.

2 Press [F7] and then [↵Enter]. The line changes color and starts blinking.

3 Move the cursor to the "Utah" line and press [F7] again.

4 Press [F9] and then [M] (write Marked area).

5 Type a filename (such as educ.dat) and press [↵Enter].

You can also use a complete pathname to save into a different directory.

See Chapter 5 for information on reading the data back into SPSS/PC+ from the data file.

PRINTING RESULTS WHILE RUNNING

It is possible to print the output as it is produced in SPSS/PC+ by running the command SET PRINTER ON. However, we do not recommend this method of operation because it slows your session to the speed of the printer. Instead, print the listing file spss.lis from DOS; or save only selected lines into separate files and print from DOS (see Chapter 4).

RUNNING SPSS/PC+ FROM THE PROMPT

If you want to run SPSS/PC+ commands from the prompt, press [F10]. Then select Exit to prompt on the mini-menu and press [↵Enter]. The prompt SPSS/ PC: appears, where you can type a command and press [↵Enter] to run it.

If there is no period when you press [↵Enter], SPSS/PC+ responds with the continuation prompt (seven blank spaces followed by a colon) and waits for more of the command. The advantage of working at the command prompt is speed; however, it does not give you much chance to correct errors in commands or to use the Menu system.

To return to the Menu system, at the prompt type

review.

and press ⏎Enter.

FINDING COMMANDS IN SPSS/PC+

The commands in this book come from the SPSS/PC+ base system and its add-on options.

- The commands in Parts 1 and 2 of this book are all in the SPSS/PC+ 4.0 base system.

- Parts 3 and 4 discuss the statistical procedures T-TEST, ONEWAY, ANO-VA, and REGRESSION, in addition to base system commands. These procedures are all in the SPSS/PC+ 4.0 Statistics option, as is NPAR TESTS, which is discussed in Appendix E.

The commands discussed in Parts 3 and 4 can be used in SPSS/PC+ if you have purchased and installed the Statistics option.

Appendix D
Formatting Information with REPORT

A t times it is useful to be able to display descriptive statistics in a compact format, either to present them to others or to study multiple variables side-by-side. The REPORT procedure is designed to present summary statistics (like those produced by MEANS) in a format you can control to a large extent. It is also useful for listing cases when you want to show variable and value labels or control the format in ways not available with LIST. This makes it particularly valuable for producing corporate and government reports; but it can also be useful in studying and presenting survey data, as this appendix will show.

A BASIC REPORT

In Chapter 12 we used MEANS to look at the average ages of people who found life exciting, routine, or dull. What if we want to look not only at the mean age for each group but also at the means for education level of respondents, their parents, and their spouses? The following commands produce a report with this information (Figure D.1).

```
get file 'gss.sys'.
sort cases by life.
set length 59.
report /format = automatic
 /variables = age educ paeduc maeduc speduc
 /break = life
 /summary = mean
 /summary = stddev
 /summary = validn.
```

REPORT requires that the file be sorted by the values of any variable or variables used to break the file into subgroups. Since we want to see statistics for the subgroups defined by *LIFE*, we name that variable on the SORT CASES command. The SET LENGTH command sets the page length to 59, the standard number of lines on a printed page.

Automatic format calls into play a number of formatting choices that make the report more attractive. (To see the alternative, run this report without the FORMAT subcommand.) The remaining subcommands simply name the variables to be summarized, name the **break variable** that defines the subgroups, and name the summary statistics. One SUMMARY subcommand is required for each line of statistics to appear in the report.

Figure D.1 Basic report

Is life exciting or dull?	Age of respondent	Highest year of school completed	Father's highest year of school	Mother's highest year of school	Spouse's highest year of school
Exciting					
Mean	42	13	11	11	13
StdDev	17	3	4	3	3
N	683	684	544	599	391
Pretty routine					
Mean	45	12	10	10	12
StdDev	18	3	4	3	3
N	700	702	483	583	398
Dull					
Mean	53	10	8	8	10
StdDev	20	4	4	4	4
N	73	73	35	49	30
Missing data					
Mean	48	12	12	10	12
StdDev	23	3	5	4	3
N	11	11	5	9	4

The report in Figure D.1 allows us to compare variables as well as subgroups, but we would like to see more precision in the means and standard deviations, and we would like to have statistics for the file as a whole as well as for subgroups. Obtaining statistics for all cases in the file is simple; just specify (TOTAL) on the BREAK subcommand. Changing print formats for the statistics requires more typing because the format for each variable must be specified separately for each statistic. A number in parentheses following the variable name indicates the number of decimal places to print, as in the following command, which produces Figure D.2.

```
report /format automatic
 /variables = age educ paeduc maeduc speduc
 /break = life (total)
 /summary = mean (age(2) educ(2) paeduc(2) maeduc(2)
    speduc(2))
 /summary = stddev (age(2) educ(2) paeduc(2) maeduc(2)
    speduc(2))
 /summary = validn.
```

Figure D.2 Report with total statistics and revised print formats

Is life exciting or dull?	Age of respondent	Highest year of school completed	Father's highest year of school	Mother's highest year of school	Spouse's highest year of school
Exciting					
Mean	41.95	13.04	10.59	10.85	12.86
StdDev	16.81	3.18	4.13	3.32	2.87
N	683	684	544	599	391
Pretty routine					
Mean	45.03	11.99	9.64	9.95	12.21
StdDev	18.13	2.94	3.91	3.38	3.10
N	700	702	483	583	398
Dull					
Mean	52.85	9.55	7.83	8.02	10.10
StdDev	19.69	3.50	4.23	4.31	4.37
N	73	73	35	49	30
Missing data					
Mean	47.82	11.91	11.60	9.78	11.75
StdDev	22.72	2.63	4.51	4.06	3.30
N	11	11	5	9	4
TOTAL					
Mean	44.00	12.36	10.07	10.31	12.44
StdDev	17.81	3.18	4.08	3.45	3.09
N	1467	1470	1067	1240	823

The report in Figure D.2 makes it easy to see how ages and education levels differed among people who found life exciting, routine, or dull. In all categories, education level seems to be going up with time; since parents' level is below that of respondents and spouses. Notice that, by default, RE-PORT includes the group of cases with user-defined missing values for the *LIFE* variable. Cases are excluded for each of the summarized variables individually, as can be seen in the different N's for the different variables.

As a next step, we might wish to look at the same report for males and females separately. This requires a second break variable and summary. In the following REPORT command, the first break variable, *SEX*, causes the report to break into two groups, while the second break variable, *LIFE*, causes a further breakdown within each category of *SEX*. Since we want the same statistics reported for the primary break (for all males and for all females) as we do for the secondary break (the *LIFE* categories), we can save some typing by using SUMMARY=PREVIOUS. To get the cases into the right order for this report, a new SORT CASES command is also required. The following commands produce the report in Figure D.3 and Figure D.4:

```
    sort cases by sex life.
report /format automatic
 /variables = age educ paeduc maeduc speduc
 /break = sex
 /summary = mean (age(2) educ(2) paeduc(2) maeduc(2)
     speduc(2))
 /summary = stddev (age(2) educ(2) paeduc(2) maeduc(2)
     speduc(2))
 /summary = validn
 /break = life
 /summary = previous.
```

Figure D.3 Report with two break levels

Respondent's sex	Is life exciting or dull?	Age of respondent	Highest year of school completed	Father's highest year of school	Mother's highest year of school	Spouse's highest year of school
Male	Exciting					
	Mean	41.40	13.26	10.46	11.05	12.65
	StdDev	16.07	3.50	4.05	3.14	2.77
	N	300	300	246	260	182
	Pretty routine					
	Mean	43.34	12.11	9.78	10.06	12.36
	StdDev	17.65	3.17	3.91	3.49	2.62
	N	267	266	186	218	160
	Dull					
	Mean	47.76	9.79	6.94	8.00	9.08
	StdDev	19.88	3.19	4.34	4.86	3.12
	N	29	29	17	16	13
	Missing data					
	Mean	58.00	10.00	19.00	12.00	11.00
	StdDev	.	.	.	.	.
	N	1	1	1	1	1
Mean		42.61	12.57	10.07	10.52	12.38
StdDev		17.02	3.44	4.08	3.42	2.79
N		597	596	450	495	356
Female	Exciting					
	Mean	42.37	12.86	10.69	10.69	13.05
	StdDev	17.38	2.89	4.20	3.45	2.95
	N	383	384	298	339	209
	Pretty routine					
	Mean	46.07	11.92	9.55	9.89	12.11
	StdDev	18.36	2.79	3.90	3.31	3.38
	N	433	436	297	365	238
	Dull					
	Mean	56.20	9.39	8.67	8.03	10.88
	StdDev	19.04	3.72	4.06	4.10	5.07
	N	44	44	18	33	17
	Missing data					
	Mean	46.80	12.10	9.75	9.50	12.00
	StdDev	23.69	2.69	2.06	4.24	4.00
	N	10	10	4	8	3

Figure D.4 Report with two break levels (continued)

			Highest year of	Father's highest	Mother's highest	Spouse's highest
Respondent's sex	Is life exciting or dull?	Age of respondent	school completed	year of school	year of school	year of school
Mean		44.96	12.21	10.07	10.17	12.48
StdDev		18.28	2.99	4.09	3.47	3.31
N		870	874	617	745	467

SPSS/PC+   PAGE   2

While this report has all of the information we need, it does not take advantage of REPORT's many titling and formatting options. A few of the more commonly used options are illustrated in the following REPORT command.

```
report /format automatic brkspace(0)
 /title = left 'Age and family education'
             'by attitude toward life'
 /title = right 'From General Social Survey'
               'Page )PAGE,   Sex = )sex'
 /variables = age educ paeduc maeduc speduc
 /break = sex (6) '' (page)
 /summary = mean (age(2) educ(2) paeduc(2) maeduc(2)
    speduc(2)) ' Mean'
 /summary = stddev (age(2) educ(2) paeduc(2) maeduc(2)
    speduc(2)) ' Std. dev.'
 /summary = validn '  Valid cases'
 /break = life
 /summary = previous.
```

- On the FORMAT subcommand, BRKSPACE controls the vertical space between the label for the break level and the first statistic reported. Note in Figure D.5 that the line for *Mean* comes right after the *Exciting, Pretty Routine, Dull,* and *Missing data* labels due to BRKSPACE(0).

- The TITLE subcommands set up left- and right-justified titles--one line of title for each string of text enclosed in apostrophes. In the right title,)PAGE (which must be capitalized) is used to print the page number, while)sex (upper or lower case) prints the current value of the variable *SEX*.

- On the first BREAK subcommand, the 6 in parentheses sets the width of the column to six characters, while the two apostrophes define a null title for the column. (PAGE) causes a new page to start every time the value of *SEX* changes.

- On the SUMMARY commands, replacements for the default summary labels are enclosed in apostrophes. To indent them, two spaces are included at the start of each label.

Figure D.5 Report with titles and formatting options

```
Age and family education                             From General Social Survey
by attitude toward life                                  Page      1,  Sex = Male

                                        Highest   Father's  Mother's  Spouse's
                      Is life           year of   highest   highest   highest
                      exciting or  Age of  school  year of   year of   year of
                      dull?        respondent completed school    school    school
                      _____

Male    Exciting
          Mean        41.40     13.26     10.46     11.05     12.65
          Std. dev.   16.07      3.50      4.05      3.14      2.77
          Valid cases   300       300       246       260       182

        Pretty routine
          Mean        43.34     12.11      9.78     10.06     12.36
          Std. dev.   17.65      3.17      3.91      3.49      2.62
          Valid cases   267       266       186       218       160

        Dull
          Mean        47.76      9.79      6.94      8.00      9.08
          Std. dev.   19.88      3.19      4.34      4.86      3.12
          Valid cases    29        29        17        16        13

        Missing data
          Mean        58.00     10.00     19.00     12.00     11.00
          Std. dev.      .         .         .         .         .
          Valid cases     1         1         1         1         1
Mean                  42.61     12.57     10.07     10.52     12.38
Std. dev.             17.02      3.44      4.08      3.42      2.79
Valid cases             597       596       450       495       356
-----------------------------------------------------------------------
Age and family education                             From General Social Survey
by attitude toward life                                  Page      2,  Sex = Female

                                        Highest   Father's  Mother's  Spouse's
                      Is life           year of   highest   highest   highest
                      exciting or  Age of  school  year of   year of   year of
                      dull?        respondent completed school    school    school
                      _____

Female  Exciting
          Mean        42.37     12.86     10.69     10.69     13.05
          Std. dev.   17.38      2.89      4.20      3.45      2.95
          Valid cases   383       384       298       339       209

        Pretty routine
          Mean        46.07     11.92      9.55      9.89     12.11
          Std. dev.   18.36      2.79      3.90      3.31      3.38
          Valid cases   433       436       297       365       238

        Dull
          Mean        56.20      9.39      8.67      8.03     10.88
          Std. dev.   19.04      3.72      4.06      4.10      5.07
          Valid cases    44        44        18        33        17

        Missing data
          Mean        46.80     12.10      9.75      9.50     12.00
          Std. dev.   23.69      2.69      2.06      4.24      4.00
          Valid cases    10        10         4         8         3
Mean                  44.96     12.21     10.07     10.17     12.48
Std. dev.             18.28      2.99      4.09      3.47      3.31
Valid cases             870       874       617       745       467
```

It is often useful to examine the cases with missing data, to see if there is some pattern associated with not answering a question. Many techniques can be used, but a simple listing is a good start. In many chapters of this book, the LIST command is used to list the values of individual cases. REPORT can produce case listings that include the value labels in the data and use the variable labels as default column headings; just specify LIST on the FORMAT subcommand, as in the following commands, which produce Figure D.6.

```
select if (missing (life) or missing (sex) or missing(age)
          or missing(educ)).
report /format = automatic list
 /variables = id life (label) sex (label) age educ.
```

Figure D.6 Report for case listing

Identification number	Is life exciting or dull?	Respondent's sex	Age of respondent	Highest year of school completed
204	Pretty routine	Male	60	.
304	Missing data	Male	.	.
1056	Missing data	Male	58	10
1062	Exciting	Female	.	12
1	Pretty routine	Female	.	12
147	Pretty routine	Female	.	9
148	Pretty routine	Female	.	12
359	Pretty routine	Female	.	12
766	Pretty routine	Female	82	.
31	Missing data	Female	86	16
348	Missing data	Female	31	16
415	Missing data	Female	28	12
692	Missing data	Female	31	12
694	Missing data	Female	40	12
698	Missing data	Female	80	8
729	Missing data	Female	60	12
731	Missing data	Female	64	12
789	Missing data	Female	23	8
1199	Missing data	Female	25	13

You can combine case listings with summary statistics in a report by including both LIST on the FORMAT subcommand and by including a BREAK subcommand and associated SUMMARY subcommand. The following REPORT command produces Figure D.7.

```
report /format = automatic list
 /variables = id life (label) sex (label) age educ
 /break = sex
 /summary = validn.
```

Figure D.7 Report with case listing and summary statistics

Respondent's sex	Identification number	Is life exciting or dull?	Respondent's sex	Age of respondent	Highest year of school completed
Male	204	Pretty routine	Male	60	.
	304	Missing data	Male	.	.
	1056	Missing data	Male	58	10
N	3	1	3	2	1
Female	1062	Exciting	Female	.	12
	1	Pretty routine	Female	.	12
	147	Pretty routine	Female	.	9
	148	Pretty routine	Female	.	12
	359	Pretty routine	Female	.	12
	766	Pretty routine	Female	82	.
	31	Missing data	Female	86	16
	348	Missing data	Female	31	16
	415	Missing data	Female	28	12
	692	Missing data	Female	31	12
	694	Missing data	Female	40	12
	698	Missing data	Female	80	8
	729	Missing data	Female	60	12
	731	Missing data	Female	64	12
	789	Missing data	Female	23	8
	1199	Missing data	Female	25	13
N	16	6	16	11	15

MORE ABOUT THE REPORT COMMAND

REPORT provides a large number of options for custom formatting, only a small portion of which are covered here. More information is available not only in the *SPSS/PC+ 4.0 Base Manual* but also in the help text that accompanies the Menu system.

If you are preparing the report for printing, you can set the page length to 59, or whatever number of lines is standard for your printer. Use the command SET LENGTH 59.

REPORT requires a VARIABLES subcommand that names the variables to be listed or summarized. It also requires either a FORMAT subcommand with LIST specified or a BREAK subcommand and SUMMARY subcommand to indicate the statistics to be calculated and the subgroups for which statistics are desired. It can have all of those, plus multiple combinations of BREAK and SUMMARY and other optional subcommands. The order of subcommands is important; the following will work:

```
/FORMAT
/OUTFILE
/TITLE
/VARIABLES
/BREAK
/SUMMARY
```
additional BREAK and SUMMARY subcommands

The FORMAT Subcommand

The FORMAT subcommand accepts a number of keyword specifications to control spacing, margins, and overall layout. For most reports, the AUTO-MATIC keyword creates a good looking report with little effort. Other keywords often used in conjunction with AUTOMATIC are

LIST(n)   List individual cases. The optional *(n)* causes a blank line to be skipped after each *n* cases.

BRKSPACE(n) Number of blank lines between the break head and the next line. BRKSPACE(-1) puts the break head and the summary on the same line, eliminating the summary title.

MARGINS(l,r) The columns for the left and right margins. Useful for making titles and report contents align.

Example:
```
REPORT /FORMAT = AUTOMATIC LIST MARGINS(1,72)
  /VARIABLES = VAR1 VAR2 VAR3.
```

The OUTFILE Subcommand

Specify OUTFILE = 'filename' to have the report written to a separate file instead of the listing file. This allows you to print the file by itself without editing the listing file.

The VARIABLES Subcommand

The minimum specification is a list of variables to be summarized and/or listed in the report. After each variable name you can include, in any order, the following specifications:

(LABEL)   In a case listing, print value labels instead of values. The default is (VALUE).

'column title' The title for the column. You can specify multiple lines, each enclosed in its own set of apostrophes or quotation marks.

(width)   The column width. With FORMAT=AUTOMATIC, REPORT attempts to make column widths accommodate the width of the data or the longest element in the column title. A number in parentheses overrides the default.

Example:

```
/VARIABLES= EDUC 'Education' 'Level' (9)
            INCOME 'Income' 'Category'
            AGE 'Age' (3)
```

The BREAK Subcommand

Specify the variable that defines categories for which you want statistics. If you include more than one BREAK subcommand, the second one defines subgroups within categories of the first, and so on. The BREAK subcommand must be followed by a SUMMARY subcommand. In addition to the name of the break variable, you can specify

(LABEL)   Print the value labels instead of the values of the break variable. This is the default with FORMAT=AUTOMATIC. You can specify (VALUE) to print values.

'column title'   The title for the column. You can specify multiple lines, each enclosed in its own set of apostrophes or quotation marks.

(width)   The column width.

(TOTAL)   Calculate summary statistics not only for each category but for the report as a whole. Useful only on the first BREAK subcommand in a REPORT command.

(SKIP|PAGE)   Number of blank lines (SKIP(n)) to precede each new category within the break. Alternatively, start a new page each time the break category changes.

Example:

```
/BREAK = SEX 'Gender' (6) (TOTAL) (SKIP(2))
```

The SUMMARY Subcommand

Each BREAK subcommand must be followed by one or more SUMMARY subcommands. Each SUMMARY subcommand defines a separate line of summary statistics.

The following summary statistics are available:

VALIDN	Valid number of cases. Computed for string as well as numeric variables.
SUM	Sum of values.
MIN	Minimum value.
MAX	Maximum value.
MEAN	Mean.
STDDEV	Standard deviation.
VARIANCE	Variance.
KURTOSIS	Kurtosis.
SKEWNESS	Skewness.
PCGT(n)	Percentage of cases with values greater than n.
PCLT(n)	Percentage of cases with values less than n.
PCIN(m,n)	Percentage of cases with values between m and n, inclusive.

Specifying Variables and Print Formats for Summaries

Unless you indicate specific variables, summary statistics are printed for all numeric variables. You can specify a set of variables for a summary statistic and even specify different statistics on the same line, so long as you don't ask for more than one statistic for the same variable. The variable names go in parentheses following the keyword for the statistic, as in

```
/SUMMARY = MEAN (AGE SIBS) VALIDN (ID)
```

You can also specify a one-line title for each summary line by enclosing the line in apostrophes, as in

```
/SUMMARY = MEAN (AGE SIBS) VALIDN (ID) 'Mean/Count'
```

If you specify variables, you can also specify print formats for the summary statistics by placing the print format in parentheses following the variable name. By default, the system uses the variable's own print format for statistics reported in the same units as the variable itself (such as sums and means). You can choose among keywords (DOLLAR), (COMMA), and (PLAIN) to override the default. You can also include a number in parentheses to indicate the number of decimal places to print, as in

```
/SUMMARY = MEAN (AGE(2) SIBS(2))
```

Using the Previous Summary

If you specify more than one BREAK subcommand, on those after the first you can specify just PREVIOUS, which means to apply all SUMMARY subcommands from the previous break to the current one.

Titles and Footnotes

You can specify as many lines of titles and footnotes as you have room for on your report page. /TITLE and /FOOTNOTE produce centered titles and footnotes:

```
/TITLE = 'Report on Attitudes Toward Life' ' '
         'Data from General Social Survey'
/FOOTNOTE = 'Sociology 101'
```

which sets up a three-line title (the middle line blank) and a one-line footnote, all centered. Using keywords LEFT, CENTER, and RIGHT, you can justify title and footnote lines to the report margins as well as center them:

```
/TITLE=LEFT 'Report on Attitudes Toward Life' ' '
            'Data from General Social Survey'
/TITLE=RIGHT 'Prepared by Timothy Williams' ' '
             'July 22, 1991'
```

Within titles and footnotes, you can use one of three special keywords to print the date, page number, and the value of a specific variable:

)PAGE   Page number. Must be specified in capital letters.

)DATE   Current date. Must be specified in capital letters.

)var   Print the value label (or value if no label is defined) for the current value of the specified variable.

Example:

```
/TITLE=LEFT 'Report on Attitudes Toward Life'
            'Prepared )DATE'
/TITLE=RIGHT 'Page )PAGE'
```

Missing Values

By default, REPORT treats missing values separately for each variable named on the VARIABLES subcommand. It prints cases with missing values in case listings, but it excludes missing values from calculation of statistics on a variable-by-variable basis. You can control the handling of missing values with the MISSING subcommand, on which you can specify NONE or LIST. NONE takes all user-defined missing values as valid. LIST can be qualified by a set of variable names in parentheses; a case is excluded from all statistics if it has a missing value on any of the variables in the list. If you don't include a variable list, the default for LIST is all variables, so

```
/MISSING = LIST
```

excludes a case from all statistics if it has a missing value on any of the variables on the VARIABLES subcommand.

Appendix E
Nonparametric Procedures: The NPAR TESTS Command

Most of the statistical procedures we used in this book required assumptions about the populations from which the samples are selected. For example, in the two-sample *t* test, we had to assume that the data are from populations that have normal distributions, or that the sample sizes are large enough so that the distribution of sample means is normal. To use an equal-variance *t* test, we also had to assume that, in the population, the two variances are equal. Procedures that require assumptions about the shapes of the distributions from which data originate are known as **parametric** procedures. Many parametric procedures depend on the assumption of normality.

In data analysis, however, there are many situations in which the assumption of normality does not appear reasonable. Data are often nominal or ordinal. Interval data may originate from markedly non-normal distributions. Or we may have little information about the distribution of the data. In these situations, procedures that require very limited assumptions about the distribution of the data can be used. Collectively, these procedures are termed **distribution-free** or **nonparametric** tests.

The advantage of nonparametric tests is that they require few assumptions about the data. The disadvantage of nonparametric tests is that they are usually not as good at finding differences between groups or variables when the differences do, in fact, exist. Another way of saying this is that nonparametric tests are not as powerful as their parametric counterparts, and this is true because they usually ignore some of the available information. For example, they replace actual data values with ranks. In general, if the assumptions of a parametric procedure can be met, you should use the parametric procedure.

Let's now take a look at several nonparametric procedures that are available in SPSS/PC+. The first is a nonparametric equivalent of the *t* test for two independent samples.

THE MANN-WHITNEY TEST

The **Mann-Whitney test,** also known as the **Wilcoxon test,** can be used to test the hypothesis that two independent samples come from populations having the same distribution. You don't have to specify what type of distribution they have. The data can be measured either on an interval or ordinal scale. The Mann-Whitney test requires only that the observations be a random sample and that values can be ordered from smallest to largest. The hypothesis tested by the Mann-Whitney test is similar to that of the two independent samples t test. However, normality and equality-of-variance assumptions are not needed.

To see how the Mann-Whitney test can be used, consider the data used in Chapter 9. We had two groups of students, those on probation and those on the Dean's List. We recorded the number of hours of TV watched in a week. Let's see how we could test the hypothesis that the distribution of TV watching might be the same for the two types of students. First we must combine the hours of TV watched in the two groups and arrange them from smallest to largest. This results in the following table:

Table E.1 Ranked data on TV viewing

TV hours	Rank	Tied rank	Group	TV hours	Rank	Tied rank	Group
0	1	3	Probation	5	11	11.5	Dean's List
0	2	3	Probation	5	12	11.5	Dean's List
0	3	3	Probation	5	13	11.5	Dean's List
0	4	3	Probation	5	14	11.5	Dean's List
0	5	3	Probation	6	15	15.5	Dean's List
3	6	6	Probation	6	16	15.5	Dean's List
4	7	7.5	Dean's List	10	17	17.5	Probation
4	8	7.5	Dean's List	10	18	17.5	Probation
5	9	11.5	Dean's List	12	19	19	Probation
5	10	11.5	Dean's List	15	20	20	Probation

The first column of the table contains the actual hours of TV watched; the second column tells you the sequence of the case in the ranked table. The last column tells you the group to which a student belongs. You will notice that the first five students in the table didn't watch any TV. The first five sequence numbers, or ranks, are assigned to them. Since we have five cases that are "tied" in value, we will average the sequence numbers assigned to all of them and use this averaged value to represent the five cases in the analysis. The average rank assigned to the first five cases is $(1+2+3+4+5)/5 = 3$. This average rank appears in the third column (Tied Rank). Whenever ties occur in the data, the average rank is used.

The Mann-Whitney test is based on the average ranks assigned to the cases in the two groups. If the two groups come from the same population, then we would expect similar ranks in the two groups. That is, neither group would have a preponderance of either large or small ranks. If one of the groups has more than its share of small or large ranks, there is reason to suspect that the two underlying distributions are different.

To run the Mann-Whitney test for this example, use the command:

```
npar tests m-w tvhours by group(1,2).
```

Figure E.1 shows output from the Mann-Whitney test. For each group, the mean rank and the number of cases are given. (The **mean rank** is the sum of the ranks divided by the number of cases.) The entry printed under W is the sum of the ranks for the group with the smaller number of observations. If both groups have the same number of observations, W is the sum of the ranks for the group named first on the NPAR TESTS command. In this example, W is 115, the sum of the ranks for students on the Dean's List. The number identified as U on the output is the number of times a value in the Dean's List group is smaller than a value in the probation group.

Figure E.1 Mann-Whitney test

```
- - - - - Mann-Whitney U - Wilcoxon Rank Sum W Test

     TVHOURS
  by GROUP


    Mean Rank    Cases

        11.50       10   GROUP = 1   Dean's List
         9.50       10   GROUP = 2   Probation
                     --
                     20   Total

                                  EXACT           Corrected for Ties
         U              W       2-tailed P         Z      2-tailed P
        40.0          115.0        .4813         -.7730      .4395
```

The observed significance levels associated with U and W are the same. They are obtained by transforming U or W into a standard normal deviate (Z). If the total sample size is fewer than 30, an exact significance level is also printed. If there are ties in the data, a significance level corrected for ties is also printed. For this example, the observed significance level corrected for ties is large (p=0.4395). Therefore we can't reject the null hypothesis that the two groups come from the same distribution.

THE SIGN TEST

In Chapter 18, we used the paired t test for means to test the hypothesis that the average years of education is the same for husbands and wives. We had to assume that the average differences are normally distributed in order to calculate the observed significance level.

The **sign test** is a nonparametric procedure used with paired samples to test the hypothesis that the distributions of two variables are the same. This test doesn't require any assumption about the shape of the distributions.

To compute the sign test by hand, you would first compute the difference in years of education between husband and wife for each couple. Next, you would count the number of positive and negative differences. If the distributions of the two variables are the same, you should expect to see similar numbers of positive and negative differences.

SPSS/PC+ computes the differences for you. Just run the command

```
npar tests sign = hused wifed.
```

The output in Figure E.2 shows that, for this example, the number of negative differences is 295, and the number of positive differences is 269. Of the total, 258 of the pairs had exactly the same years of education. These are labeled as *ties* on the output. The observed significance level is large (p=0.2925), so the hypothesis that the distributions are the same is not rejected.

Figure E.2   The sign test

```
get file 'gss.sys'.
if (sex=1) hused =educ.
if (sex=1) wifed = speduc.
if (sex=2) wifed = educ.
if (sex=2) hused = speduc.
npar tests sign = hused, wifed.

- - - - - Sign Test

      HUSED
with WIFED

            Cases

            295  - Diffs (WIFED Lt HUSED)            Z =     1.0527
            269  + Diffs (WIFED Gt HUSED)
            258    Ties                    2-tailed P =       .2925
            ----
            822    Total
```

THE RUNS TEST

The **runs test** is a test of randomness. That is, given a sequence of observations, the runs test examines whether the value of one observation influences the values of later observations. If there is no influence (i.e., the observations are independent), the sequence is considered random.

A **run** is any sequence of like observations. For example, if a coin is tossed 15 times and the outcomes recorded, the following sequence might result:

HHHTHHHHTTTTTTT

There are four runs in this sequence: HHH, T, HHHH, and TTTTTTT. The total number of runs is a measure of randomness, since too many runs, or too few, suggest dependence between observations. The runs test converts the total number of runs into a Z statistic having approximately a normal distribution. The only requirement for this test is that the variable must be dichotomous (i.e., it can have only two possible values).

Suppose, for example, that a weather forecaster records whether it snows for 20 days in February and obtains the following sequence (1=snow, 0=no snow):

01111111010111111100

To test the hypothesis that the occurrence or nonoccurrence of snow on one day has no effect on whether it snows on later days, the runs test is performed. The commands are

```
data list free / snow.
begin data.
0 1 1 1 1 1 1 1 0 1 0 1 1 1 1 1 1 1 0 0
end data.
npar tests runs(1) = snow.
```

The output is shown in Figure E.3.

Figure E.3 Runs test

```
- - - - - Runs Test

    SNOW

        Runs:    7          Test Value = 1.00

        Cases:   5    Lt 1.00
                15    Ge 1.00            Z =   -.6243
                --
                20    Total    2-tailed P =   .5324
```

You must supply a **cutting point** to the runs test. The cutting point goes in parentheses after the keyword RUNS. Cases with values greater than or equal to the cutting point go into one group; cases with values less than the cutting point go into the other group. You can also use an in-between value, such as 0.5 in this example.)

Since the observed significance level is quite large (0.5324), the hypothesis of randomness is not rejected. It does not appear, from these data, that snowy (or nonsnowy) days affect the later occurrence of snow.

THE ONE-SAMPLE CHI-SQUARE TEST

The chi-square statistic was applied in Chapter 10 to test the null hypotheses that the row variable and column variable in a crosstabulation are independent. The same statistic can be applied to many other types of hypotheses. Here we will test the hypothesis that deaths from cardiac failure are equally likely to occur on each day of the week, using data from the Western Electric study, in which the incidence of coronary heart disease in 2,017 men was monitored for 20 years.

To test the hypothesis that deaths occurred with equal frequency on each of the seven days of the week, a **one-sample chi-square test** can be used. This nonparametric test requires only that the data be a random sample.

To calculate the one-sample chi-square statistic, the data are first classified into mutually exclusive categories of interest—days of the week in this example—and then expected frequencies for these categories are computed. Expected frequencies are the frequencies that would be expected if the null hypothesis is true. For this example, the hypothesis to be tested is that the probability of death is the same for each day of the week. The day of death is known for 110 subjects. The hypothesis implies that the expected frequency of deaths for each day is 110 divided by 7, or 15.71. Once the expected frequencies are obtained, the chi-square statistic is computed exactly as it is for a crosstabulation. For each category, the squared difference between the observed and expected frequencies is divided by the expected frequency. The chi-square statistic is the sum of these quotients for all the categories.

If the null hypothesis is true, the chi-square statistic has approximately a chi-square distribution. This statistic will be large if the observed and expected frequencies are substantially different.

To run the one-sample chi-square test on SPSS/PC+, use the command

```
npar tests chi-square dayofwk.
```

Figure E.4 shows the output from the one-sample chi-square test for the death data. The observed chi-square value is 3.4, and the associated significance level is 0.757. Since the observed significance level is large, the hypothesis that deaths are evenly distributed over days of the week is not rejected.

Figure E.4 One-sample chi-square output

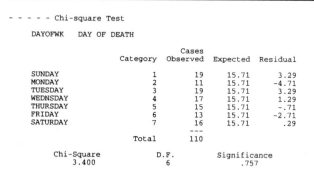

```
- - - - - Chi-square Test

    DAYOFWK    DAY OF DEATH

                               Cases
                  Category   Observed   Expected   Residual
       SUNDAY        1          19        15.71       3.29
       MONDAY        2          11        15.71      -4.71
       TUESDAY       3          19        15.71       3.29
       WEDNSDAY      4          17        15.71       1.29
       THURSDAY      5          15        15.71       -.71
       FRIDAY        6          13        15.71      -2.71
       SATURDAY      7          16        15.71        .29
                                ---
                  Total        110

       Chi-Square              D.F.           Significance
         3.400                  6                 .757
```

Expected Frequencies

When you use the chi-square test by itself, as above, SPSS/PC+ assumes that the expected frequencies are equal in each category. If this isn't so, you can use the EXPECTED subcommand to specify the proportion of cases that you expect in each category. For example, if you were testing the hypothesis that there is no association between cases of spring fever and month of the year, you might wish to take into account that all months are not equally long. You would expect more incidents to occur in January than in February. You could specify the expected proportions like this:

```
npar tests  chi-square month
/expected=31,28.25,31,30,31,30,31,31,30,31,30,31.
```

Note that you can enter expected *counts* on the EXPECTED subcommand. SPSS/PC+ divides each count by the sum of all of them to determine the expected proportions.

MORE ABOUT THE NPAR TESTS COMMAND

You can perform all of the nonparametric tests discussed in this appendix with procedure NPAR TESTS. (See Siegel, 1956, for further information about these tests.) In addition to obtaining the test statistics, you can request additional statistics, specify missing-value treatments, and use a random subsample of your data for NPAR TESTS.

The general format for an NPAR TESTS command is

```
npar tests testname[(parameters)]varlist.
```

Each subcommand requests a specific test and lists the variables to be tested. The equals sign is optional. You can use the TO keyword to refer to adjacent variables in the file. The form of the variable list depends on the type of test specified. More than one test can be requested on one NPAR TESTS command.

One-Sample Tests

The one-sample tests available in NPAR TESTS are the one-sample chi-square test and the runs test.

The One-Sample Chi-Square Test

Use the CHISQUARE subcommand to obtain a one-sample chi-square test. The format is:

```
npar tests chisquare varlist[(lo,hi)].
```

The range following the variable list is optional. If it is not specified, each distinct value of the variable named is treated as a separate category. If the range is specified, noninteger values are truncated to integers, resulting in categories with only integer values. Cases with values outside the specified range are excluded from the analysis.

For example, the output in Figure E.4 was produced with the command:

```
npar tests chisquare=weekday.
```

For each chi-square test, the output shows the observed and expected numbers of cases in each category, the residual (observed minus expected) for each category, and the chi-square statistic with its degrees of freedom and observed significance level.

By default, the expected frequencies are assumed to be equal. You can specify other frequencies, however, by using the EXPECTED subcommand, which has the format

```
/expected f1,f2,...,fn
```

where *f1* through *fn* are the expected frequencies to be used. You must specify a frequency greater than zero for each category of the variable. The values listed on EXPECTED are treated as proportions rather than actual numbers of cases expected. That is, the values are summed, and each value is then divided by this sum to calculate the proportion of cases expected in the corresponding category.

For example, the command

```
npar tests chisquare=flowers /expected=1,2,2,2,1.
```

specifies 1/8, 2/8, 2/8, 2/8, and 1/8 as the expected proportions for the values of FLOWERS.

The EXPECTED subcommand applies to all variables listed in the *preceding* CHISQUARE subcommand. If you want to specify different expected frequencies for each variable, use separate CHISQUARE and EXPECTED subcommands for each variable. Several CHISQUARE and EXPECTED subcommands can also be used to test different expected frequencies for the same variable.

The Runs Test

Use subcommand RUNS to obtain the runs test. This subcommand has the general format

```
npar tests runs(cutpoint) varlist.
```

The cutting point dichotomizes the variables in the variable list. Even if a variable is dichotomous to begin with, a cutting point must be specified. Values *equal* to the cutting point go in the second (upper) category. For example, a variable that takes only the values 0 and 1 would have 1 for the cutting point, as in the command

```
npar tests runs(1)=snow.
```

which produces the output in Figure E.3. You can specify the mean, median, mode, or a value for the cutpoint in parentheses.

MEAN *Mean.* All values below the observed mean make up one category; all values greater than or equal to the mean make up the other category.

MEDIAN *Median.* All values below the observed median make up one category; all values greater than or equal to the median make up the other category.

MODE *Mode.* All values below the observed mode make up one category; all values greater than or equal to the mode make up the other category.

value *Specified value.* All values below the specified value make up one category; all values greater than or equal to the specified value make up the other category.

The RUNS output shows the cutting point, the number of runs, the number of cases below the cutting point, the number of cases greater than or equal to the cutting point, and the test statistic Z with its observed significance level.

Two-Sample Tests

The two-sample tests available in NPAR TESTS are the sign test and the Mann-Whitney test. The sign test applies to two related samples, while the Mann-Whitney test applies to two independent samples.

The Sign Test

The SIGN subcommand requests sign tests for paired variables. The format of SIGN is

```
npar tests sign varlist [with varlist].
```

For example, the output in Figure E.2 was produced by the command

```
npar tests sign hused wifed.
```

If there are more than 25 cases, the observed significance level of the test statistic is based on a normal approximation. If there are 25 or fewer cases, the binomial distribution is used to compute the exact observed significance level.

When only one variable list is specified, each variable in the list is paired with every other variable in the list. For example, the command

```
npar tests sign rating1 rating2 rating3.
```

produces three sign tests: *RATING1* with *RATING2*, *RATING1* with *RATING3*, and *RATING2* with *RATING3*. When you supply two variable lists, separated by the keyword WITH, each variable in the first list is paired with each variable in the second list. For example, the command

```
npar tests sign rating1 with rating2 rating3.
```

produces tests of *RATING1* with *RATING2* and *RATING1* with *RATING3*.

You can also pair variables sequentially by specifying Option 3 on the OPTIONS subcommand.

Option 3   *Sequential pairing of variables for two related samples.*

When Option 3 is requested with a single variable list, the first variable in the list is paired with the second, the second variable with the third, and so on. For example, the command

```
npar tests sign=rating1 rating2 rating3 /options=3.
```

performs two sign tests: one for *RATING1* with *RATING2* and one for *RAT-ING2* with *RATING3*.

If Option 3 is specified with the keyword WITH and two variable lists, the first variable in the first list before WITH is paired with the first variable in the second list, and so forth. For example, the command

```
npar tests sign rating1 rating2 with rating3 rating4
/options=3.
```

requests sign tests for *RATING1* with *RATING3* and *RATING2* with *RATING4*.

The Mann-Whitney U Test

Request the Mann-Whitney test with the M-W subcommand, which has the format

```
npar tests m-w varlist by variable(value1,value2).
```

The variable named after BY is the variable used to group the cases. All cases with *value1* are in the first group and all cases with *value2* are in the second group.

For example, the command

```
npar tests m-w tvhours by group(1,2).
```

was used to produce the output in Figure E.1.

The output produced by M-W includes the mean rank for each group, the Mann-Whitney U statistic, and the Wilcoxon W. For samples with fewer than 30 cases, the exact observed significance level is displayed. For larger samples, a Z statistic with its (approximate) observed significance level is displayed.

Optional Statistics

You can obtain additional summary statistics for all variables named on NPAR TESTS subcommands by specifying Statistics 1 or 2 on the STATISTICS subcommand. All cases with valid values on a variable are used in calculating the statistics for that variable. The following statistics are available:

Statistic 1   *Univariate statistics.* The mean, maximum, minimum, standard deviation, and count are displayed for each variable named on a subcommand.

Statistic 2   *Quartiles and count.* The values corresponding to the 25th, 50th, and 75th percentiles for each variable named on a subcommand are displayed.

Missing Values

By default, cases with missing values are excluded on a test-by-test basis. That is, cases with missing values for any of the variables used in a particular test are excluded from calculations for that test only. You may request two alternative missing-value treatments with the OPTIONS subcommand.

Option 1 *Include user-missing values.* Cases with user-missing values are included in all tests requested on the command.

Option 2 *Exclude missing values listwise.* Cases missing on any variable named on any subcommand are excluded from all analyses.

Subsampling

NPAR TESTS stores cases in memory in order to calculate its statistics. If you do not have enough computer memory to store all the cases, you will need to use Option 4 on the OPTIONS subcommand to select a random subsample of cases for analysis.

Option 4 *Random sampling if there is insufficient memory.*

Because such sampling would invalidate a runs test, this option is ignored when the RUNS subcommand is used.

Appendix F

Areas under the Normal Curve

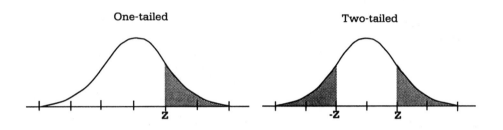

One-tailed   Two-tailed

Z Score	Probablity One-tailed	Two-tailed	Z Score	Probability One-tailed	Two-tailed
.0	.50000	1.00000	2.5	.00621	.01242
.1	.46017	.92034	2.6	.00466	.00932
.2	.42074	.84148	2.7	.00347	.00693
.3	.38209	.76418	2.8	.00256	.00511
.4	.34458	.68916	2.9	.00187	.00373
.5	.30854	.61708	3.0	.00135	.00270
.6	.27425	.54851	3.1	.00097	.00194
.7	.24196	.48393	3.2	.00069	.00137
.8	.21186	.42371	3.3	.00048	.00097
.9	.18406	.36812	3.4	.00034	.00067
1.0	.15866	.31731	3.5	.00023	.00047
1.1	.13567	.27133	3.6	.00016	.00032
1.2	.11507	.23014	3.7	.00011	.00022
1.3	.09680	.19360	3.8	.00007	.00014
1.4	.08076	.16151	3.9	.00005	.00010
1.5	.06681	.13361	4.0	.00003	.00006
1.6	.05480	.10960	4.1	.00002	.00004
1.7	.04457	.08913	4.2	.00001	.00003
1.8	.03593	.07186	4.3	.00001	.00002
1.9	.02872	.05743	4.4	.00001	.00001
1.96	.02500	.05000	4.5	.00000	.00001
2.0	.02275	.04550	4.6	.00000	.00000
2.1	.01786	.03573	4.7	.00000	.00000
2.2	.01390	.02781	4.8	.00000	.00000
2.3	.01072	.02145	4.9	.00000	.00000
2.4	.00820	.01640	5.0	.00000	.00000

Appendix G
The *t* Distribution

t Value	0.0	0.25	0.50	0.75	1.00	1.25
df	Two-tailed Probability*					
1	1.0000	.8440	.7048	.5903	.5000	.4296
2	1.0000	.8259	.6667	.5315	.4226	.3377
3	1.0000	.8187	.6514	.5077	.3910	.2999
4	1.0000	.8149	.6433	.4950	.3739	.2794
5	1.0000	.8125	.6383	.4870	.3632	.2666
6	1.0000	.8109	.6349	.4816	.3559	.2578
7	1.0000	.8098	.6324	.4777	.3506	.2515
8	1.0000	.8089	.6305	.4747	.3466	.2466
9	1.0000	.8082	.6291	.4724	.3434	.2428
10	1.0000	.8076	.6279	.4705	.3409	.2398
11	1.0000	.8072	.6269	.4690	.3388	.2372
12	1.0000	.8068	.6261	.4677	.3370	.2351
13	1.0000	.8065	.6254	.4666	.3356	.2333
14	1.0000	.8062	.6248	.4657	.3343	.2318
15	1.0000	.8060	.6243	.4649	.3332	.2305
16	1.0000	.8058	.6239	.4641	.3322	.2293
17	1.0000	.8056	.6235	.4635	.3313	.2282
18	1.0000	.8054	.6231	.4629	.3306	.2273
19	1.0000	.8053	.6228	.4624	.3299	.2265
20	1.0000	.8051	.6225	.4620	.3293	.2257
22	1.0000	.8049	.6220	.4612	.3282	.2244
24	1.0000	.8047	.6216	.4605	.3273	.2234
26	1.0000	.8046	.6213	.4600	.3265	.2224
28	1.0000	.8044	.6210	.4595	.3259	.2216
30	1.0000	.8043	.6207	.4591	.3253	.2210
35	1.0000	.8040	.6202	.4583	.3242	.2196
40	1.0000	.8039	.6198	.4576	.3233	.2186
45	1.0000	.8037	.6195	.4572	.3227	.2178
50	1.0000	.8036	.6193	.4568	.3221	.2171
∞	1.0000	.8026	.6171	.4533	.3173	.2113

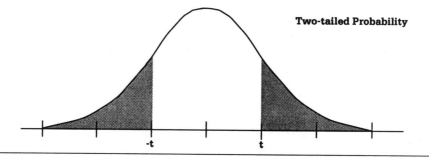

Two-tailed Probability

1.50	1.75	2.00	2.25	2.50	2.75	3.00	t Value
Two-tailed Probability*							df
.3743	.3305	.2952	.2662	.2422	.2220	.2048	1
.2724	.2222	.1835	.1534	.1296	.1107	.0955	2
.2306	.1784	.1393	.1099	.0877	.0707	.0577	3
.2080	.1550	.1161	.0876	.0668	.0514	.0399	4
.1939	.1405	.1019	.0743	.0545	.0403	.0301	5
.1843	.1307	.0924	.0654	.0465	.0333	.0240	6
.1773	.1236	.0856	.0592	.0410	.0285	.0199	7
.1720	.1182	.0805	.0546	.0369	.0251	.0171	8
.1679	.1140	.0766	.0510	.0339	.0225	.0150	9
.1645	.1107	.0734	.0482	.0314	.0205	.0133	10
.1618	.1079	.0708	.0459	.0295	.0189	.0121	11
.1595	.1056	.0687	.0440	.0279	.0176	.0111	12
.1575	.1037	.0668	.0424	.0266	.0165	.0102	13
.1558	.1020	.0653	.0411	.0255	.0156	.0096	14
.1544	.1005	.0639	.0399	.0245	.0149	.0090	15
.1531	.0993	.0628	.0389	.0237	.0142	.0085	16
.1520	.0981	.0617	.0380	.0229	.0137	.0081	17
.1510	.0971	.0608	.0372	.0223	.0132	.0077	18
.1500	.0963	.0600	.0365	.0217	.0127	.0074	19
.1492	.0954	.0593	.0359	.0212	.0123	.0071	20
.1478	.0941	.0580	.0348	.0204	.0117	.0066	22
.1467	.0929	.0569	.0339	.0197	.0111	.0062	24
.1457	.0919	.0560	.0331	.0191	.0107	.0059	26
.1448	.0911	.0553	.0325	.0186	.0103	.0056	28
.1441	.0903	.0546	.0319	.0181	.0100	.0054	30
.1426	.0889	.0533	.0308	.0173	.0094	.0049	35
.1415	.0878	.0523	.0300	.0166	.0089	.0046	40
.1406	.0869	.0516	.0294	.0161	.0086	.0044	45
.1399	.0863	.0509	.0289	.0157	.0083	.0042	50
.1336	.0801	.0455	.0244	.0124	.0060	.0027	∞

*For one-tailed probability, divide by 2.

Bibliography

Basic Statistics Textbooks

Blalock, H. M. 1979. *Social statistics.* New York: McGraw-Hill.

Hays, W. M. 1973. *Statistics for the social sciences, 2nd ed.* New York: Holt, Rinehart & Winston.

Loether, H. J., and D. G. McTavish. 1976. *Descriptive and inferential statistics: An introduction.* Boston: Allyn & Bacon.

Books on Designing Experiments and Surveys

Kirk, R. 1968. *Experimental design: Procedures for the behavioral sciences.* Belmont, Calif.: Brooks.

Sudman, S., and N. M. Bradburn. 1982. *Asking questions: A practical guide to questionnaire design.* San Francisco: Jossey-Bass.

Williams, B. 1978. *A sampler on sampling.* New York: John Wiley & Sons.

Other References

Cedercreutz, C. 1978. Hypnotic treatment of 100 cases of migraine. In *Hypnosis at Its Bicentennial,* eds. F. H. Frankel and H. S. Zamansky. New York: Plenum.

Hooke, R. 1983. *How to tell the liars from the statisticians.* New York: Marcel Dekker, Inc.

Kleinbaum, D. G., L. L. Kupper, and H. Morgenstern. 1982. *Epidemiological research: Principles and quantitative methods.* Belmont, Calif.: Wadsworth, Inc.

Kraemer, H. C. 1982. Kappa coefficient. In *Encyclopedia of statistical sciences,* eds. S. Kotz and N. L. Johnson. New York: John Wiley & Sons.

Siegel, S. 1956. *Nonparametric statistics for the behavioral sciences*. New York: McGraw-Hill.

Tanur, J. M. 1978. *Statistics: A guide to the unknown*. San Francisco: Holden-Day.

Winer, B. J. 1971. *Statistical principles in experimental design*. New York: McGraw-Hill.

SPSS /PC+ Manuals

Norusis, M. J., and SPSS Inc., 1990. *SPSS/PC+ 4.0 base manual*. Chicago: SPSS Inc.

____. 1990. *SPSS/PC+ statistics 4.0*. Chicago: SPSS Inc.

Index